William Temple

WILLIAM TEMPLE

Twentieth-Century Christian

❀ ❀ ❀

JOSEPH FLETCHER

New York

1963

Acknowledgments

Grateful acknowledgment is made to the following publishers and authors for permission to quote from the copyrighted titles listed:

Abingdon Press—Gordon D. Kaufman, *The Context of Decision.*
Eyre & Spottiswoode, Ltd.—William Temple, *Citizen and Churchman.*
Macmillan Company—William Temple, *The Church Looks Forward* and *The Hope of a New World.*
Macmillan & Co., Ltd., London, and Mrs. William Temple—William Temple, *The Faith and Modern Thought, The Kingdom of God, Nature, Man and God,* and *Repton School Sermons.*
Oxford University Press, London—F. A. Iremonger, *William Temple.*
G. P. Putnam's Sons—H. Begbie, *Painted Windows.*

I want to express my deep debt of gratitude to two people who have helped me immeasurably in seeing this book to the press—my wife, without whose labors the book would never have been published, and the Rev. William H. Crawford, Jr., whose editorial acumen and vocational concern have improved it in countless places.

To My Wife
and
England

Preface

This book is written for the reader who is interested in theology but is not a theologian; in philosophy, but not a philosopher; in society, but not a sociologist. There is one other assumption about the reader: he is either an active or a latent Churchman—and, according to Temple, this covers everybody! Whatever his interest, the reader will find here not a definitive biography but a portrait. A portrait is both selective and interpretive; it is not a photograph or facsimile. This book, therefore, makes no attempt to match the rich detail of full-length studies like that of Dean Iremonger; neither does it try to do more than "picture" the vast extent of William Temple's thought. To keep its length within reasonable bounds I have had to choose facts and materials, and we all know that selection is inherently interpretive. I can only claim that there is no attempt in the text to interpret Temple in the sense of supplying any connective tissue which is lacking in the sources themselves. The lucid style and structure of his thought leave no ground to fill in. All deliberate interpretation has been put in the Notes. For the most part, also, I have kept what scholarly and academic apparatus I have used to a minimum, restricted to the Notes.

If there is complaint about leaving out this or that, let me plead my basic purpose: to produce an account which I hope will have some usefulness and readability for non-professional readers. For example, I have not discussed Temple's disagreement with Gore over the "kenosis" theory, and there are several other matters—all minor, however. In the same way, I have set aside all personal references. But let me say here that my acquaintance with Temple spanned the last thirteen years of his life. It began when he wrote a Foreword for the first number of *Christendom:*

A Journal of Christian Sociology in March 1931, and I contributed a review article about Olive Wyon's English translation of Ernst Troeltsch's *Soziallehren*.

No attempt has been made to cite all of the places where a quotation or its near equivalent can be found. For example, Temple refers in several places to Plato's final affirmation of the God behind the good; only one such reference is given. Ordinarily this rule has been followed unless there is some change or significant deviation; this avoids the odor of pedantry and magpie research. The close student of Temple's works quickly learns that he rewrote or re-used many ideas, not only in germ but often in actual phrasing. It is amazing, for instance, to trace the persistent development of many concepts that first appeared as early as his editorials in *The Pilgrim* from 1920 to 1927.

I have tried to do justice to Temple as a person in his own times and context, and to be sufficiently circumstantial and explanatory for that purpose. But beyond that it has seemed better by far to let him speak for himself, either through direct quotations or carefully telescoped reporting. While this is not a biography, neither is it anything so disinterested and bareboned as an abstract in a professional journal. I have tried to fit together the enduring parts for Christian or enquiring readers.

My own phrasing often seems poor and labored compared to Temple's felicity. Dean Matthews once said that he "spoke in pamphlets"—meaning that his style and construction were very simple, colorful and easily grasped. He had an English dislike of flowery speech and purple passages, and he put his premium on *what* he was saying, confident that if the reasoning were sound the language would be clear. If at times there seems to be an over-elaborate machinery of quotation and citation, it is for a simple and sufficient reason: of all Temple's books only two, *Nature, Man and God,* and *Christianity and Social Order,* have indices. The thorough student will have his task made easier by my research, even if I risk being suspected of "academitis." (The contrast between Canon Baker's seventy-odd list of Temple's writings, and the 221 in this book's bibliography shows what continuing investigation can accomplish.)

Temple's is far and away Anglicanism's most creative and comprehensive contribution to the theological enterprise of the West. Theological architects and scholars in other communions will have to take him into account because of his *process* theology, his *incarnational* theology, his *social* theology, his *personalist* theology, and his *relationship* theology. These five "organizing principles" of his work have enduring importance. The evangelical "recital theology" was threaded throughout all of them. It is almost a cliché to say that much of his writing was seminal, but much of it was also well germinated and gestated.

At Malvern in 1941 Temple said, "Few of the younger generation have heard . . . of the great tradition of Christian social teaching associated with the names of Ludlow, Maurice, Kingsley, Westcott, Gore, Scott Holland. The world has to be reminded of it if the tradition itself is not to fade." [1] The purpose of this book, most obviously, is to add Temple's name to the roster of that great tradition. When the search for a successor to Archbishop Lang at Canterbury began, Cyril Garbett of York said that Geoffrey Fisher would make a "good" one and William Temple might make a "great" one.[2] Did he live long enough to settle the question? Was he not already a great man? The answer is plainly affirmative on both scores.

It is impossible to divorce the thinking of a man from the historical accidents of his life. This is supremely true in the case of William Temple, ninety-eighth Archbishop of Canterbury, who lived and worked in one of the most revolutionary periods of English history. To do him justice in a biographical sketch required a chapter of greater length than I deemed wise to place at the beginning of this study. The chapter is long, too, because it contains a considerable amount of material never before published. If one is familiar with the main outlines of the life of Temple, he may defer the reading of this chapter until he has finished the book. If the twenty-one years which have elapsed since Temple's death have blurred the outline, the reader would do well to start with this chapter which begins on page 234. In either case, it must be remembered that William Temple's thinking on all subjects was always in close relation to the times in which he lived; and in order to attempt to understand his mind it is necessary to understand, insofar as one can, the forces that were at work in the world during the sixty-one years of his life.

It may still be too early to attempt this "portrait," although I find comfort in knowing that even a not too sympathetic critic agrees that it can be done.[3] And I have relied on my being an ordinary man to guide me in picking out the things in Temple's life and thought which will touch and illuminate our common life and thought, and needs. *Audite haec, omnes.*

JOSEPH FLETCHER

Cambridge, Massachusetts
Eastertide, 1963

A NOTE ON THE USE OF THE REFERENCE MATERIAL

The superior numbers in the text indicate References which are consecutive by chapters and begin on page 341.

The numbers in brackets in the text refer to the Notes beginning on page 285.

Capital letters in parentheses in the Notes abbreviate the titles of Temple's works already referred to in text. These are arranged alphabetically before the titles in the Bibliography, and will serve as a quick reference to this section.

Contents

Part I

CONSTRUCTIVE THEOLOGY

❖ ❖ ❖

I

Theology as a Method

William Temple's enduring passion was theology, and it was along theological lines that he tackled everything he encountered in life—facts and ideas alike. To him theology was a method, a way of looking at things, a standpoint or perspective—an "angle" of approach.

From first to last, he was convinced that in order to succeed at understanding or doing anything it has to be theologized, i.e., set in a framework of Christian faith. And he pressed his theological quest with great confidence: "I know of no problem which does not yield in some degree to the application of Christian faith when that is brought to bear upon it." [1] His whole outlook and attitude, and his basic response to life, were so pervaded by Christian faith that he had no "religious experiences" in the usual sense of the term, because all his experience was religious.

It was a mistake, as he saw it, to consider theology primarily as a body of dogmas or a system of doctrines. He thought of it as a living, changing, growing method of understanding both personal and social problems. [43] He liked to tell a modern parable of the foolish man who bought a basket of fruit, chewed the basket along with the fruit and, finding it not good as food, threw it away with the fruit inside it, and went hungry. Another foolish man found it in the ditch and ate both fruit and basket: he got bad indigestion. Temple sought constantly for ways to bring home to Church people and skeptics alike that those who cannot separate the truth from the formula, the dogma from the doctrine, are going to suffer whether they keep them or throw them away.

In large measure it was this that accounted for his remarkable ability to make theology a "lively" subject wherever he went, for

3

whomever he met. It was only to be expected, somehow, that when about two dozen Americans described their conversions to Anglicanism recently, in *Modern Canterbury Pilgrims,* they would dedicate their confessions of faith "To the late William Temple, for many a guide on the pilgrimage." He was very close in method to Socrates reasoning in the market place, very far from Moses handing down rulings on tablets of stone.

❋ FAITH AND REASON   Being a man of both reason and faith, he naturally gave serious attention to the relation between the two. Some men try to live by reason alone, by the facts of sense experience and the use of logic, without any faith assertions at all. Others live by faith alone, ignoring any intellectual difficulties raised by their faith. With Temple faith came first, but he always sought to refine and validate it with both logic and the facts of common observation. He liked to quote St. Paul's counsel to the early Christians on matters of faith: "Occupy your *minds* with these things." When, as a small boy, he read Plato's suggestion about government in *The Republic,* he asked his father if it wouldn't be a good thing if philosophers ruled the world; and his father replied, "They *do* rule it, silly, five hundred years after they are dead." [2] He never forgot that.

To put this directly, then, theology's first-order problem is the connection between faith and reason. But before we look at Temple's treatment of it, we should understand that, in Christianity, faith is not all alone as it seeks a partnership with reason. It has *revelation,* or self-disclosure, alongside it as a coequal. Christianity, like the other two Semitic religions, Judaism and Mohammedanism, is a faith based in part upon divine acts of revelation, not only on human acts of faith and reason. Biblical religion is a matter of God's disclosures as well as of man's discoveries. Part of its data, therefore, along with reason and faith decisions, are revealed truth and meaning. Thus the theological method is three-pronged: it involves revelation as well as faith and reason.

Temple always made it quite clear that God's revelation is

never in the form of complete, utter proof. Our beliefs have no finality. "How should there be finality in the finite's apprehension of the Infinite? . . . Our faith is a continuous adventure, and leads perpetually to new discoveries." [3] That is, God does not tear down the frontier between the human and the divine; He never makes the relative absolute, nor the finite infinite. Just as He does not coerce or override our wills, *making* us righteous and obedient, so He does not override our intelligences, making us believe or know what our human limitations cannot encompass.

Temple pointed out that if the factual evidence for the Incarnation, for example, were complete, then we would *have* to believe that Christ was God in human form, *even if we wished it were not true!* It would be like a logical or scientific proof. It would be assent, not discipleship; mental submission, not commitment in faith. If philosophy could *prove* faith, faith would lose its religious quality. [4] Here, incidentally, we see the vital difference between faith and belief: in faith there is only partial proof, while in belief there is full proof. This is as much a moral as it is an intellectual difference, since it means that faith is a matter of voluntary or loving relationship, whereas belief is mental conquest. A grasp of this difference between faith and belief, and the relative subordination of the latter, is utterly necessary to an understanding of Temple's theology. He always remembered that trust is the essence of faith, not of belief— because *even Satan believed, and all his angels.* [44]

Faith and reason, as Temple saw them, are related to each other as a team, yet as two definitely different functions. The priority of faith in all religious propositions was very plainly set forth in his thinking. "My own upbringing has predisposed me to believe in the promises of Christ." [5] [45] It almost took the form of Tertullian's *credo quia absurdum*—holding by faith what is absurd, i.e., alongside or beyond reason's powers. On the other hand, he never took the view that he could, by faith, embrace what is against reason. Rather than oppose the two, he used a dialectical method with which we shall grow quite familiar as we go along. [46] He took the view that it is not a question of faith *versus* reason, or faith *or* reason, or even faith *and* reason, but of the dynamic principle of faith *in* reason and reason in faith. This is surely a liberal principle; and we can all agree with Canon Baker that it is the method a man uses to arrive at his opinions, and not the opinions themselves, that mark a man as a liberal.

All his life he was looked upon by philosophers as a theologian, and by theologians as a philosopher—demonstrating that he managed fairly well to practice what he preached! Bishop Yngve Brilioth thought him possibly a little too much of each to suit those wholly in the other camp.[6] Archbishop Ramsey, another theologian-Primate, speaking of Temple's work as more that of the intellectual than the historical scholar, said, "If Temple was the amateur, he was yet, *par excellence,* the theologian . . . and, if ever a man was, a theologian by temperament and intuition." [7]

⚙ THE LEAP OF FAITH   As with Tertullian's maxim, in spirit Temple was at least very close to Anselm's *credo ut intelligam.* ("I do not seek to understand in order to believe, but I believe in order to understand.") [8] In the preface to *Christus Veritas* he said bluntly that Anselm's maxim must be "the motto of Theology." The whole of his first major work, *Mens Creatrix,* was a philosophic defense of the "credo" principle: he shows in the first part how "Man's Search" for the ultimate meaning of life does not succeed and, in the second part, how "God's Act" alone gives religious truth and certainty. But here again he was certain that even though we have to make a "leap" of faith in order to achieve religious convictions and beliefs, reason still has to enter in at once; and where faith knowingly violates reason's rules, it loses all moral claim to trust or loyalty.

If we can say that reason was the junior partner, rather than the senior, in Temple's method, it was nevertheless impossible for him to feel any agreement with Luther's outburst, "That whore, Dame Reason!" It is true that he put Luther as a man of faith in a triumvirate of giants along with St. Francis and Pascal. But while he could understand Luther's anger at any stiff-necked uses of reason to isolate and demean faith, he could never sympathize with a denunciation of reason as such and by name. [47] It was just that he put theology first and philosophy second: *Christian* philosophy is constructive reasoning about the theology (faith assertions) already in hand. "Faith," he insisted, "is not a conclusion but a starting point; reasoning will enrich its content." Yet "God is for faith not an inference, but a *datum*," because "the man of faith does not reach his faith by scientific inference." [9]

There are, he thought, three fundamental ways in which all propositions of faith vitally need to be serviced by reason and critical thinking. First, reason is a means of communication, a tool with which men of faith can "make sense" of their faith to others. Second, reason is a means of relating faith to life, to all and sundry of the private and public concerns of human beings, to deepen and illuminate and test them in the light of faith. In short, *reason is the link between the believing and the behaving*. (It was this partnership of faith and reason, as applied to controversial economic and political problems, which gained him the alert attention of the world at large, religious and non-religious.) [48] Third, reason is a method of criticizing, testing, and evaluating the faith itself against the canons of sound logic and broad human experience.

Here, too, we see that for all his admiration of Luther, he would not embrace any notion of faith which permits it to flout or ignore reasonable tests as to its internal and external consistency. He put Luther alongside Descartes as one guilty of the *faux pas* of self-imprisonment or "solipsism"—an individualistic or egocentric way of seeking truth which attempts to be its own judge and critic. The essential thing about sin or moral evil is that it is self-centered, and he regarded self-centered methods of thinking as an intellectual evil. Descartes' "I think, therefore I am" was like "I want, therefore it is mine," or "I believe, therefore it is true." [49] Temple showed that Descartes was wrong in supposing that self-consciousness precedes or arises before consciousness of the objective world—including other consciousnesses. The fact is, they go together; the self remains unknown even to itself except by contrast with the not-self. Like Heidegger, Temple claimed that even selfhood is a social achievement

—that the primal perception is not self-consciousness, pure self, but *being in the world:* Descartes could have been sure both of himself and of the cold stove in which he sat for a day, when he made his great discovery!

To paraphrase the old saying about mysticism, Temple held that solipsism, or any self-validating test of faith, is a method that begins in sole-ness or loneliness (mist), centers in I or the self, and ends in schism. Along with interpretation and application, therefore, *correlation* (but not, note, verification) is one of reason's vital services to faith. It was in this temper that he also used "analogy" in his theologizing, drawing logical parallels between what we know about man or nature to what we think about God. He followed Jesus' analogical method of reasoning, as in the conclusions He drew about the heavenly Father's love from what He knew of a human father.[10] The divine and infinite are not subject to proof positive since "the Eternal ever eludes us," and yet he thought "by analogy we may make progress" in our wondering about theology's questions, "even though we never reach their ultimate solution."[11] "I see no alternative to the acceptance of the method of analogy."[12]

In this method reason is not able to build a bridge from the side of doubt, or unbelief, to the opposite shore of faith. Temple was close to a Catholic like Kenneth Kirk and to a Protestant like Karl Barth: his foundation was dogmatic, not empirical. But while his method was not that of "natural theology" constitutively, it was regulatively. He would not agree with Barth, strongest of the positive theologians, that natural theology leads only to idols and metaphysical vagaries. Says Barth, "God is not only unprovable and unsearchable, but also *inconceivable.*"[13] Temple would deny the last assertion, accept the first two. Reason, by its scrutiny of the facts of experience, might build a platform that will put a man of faith within jumping distance of it. "A vague theism," he said, "is futile." The various proofs of God's existence have no cutting edge. "The Christian has made a *decision* for God who has spoken—in nature, in history, in the prophets, in Christ."[14] In the end a "leap" is needed to get him there. The intellect has to make "a leap in the dark such as Science may not take."[15] Temple liked to describe genuine faith propositions as *decisions,* not conclusions. But then, once the leap is made, once the faith is reached and the decision made, reason must come into play again to check the faith against logic and experience, criticizing, testing, relating, explaining, applying it.

For this reason, his method was "a policy of encirclement." He circled round and round a problem like a mongoose around a cobra, using both intuitive reasoning (from data) and deductive (from premises). [50] He would quote his teacher Edward Caird, "There is no harm in arguing in a circle if the circle is large enough." [16] Beginning with his *Mens Creatrix* he used a method combining "inner circle," or theological reasoning *from* faith to questions raised by experience, and "outer circle," or philosophical reasoning *toward* the Christian faith. One was *credo ut intelligam,* the other *intelligo ut credam.* In the end, as he saw it, the philosophical method does not succeed. As far as it goes it is sound but its result is fairly barren. The theological method, starting with a faith-premise, "is a leap only justified intellectually by its results." But Temple was convinced that it *is* so justified.

It is, of course, part of this method to assume by a faith-leap that coherence and ultimate unity are real and to be searched for. This ultimate "monism" is what the theology of monotheism rests upon. Temple would say that "pluralism is nonsense," but he meant *ultimate* pluralism and not immediate intellectual or social pluralism: for only by accepting the variety of opinions among finite humans will the method of dialectic or coherence lead us closer to the unity. Along the way we are to avoid either-or thinking. "Many unnecessary difficulties are caused, as I think, by a readiness to draw negative inferences from positive premises." [17] And we are to avoid easy and hasty blueprints of theology! [51] Of the magnificent scholastic unification of medieval thought, under the scepter of theology, he thought, "The trouble about the effort was not that it failed but that it succeeded too well. Its very completeness laid fetters upon the intellect of later generations, and when progress came it was by the bursting of a dam." [18]

One way of describing the temper or quality of Temple's mind might be in the words used to describe Edward Caird, the Master of Balliol in Temple's undergraduate days. "Nothing would content him but to be a man of *coherent* convictions." [19] His thought had to be coherent, or consistent or harmonized, within itself—as well as without in its application to the world. He thought *unitively*. If a distinction made in some quarters has any meaning, we would say that his chief excellence was in "coherent" reason rather than in "analytical" reason. [52] All of his life—in all kinds of groups and in his characteristic role as mediator between one group and another—he was able to see quickly the middle terms, the common elements and connecting links in an irenic and conciliatory reinterpretation. It was a gift of reconciliation and "at-one-ment" from which the Anglican communion, the World Council of Churches, and the public policy constantly profited.

In characteristic modesty and humor, he called this ability to harmonize divergent views his little "parlour trick." He thought *in*clusively, not *ex*clusively; and nothing was more alien to his intellectual bent than individualism in conduct and arbitrariness in thought. Dean Matthews called Temple's approach a "comprehensive" one fired by a "synthetic impulse." [20] When Anglicans were accused of trying to carry water on both shoulders, Catholic and Protestant, Temple himself would reply that far from sacrificing truth for the sake of peace, peace and coexistence are a prerequisite to reaching a fuller truth! His method was an Anglican method, in effect. In a memoir about Oliver Quick in 1944, shortly before his own death, Temple spoke of his (Temple's) "temperamental disposition, fortified by the fact that my master in logic was Edward Caird, to start from the assumption that every conviction strongly held is at least partly true, and that, as a rule, our wisdom is to find out, if we can, where this partial truth fits into the whole fabric." [21]

❂ REVELATION   Temple described revelation as a believing interpretation of experience. A typically terse and lucid discussion is seen, among others, in the first chapter of *The Cen-*

trality of Christ. Reason, he showed, is not opposed to revelation any more than to faith. Everything is revelation but not everything is revealing, he thought, because its meaning will depend upon what the receiver can receive. The whole world, God's entire creation, is a revelation of its Maker's mind and will, but the extent to which it reveals its Maker to any observer will depend on the observer's insight and openness to meaning. God's acts of self-disclosure (the essential definition of revelation) are therefore both *general*, i.e., discernible in the world of realities He has created, and *special*, i.e., deliberately given, in certain distinct and particular acts or events of the divine initiative. Temple treated both theology and philosophy as coherent studies, unitive studies of all things, with the whole of reality as their proper field.[22]

According to Temple there are two dimensions to revelation —the divine and the human. One way to put it would be to say that revelation is a two-way traffic. It is, first of all, a divine act of God's self-disclosure. In its next or second stage, it is a human perception or believing response. Fully and finally, revelation is the coincidence of event and appreciation. [53] As a faithful reader of the Fourth Gospel Temple was aware of these two sides of the process: first, "the Word was made flesh and dwelt among us, full of grace and truth," and second, "we beheld His glory, the glory of the only-begotten from the Father." [23] The beholding of God's self-disclosure is the work of theology. The human side of revelation gives us plenty of reason to be humble rather than overbearing or overconfident about our faith.

Even in respect to the Bible or "Word of God," he insisted that we remember that it is *ta biblia*—in the plural—a collection of books, by an assortment of writers in a variety of situations, dealing with plural revelations which may well be disclosures of the divine, yet they are all refracted or sifted through the finite personalities of the human writers of the books. Not the books of the Bible but the events it records make the revelation. "There has never been a devout person who in practice puts the whole Bible upon one level". [24] He would not take seriously the dictation or stenographic doctrine that it is inspired completely

and literally, word for word, by the Holy Spirit, as taught by
Roman Catholic and Protestant fundamentalists.

As Temple watched biblical theology gain a revival, he
feared that some of the young theologians were in danger of
forgetting the lessons of the nineteenth century, and even of
getting involved in "a position which is either obscurantist or
humbug." [25] He distrusted "Bible Christianity" for the same
reason he distrusted "Churchianity"—he could see the ultimate
self-centeredness behind them. The craving for an infallible and
unquestionable authority is actually often a subtle form of
hubris: it may lead to an infallible Book, then to an infallible
Church to interpret the Book, then to an infallible spokesman
for the infallible Church; but behind all this is the infallible
Self which selects and therefore undergirds all such infallibilities.

In an essay on revelation, he called it "the coincidence of
divinely controlled event, and minds divinely illuminated to read
it aright." [26] He also once told a university audience that it "is
given chiefly through events to minds enlightened to receive
it." [27] This is essentially a theory of revelation by inspiration. It
must not be taken to mean, however, that God somehow arbitrarily *chooses* one person and endows him with the faith to appreciate the meaning of revelation, while not choosing others. Temple
had no esoteric or "gnostic" idea of inspiration as given by God
in the form of secret knowledge to some but withheld from
others. There are traces of this gnostic notion of divine discrimination and favoritism in some places in the New Testament,
but it made no headway with Temple. The inspiration needed
to make a faith-full response to God's special revelation, he
thought, is itself not a special gift at all. The Holy Spirit works
constantly through reason, in fellowship and the sacraments, in
the exercise of curiosity and imagination, and by character-
forming experience. Thus the Spirit leads people to open up
their lives to His influence, to "lay them open" to faith. God
makes nobody ride second class, just as He compels nobody to
ride first. Faith is free—a free gift from God and a free choice
of men.

These two kinds of revelation, general and special, have been
treated separately in traditional theology under the headings of

"natural religion" and "revealed religion." But, as Temple showed, the categories are not too useful because they are not truly separate. After all, nature itself is a revelation, and revelation is made through or by means of natural media. Everything is a revelation, even if it is not always revealing. In any case, revelation always occurs *within* nature since it is natural man who is the receiver. Nature is revelation's context, whether God is "seen in a sunset" or encountered in the sudden blindness suffered by a Pharisee from Tarsus, on the road to Damascus. The starting point of Temple's Gifford Lectures in Glasgow, 1932-1934, was that the difference between Natural Theology and Revealed Theology, so-called, is one of method only, not of content or sphere. And by the same token he set aside the division commonly made between "philosophy" and "theology," claiming that it is intellectually unrealistic to call the first an enterprise in reason and the second an enterprise in faith. Since reason and faith cannot be so artificially disconnected or pulled loose from their true relation to each other, he held that the true task of theology is to reason closely and fully about faith.

Whether it results from studying things in creation, such as its laws of gravitation and development, or is a result of some particular event, such as the Cross or Pentecost, faith in every case has to be examined seriously and honestly. As Temple himself demonstrated in his whole life and thought, *theology is the business of philosophizing about faith,* of checking and analysing and relating and criticizing and applying the tenets of both "natural" and "revealed" faith.

He thought of his own work as more a matter of *theological philosophy* than "philosophical theology." [28] The method-difference has to do with the starting points they use; philosophy starts with no assumption except the reliability of reason applied to experience, whereas theology begins with a "primary certainty," or faith-assumption, about God. But both of them are concerned with what he called the four departments of the spiritual life— science, art, morality, and religion.[29] Therefore he could also say, on the same grounds, that the "limitation of the Church's sphere is not a matter of area, but of method." [30]

It would be superficial to suppose that philosophy is a critical and thoughtful practice, while theology is somehow authoritative and arbitrary—more a matter of willing or feeling than of thinking. That there is a great spread of merely visceral "religion" is a sad fact that has to be dealt with and guarded against. But this is not by any means a true picture of theology. And in the same way philosophy cannot be said to rule out all consideration and use of faith-assertions, even though some brands of philosophy do, such as certain radical forms of "logical positivism" which strictly limit their facts to the sense data of the scientific method. [54]

⚙ THEOLOGY IN PROCESS Temple saw the various methods men use in their thinking and believing as *dialectically interpenetrating,* rather than as watertight categories and compartments. This was part of the secret of his dynamic interpretation and his wide influence. Diagrams are helpful to some readers, not to others; but for what it is worth, here is one that sets out Temple's "epistemology"—his theory of the progression of knowledge and insight, and the method of theology. It puts science, philosophy and theology into a working relationship along a line, or continuum, of human consciousness. According to his conception, each of these channels of approach is, in its own way and place, a form of knowledge:

(direct knowledge)	(inferential knowledge)	(inferential knowledge)	(direct knowledge)
SCIENCE	PHILOSOPHY	GENERAL REVELATION	SPECIAL REVELATION
sense data	logic and values	awareness of the holy	faith in the divine initiative

Each type of "knowing" has its own distinctive kind of objective data, given just below its place in the line. Each type of knowing, furthermore, has as its full data, or material, not only what stands below it on the line but also *everything to the left.* Each kind of knowing contributes to, but does not automatically or necessarily result in, what follows it on the line to the right. Thus, for example, many men of high intelligence and good will know the facts of science, but without doing any philosophizing from them at all. Others might philosophize, but without any sense of the *mysterium tremendum et fascinans* all about us. Still others may be "theists," yet they will not give any credence to the special revelation of (let us say) Moses' law or Christ's divinity. Others follow the whole route from right to left. Some take account of the sense experience at the extreme left, but not of the religious experience at the extreme right. As a matter of fact, the only point at which we *all* stand, of necessity, *is* on the left end. It is the starting point of knowledge for everybody. And philosophy *as such* may use theism as a hypothesis, but that is all it can be—for philosophy.[31]

Revelation comes at the summit of Temple's knowledge hierarchy, so to speak. We might sum up what he had to say about it by using the "seven queries" of the journalist who writes a newspaper story: the who, the what, the where, and so on, of revelation.

Who? It is God Himself who initiates certain specially revealing acts or events, in addition to the revelation of the basic creation itself. Therein He discloses His nature and will to men. The Bible, which is often described as the story of the mighty acts of God, is the supreme and normative revelation of the Christian faith. But God's self-disclosure in creation, history, and in personal religious experience goes on continually: it is progressive—not hardened once for all in any time, place or manner.

What? The best way to describe revelation is as a "dialectic" or mutual combination of mind and event, consciousness and phenomena, perception and experience, insight and data. [55] The data may lie in nature and history, or in some special episode or fact. But in revelation there is both *what God does* and *what man discovers.* As a student and young don at Oxford he learned much from Plato, the idealist, and often quoted Plato's maxim, "Comprehension is dialectic, nothing else"—a maxim by which even a materialist like Marx could do his reasoning. Temple's method, incidentally, had been suggested to him by reading Plato and Kant, not Hegel and Marx.

Where? Everywhere. God is revealed everywhere if He is revealed anywhere. The God of Christian faith is omnifacient (Maker of all things) and all things reveal Him. It is all His handiwork, not only the Babe in the manger but the tree from which the manger was cut and shaped.

When? Revelation comes in the *regularities* of nature, in such "laws" and processes as Mendelian genetics and interplanetary attraction. But it comes about also in *departures* from regularity (not violations) by which God acts directly in His "search" for man. Examples would be the Resurrection appearances described in the gospels and Acts, and above all in the Incarnation. In Temple's understanding, God's revelation is a process exactly as His creation is a process. They are not mere episodes, or only events. They are dynamic, not static. They are *processes*. As early as 1912, in the essay on the Church which he wrote for Canon Streeter's *Foundations*, he declared that even if Christianity is the "final" religion, the Church is still in its infancy. Two thousand years are as two days in God's plan. Any appeal to the "primitive" Church is misleading because *we* are the primitive Church!

How? Revelation, we have said, comes both in a general way and in a special way: through nature and history, and in single events in the lives or persons of men. As we shall see, it was by the last named means, through personality, that Temple found revelation's supreme "opening" into human experience. "Knowledge of the living God comes not from Greece and philosophy but from Palestine and from religious experience." [32] He expressed this by constantly quoting II Corinthians 5:19, "God was in Christ, reconciling the world . . ." [56] The highest, truest revelation is in persons, and the highest, truest person is Christ. Christian theology interprets or accounts for the universe in terms of personality, for it traces all things to God the Father as the Alpha and Omega. Precisely, it interprets personality in terms of Christ as the norm.

As a devoted student of the Fourth Gospel he was struck by

the story of Philip's saying, "Show us the Father and it sufficeth," and Jesus' reply, "He that hath seen me hath seen the Father." [33] In a letter to Ronald Knox in 1913, he wrote, "The whole of my theology is an attempt to understand and verify the words: 'He that hath seen me hath seen the Father.' " [34] Temple went so far as to say that knowledge of God can be fully given only in a person, never in a doctrine, still less in formless faith, whatever that might be. It was his Incarnational or Christocentric faith that lay behind his "personalism" and the entire scheme of his values. Personality is the highest good and the chief medium of our knowledge of God. "So long as people discuss God in the third person—whether He exists and of what nature He is— they are in a frame of mind for which apprehension of the Truth about Him is impossible. God must be to us neither *It* nor *He,* but *Thou* . . . Knowledge *about* God is valuable in its place; but knowledge *of* God alone has saving power." [35]

Why? God's purpose or aim in revelation is not primarily intellectual or cognitive. It is not essentially the uncovering of mysteries or the overcoming of ignorance. It is an interpersonal divine-human encounter. Temple saw that God comes Himself in the experience of revelation. He meets us in person—not by sending a letter or an impersonal message or formula, or even an agent. He came Himself. Christianity is not a *gnosis.* Thus Temple insisted that faith is not the holding of correct doctrines, but personal fellowship with the living God. He was sure that what is offered to man's apprehension in a specific revelation is not truth concerning God, but the living God Himself. Theism, belief that there is a God, can give what he called "a comfortable warmth," but it won't "kindle fire"; for "it is not belief in a diffused Goodness pervading the universe that has the power to change men's lives, but [as Galatians 2:20 expressed it] faith in the Son of God, Who loved me and gave Himself up for me." [36]

Here we see two cardinal elements in Temple's theology: first his sharp emphasis that men with their finite intelligences can at best by reason and revelation only *ap*prehend God, not *com*prehend Him; and second, that faith is essentially not belief *about* God but a *relationship* of trust (*pistis* in the New Testament)—that, in short, faith is a moral rather than an intellectual matter. [57]

Finally, *Which?* Although it respects reason, revelation in the last analysis is faith-tied. In Temple's view, the so-called "logical proofs" of God's existence (the cosmological from a first cause, the teleological from design, and so on) are at best only arguments. God is not to be found at the end of a syllogism, or a microscope or telescope. Faith is *direct* knowledge, not inferential. Intellectually regarded it is—to repeat an important phrase —a matter of decision, not of conclusion. [58] Theology is like the judicial process in this respect, not like the scientific procedure; its end product is a *decision*. "The primary assurances of religion are the *ultimate questions* of philosophy." [37]

This is why the simplest, philosophically untutored person can "theologize"; it is not something only for the specially learned. In his personal copy of J. M. Thompson's *Jesus According to Mark,* Temple underlined the reminder, "Jesus was not a theologian." [59] This is needed to correct the highly technical and professionalized image of the theologian. In a sermon in Oxford in 1914, Temple pointed out that "Christ answered no speculative questions." [38] But possibly Temple underlined Thompson's remark for another reason altogether—maybe he was thinking that theology is God-centered thinking by anybody on any subject and that, thus understood, Jesus was the Great Theologian for us all.

II

God's Search for Man

First, last, and always Christianity is faith in Christ. Jesus' query put to the disciples at Caesarea Philippi, "Who do men say that I am?" is the core question.[1] With William Temple the doctrine of the Incarnation was the focal point of his whole picture of the world. He centered everything on the belief that God in Christ has taken on human form, dwelt as a man among men, died and rose again for their salvation and to fulfill the purpose of Creation. Thus, quite simply, to know Christ is to know God. "He that hath seen me hath seen the Father." Jesus Christ is the self-expression of God.

To understand Temple's outlook, it is necessary to appreciate his simple starting point—"simple" not in the sense of naive or superficial, but in the sense of definite and particular. Everything centers in Christ, the incarnate Word. "The whole process of that revelation which has been going on through nature, through history and through the prophets, comes to complete fulfillment in the Incarnation." [2] Therefore, to Temple, Christian theology (in the precise sense of the term) was "God in the Light of the Incarnation." And anthropology was "Man in the Light of the Incarnation."

❈ THE NECESSARY INCARNATION Temple did not hesitate to say that this supreme act of God's self-disclosure, His incarnation in a human personality, was a necessity inherent in the very nature of the divine being. Love could not keep itself secret or hidden. The Incarnation is a moral necessity, if not a "metaphysical" one. [60] To put it another way, God is personal—a

19

loving Person—and what is personal can only be communicated and *must* be communicated in personal action. [61] The divine Person reveals Himself to human persons in the historic Person of Christ: the Incarnation is a Person reaching out to persons through a Person. Truth comes in personalities rather than in propositions. "It is the only way in which divine truth can be expressed, not because of our infirmity but because of its own nature. What is personal can only be expressed in a person." [3]

In addition to God's own nature as love, as a rationale for the Incarnation, Temple held that His gift to men of moral or "spiritual" freedom is also a reason for it. The divine self-disclosure had to be an intelligible one for men. "For God had made men so that their full response could only be to what they understand." [4] If God forced our obedience to His will or arbitrarily remade our character to fit in with it, He would thereby violate His own nature as love and vitiate our freedom. To escape from our natural human self-centeredness, and to entrust ourselves to God, we have to be *drawn* to His service, not driven. And there is, Temple explained, only one power—God's love—which can be so compellingly attractive. (This conception, a dialectical combination of compulsion and attraction, is a genuine paradox. The grammatical term for it is "oxymoron," meaning the combination of two terms which are ordinarily contradictory.)

God's love, alone among loves, is *ultimately* irresistible, yet immediately it is always a matter of free choice, either requited or unrequited. "When a man acts to please one whom he loves," said Temple, "doing or bearing what apart from that love he would not do or bear, his action is wholly determined by the other's pleasure, yet in no action is he so utterly free—that is, so utterly determined by his apparent good!" [5] [62] Only love can call love forth. It shapes its own response. This is what God did in the self-sacrificing love He showed in humbling Himself to become Man and dying ignobly on a cross. Yet He refused in His work to infringe on any one's liberty. "All response was to be free, and if no free response was forthcoming He would seek no other." [6]

When he spoke of God "humbling Himself to become Man,"

Temple definitely meant both things—that the Incarnation is humbling to God (although not humiliating), and that by it God identified Himself with all mankind and not with just one individual. Propositionally, in some metaphysical sense, God is "wholly other" as some theologians say. This is the "transcendental" side; He is surely beyond and apart from His creation. But *experientially* speaking, God is here and now, to be met, accessible in prayer, and an Actor with His own role in history. To the Greeks, as St. Paul pointed out (I Corinthians 1:23), the Christian faith that God could be human was, in spite of their own popular mythology, an absurdity. And to the Jews, the Christian faith that the Messiah had died on a cross was a scandal. Yet Temple never flinched from the affront to "polite" opinion in such an absurd and scandalous doctrine. He never lost sight of the point that the heart of Christian belief is in a God who could not only "come down to man's level," but actually be executed by capital punishment under a civil-ecclesiastical sentence. This is a God who not only dared to become a man but a criminal—a divine act of shocking sacrificial love. [63]

❁ MAN—NOT ONE MAN ONLY But is it enough or correct to say that God became "a" man? Not according to Temple.[7] He saw our Lord as the Second Adam, the new or renewing progenitor of the human race. Adam in the Genesis myth means, of course, "mankind" collectively, not a single individual. [64] So God in Christ entered into human nature and humanity as a whole. He took upon Himself mankind. This is the supreme instance of "the immanence of the transcendent." [8]

Temple held, as in *Foundations*, that in the eternal Christ, the everlasting Son, there abides a "Divine Humanity" which always underlay created humanity and was made fully manifest at the Incarnation—"the humanity of God, if the expression may be allowed, took flesh in the fulness of time." And a major part of the total process of continuing creation, he believed, is created man's "growing up into Christ," into Man.

Thus he reasoned that the Incarnation was not only, or primarily, the addition of another individual to the human race. It was the confluence of deity and humanity, "the inauguration of a new system of mutual influence" which will ultimately embrace all men. He therefore taught that to be "saved" means to know and to believe gladly that we *have* been lifted up, that "I live, yet not I, but Christ liveth in me." [9] He quoted a phrase of his father's that in the Incarnation God "raised our humanity to an entirely higher level, to a level with His own." He also quoted Moberly: "Christ is Man, not generically but inclusively," just as He is God "not generically but identically." Temple made his own a saying of Frederick Denison Maurice, "He is the Head of the Body." [10] It was a strong Christocentric doctrine of human and social solidarism.

However, he offered no merely mechanical identification of God and men as an incarnational *event* only. It was the "inauguration" of something, too. In keeping with his method of process or development, he regarded our human solidarity with and in Christ—at least as far as our knowledge and acceptance of it are concerned—as something being wrought out through time and the course of history. For this reason he favored the analogy of Christ as the Vine in the Fourth Gospel, growing and absorbing and embracing all about it: Christ the root, men the branches (John 15). What was in fact accomplished potentially in the Incarnation, this at-one-ment or reconciliation of all men with God, would in the end be certainly and fully realized in a conscious fellowship. God will not be mocked, His loving purpose will not be frustrated, His Kingdom is begun and will surely come at last in full completion. It is now already "in process," he believed, and therefore he discarded all millennial notions of a "second coming" to establish the Kingdom. He was convinced that the scriptural grounds for such an idea are confused and inadequate. "But not all have eyes to perceive; and the time when 'every eye shall see Him' is still future, and this is the truth in the expectation of a Return or Second Coming." [11]

Because of his dislike and distrust of doctrinaire rigidity, Temple was glad that this most important part of the Christian faith has never been exactly defined and formulated. No orthodoxy tests have ever been applied. [65] The upshot of the Christological controversies that ran from one ecumenical council to another in the early Church was a decision formed in Chalcedon, 451 A.D. It simply declared that Jesus Christ was both human and divine—but as to *how,* it said nothing. "The truth is that this great formula derives part of its value from the clearness with which it refuses to explain . . . it marks the definite failure of all attempts to explain the Incarnation in terms of Essence, Substance, Nature, and the like . . . Interpretations will vary from age to age, according to the concepts supplied to the interpreters by current thought. It would be disastrous if there were an official Church explanation of the Incarnation." [12] Thus the Maurice-Temple doctrine of solidarism was, as they were both always careful to remember, only *their* theory of the "how" of the Incarnation.

❄ THE WORD MADE FLESH In his *Citizen and Churchman,* published in the early stages of the Second World War (1941, the year of the Malvern Conference), he said that the Incarnation is the heart of the Christian philosophy because it challenges the common habit of treating the "material" and the "spiritual" as if they were mutually exclusive. As the core doctrine of Christian faith, he thought, the Incarnation asserts—as Marxism does—a dialectical interpenetration of the two. By claiming that the divine and the human—the spiritual and the material—are one in Christ Jesus, their alleged opposition and contradiction are once and for all denied. "Christianity," he said, "is the most avowedly materialist of all the great religions." [13] It makes the astounding claim (John 1:14) that the Word was made flesh and dwelt among us!

This Incarnational doctrine makes Christianity a far more radical form of "dialectical materialism" than Marxism ever dreamed of being. For Christianity sees life and growth taking place not only through dialectic, the mutual penetration between things and the human spirit, but also through the interpenetration of the *very flesh* of men with no less than the Holy Spirit of God. No more *cosmic* and, at the same time, intimate dialectic than this is imaginable.[14]

People often say that theology's insoluble problem is the presence of evil in God's creation. (Not so much the moral evil of sin as the "cosmic" or natural evil of error and suffering.) This may be so, although we shall see that Temple nevertheless boldly wrestled with it. But, logically, there is a prior and equally perplexing question. Before wondering how a loving Creator could devise or allow evil in any form, we might well wonder why He would create a finite world at all! Why would God produce the relative out of the absolute, the finite from the infinite, the conditional alongside the unconditioned, the imperfect beside the perfect? Temple, refusing to evade the question by a bland disregard, explained it on the ground that, although He had no need of us for the fulness of His being, He has need of us for the satisfaction of His love.[15]

Just as love is the cause of the Incarnation, so is it the cause of the Creation. It is the reason for *both* creations, the old as well as the new. Love, for Temple, was the creative power behind both nature and grace. To use the language of the Scholastics, he saw in love the "efficient," or beginning, cause of both nature and redemption, and the "final" cause—the goal of "the Kingdom of God, the sovereignty of Love." God being love, indeed, love is the First Cause of all things. God "needs" objects for His love, but not in the sense that God could not be God without men as His beneficiaries or love objects. "The World — God = O: God — the World = God." [16] This is because love of its own nature conceives and creates; while it does not need objects, it necessitates them. The creation of man in particular is thus a parallel to the creation in general, "necessary to God only in the sense that, being what He is, His nature leads to its creation." [17]

⚙ THE SUFFERING OF GOD   There is too close a relation between God and man (God the origin or original, man the image or likeness) to imagine either of them being without some of the qualities of the other. This mutuality extends to other things besides the primary capacity of love. One of these is suffering. [66] There is a radical difference between the Greek metaphysical theology and the Jewish personal theology here. Temple felt that Israel's refusal to accept the Gospel had "led to the excessive influence of Greek intellectualism over the moral and prophetic witness of the Church." [18] To the Greeks deity, or the divine nature, is so perfect and remote and impersonal ("substance" or "essence" or "being") that it is beyond the suffering of imperfect and vulnerable human beings. For them God is "impassive" or apathetic. He feels nothing, being beyond emotion. His nature transcends all such human traits.

But in the Hebraic, biblical faith it is different. There God is "human" or "personal" in the sense that His nature is not at all different from man's in its qualities, only in its perfection of those qualities. The divine life, like the human, is marked by "mind" and "will" and "feeling," all three of the basic psychological workings of personal being. To think of God as personality may be inadequate analogy, for His ways and thoughts are not ours. It may only be the highest or "last term" we can conceive with finite minds. But, said Temple, it is a mode by which we may think of God "more accurately" than in any other way.[19] In any case, the biblical understanding of God is a highly personal one, almost "anthropomorphic" in its vivid way of projecting a human image. [67] This is because of the Bible's creationist faith that men are *theomorphic,* made in God's image. The "likeness," that is to say, logically has to run in both directions.

"Only a God in whose perfect Being pain has its place can win and hold our worship; for otherwise the creature would in fortitude surpass the Creator." [20] This insight of Temple's cuts straight across the Greek distaste for the idea that the heavenly Father could suffer. As a "patripassian" error they often condemned it, but never actually declared it a heresy. In spite of his sometimes almost lyric admiration for the Greeks' literature and philosophy, Temple was never a "classicist" at any point where it could cut across his position as a Biblicist. God in Christ suffered the agony of Gethsemane and the Cross. [68] Continuously He is suffering from the refusal of men to accept Him into their lives. Any and all unrequited love is divine suffering.

But Temple had an answer for those who are too metaphysical about God and who suppose that suffering would demean and dethrone him as divine. "Suffering," he said, "is not the ultimate evil. Hate is the ultimate evil." Even more to the point, he argued that suffering is not an evil at all when, as on the Cross, it is voluntary and a matter of sacrificial love. Suffering *when it is wholly voluntary* is redemptive: this is the positive Christian faith.

As he departed from Greek metaphysics about God's suffering, so Temple, in his emphasis on Christ as the "suffering servant," departed from the somewhat metaphysical and Hellenistic leanings of the Fourth Gospel. Much as he drew upon St. John in other respects, here he tended with the earlier evangelists in the synoptic gospels to think in terms of the messianic figure in Second Isaiah, whose suffering would recall men from their disloyalty to God. Although he saw some validity and meaning also in the Johannine idea of the Logos ("Word" or divine reason), he laid much greater emphasis upon this Old Testament saviour, the Suffering Servant. He had an unshakeable faith in redemption, as it is effected through the power of sacrifice, to win men's hearts.

Combining the Old Testament figures of the Servant and the Son of man, in such phrases as "the Son of man must suffer," he explained that our Lord had departed from all popular Jewish ideas of the Son of man as one who would be conqueror through glory and victory. For this reason his stress fell on the dramatic symbolism of Jesus' washing the disciples' feet at the feast of the Passover. Above all, he was influenced by the combination of suffering and salvation, in the paradoxical conception of the Great High Priest who is also the Paschal Lamb. It was only an apparent contradiction, of course—this conception of a Son of God who is the Lamb of God. Temple found it implicit in St. John's Gospel and quite explicit in the Epistle General to the Hebrews. [69]

By the same token, Temple found in the Incarnation another important moral or personal trait of God. "Christ," he said, "does not reveal all that is meant by the word God. There ever remains the unsearchable abyss of Deity. But he reveals what it vitally concerns us to know; he reveals God the Father." [21] Here is another example of the biblical analogy between the divine original nature and its human likeness (*similitudo*) in men. In fact, Temple went so far as to claim that "what was novel in the religious language of the Lord was His constant, His almost invariable, use of the word 'Father' as the name of God." [22] This was a unique element in our Lord's own teaching, not only missing in other religions but also from Judaism itself. In the old covenant God was worshipped as Judge and Law Giver, in the new as Father—combining judgment and authority with love and mercy. And he saw a regretable polytheism (bi-theism) lurking behind the kind of Christian church school education in which it is "not uncommon to find children who . . . feel differently toward God and toward Christ. When that occurs, it proves that their teaching has been greviously at fault." [23] He meant, of course, the kind of teaching which leads people to think of Jesus as generous and His heavenly Father as wrathful.

❀ INCARNATION-ATONEMENT   For Temple the Incarnation was practically an umbrella concept, it covered so many sides of Christian belief. Its scope included our Lord's life and death and resurrection, and all of their consequences. By Incarnation he meant, to put it in topical terms, a five-part complex of revealing-saving events: the birth of Jesus, His ministry of teaching and healing, His crucifixion, His resurrection, and His ascension. Taken together, these things—often called "the work of Christ" —resulted in, or effected, the Atonement. They brought about a reconciliation between God and wayward, sinful mankind. Just as in the person of Christ there was the perfect prototype of "at-one-ment" between man and God, so all men, by virtue of their creation *imago dei,* shared in the at-one-ment. [70] Therefore in contemplating Christ and His loving obedience "we see Man fulfilling his true destiny." [24]

Over the centuries the word Atonement has often carried different meanings. Some have believed that by His descending to man's estate, entering history, and suffering the Cross, Christ had "atoned" or made up somehow to God for the sins of men, thereby "getting them off the hook." This notion developed into various "satisfaction" or "substitutionary" theories, so-called. Sometimes the hook was Satan's hold over human sinners, which had to be bought off as in a ransom; sometimes the hook was God's wrath, which had to be appeased by the death of the only One important enough to substitute for them—His own Son.

In the eleventh century Archbishop Anselm developed this last mentioned notion that God's *honor,* rather than His anger, had to be satisfied somehow for man's misbehavior, and only His Son was perfect enough to compensate Him. Temple, of course, had no truck with any of these traditional views of the work of Christ in the Incarnation. They were discarded because they centered its atonement-consequences on God's honor or anger rather than upon His love. The Incarnation as he understood it was not a duel or a pay-off. [71]

An impression has grown up among some students of recent British and Anglican theology (although not the most careful ones) that while Temple was strong on the Incarnation, he neglected or minimized the Atonement. The idea seems to be due mainly to something he himself said toward the end of his life in an article ('Theology Today," 1939) on the eve of the Second World War.[25] In the Hale Lectures at Seabury-Western Theological Seminary, Archbishop Ramsey spoke of Temple's having "the courage of rare intellectual humility" because he pointed to the recent development of a "theology of redemption" in place of "a theology of explanation." [26] Temple thought that mid-century disorders, upheavals, wars and revolutions had brought an end to the atmosphere in which he and his contemporaries had lived most of their lives. [72]

He described his own era as one in which people generally had still wanted to live by Christian morals, making it possible on at least that much common ground to discuss and re-argue the case for Christian doctrine. Now, he advised, "Christian standards of conduct are challenged as radically as Christian doctrine." In such a milieu he thought it would be unstrategic to carry on this *theological* work of making a "Christian map" of the world in a Christological frame of reference. He suggested, tentatively, that it would be better to try "less imposing structures" theologically and something more in the way of direct conversion appeals. Years before, in his preface to *Doctrine in the Church of England,* he had explained that an incarnational theology leans to descriptive concerns, whereas a theology of "redemption" (he did *not* say Atonement) tends to be more prophetic and challenging. Yet he took that opportunity to drive home the point that these are only emphases, and that both theologies are part and parcel of each other.[27]

What he was after was to encourage a sensitivity to the times in the younger theologians. [73] The tactics of theology, as he saw it, called for an evangelical emphasis on redemption rather than the "metaphysics" of creationist theology. But never did he suggest that Atonement and Incarnation could be separated and one chosen rather than the other. (One who actually did was J. R. Illingworth, of an earlier generation, in *Lux Mundi.*) On the contrary, logical man that he was, he saw the Atonement as the meaning and effect of the Incarnation, and he viewed the Incarnation as an all-in-one: the birth, ministry, death, resurrection and ascension of Christ. They are all tied together as means and end. The Nativity is as much a necessary part of the Drama of Redemption (Atonement) as the Crucifixion and Resurrection; the Manger as much a part as the Cross or Empty Tomb; the Incarnation as much as the Loving Sacrifice and the Triumph over Death. At the same time, he realized what was the Church's great difficulty: that the world has lost "any sense of sin, and consequently any sense of the need for atonement." [28]

✿ THE AT-ONE-MENT   The Cross and Resurrection were the focal points of the At-one-ment or "togetherness" of God and man, brought about in and by the Incarnation. As Temple understood the Atonement, it had two sides to it, the objective and the subjective. The objective side was what God had done for man—His revelation of Himself by the Incarnation's demonstration of His unchanging love. Temple thought of the Fall myth as a story of the crucial step *forward* in the moral and spiritual development of man. At that crucial point in the *process* of man's spiritual creation he suffered no degradation. Men did not lose their status as children of God or their relationship with Him. [74] For this reason, therefore, Temple never treated the Incarnation as a restoring of mankind to a right relationship with God *so far as God was concerned.* "Christ's death and Resurrection did not cause God to be after their occurrence what He was not before." [29] Nevertheless, the revelation of God's love was an objective event and a new fact without which men could not be "saved"—that is, enter consciously into a right relationship with God in free loving obedience.

The subjective side is, of course, our response to this decisive event. Whereas the objective side is the saving revelation, the subjective side is the willing response. [75] The completion of our Atonement "is accomplished through our realization of the love of God." [30] It was an equation-process: God's outreach to man in His Self-disclosure, man's response in faith—not something done *to* us, but *for* us and *with* us. "The Love displayed in the Passion has transforming power, and will, if we submit our souls to its influence, mould us into its likeness." [31] So-called "moral influence" theories of the Atonement held part of the whole truth, as Temple saw it. He said that every Christian is prepared to believe with Abelard, even if he wishes to add more, that "Christ by His manifestation of His love awakens love in us, and that this is the Atonement." [32] The revelation "at-ones" us with God and each other. The unconquerable love of God is manifested in the objective fact; human freedom is respected in the subjective fact—in the ability of men to respond by Yes, or to say No, even unto death.

As early as 1909, in lectures to students in St. James Hall, London, Temple expressed his faith in the following terms, which never altered: "I believe that if we work out that theory—thinking of the effect which love always has, when it is understood, upon any heart, and remembering that the world has progressed a good deal since the earliest ages that we know, and progressed in love more perhaps than in any other quality—we shall find that it may be true that the whole world is moving onward forever under the impulse of the infinite love of God to a more and more adequate return of that love; we begin to think of the whole Universe as knit together in that love as its one controlling principle." [33]

He knew that those who were wedded to traditional ransom and satisfaction doctrines of the Atonement might regard his view as "purely subjective," insisting against his interpretation that the Christian experience demands something "more objective." But Temple never could see exactly what that demand means. Does it call for belief in something accomplished altogether *outside* us, or something done *for* us? These two ideas are compatible but not identical. It was the latter that he held: the Atonement is what we could not do for ourselves, yet it is accomplished *in* us. The notion that such a view makes sin only a matter of moral growing pains he called a travesty; for to treat sin as no more than that is "a pernicious lie"—the danger of which comes from its being a half-truth. [76] He denied that his view left God's justice out of account by saying that God treats all men equally, and that penal justice in the form of retribution is immoral and impossible with God. Of course, God is angry at man's sin in the same way that a father is angry at his son's ingratitude: without wanting to damn him, never wishing him evil. If his view suggested that man's sin is not important, then (he said) look again at the Cross, and at God upon it!

"Keeping a sturdy hold on the Love of God is our one all-sufficing principle, and making a wise use of the conceptions of Personality and Evolution, which play so large a part in our modern thought, we shall be able to catch more of the meaning of the revelation of God in Christ than was possible, perhaps, in earlier times." [34] And, as in the case of the Incarnation, Temple was glad that "the Church as a whole has never formally accepted any particular explanation of the fact" of the Atonement.

This way of looking at it suggests, of course, that after man's existence has ended in this life—if he dies in ignorance of what Christ has done for him, or stubbornly refuses all his mortal life to believe or abide by it—then he must learn the good news and finally be won over to accepting it sometime, somehow, hereafter in eternal life. On this question, interestingly enough, Temple was somewhat equivocal or at least undecided. His in-

decision no doubt reflected a common uncertainty in the minds
of many Christians. Only the unreconstructed hell-and-damna-
tion, now-or-never salvationists seem to be sure that non-Christians are lost. He often called the problem a dilemma between
God's all-powerful love and man's radical freedom here on
earth.[35] His tendency was to fall back on the confession that
"what its ultimate issue is to be lies beyond the bounds of
terrestrial experience." [36] He held the conviction that "every
personality survives bodily death," but he could not and would
not put any soul in a hell as lost to the love of God.[37] Only if and
while we say No to God, "we are shut out utterly (but not
finally) from His Presence; that is Hell." [38] Once when he told
Baron von Hügel that he had first leaned toward universalism
but now leaned away, von Hügel replied that *he* was moving
toward it! In the Gifford Lectures Temple quoted Browning's
Ring and the Book about God's giving stubborn people a second
chance. In another world beyond this "God unmakes but to
remake" those who have finished their mortal, natural lives
outside God's fellowship.[39] (He never discussed the case of those
who die merely ignorant instead of defiant—probably because he
couldn't imagine anybody in the modern world who would want
or try to put them in a "hell" or "limbo," through no fault of
their own.)

⚙ CHRIST THE CRISIS POINT Temple's understanding of
the Incarnation-Atonement in non-ransom, non-satisfaction terms
is a coherent part of his whole theology. He was definite that it
was something that God did and to which men make a response
—say a Yea or a Nay. But like everything else in his theology,
it is a process as well as an event. The event is the Incarnation,
the objective side; the process is the subjective or moral side—in
which "gradually our hearts learn to respond . . . This is the
Atonement of the World." [40] It goes forward, with ups and
downs. The war against sin and self-centeredness was won on the
Cross, so to say, but the battles of evangelism, of the Church as
a mission, remain as a mopping-up operation. For a while some
battles will be won and others lost. "What was to appear immedi-

ately was the power sufficient for that accomplishment, so that
thenceforward the victory in principle was already won." [41]

❀ WORLD SAVING, NOT SOUL SAVING   But more than this,
he was also definite that, in the whole salvation-drama, more was
at stake than simply remitting the sins of wicked individuals.
His was no mere "extricationist" interpretation, which treats
redemption as the soul-saving business of extricating individuals from "this wicked world" and getting them into heaven. On
the contrary, he thought redemption was *world*-saving, the redemption of the world through our Lord Jesus Christ—and,
therefore, the souls within it, too. He remembered St. John's
explanation (3:16) that "God so loved the *world*." It was a this-
worldly redemption, not other-worldly. Both Alec Vidler and
Simone Weil have called it "worldly holiness."

In Temple's process-theology redemption, so-called, is a part
of creation, so-called, and vice-versa. He never set redemption
as a category of Christian theology to be held over against the
category of creation. He never dreamed of embracing a theology
of redemption *rather than* a theology of creation, as Barth used
to do. Temple held that the Incarnation and its result in at-one-
ment, or God-man fellowship, was a decisive point in the total
process of creation. The process is to end ultimately in the Kingdom of God, the reign of Love, the "Commonwealth of Value."

He put it this way: "The fact that in human history the
Atonement takes the form of the Passion is largely due to human
sin"; but "still the Cross is not merely the reaction of the Divine
Nature to human sin." [42] It is much more than that. Like Duns
Scotus and William of Ockham before him, Temple insisted that
the Incarnation, broadly enough understand, was the crucial or
nodal event of *creation*—the "theosis" of the world in an ongoing
creation. Thus if men had *not* been sinners, the Incarnation
would have capped God's creative process anyway. The incarnate
Lord is *Christus Consummator* as well as *Christus Salvator*.
Norman Pittenger has recently dealt with the question in much
the same manner. He said he regarded himself as a Scotist,
and declared his conclusion that God in any case "would have

crowned his creative work by his supreme creative act"—the
specific, prototypical unifying of the divine and human natures
in Christ.[43] For the difference between Christ and men is one
"of almost immeasurable degree and not of absolute kind." [44]
This same unity, as it comes to mankind, will be the result of
a process, of course, and not a simple event. It has to develop,
with history, in the social process, and with nature as God's
creative medium. As Jesus expresses it in a process-saying, "My
Father is working still, and I am working." [45]

Patristic and medieval theology, being prescientific, for the
most part supposed that creation was complete. It literalized the
myths of Creation and the Fall, and therefore supposed that
the only purpose of the Incarnation was to "redeem" the created
world from the Fall. [77] They actually thought that once, in
the remote past, men were aboriginally virtuous and God-fearing
and neighbor-loving! They knew nothing of modern zoology and
anthropology and their over-whelming evidence to the contrary.
A St. Thomas or Martin Luther believed that the Incarnation
was for the salvation of souls—period. It was only for the redemption or *re*-storation of individual personalities, to their
presumed, aboriginal righteousness. Catholic Doctor and Protestant Reformer would both have answered No to the question:
"Would Christ have been born among men except for the Fall?"

The creative-redemptive process conceived by Maurice and
Temple was never a part of their pre-evolutionary Christian
thinking. Students of modern Anglican theology would find
interest in comparing Gore's Bampton Lectures of 1891, *The
Incarnation of the Son of God,* which treated the Incarnation
as the rectification of a fallen world, to Temple's *Christus Veritas*
which treated it as the fulfillment of creation.

Even today there is a great deal of individualistic pietism tied
up with notions of an actual "Fall" away from Eden-innocence.
It waited for modern Christians with a developmental, historical,
evolutionary perspective to see Christ as a cosmic Lord, author
of "a new creation" and "a new life" as part of God's creative
purpose. When a Catholic theologian, Lionel Thornton, and a
Protestant theologian, Paul Tillich, speak this way, they follow
Temple, even though not in his language nor exactly as he
would interpret it. [78]

III

Kingdom and Church

The Kingdom of God is of key importance in the Gospels, and it holds the same place in Temple's faith-outlook. "The prominence of the Kingdom in the teachings of our Lord is the great discovery of recent study. To us it is obvious; but till the middle of the nineteenth century it was little noticed." [1] As early as 1912 he published the thorough canvass of the Kingdom idea which he had first offered as a series of lectures to the Cambridge Christian Evidence Society. From then on it was a thread that ran consistently through his interpretation of both religious and social questions.

It would be well, at the outset, to see definitely what he meant by the term "Kingdom." As Temple used it Kingdom meant primarily king*ship,* God's sovereignty or reign over His world and His people. It is true, of course, that every reign implies a realm, and that God's kingship has its kingdom. The *locus* or place of God's rule ought to be both in the hearts of the people He created and the social structures of the world He created. [79] For example, it ought to obtain equally in their economic attitudes and their economic institutions. The Kingdom conceived as God's rule means, therefore, the rule of the law of neighbor-love. The extension of the Kingdom is signalled and shown not merely in what men desire in their hearts but what they do in their lives. To pursue the economics example, it will manifest itself in their exchange values as well as in their marketing policies. But the essence of the Kingdom lies in the fellowship of faithful believers.

"If the Kingdom of God is to come on earth, it must be because God first came on earth Himself." [2] The Kingdom's founder or inaugurator was Christ. He started it on its course of overcoming the world by showing it forth in His own life and death. This was because "the spiritual power of God over the spirits of men could only be complete when its nature was revealed in an intelligible form so that men should render it a free response, [and] so the Kingdom comes with power only through that revelation." [3]

Yet we must note his warning to those who are moved by "the Christian hope"—the Kingdom "cannot come in all its *perfection* in this world," because, no matter how much it progresses in its growth, "every child that is born, being a nucleus of that Original Sin which is self-centeredness, disturbs any such degree of approximation as has been reached." [4] Nor will the Kingdom come in its *permanence* in this world. Science has told us this: the second law of thermodynamics serves notice to all who want to believe in endless progress that entropy, the dead-level energy trend, will reduce the world in some theoretical future to an undifferentiated mass of cold and lifeless material. Yet these are questions beyond the calculations of man. As God's co-workers and servants we live in the faith that because He is the Creator, His purpose is the key to history, and its realization will surely turn on His character—love. In working and praying for the Kingdom we are relatively indifferent to the *extent* it may be accomplished on earth. "Our duty is to do our utmost; of that there is no doubt." [5]

Temple has been charged, perhaps inevitably, with being "utopian" because of his faith in the power of God's Kingdom (Love's reign), but at least his utopianism was not perfectionist. In recent times the word "utopian" has been turned into a theological epithet. For his part, Temple regarded as cynical a view, such as Emil Brunner's, that all points in history are "equidistant from eternity." He might tolerate it if it carried nothing more than a merely metaphysical meaning, but even then it was alien to his sense of the importance of time and history. He confidently believed that God's lordship over history means that history is progressive, and that civilization (for example) is an improvement over barbarism and a closer approach to the Kingdom. [80]

⚙ PROPHETIC, NOT APOCALYPTIC Temple was convinced that the prophetic view of the Kingdom was the one Jesus taught, and that this was what most of his hearers in Palestine understood by "the Kingdom." [81] Two views of the Kingdom were held in Jesus' day. One that it would come by political and social means, maybe even using force, but in any case, God's will is its guarantee. This was the prophetic faith. The other idea was that it would come by cataclysm or apocalyptic, through the action of the Son of man, by a miraculous act of God. Jesus combined them: the Son of man was to bring the Kingdom through the developing course of political and social means. He cast aside the superstition of apocalyptic as well as the notion that the Messiah was to be a strong man of arms. While the apocalyptic idea was not so widespread among the people of the land, the hope for a conquering Messiah was. And it was on this latter course that Jesus made his most radical departure from popular beliefs. His teaching about Messiahship and the peaceful, gradual process of the Kingdom by the Suffering Servant perplexed and offended them.

The new conception is to be seen in the temptation story in Matthew's and Luke's Gospels. As Temple understood the story, our Lord made three striking points. First, by refusing to turn stone into bread, He rejected the use of power for Himself, thus choosing the Suffering Servant role foreshadowed in Second Isaiah. Second, by refusing to worship Satan to gain the Kingdom (rule), He rejected quick-power, *coup d'état* methods of realizing the Kingdom. Third, by refusing to cast Himself down from the pinnacle of the Temple He rejected the use of miracles, and any supernatural coming "on the clouds of heaven."

In this way (1) Jesus put aside Messianic glory in favor of redemptive love and reliance on the power of sacrifice; (2) He spurned Jewish nationalism in favor of a universal fellowship; and (3) He repudiated apocalyptic magic in order to embrace a creative *process* which took human freedom and the time dimension seriously. Unfortunately, the apocalyptic *deus ex machina* "hope" continued to infect the early Church, as we

can see by a close scrutiny of Mark 13 and—a great deal more
—of the Gospels and Epistles. In a letter to "Ronnie" Knox in
1913, Temple said quite deliberately, "If I thought He expected
an immediate catastrophe other than His own death and Resurrection, I think I should have to renounce Christianity." [6]

◉ ASPECTS OF THE KINGDOM Temple's interpretation of
the Kingdom included five aspects of significance. (1) It had
its *preparation* in the prophets of Israel whose preaching foretold God's demands upon society, and whose teaching included
an eschatology or hope of a new age to come in the world, to
be inaugurated by Messiah.

(2) Its *founding* was by Christ on the Cross, "triggered," as it
were, by a moral device rather than by conquest through the use
of physical power. "The whole Church exists in Jesus Christ and
was complete on the Resurrection morning. We are joined to it,
but we never constitute it." [7] It relies for its spread on the
contagion of love rather than the compulsion of fiat and force.
Men of their own powers do not build the Kingdom. Rather,
He who began it builds it, using men as His agents and ves-
sels. "God can and does effect the increase of the Kingdom by
His own activity in the society of Christian people. Our duty is
to put ourselves under the control of that Spirit and let Him
guide our action private and public, individual and corporate.
Thus we became His agents in the increase of His Kingdom as it
is, and in preparation for its perfect coming." [8]

(3) The *dimensions* of the Kingdom are total, at the same
time both subjective and objective—the Kingdom "within you"
but also "amongst you." As God's rule over our lives it entails
His moral-spiritual rule internally in our hearts as well as the
expression of His will in the institutional-structural ordering of
our external relations and social affairs. With Temple things
were never treated arbitrarily as either/or, entirely one thing
or the other. Using his dialectical approach, he conceived the
Kingdom as personal *and* social. It was salvation (literally,
wholeness or health) both for individual souls and corporate

bodies. Christianity, he said, aims "not at the Salvation of individuals one by one, but at that perfect individual and social
welfare which is called the Kingdom of God." [9] By the same
token, it is both present and future, already at work and yet to
be fulfilled, a present reality in the existing fellowship of faithful
believers, but still to be realized or fulfilled as their obedience
widens to include more and more of God's people. [82]

(4) The notion that the Kingdom is a *process,* and not only an
event, was a most essential part of Temple's view. [83] It is
both a "distant desire" and an immediate duty. He applied the
concept of process to the realization of the Kingdom just as he
did to the creation of the world and the course of redemption.
His principal idea that process characterizes everything, markedly
close to the process principle of reality in Whitehead's philosophy, justifies us in speaking of Temple's thought as a process-
theology. [84] Indeed, the Kingdom in Temple's outlook was
the direction-giving goal *(telos* or *eschaton)* toward which creation and redemption move. Both creation and redemption are
processes of progressive development.

"I have overcome the world," said our Lord in the Fourth
Gospel, and Temple took this to mean, as does T. W. Manson
in *The Beginnings of the Gospel,* that "the victory in principle
was already won" by Christ.[10] He *had* overcome the world, but
at the same time He was still *overcoming* it. Temple with St.
Paul (I Corinthians 15:57) prayed, "Thanks be to God who
gives us the victory through our Lord Jesus Christ." He offered
not the slightest encouragement to any stalemate theology about
the future, in which there is to be only a perpetual and unresolved conflict of good and evil. [85]

(5) Finally, he understood that the Church and the Kingdom
stand in a means-and-end relation to each other. The Church is
an instrument of the Kingdom's coming. "As Christ's purpose
was to found a Kingdom, so we should think of the Church as
the army of that Kingdom." [11] Temple never swallowed the
"Catholic heresy" which tends to treat the Church as the highest
good and an end in itself. In a letter to a military chaplain in
1943 he said, "I believe that all the doctrinal errors of Rome
come from the direct identification of the Church . . . with the

Kingdom of God." [12] In much the same way as he saw society
related to the Kingdom as batter is to the cake, so Temple
looked upon the Church as God's instrument—the chief (but
not the only) divine *tool* or implement of the kingdom-process.
[86] Knowing this, the Swedish Bishop Brilioth remarked that
"the common criticism against Anglo-Catholic theology as
founded on a superficial conception of the Kingdom of God
cannot be applied to him." [13]

⚙ THE BECOMING CHURCH   The Church loomed large in
Temple's outlook. "I do not see how anybody in his right senses
could believe in the deity of Christ who did not also believe
in that society which we call the Church." [14] Being God's chief
instrument for the conversion or transformation of the world
into the Kingdom, the Church was set squarely at the center of
his attention. "The Church will only manifest the whole power
of Christ when it embraces all mankind; here and now it fully
manifests His Spirit only in the degree in which it is missionary.
Christendom will only be complete when it is all the world, and
now is only truly Christian so far as it is concerned for the
bringing of the world into the Kingdom of God, of which it is
at once the earnest and the servant!" [15] The Church, then, has
as its purpose *to eliminate itself* or, alternatively expressed, to
become one and the same with the Kingdom. However we put
it, the Kingdom is the Church's first and final order of business.
The Kingdom is to "take over" the world: society is the batter,
the Kingdom the cake, God the baker, the Church His most
prized mixer.

Here again Temple applied his process-theology directly and
firmly. The Church is not a finished creation, sprung like Athena
full-fledged from the brain of Zeus. Like all of God's creation,
the Church is *becoming* the Church. As he said, when he was a
rector in London's Piccadilly, "The true Church is still coming
slowly into historic existence; that process is the meaning of
history from the Incarnation onwards." [16]

Many years later, as Archbishop of Canterbury, he declared
flatly, in speaking of the apostasy of disunity, "I believe in the

Holy Catholic Church, and sincerely regret that it does not exist." [17] As a matter of fact, even if the present tragic divisions between the churches in the Body of Christ were fully healed, Temple would continue to say what he did, until Christ is all in all. And in addition to this qualification about the Church, Temple had another. God's work through and in the historic process, he said, is not restricted to, or a monopoly of, the Church. "It is perfectly possible, as indeed it frequently happens, that in this respect or that, the operation of the Holy Spirit is more potent among those who are not members of the Church." [18] In dealing with secular idealists and leaders he never lost sight of what, in *Foundations,* he called the Church's "abundant capacity for taking the wrong side in moral issues." [19] Too often, he would say, the Church is a draped lantern. The light is not at fault but *we* are, for obscuring it.

⚙ ASPECTS OF THE CHURCH   Temple's interpretation of the Church included several points worth noting, and for the sake of brevity and clarity we can put them down in headings.

The Church gave us the Bible.   Like the Lutheran Pastor Gruntvig, and his "unparalleled discovery" in controversy with Søren Kierkegaard in Copenhagen, Temple believed that the Church gave us the Bible, not the other way round. In 1905, writing from Germany, Temple noted that Lutherans stand while the Bible is read in church. He thought it "a horrible and idolatrous worship of the text." "If one has to choose," he said, "between the sole authority of the Bible and the sole authority of the Church, in Heaven's name let us have the Church, which is alive and, because plainly subject to error, is also capable of truth." [20]

This always remained his attitude. He was no "biblicist" in the sense of being anti-ecclesiastical or Book-sufficient. He held firmly to the opinion that to be loyal to itself and preserve its integrity the Church must measure its life and thought by *its own standard.* He pointed out, however, that the Church's standard *is* the Bible, produced in and by the Church for that very purpose. [87] As he saw it, the fellowship of faith, the society of the disciples, came first both in history and in importance. Consequently it was in and through that fellowship that the Spirit produced a polity, canons, a *kerygma* and *didache* (faith proclamation and discipline), *and* the Book. Churchmen wrote the Book, and churchmen decided what went into "the canon of scripture" and what was cast aside.

The Church carries civilization. In the history of the West the Church has combined and preserved the three greatest gifts and traits of civilization: (1) the religious morality, or ethical monotheism, of Palestine and Judaism, (2) the intellectual vigor and outreach of Greece, and (3) the Roman love of law and social order.[21] Temple always tried to keep in balance these three geniuses—the ethical, intellectual and institutional. Like his friend, Baron von Hügel, he avoided any theology which reduced the Church to only one of these things, or which tended to ignore any of them. Time after time he recurs to this ancient doctrine of the Fathers—the *praeparatio evangelica.* Thus he had no great patience with pietistic indifference to social justice, or with anti-rational mysticism, or with a sectarian, non-church type of Christian fellowship.

But above all he was a "church" Christian, in the sense that Troeltsch has distinguished it as a type from "sect" Christianity. The Church is not a sect with a small exclusive in-group arrogance, keeping people out by rigid orthodoxy and behavioral tests. The Church is *for* the world! He preferred Revelation's ideal of the New Jerusalem (21:22-26)—the whole, entire city being the Holy of Holies—to Ezekiel's remote ideal (40:2) of the Temple apart from the world, alone on the hill of Zion. His paper in *Foundations* on "The Church" (1912) made this perfectly clear. He was positive that we cannot be Christians all by ourselves, and that only a Society can witness to society about what society should be.

As he resisted sectarianism, so he resisted individualism and private religion. He constantly struggled against the tendency in "bourgeois" culture to regard religion as a private affair, and to treat it as a matter of individual soul-saving. "All relevant analogy suggests that a spirit must take definite and concrete form before it can be effective in the world, even as God himself must become incarnate in order to establish His Kingdom upon earth." [22] Not only in *Readings in St. John's Gospel* but in all that he wrote, there was a constant recurrence to the analogy of the Church as a Vine, or to St. Paul's figure of the Body. The Church is not to flee the world but to take its social and material interests up like sap through its roots into its body, transforming it. He lived and breathed by Bishop Talbot's reply to the question what he meant by "being a Catholic." "I mean that it doesn't much matter what happens to me as long as the life of the Church goes on."

The Church is democratically inclusive. Temple was certain that the power of the Holy Spirit, working through the evolutionary process, is on the side of democracy. Indeed, he said so quite plainly and added that "Our belief in a tendency of the world to improve is a belief in the Holy Ghost." [23] He held history to be essentially a *social process,* and believed that the process of socialization is the work of the indwelling Spirit. Love's (i.e., God's) sovereignty and control increase their place in the world He created and for which He holds His one increasing Kingdom-purpose.

Merging St. Paul's description of the Church in Galatians 3:28 and Colossians 3:11 (a profile of those whose lives are hid with Christ in God), Temple said, " 'There is neither Jew nor Gentile' —the deepest of divisions based on religious tradition has disappeared; 'there is neither Greek nor Scythian'—the deepest of divisions based on culture has disappeared; 'there is neither bond nor free'—the deepest of social and economic divisions has disappeared; 'there is neither male nor female'—even the division of the sexes has disappeared. [88] In place of them all is 'one man in Christ Jesus.' " [24] Temple read the New Testament carefully. He knew the teaching (Ephesians 1:10) that God works "according to His purpose which He set forth in Christ" as a plan for "the fulness of time, to unite all things in Him, things in heaven *and things on earth.*" And Temple was also perfectly well aware that, by this exciting and comprehensive standard, much of what passes for "church life" and "church membership" is fraudulent.

The Church is a corporate community. By the same radical or "ideal" definition, the Church is the organism of the Kingdom growing in the world's soil. It is a fellowship (*koinonia*) of all things, of goods as well as of faith. To Temple, a lifelong Christian Socialist (perhaps we should say Socialist Christian), there was nothing too hard to bear in the life of radical solidarism—sometimes called "religious communism"—of the Jerusalem congregation.[25] As he saw it, the Church's "paradigmatic" task is to set forth or exemplify the coming Kingdom *now*. This means, he believed, Christian fellowship in theological outlook, political policy, and economic assets. We cannot be in "spiritual" Christian fellowship or community if we are not in material fellowship too: fellowship must, in short, be sacramental.

"The Kingdom," he said, "can be made known only by living according to the principle of its fellowship." If the world is to know it, the Church must show it. The recreative Word of God is a word for demonstration, not only for proclamation. And this was why, for example, he welcomed and happily endorsed *Putting Our House in Order,* in 1941, along with thirty-eight other bishops, sixty clergy, and thirty-one prominent laymen. This volume was an appeal to the Church of England to follow up the recommendations made in an earlier manifesto, *Men, Money and the Ministry,* to pool the Church's funds under the ecclesiastical commissioners. Temple was certain that we must transcend our present-day parochial ("private") ownership of the Church's resources. He called for a decision to redistribute endowments and set up a "basic stipend" plan whereby clergy salaries would become equal, yet with variable extra allowances according to individual needs. In a sacramental community, the spirit has to be materialized.

The laity are the ministry. In a paper entitled "The Apostolate of the Laity" Temple explained that our Lord was the Church's first Apostle ("one who is sent"). He was sent into the world by the Father. He then in His turn sent other apostles. Every one of His disciples or followers is "called," or has it as his "vocation" (calling), to represent Him in the world. Here, in this sense at least, is an unchallengeable apostolic succession!

"As my Father hath sent Me, even so I send you." Because Christians are members of the Apostle Christ, they are all apostles. As Temple looked at it, every Christian is also a pastor and shares in Christ's priesthood. [89] The clergy have been ordained to a *special* ministry, he said, "not so that they may do it on behalf of the laity who are thus relieved of the responsibility for it, but so that the laity may be reminded by them of their own share in the work" of the Church's ministry.

And what is that work? "All Christians are called to serve God in their daily work and to use their influence so to draw men nearer to Christ." It is impossible, he pointed out, to live at all without exerting an influence which is "either drawing men to Christ or driving them farther from Him." This vocation and calling is the same for all Christians. The kind of *work* through which they fulfill it—professional, business, domestic, governmental, or whatever—to a large extent is a matter of personal choice or talent. And the specific *job* in which they do their work will depend upon a host of partially chosen factors, partially accidental conditions. Any decent employment is a channel of Christian ministry, or of what Temple called "a week-day apostolate." He mourned the fact that church organizations and committees lead people "to think nothing else is really church work. But nine-tenths of the work of the Church is carried on by ordinary Christians doing their ordinary job in a Christian spirit."

The laity are not called to "do church work" but to *be* the Church in the world, because God's redemption comes into play at the point of intersection between the Church and the world where the laity (far more than the clergy) are. God does not work in the world *for* the Church. He works in the world *through* the Church for the world.

In Ephesians Temple found the fullest account of "salvation-history." There he found an interpretation of history in which (1) the *end* is the Kingdom, a society of free spirits moved and united by the love of God; (2) the *means* is the Church, the society of those who already know the end and are in the power of the Holy Spirit; and (3) the foundation and impetus is the revelation of the love of God in Jesus Christ.[26]

IV

Personality in Fellowship

Simple, capsule definitions are often the best because we can keep them in mind without any great feat of memorizing. But in such brevity there is often a lot more than meets the eye. So it is with a short, quick way of expressing Temple's view of divine and human personality: "Purposive will organized for action." The core of his idea is that we are "persons" because our lives are integrated with, and devoted to, a purpose beyond ourselves. We are persons "because" we live for a cause. The key to personality is something like the "life line" in Alfred Adler's psychology. [90] As Temple once phrased it, "The essence of personality is intelligent choice or purpose." [1] To see right to the heart of his theology we have to spell out what these phrases mean.

❀ WILL AS A PERSONAL UNITY   What, to start with, is will? As a modern man Temple had discarded the old faculty psychology of Plato, Aristotle, and Augustine in which man had been divided up into three separate and distinct components called "intellect" and "feeling" and "will." He knew that our psychic activity always blends together the intellectual, emotional, and volitional elements. Sometimes these dynamic forces are blended smoothly and sometimes they are only jumbled chaotically. That is to say, sometimes we are integrated or unified persons and sometimes we are divided "against" (within) ourselves. On this basis he held that "will" is not a faculty with a separate existence of its own, able to oppose the intelligence or defy the emotions. People often say, "I know what is right,

46

but my will is perverse," or, "He *wants* to do the right thing, but his self-will gets in the way."

However, as Temple pointed out, will is the union, or unity, of mind and feeling. Will comes into being as a function of their union. Will equals mind plus emotions. "The will, then, is not an original endowment of our nature, but is something in process of formation throughout life." [2] When desire seeks what the mind also affirms, then will is born and comes into play. When that happens we are able to make a choice and act "wholeheartedly." And when feeling, either positive or negative (i.e., desire or distaste), runs counter to the suggestion of reason, then there is no will at all. In that case we are unintegrated, not personalities at all. Or, to put it another way, to the extent that we are "conflicted" (not a term Temple ever used), we are minus-personalities. We are only capable of purposive living, of choosing our goals and causes, when we are enough at one within ourselves. Then we are integrated enough to *want* what we "believe in," and that, when it happens, is not only will but *faith*. Temple had a biblical basis for his conviction that we can and *do* do what we *want* to do: "If you love me, you will keep my commandments"; he added, "And if we don't, we shan't. Let no one deceive himself about that." [3]

This means, among other things, that the age-old debate over the question, "Is the will free?" is nonsense.[4] The question is not a real question. It is merely circular because it only asks, "Has the power to choose got the power to choose?" [91] He was helped to see this side of things, he said, by reading the chapter on Power in John Locke's *Essay on Human Understanding*. He learned the same lesson from Aristotle's definition of choice, or resolution, as literally *emotion intellected* (*orexis diathontikei*). Thus another word for that unity, which is personality or purposive will, is *freedom*. Freedom is the power to choose. [92] A person, Temple decided, is "a self-conscious and self-determining system of experience in process of achieving unity or, morally speaking, freedom." [5]

❂ REAL FREEDOM IS PERSONAL   Moral freedom is what is
at stake. Physical freedom is something else entirely. We may
choose, in the sense of affirming or willing what we cannot get or
do, because of forcible restraint or some physical impossibility.
The capacity to choose is moral ("spiritual") freedom—the essence of being a person. Without this freedom we are not only
sub-personal, we are also sub-human. For it is precisely freedom
which is the postulate of human acts and human status, distin-
guishing human beings from all other animals. The goals of
sub-human animals are *given* rather than chosen. They are instinctual, not cultural. What makes the difference is the factor of
rationality. The emotions are common to both human and sub-
human creatures; what makes the difference is the intellect. And
because the beasts lack the cognitive capacity to choose whether
they will go with or against their *desires,* they are never free,
they never achieve true "will." Two things, said Temple, are
true—that "a human personality is a self-determining, self-
integrating system, and that ideas are the chief instrument of its
self-determination." [6] Personality is "moral being," but we need
to understand that the "noetic" or intellectual component is
decisive. And the self or person, in Temple's understanding, is
a *becoming* being, a process, a growing system of life.

Self-determination is the characteristic of a moral being, he
maintained, adding the theological observation, "without it he
could never be called into fellowship with God." [7] Making use
of the language of the Hasidic philosopher Martin Buber, which
in recent years has been widely taken over into Christian "an-
thropologizing," there must be an *I* to meet a *Thou.* [93] This
is true not only as between man and man in the horizontal
dimension of relationship, but also as between man and God
in the vertical dimension. Like human intercourse, the divine-
human encounter is a personal one.

In an essay on *Christianity As a Historical Religion,* written
in 1935, Temple explained how we have nowadays discarded the
notion that persons are hard, atomic cores of individuality.
"Personality is inherently social. We only become fully personal
through the interaction of our own and other selves in the
fellowship of society. Not only must every one who speaks of

himself as 'I' recognize that every other one also speaks of himself as 'I,' but he must recognize that 'I' am only 'I' at all because 'Thou' art 'Thou' and 'Ye' are 'Ye.' Our personality is a social product, and spiritual liberty is a resultant of social determinations." [8] No Christian theologian had yet written in exactly these terms; but Buber's "dialogic" thesis, identical almost word for word, has helped to shape the man-theory of such theological philosophers as Maritain, Berdyaev, and Tillich. [94]

We cannot enter into fellowship without freedom, i.e., selfhood, any more than we can be called to account (held responsible) without it. Only persons are morally free, whether God or man. Therefore only persons can act in the forum of conscience. *Self*-determination is the most important determinant at work in what persons do or do not do, in their commissions or omissions.

⚙ PERSONALITY: TOP VALUE In a non-doctrinaire way Temple was unquestionably a "personalist," although he never attached that label to himself. And there are, we should recognize, quite a number of Christian and non-Christian forms of personalism with which he would have had only relatively little in common. But his belief that men are persons, and that they share that status with God, was a pillar of his thought. The Creation story's claim that man is made "in the image of God" was basic to his whole scheme of things. Like God, men are personal; unlike God, they are not perfectly or completely personal. For, be it carefully noted, in Temple's thought and worship God is never a philosophical or metaphysical entity—such as "ultimate being" or "the ground of reality." These things are true of Him, too, since God is the source of all things, omnifacient, the author of the universe, the maker of all things. But first and foremost for Temple, as in the biblical faith of Jews and Christians, God was a *personal* God, a heavenly King and Father whom one encounters, addresses, and to whom one relates. His was a personalist theology through and through.

And since God is personal, then personality is the highest

good, the *summum bonum,* the paramount value. For this theological reason, the only value or good which is intrinsically and uncontingently "valuable" is personality. Democracy or any other kind of human social order must respect, protect and treasure each person primarily because he is a person, and not because of such accidents as reputation and rank, race or income. For this theological reason the validity, for example, of any political system, and the allegiance it can expect of Christians, will depend on whether in it "men do or do not believe that personality in man has a status independent of all associations or allegiances because of its kinship with the personality of God." [9] This is a radical, theological kind of democracy. [95] By comparison all secular versions seem pretty cautious and qualified. It makes no attempt to rest its case for respecting the individual, or for sharing the benefits of society, on the flimsy (indeed, partially untrue) claim that all men are born equal. Instead, it says that *equal or not* they are personalities, as God Himself is, and for *that* reason they claim our love and care.

Temple was no Kantian, but he accepted Kant's second maxim: "Treat personality in yourself and others always as an end and never as a means." It was this personalist view of man which in his eyes made sense of the ethical maxim, "Love thy neighbor as thyself." As we shall see in detail later on, it was on this ground that he resisted the commodity theory of labor— a theory under which workers are to be paid according to the impersonal workings of supply and demand, as if they were things.

❂ No Person, No Good   While calling personality the highest value and the only intrinsic one, the only one which is always good in itself, Temple gave it yet an additional importance. He also held that there is no value of any kind at all, that nothing is good, *apart from persons.* The goodness of any thing or action "depends for its actuality upon the appreciating mind." [10] [96] Things to be of value must be related to, and

apprehended by, *an appreciating intelligence.* Value or goodness could not be a quality of anything without either God or
man to know it. (Knowing is to comprehend in God's case, but
only to apprehend in man's.) In short, the only reason anything
is worth anything is because of personality. In biblical theology
this is the same as saying that without God there is nothing
worth, all is vanity. As the philosophers would say, even Temple's
"axiology" or value-theory is personalistic. [97]

There is an obvious linkage here between Temple's personalist view of value and his personalist view of revelation. Just as
an appreciating mind is needed to establish value or worth, so an
appreciating mind is required as a "receiver" for a revelation.
Event + appreciation = value; event + appreciation = revelation. And he theologized in this same personalist way about the
Incarnation, by observing that the highest truth comes only
through the highest good. [98] A personal God can only confront
human persons revealingly through personality. This He did
decisively in the Person of Christ. The Christian revelation is a
disclosure of a Person through a Person to a person.

⚙ No Society, No Person Alongside the formula "Will
= mind + emotion" we can set another of Temple's conceptions:
"The individual plus society equals the person." He had no individualist or bootstrap theory of personality, any more than he
had a bootstrap or do-it-yourself idea of salvation. He took care
to warn Christians that "the sacredness of personality might work
out as a kind of egoism all round if it were not at once balanced
by the other great principle of fellow-membership, that we belong to one another." [11] Relationship was "a fundamental truth
of human nature." It is a given fact about all human existence,
even though it will be fully realized only in the fellowship of
Christ.

The belief that personality is intrinsically good was never, in
his book, a reason for exalting the rights of the individual over
against the community. This cannot be done, as he pointed out,
for the simple reason that a person is a socialized individual.

"Personality is always a social product." [12] No community, then no personality. The individual of and by himself is a biological entity only. The family, friends, work, education, marriage and citizenship of the individual are the things that convert the mere psychophysical organism into a personality. It is acculturated. Persons do not grow or emerge all by themselves. Even *if* a baby could survive and grow to adult years in utter isolation from its fellow humans, whatever else that creature could be called, it would not be a "person" by even a minimum definition. As he put it, "I am only I in my relationships with You, and You are only You, or capable of being called an I, in your relationships with Me." Just as the Church, in Christ, was prior to its members, so society is "prior to the individual."

Since all things, except their Creator, come into being by means of becoming—that is, since *process* is the dynamic key to life and reality—Temple's theology conceives of personality under the rubric of process. He had a kind of developmental hierarchy which moves up through three strata of being, through things to brutes to persons. [99] Things have no consciousness, therefore no intelligence, therefore no will. For them there is no good or evil, no value. They are, therefore, outside the forum of conscience: they are acted *upon* but do not act, and their fate is determined by external forces. Temple called them the "billiard balls" of the world. (Such "objects" may be either mineral or vegetable, inorganic or organic.) Then under the dynamics of development, or to put it theologically, through the creative evolution of God's purposive will, there emerges in sub-conscious things some element of mind. This is when the "animal," or self-propelling spirit, comes into being. Then we have a brute.

The brute is conscious, but its consciousness is sub-volitional. It hasn't sufficient intelligence to stand in critical judgment over the impulses of desire, and therefore has no will—no power to choose, no freedom. Brutes are governed by instinctual drives. Their ends or goals are given, not chosen; at most their range of selection lies only between the available means to imperious ends that are already given—sex, food, comfort, sleep, play, and safety. Brutes are not, like humans, cultural animals. Their time-sense copes only with the present.

But persons, at the third level of this creative process, are intelligent and therefore capable of integrating their minds and their desires or feelings. Thus they are, or can be, willful or voluntary, free creatures. (It varies among them; they are, after all, only finite beings.) They are able to choose, in a measure, between ends as well as between means. Their time-sense covers not only the present but the past and future. In short, possessed of higher intelligence and genuine time-consciousness, they become capable of *purpose,* which is compounded of memory, foresight, and values. Thus a person, as Temple said, is "purposive will organized for action."

⚙ PEOPLE ARE FOR LOVE   There are three paramount features of personality in Temple's conception. Besides the purpose and fellowship, already discussed, love is of first-order importance. Love is the highest good for which true persons always reach, even though (to use Browning's old phrase) their reach exceeds their grasp. As he believed, the goal of life and the purpose of God's continuous creation is "fullness of personality in the widest possible fellowship." [13] Personality and society are, as we have seen, interdependent, *and their nexus and dynamic is love,* neighbor-regard. From this perspective it is a sad but obvious fact that people strive for all sorts of lesser goals, a variety of false gods or idols. Temple's critique of the cultural *status quo* pinpointed many of these idolatrous goals in human society. With some the idol is the state; with others it will be race or wealth or status, or even romance.

But Temple's understanding of the authentic *Christian* purpose, and hence his ideal image of the true Christian, was to be "by love possessed." This is much the same, theologically, as saying that genuine persons are God-possessed, for God *is* Love. Love (God) is the Alpha and Omega of the Christian life, the first and last word. True love is a function of true personality. We could say on this basis, for example, that while *character* will get us out of bed inconveniently early to fulfill some private purpose of our own—self-interest being the discipline—only

personality will get us out of bed inconveniently early for somebody else's sake. Neighbor-concern (agapeic love) is its discipline
and directive. Temple's theological comment here was: "Personality is nowhere fully realized except in the Godhead." [14] Among
human beings Christ alone is the perfect type of personality, because he was God incarnate and not only an image and likeness.
As St. Paul repeatedly reminded us, He is our example.

Because human persons are still struggling with self-centeredness in one measure or another, they can only express or do
agape (Christian love) in response to the contagion and power of
God's love. Temple frequently quoted I John's "We love because
He first loved us"(4:19). This divine origin and source of love
is the first theological observation about it. Only because it
comes to us from God can it go out from us to our neighbors and
back to God who gave it. The second theological point is, using
Temple's own words, "The love wherewith we love is the Holy
Ghost." [15] God isn't just a loving God, He *is* Love. [100] "God is
love," we are told in I John (4:16), and this is the primary or
bedrock proposition in all of Christian theology. Of this theology
Temple once said, in Jerusalem, that Christians usually close
their minds to it, for "if they really believed it, it would frighten
them out of their wits." [16] He was saying the same thing years
later when he wrote: "If Christianity has never frightened us,
we have not yet learnt what it is." [17] You may, he thought, have
all the spiritual gifts there are; but, according to St. Paul, if "you
have not love or charity, you are no more a worshipper of Christ
than Dionysus." [18]

The New Testament is saying that *God* is love, not God is
love! [101] In a sense we cannot even really say that God loves,
since love is His *being* and not just an activity of His being.
In God's case love is a noun, and substantive. In man's case it
is a verb, and adjectival. The works of love are the work of the
Holy Spirit. Love is actually God "in" us. It is this radical and
bemusing doctrine of "enthusiasm" (which literally means God-
filled) which prompted Temple to say without hesitation that
"the atheist who is moved by love is moved by the spirit of
God; an atheist who lives by love is saved by his faith in the
God whose existence (under that name) he denies." [19] He was

sure that if anybody were to be lost or "damned," it would not
be the unbelieving but the unloving.

⚙ LOVE IS SOCIAL Still, there are many who fly a flag with
"love" on it, but not all of them mean what the New Testament
means by it. In the first place, what is sometimes called self-love
or narcissism is not truly love at all: "A man may be of a loving
disposition, but he actually loves only when another person exists
to be the object of his love." [20] Love is a social and relational
thing, not private or individual.

In the second place, *agape* is not "romantic" love between only
two people, or even friendship-love which is a matter of selective
affection. It is *loving;* it is not a question of "liking" at all. There
is nothing exclusive or discriminating about it. It is inclusive,
not selective. It is universal, neighborly, and for all without "respect of persons." It is even for enemies, since "if you love those
that love you, what reward have you?" [21] When we manage to
grasp that *Christian* love is a disposition or attitude, a matter of
the will rather than a romantic or emotional attachment, there
is "no conceivable combination of circumstances in which it is
not possible to show love." [22]

This love is the only Christian absolute: the "law of love" is
the only norm or principle that we are always obliged to obey.
Christianity is not a rigid code-system any more than it is a
rigid creed-system. We are saved, said St. Paul, by love, i.e., grace
—not by law. Said Temple in his Gifford Lectures, "What
[things] are right may depend on circumstances . . . But there
is an absolute obligation to will whatever may on each occasion
be right." [23] This *willing what is right,* according to the situation
in which the decision is made, is precisely *agape,* or Christian
love. [102] Our poor attempts to *will* it are due to our lack of
personal integrity (maturity), not to love's weakness. "Over and
over again we are filled with despair because our love is so cold
and feeble. No; it is not feeble; it is almighty; for it is God the
Holy Ghost, waiting until we give Him opportunity." [24]

Christian love, which was dramatized and portrayed on the

Cross, is a sacrificial kind of love. It seeks to give rather than to get. "The greatest thing that can happen to any human soul is to become utterly filled with love; and self-sacrifice is love's natural expression." [25] Yet we can easily distort the meaning of sacrificial love, as if it were self-destructive. Actually it is self-realization, for Christian love—like so much in the New Testament faith—is a paradox. Temple perceived that "love is the consciousness of survival in the act of self-surrender; the consciousness of dying for another and thereby being one with that other." [26] This is the "mechanism," if we may use such a word, of "mystical union" with Christ. This is the process of dying daily unto self in order to rise with Him in His resurrection to a new kind of life. It is what the love of Christ means. And the result of sacrificial love is not loss but gain; it is edifying or building-up. For love is God's kingship, the Kingdom of God. "The Kingdom of God," said Temple, "is the Sovereignty of Love—since God is Love." This is the basis of Christian and theological optimism, the faith that "every purpose or policy prompted by love—by the desire to serve rather than to gain—will reach its fulfillment, whatever the sacrifices that may first be required of it, because it is allied with the supreme power." [27]

One last word about love in Temple's theology is in order here. He perceived closely what most of us never see, that the opposite of love is indifference, not hate or malice. "The essence of sin is self-will . . . Of the forms of self-will, complete indifference to other people is the worst. Hatred at least recognizes the other person as being of importance and, in essence as well as by our psychological tendencies, is nearer to the moral relation with its culmination in love than is indifference." [28] The common mistake of regarding hate as the opposite of love is not only a psychological error; it is also a result of the *theological* error of treating love as an emotion—like hate.

V

History, Freedom and Necessity

We have seen how Temple looked upon history, the every-day, down-to-earth world, as the place where God's creative activity is going on. Furthermore, the divine activity is pur-posive and value seeking. Good is at stake, and a goal. A purely scientific view tends to concentrate on the *what* and *how* of things, neglecting the *why,* and therefore in this era man's thought tends to find causation more important than purpose or judgment. [103] But value questions and ultimate issues are essential in the theological approach.

Christian theology begins with the belief that God not only made the world and "saw that it was good," He actually loves the world so much that He gave it His only begotten Son. That gift is the hinge of history, the crucial or dialectical point in the story of creation. God is the Author of the unfolding drama, and His writing of the script and direction of the action is theolog-ically known as *providence.* The process of history is the Creator Spirit's purposive will becoming manifest in "the moral struggle and progressive effort both of individuals and communities." [1] This faith of Temple's is the same that Tennyson expressed in *Locksley Hall:* "Yet I doubt not, through the ages, one increas-ing purpose runs," and that purpose reaches beyond history's finite possibilities.

Nevertheless, as Bishop Robinson has said, in Temple's spirit, Christians "no more than the Communists are other-worldly, in the sense that their hope is not a hope for history. Their concern for it is just as serious; in fact it must go much deeper, since they see it, not as a fortuitous concourse of atoms, but as God's cre-ation. Their prayer is precisely that His Kingdom shall come *on earth as it is in heaven.*" [2] That hope may be "out of this world," but as followers of history's greatest visionary, Christians are bound, Temple thought, to be called visionaries. Not to be "guilty" of it is not to be Christian.

◉ HISTORY IS PROCESS IN PROGRESS   The logic of Temple's interpretation of God as purposive will, of creation as a process, and of the Kingdom as for yet not "of" (i.e., not from) this world, led him inevitably, in his theology, to a consistently *developmental* view of history and of man. In the background of his discussions is a concept he often called "the structure of reality," by which he meant created and becoming reality. He held that all things exist in dynamic, ascending grades. They develop upward, from matter to life, from life to mind, from mind to spirit, in a gradient somewhat parallel to the life-ascent he traced from things to brutes to persons. [104] Each of the four grades of being "finds its own completion or perfect development only in so far as it is possessed or indwelt by that which is above it." "Life," he said, "is unknown apart from living organisms, which are matter informed by life. Mind is unknown except in reasoning, living organisms. Spirit is unknown except in conscientious, reasoning, living organisms." [3]

All of this means that the process of creation is marked by value achievement or "progress." Progress is process making moral gain or value. John Baillie has described it, with Pauline echoes, as the progressive embodiment in the life of humanity of the mind that was in Christ. It is, he said, what the New Testament called a "growing up in all things unto Him who is the Head" (Ephesians 4:15). Temple would have applauded with theological satisfaction, however, when Baillie called the modern non-theistic, bootstrap idea of *natural* progress "a Christian heresy." [4] But on his own theistic grounds Temple always emphasized how radical the difference is between the Greek view of history, as a series of pointless cycles, and the biblical *linear* view of history as going somewhere, creative and purposive. The Bible is preponderantly concerned with history. "It is very largely a History Book, or rather an historical library." [5] "The purpose of God is for Eternity, but it includes Time in its scope; the supreme values are spiritual, but spirit is chiefly manifest in control and direction of the material," and therefore the Church "is no refuge of escape from the evils of this world to the bliss of the next." [6] There was never any doubt, given his theological foundation, that Temple's conviction was on the side of what he called "the optimistic hypothesis" (God's sovereignty) and against "pessimistic agnosticism." [7]

Among other things, his providential view of history entailed confidence in *moral* progress. If history is God's drama, it is not enough to give credence only to technical progress. That is obvious enough in the development from raw meat in caves to fire and cooked meals, from wheels and levers and the like up to mass production, air transport, and nuclear power. There is a comparably plain record of progress also in social and cultural life, from the struggles of primitive food-gathering packs up through nomadic, pastoral, agrarian, localistic and "backward" societies and cultures. All along there has been a "secular" (i.e., on the whole) gain in mutual aid and social security, now including more and more trans-cultural associations and international corporations in an emerging modern one-world community. With painful ups and downs (without any nonsense about "automatic" progress) these things have come along. Still, thought Temple, over and beyond all this, there has been moral progress as well. God, who is the Lord of history, is a God of love and righteousness and He will not be frustrated ("mocked," St. Paul said). "To deny the reality of moral progress, or that moral progress is an increasing conformity to the Divine, is wanton." [8]

Man's disobedience, his misuse of his freedom in order to sin, means that progress follows no smooth curve. The notion of nineteenth-century liberals about automatic progress (which among Christians, is a Protestant rather than Anglican or Roman conceit), was no part of Temple's thinking. [105] "The greatest delusion that can possibly seize upon the human mind is the supposition that whatever happens next is bound to be better." [9] To put his conception briefly but fairly, it comes to this: Men move forward, unevenly and irregularly, from primitive, unenlightened selfishness to more and more enlightened selfishness. The *secular* (i.e., general) trend is toward God's righteous will and purpose; and, *on balance,* it appears that "those who embark on selfish courses must bring calamity upon themselves and others, because they are going contrary to the fundamental nature of reality, which is the character of God." [10] The history of civilization is the story of this progress measured in terms of socialization and the common good, and it is a real progress. [106]

But when we look at it from the perspective of *agape's* radical demands, in the light of what Christian love requires, there is no ground, alas, for claiming any general success in moving from enlightened selfishness (prudential morality) to disinterested love. Such progress only occurs in particular cases of truly converted persons who have given themselves over to the demands of their divine son-ship.[107] Yet God works through love at all its levels, "so that progress consists in the increasing preponderance of goodwill and love over self-interest and ill-will." [11] While Temple understood that a balanced social optimism is ready to concede that good will's gains are more often a personal than a corporate achievement, he still claimed that he saw evidence, *in general,* of headway in God's creative love: "There is more love in the world now than there was. The cause goes forward slowly and with difficulty; but it goes forward." [12]

Temple's essential belief can be summed up in his own words. "The whole progress of social and civic development is the parallel growth of two things: the richness of individual personality with completeness of social intercourse. The development of personality in fellowship is no bad definition of what we mean by progress." [13] His conception of history is both teleological and eschatological. [108] And it affirms strongly the biblical view that history is *not* circular, as the Greeks thought, but end-pointed— a divine enterprise of significance and purpose. It is to be taken seriously because God is the Potter who turns the wheel and shapes its destiny. [109]

Because it is a development, the history process cannot stand still or come to rest for the sake of any *status quo.* This is the *theological* reason for opposing all forms of reactionary, or even conservative, social opinion. All orders and structures will change, for change is the only thing certain this side of the Kingdom of God fulfilled! What has been called "the idolization of the ephemeral"—whether of the self or of social institutions—is, because of its idolatry, doomed.[14]

In Temple's analysis of history—the process of God's creation —there are two main goals or *teloi* (*eschatoi,* too) to be attained: personality and sociality. As he interprets it, personality is the precious achievement of personal unity or integrity, of purposive will and moral stature. Sociality or community is conceived as essential to personality. "Personality is the capacity for Fellowship." Community is the matrix or setting in which personality has to develop. Unity or "integration" between persons is the *sine qua non,* both *within* persons for their own sakes and *between* them for the sake of a fellowship fit for personality. Producing or maturing personalities is history's work, but deepening fellowship is history's task, too. [110]

This interdependence of integrated persons and integrated societies makes politics and economics, education, the arts and sciences—all socio-cultural concerns—of prime importance. For this reason, primarily, Temple was concerned with social issues and social justice. His principle of unity or integration—for both persons and societies—led him to adopt the view that history's *direction* is "from heterogeneity to homogeneity," from the diverse to the united, from the individualistic to the collective or corporate. [111] He saw nothing baffling or ominous in the growth, for example, of corporations in place of small-scale competitive enterprises, or in the many signs that socialism is replacing individualism, or that economic unions (e.g., "Benelux" or the European Common Market) are crowding out crippling customs barriers.

☼ FREEDOM But where in this whole process do human beings stand? Have they any freedom and purpose of their own or does fate rule them? Have they some part of their own in shaping the Potter's clay?

Like personality, freedom is an emergent out of the creative process—out of what is often called the "evolutionary" process. Indeed in Temple's interpretation, as we have seen, freedom and personality are inherent in each other. Freedom is what is born out of the unity or integration of a personality-in-community. It is the human capacity that first got its start in the process-ascent when *homo sapiens* made the leap, or mutation, from instinctive beast to rational human. In the Genesis myth this is described as "the Fall" upwards out of the Garden of Eden. (The Garden is, of course, the jungle of pre-voluntary, animal innocence.) It is a paradox that in achieving the "power to choose," which makes love and fellowship possible, sin or selfishness arises along with love as equally possible. Having the capacity to choose between them, man becomes responsible. This turns him into a "tragic" animal who stands in judgment over himself.

According to Temple, the growth and maturity of freedom is the story of the human race as of the human individual. The old phrase "ontogeny recapitulates phylogeny," meaning that each individual's development repeats the species' development, is not too far from what he taught. [112] With time and experience mankind enlarges its areas of freedom—especially, as we have seen, its technical and social freedom. So does the person. It is an uneven development, both individually and socially. The struggle away from immaturity of the species, its rise from primitive savagery, and of the individual from the immaturity of infancy, is often painful. Often its gains are more apparent than real. But such freedom does come, Temple was certain. It comes to men, indeed, whether they want it or not. And many do *not* want it, as Dostoevski's legend of the Grand Inquisitor in *The Brothers Karamazov* brings home so forcibly.

We have seen how Temple linked purpose (or will) and personality (or freedom): personality is purposive will organized for action. A real person is goal-directed. Yet the freedom that counts, true freedom, is not freedom to satisfy merely momentary desires. Sub-human animals have that freedom, if they are physically free to act at all. What matters is freedom to pursue and fulfill a steady and constant *purpose*. Temple therefore took it to be the main business of education to strengthen our capacity to form and follow an adequate purpose —the "lifeline" men-

tioned earlier. Theology gives to the lifeline the title of vocation.
This is what makes the difference between a man and a brute.
Before he ate the apple Adam was a brute. Brutes are innocent,
like babies. They have the physical and psychological freedom
to choose between means; but that is all. Their ends or goals are
fixed by instinct. Their goals are really hungers. As Temple
pointed out, it would never occur to us to ask a puppy what
manner of dog he meant to be when he was grown up. A human
person can choose between ends as well as between means. That
is freedom, and real choice. "As consciousness develops into mind
with its free ideas, choice becomes possible, not only as between
means to a fixed end (such as the satisfaction of an appetite) but
between alternative and incompatible ends (as between duty and
pleasure). Only at *this* stage is there real freedom." [15]

In Temple's view of creation as a gradient ascent from matter
through life to mind, the fourth and top level is spirit. Spirit
is, quite simply, that quality of being which is achieved whenever
freedom crosses beyond the frontier of normal human freedom,
and climbs the ascent high enough to make its choices and decisions from a God-centered instead of a self-centered standard.
This is the "life of the spirit." At such points in this "stage along
life's way" a person lives by love's law rather than by the calculations of self-interest. It is *theo*centricity rather than *ego*-
centricity. The stellar instance of "not my will but thine be
done" occurred in the Garden of Gethsemane, but there are
other cases in other times and places. They occur more often in
some lives than in others. But that is what "spiritual" is—God-
centeredness.

⚙ FREEDOM-IN-ORDER However, warning signals are usually
needed at this point in Temple's theology. Some people run
away with, or are run away with *by,* this principle of freedom.
Freedom is not absolute, any more than anything else is. Nor is
it to be thought of as the absence of all determination or conditions. Since freedom is not an abstraction of the creative
process, but a dynamic part of living, it is an emergent within

the realm of natural order and law. Just as man knows nothing about grace or "the supernatural" apart from nature, so he knows nothing of a freedom that transcends limiting conditions. As a matter of fact, *freedom is possible only because it is limited*. It requires order as a precondition. Freedom without order is chaos and license, just as order without freedom is tyranny and petrifaction. This is a paradox which is true of morality and politics as well as of physics and biology. For if in our moral striving there were no cause-and-effect between the means we employ and the ends we seek, what would be the use of trying? What would our freedom amount to?

Our efforts and actions must be "consequential" if they are to have any ethical or spiritual meaning. Without the order of cause-and-effect all of our aspiration, along with all scientific investigation and all social intercourse, would be random and unpredictable, chaotic and pointless. Temple's method of dialectic if applied here will refuse to accept an either-or formula, either freedom or necessity. His theological method will, to start with, formulate it as the question of *the necessity of freedom*. The whole process of creation is directed to the transformation of chaos into cosmos, and therefore to ignore, minimize or try to bypass law and order is, theologically, a rejection of monotheism—an absence of faith in the one God whose unitive purpose controls reality.

Temple applied his principle of theistic law and order to God Himself. On the subject of miracles, for example, he took the position that a miracle is a purposive and free act of God. It is not a breach of natural law but an illustration of a law which finds comparatively few occasions for its action. Science is always finding new things. Miracles are only a *philosophical* problem, and even as such they are only a problem for those who start by assuming a closed universe under mechanistic determinism. This is incompatible with the Christian theology of God who is personal Reality—which is what the historic term "Living God" means. The Creator Spirit or Logos, because personal, is purposive and free. He therefore has to act, His is the initiative, as He shapes His unfolding creation. His miracles may be unusual, but not unlawful. He never subverts physical or moral law.[16] We may not agree as to any particular instance, but we cannot in principle rule out miracles. "To the religious man, the verbs 'to explain' or 'to understand' mean to see the phenomenon in relation to the Divine Purpose."

By the same token the opposite of utter freedom also holds good, for "stark determinism is stark nonsense."[17] Purely deterministic theory claims that all things are determined or shaped by their external relations—that every thing or person is the product of something other than itself. If this were really true nothing could happen: the course of mutual determination between things could never get going. [113] Determinism, said Temple, "tells us that in a system ABC, A is only A in virtue of its relations to B and C; B and C *determine* it as A. And that seems easy; but why is B, *B*? It must be determined as B by *A* and C. And, similarly, *C* by A and B. If then each term is nothing *until* its external relations constitute it, we are confronted with the spectacle of nothing at all developing internal differentiation by the inter-action of its non-existent parts."[18] Here, in a few brief words, is as neat an answer as can be found in theological literature to one of the most persistent theories put forward in college hall debates—though not often encountered elsewhere!

The libertarian notion of limitless liberty is a false one based on the perfectly sound realization that to be responsible we have to be free. But in utter freedom there would be no responsibility actually, because a completely free person would be undermined in every way. In his own case his choices would not reflect his own character—they would be pure chance. [114] And even if his own actions were consistent and purposive, their consequences would be unpredictable. He couldn't "get anywhere." Responsibility requires both a certain "continuity of character" and the ability to foresee consequences and to decide our choices accordingly. We would not blame a man for stealing if he could always say, "Oh, that wasn't really *me;* I acted simply out of chance," or, "How could I tell what was going to happen?" On the other hand, if stark, mechanistic *unfreedom* were the theory, the same man could say, "Oh, it wasn't *I* that stole; I was driven to it." On either of these polar extremes people would be puppets—moral billiard balls.

Our personal status therefore depends upon understanding correctly the relation between freedom and necessity. Necessity is "blind" only when it is not recognized and accepted, and freedom is an "illusion" only when it is guilty of this error of ignoring necessity. As Engels pointed out long ago, freedom is "founded on knowledge of natural necessity." [19] Engels' epigram is a typical bit of dialectic. Temple put it theologically: "We are clay in the hands of the Potter, and our welfare is to know it." [20] He was following Isaiah 64:8—"Yet, O Lord, Thou art our Father: we are the clay, and Thou art our potter; we are all the work of Thy hand." As the great Reformation theologians tried to explain it, while we are "psychologically" free to defy either God's moral law or His physical order, we are nonetheless "metaphysically" bound to accept the consequences of our choices. We are free to choose but we are not free to escape the consequences. We can decide against God's laws, but then we choose the losing side. The prophetic law of harvest works, and we reap what we sow either sooner or later, however God's orderly purpose requires.

This paradox of freedom-in-order is a main theme in Temple's work. It is the subject of his last closing pages in the Gifford Lectures. He was convinced that ultimately it is only in willing obedience to the highest law and order of all, love, that freedom can come into its own. As we have seen, he held that "one thing only" can control us by actually exerting its control through, and *by means of, freedom itself.* That is love.[21] For freedom is not an end in itself, or a thing in itself like Kant's autonomous *ding an sich.* Freedom is not only *from* something but *for* something. Negatively freedom is escape from restraint and constraint, whether internal or external; positively it is the power to choose, to select, and to decide. Vegetables have neither kind; animals have only negative freedom; persons have *positive* freedom.

Theologically expressed, freedom is from the self for God—for His loving service, and "to enjoy Him forever." From the human selfhood point of view we are free until we become slaves of Christ; from the divine sonship point of view we are slaves and unfree until we become free in Christ—to use the language St. Paul used over and over. This is the paradox in the Collect for Grace in Morning Prayer, "whose service is perfect freedom." Our true freedom is gained when we die to the illusion of self-centered freedom and rise with Christ our Head, in His resurrection from sin and its wages of death to the freedom of conscious communion with God, the beatific vision for which God destines us.

⚙ MAN'S FREEDOM AND GOD'S We are provisionally free, then, to reject grace. It is not irresistible. But we are dependent upon it (i.e., upon the power of the love of God) if our freedom is to get its full growth. Only by His help can we escape from that self-centeredness which is the last and most deceptive form of captivity. "Whatever freedom of the will may mean," Temple once said, "it is sheer nonsense if it means that a selfish man can make himself unselfish. What, then, *can* you do about it? You can make what is far the most important choice anybody ever has to make at all; that is the choice of those influences by which you deliberately submit yourself to be moulded." [22] Among the influences he had in mind were, supremely, the fellowship of the Christian Church and its sacraments.

At its best, natural freedom is only the ability *not* to sin (*posse non peccare*). It is within our human powers to make a stubborn even though not always successful refusal to submit to self-centeredness. But spiritual or Christian freedom is the *inability* to sin (*non posse peccare*). And this is the *gift* of grace, from outside our own powers. The prototype and perfection of such radical and complete freedom is seen, of course, in the divine nature. For God *cannot* contradict His own nature. He cannot trample love. The paradox of freedom is that its ultimate achievement is reached when we become bound by our own highest potential character, as God is. "Such would be true freedom; and it is not ours." [23] Only God is completely controlled by His own purpose and His own character. Man, by comparison, is only finitely good and finitely free, and then only if and when he manages to get to the level of grace-freedom as distinguished from human or self-freedom.

In the Christian scheme of things, then, the optimum freedom possible to men is freedom from self-centeredness in spite of self-centeredness. And this is only possible by God's grace, not by the nature of man himself. Only God's freedom from self-love and for neighbor-love is due to His own Self, His own nature. But the finite freedom of man is achieved by a double course of God's creative activity. First He brings it about indirectly through His process of development in human selfhood, where personal integration and moral responsibility are achieved. Then He acts directly by grace, whereby His Love's power enables men to raise their human freedom to spiritual freedom in voluntary self-oblation, in free and loving obedience. On this theological view men may make their way to *two* freedoms: (1) human freedom, as the ability either to sin or not to sin, and (2) grace freedom, as the inability to betray God's love (*nota bene:* only imperfectly or finitely attained at best, even at the heights of saintliness).

The mode or operation of freedom is also twofold. In its human form it is *self*-determination, as distinct from physical or psychopathic determinism. It is our determination of our choices by what seems good to us. In its grace form it is our determination of our choices by what seems to be *God's* choice. But at either level freedom is certainly not the absence of determination. It is, rather, self-determination. In either human freedom or grace freedom, if it is the real thing, we must be able to say of any act, "I did it, and what made me do it was myself." [24] The *theological* question is whether this free self is self-centered or God-centered. It is a question of "character," or the posture of personality. "True freedom is not only or chiefly a freedom from external control, but from internal compulsion; it is found, not only when a man says, 'I did it, and no one else,' but when a man says, 'I did it, and I am glad I did it, and if opportunity arises I will do it again.' " [25]

There are many practical applications of all this. For the sake of illustration let us look at just one, in the field of politics. Temple's maxim was "Freedom is the goal of politics." [26] In an article in *The Spectator* in 1932 he declared there are two sanctions for it. One lies in human selfhood, for individuality has a right to be expressed. (A danger lurks here, because while it can only be creative if it is respected, private right becomes anarchic and destructive if it is *reverenced!*) The other sanction lies in man's sonship to God. (A danger lurks here, too, for the State may ignore this second sanction even if it honors the first! But, warned Temple, if man is a child of God, "his first duty is to God, and if it seems to him that this duty requires disobedience to earthly rulers, he will not hesitate." [27]) The theological sanction is the first-order one.

"The real reason," he explained, "why the State must not presume to dictate to me my manner of life and thought is not that I am myself, but that I am a child of God. Historically, the first claim to liberty successfully asserted against the modern State was the claim to worship God according to conscience. It is this which makes the Dutch Protestants, who rose against Philip II of Spain, the true pioneers of European liberty; and in our own country the successful assertion of the same claim by groups attached to different beliefs in a series of political upheavals was the well-spring of English liberty as we know it today. [115] Freedom of conscience—that is the sacred thing: not freedom to do what I choose or to fulfill my own purpose, but freedom to do what I ought, and to fulfill God's purpose for me." [28]

VI

Grace and Sin

In the great tradition of Christian evangelism the first things in the Gospel or "Good News" were good and encouraging, namely, the proclamation that this is God's world and in Christ is eternal life. [116] The Fourth Gospel, Temple's guideline in the Scriptures, began in just that way. First this proclamation, then the account of God's mighty acts of self-disclosure in the Incarnation. It was not until the question was raised why God had so acted through Christ's life, death and resurrection that the apostolic preacher pointed to the obvious—the fact that men are sinful and weak and in need of help. In other words, the classical apologetic started with grace, not with sin.

It has been characteristic of Reformation orthodoxy, and of some modern attempts to renew it, to reverse the order. But Temple was classical in his approach to the sin-grace equation in Christian theology (his "soteriology"). He was convinced that modern men are not half so blind to the reality of sin as they are skeptical about the reality of grace. His approach was that the essence of sin is selfishness ("self-centeredness and all the welter of evil flowing from it"), but that the clinical evidences of egoism's widespread and disastrous power in the world are generally recognized. Men know they are in trouble; this Age of Fratricide makes it painfully, fearfully obvious. They may not—in fact, they do not—any longer understand their dangerous fault in the theological perspective of "sin," but they see the fact itself. What they do not know or believe is that there is a power greater than their own available to help them. They do not perceive this in any terms, either secular or theological; and what has to be effectively recommended to modern people, he thought, is the reality and power of grace.

☼ GRACE IS LOVE IS GOD   "Grace," he said, "is not something other than God, imparted by Him; it is the very Love of
God (which is God Himself) approaching and seeking entry
to the soul of man." [1] Just as God *is* love rather than "having"
it, so God *is* grace rather than "giving" it. He gives Himself, as in
the Sacrament of the Altar. Grace, we may say, is God at work
in the world through persons. As Ephesians 3:20 has it, it is "a
power that worketh in us." He conceived of religious experience
as being in part the experience of grace, which comes as the
impulse "to throw oneself back upon a Power greater than oneself, and the sense, the perfectly sure sense, that the Power has
received one and is supporting one." [2] God does for us what we
cannot do for ourselves. Temple's line of attack on all bootstrap
theories, in which man finds salvation through his own powers,
went straight to the point. It is worth quoting one passage at
some length:

"I am the centre of the world I see; where the horizon is depends on where I stand. . . . So each of us takes his place in
the centre of his own world. But I am not the centre of the
world, or the standard of reference as between good and evil;
I am not, and God is. [117] In other words, from the beginning
I put myself in God's place. This is my original sin. I was doing
it before I could speak, and every one else has been doing it
from early infancy. I am not 'guilty' on this account because I
could not help it . . . Education may make my self-esteem
less disastrous by widening my horizon of interest; so far it is
like the climbing of a tower, which widens the horizon for
physical vision while leaving me still the centre and standard of
reference." [3]

We had to learn that the Ptolemaic viewpoint, which makes
the earth the center of things, was wrong because the sun is; and
just as we accepted a solar system, we must accept a theocentric
system. Each of us needs a spiritual "Copernican revolution"
to stop seeing himself as the center of reality and acknowledge
that God is. Only thus can we take our real place among our
neighbors, in human society and God's family.

Temple taught that "the self cannot by any effort of its own

lift itself off its own centre" by spiritual gymnastics. If the world
and the men in it are to be lifted out of their present state, as
Archimedes knew long ago, a point outside must be found to
act as a fulcrum for the lever.[4] "Something impinging on the
self from without must deliver it," and that something is grace—
God's love. It (more properly, He) alone has the power of
"winning the freely offered love of the finite selves which He has
created." [5] This is how "salvation" comes about, as the response
of the self to the divine love revealed in the "loving" life, death,
and resurrection of Christ. The *new* self it makes possible becomes open and eager for wider love, wider fellowship. To be
"saved" means to be healed, made whole or wholesome, and
this comes as the self-centered-ness of a man is *cured*.

St. Matthew (16:25) says, "For whoever would save his life
will lose it, and whoever loses his life for my sake will find
it." [118] And in that light Temple said, even more pointedly,
"The true aim of the soul is not its own salvation: to make that
the chief aim is to ensure its perdition; for it is to fix the soul
on itself as centre." [6] The merciful love of God, often received
unawares, carries forgiveness and brings the wayward self into
full fellowship with God and his faithful children. This is the
"justification" of which dogmatic theology speaks. It illuminates
the mind and soul thus opened to the Spirit's leading. It sup-
plies a strength or power for sharing and fellowship not the
natural self's own. Grace, in brief, is transforming and socializ-
ing.

II Corinthians sums it up: "The grace of our Lord Jesus
Christ, the love of God, and the fellowship of the Holy Ghost."
Grace equals love equals fellowship. As the three persons of the
Trinity are one God, so these various "attributions" of the Per-
sons are one attribute—love—*the* attribute of the divine nature.
All are one and the same—God, love, grace, fellowship. [119]

✺ LOVE LOVES FREEDOM   Grace is love, and love "loves"
freedom. As freedom is essential to personhood, so love is a
relationship between persons: it does not come into play between

things or brutes. Therefore grace and freedom are partners, in that grace always presupposes freedom. For this reason Temple's theology never had any room in it for the Calvinist notion of irresistible grace. There can be no love unless there is the possibility of its being unrequited, which is to say, unless its response is free. Grace must be resistible. Experience teaches us that it is, anyway; we know we can say *No* to God and man. The Calvinists, builders of a Protestant scholasticism every whit as *logical* as the Catholic version, started with doctrines of man's total inability through his own power to respond even tentatively to God's love, and with "predestination" (foreordained salvation for some only). These ideas were presumed logically to protect the belief that men need grace, but all they resulted in was an in-group claim for its operation which flies in the face of common sense and the logic of the love of God! Temple's "agapeic" theology had another starting point—in the belief that men have freedom. He therefore came to another conclusion about how grace operates. In his view grace does not compel us, it impels us; it does not push, it pulls; it does not force, it attracts. Otherwise, he held, our supposed freedom and responsibility are "essentially fictitious."

But, given the natural human condition of self-centeredness (what used to be called Original Sin and what the philosopher calls "egocentric predicament"), how can we account for our ability to respond, however feebly, to God's overtures? Certainly we cannot claim any natural capacity for humility and loving obedience. Temple called the "Pelagian" idea that we can of our own human power overcome our selfishness "the only intrinsically [sic] damnable heresy." [120] If we are so self-centered that we naturally resist and resent any call to forsake "the fortress I" and turn over our lives to God and His service, by what means can this be brought about? Just how are we enticed to come out of our centers or down from our towers?

Temple's answer was fairly simple. If God does not open us up by irresistible force, then it must be by irresistible attraction! "The love of Christ controls us" (II Corinthians 5:14). And what is there that can at one and the same time respect and acknowledge my freedom to say No and still overcome my No?

One thing, replied Temple, and one thing only—love. "Is there anything known in the world which does control by means of and not by over-riding freedom? Yes; one thing only—the sacrifice of love." [7] He agreed with Samuel Coleridge that the important promise in the Gospel is not forgiveness to the repentant but repentance to the sinner. There is no good in telling a man he'll be forgiven if he repents, if he *doesn't!* We have to tell him how on the Cross Christ demonstrated His love, showing us what our self-centeredness costs Him, and confronting us with the only shock that can bring us to our knees.

"When a man finds that someone else has such love for him that he is willing to suffer for that love, there is hardly anyone so hard as to remain indifferent. I do not say that such knowledge will always and at once overcome all selfishness in that regard, but it will be a strong pull. We know that there is no action in life in which we feel so free as an action that we undertake in order to please a friend; yet the content of that action, the thing we do, is then determined by the pleasure of our friend; it is, so to speak, he who has really chosen what shall be done, and yet there is nothing that we do so freely. [121] It is in the mutual interaction of love that there is to be found the power which does control the will through and not against its freedom." [8]

A common objection to Temple's view of how God's love ("moral influence") invades our selfishness is that it does not take account sufficiently of man's sin-ridden inability to be moved by God's suffering. This objection carries the assertion that we are too hardened by sin to respond. Thus it is suggested that there is an unintentional element of cruelty in Temple's explanation, because it presupposes an ability man lacks. But this is not the real issue, of course. The issue is around *faith*, i.e., whether a person *believes* that Christ is God Himself. If he does, then he *will* be moved by the spectacle of God's humility and suffering. But only if he believes, only if he has that faith. I do have the ability to respond to God's suffering *if* I believe that Christ on the Cross is the Lord Incarnate—actually He. If I don't truly believe, I won't respond.

✸ AND THEN SIN CAME   But how then is sinfulness itself accounted for, "that perverted use of self-consciousness which is called the Fall of Man?" [9] Temple's answer is that its source is psychological, not historical. Self-centeredness is man's No to God's sovereignty. Sin is self-assertion, egocentricity. Human beings are "naturally" that way; it is the condition into which they are born. [122] Hence his remark quoted above that no blame or guilt attaches to the human condition of original, or birth, sin. It is nonsense to imagine that *we* are guilty because our nature is "fallen" (self-centered), a sinfulness (self-assertiveness) which comes to us through Adam's (humanity's) very given nature. This could only show that "Adam" is responsible for our sin, not we for *his!* Only for the evils we choose *knowingly,* called "personal" (actual and habitual) sins to distinguish them from "original" sin, are we responsible or culpable. [123] Personal sins are a deliberate, conscious disobedience to God.

The old-time belief was that Adam was an individual human being, the ancestor of all men (the theory of monogenesis). It was thought that *his* personal sin—eating a forbidden apple —was somehow transmitted to all his descendants, so that they are born both corrupt and guilty. On this prescientific basis a notion of man was evolved that gave him a static constitution and allowed the slogan so dear to all conservatives and reactionaries: "You can't change human nature." Temple said, "There is no 'Human Nature' apart from human beings." [10] There is a humanity, yes, because individuals are linked and mutually constitutive. But a person is a process, not a delivered package.

It was further believed that Baptism "washes away" that sin. The old way of thinking literalized the Genesis myth and turned its psychological truth—that we are all selfish to start with—into false history about an actual "Fall" from an imaginary, aboriginal righteousness in which we lived at some time in the dim past. None of this was a part of Temple's theology.

In the first place, he regarded the sacrament of Baptism as a matter of receiving children into the fellowship of the Church, not of relieving them of a non-existent guilt. As for any claim

that Baptism will do away with, or put an end to, original or
personal sin, either one, that is most obviously not the case. As
he understood and administered it Baptism is a rite of initiation,
but not of "regeneration" in any sense but that of a "new birth"
which comes by consciously acknowledging membership in
Christ. This new being is the eternal life which has in fact already been the baptized's all along, in God's creative love, revealed now with saving power in the life and death of Christ.
In the rite it is ceremonially confessed among the brethren in
the household of faith. Baptism recognizes what is already a fact,
that the child *is* a child of God and that the Church accepts
responsibility to help nurture it to maturity in the fellowship. It
is primarily a membership act.

The Fall myth, like all good myths, tells an important truth
in poetic and imaginative form *as if it had really happened.* [124]
Temple said that human history began with the first human
glimmerings of the difference between right and wrong, between
good and evil, love and indifference. He quoted Emerson's essay
on Experience: "It is very unhappy but too late to be helped,
the discovery that we exist; that discovery is called the Fall of
Man." With the first early phase of self-consciousness—the ability
to stand off from and look at himself—man was raised to a
stratum of life higher than the brutes. Brutes, by definition,
know nothing but satisfaction and frustration. To use the language of biology, they have not yet developed a high or complex
enough brain center or cerebral cortex. When they do develop it, when self-consciousness comes, presto! Simultaneously
both obedience and disobedience, sin and righteousness, are
born. "Self-hood, or being a self, is the basis both of all spiritual
good and all spiritual evil . . . The seat of sin is the very organ
of our moral improvement and of our communion with God. It
is the spiritual life itself and that is why we cannot cure it." [11]

The wisdom of the myth in Genesis, as Temple interpreted
it, rests on four points. It declared (1) that God made the world
and it was good for that reason; (2) that man reached "conscious
realization of value," i.e., knowledge of good and evil—for although what he found himself doing in the symbolic figure of
Adam was actually wrong, he had not known it until then, so

that in doing wrong he discovered it; (3) he thereby became a conscious sinner, aware of his selfishness, turning man into what has been called the "tragic animal"; (4) yet thereby he became capable of fellowship with God. As Temple saw it, this is the story of all human progress. "Man stumbles, by the impulse of his nature into something which, by his misunderstanding of it, is first a source of new evils, but is the condition of a hitherto impossible good." [12]

The Fall was, as it were, a fall *upstairs*. Any notion that mankind as a whole, or any individual, has at any time in the past ever been free of self-centeredness (a view actually held seriously in the pre-scientific era) is simply not to be entertained. [125] Evolutionary biology, anthropology, and modern psychology with its ego-theory—these things have discredited the "primitive innocence" idea in any sense, except in the sense that a dog or chicken or a snake is innocent. That was man's innocence in the Garden of Eden. Temple always recognized two sources of human sinfulness, the biological and the sociological. "What the old theologians put down to Adam we attribute in part to our evolutionary descent from non-human ancestors, and in part to 'social heredity' [126]—the evil influence of the actual society into which we are born, its tradition of self-seeking and moral indifference." [13]

However, besides the ego-axis which holds the personality together but self-centers it, and the corruptive influence of other persons and of society's structures and conventions, there is a third source, or cause, of even greater moral or spiritual significance. Temple was firm about this. "But none of these evolutionary theories touches the center of the problem, for no man who is really conscious of sin will be content to have that consciousness explained as merely an indication that his growth is as yet incomplete . . . It is not simply that he sees before him a goal he has not reached, but that he has seen a goal before him and has turned his back upon it; and every one of us knows in his own heart that the secret of his sin is a quite definite refusal of the claim of God and the call of God." [14]

There are, then, three sources of sin: our as yet ungrown-out-of primitive egoism, our "conditioning" by the sin-centered evils of our social culture, and our personal or deliberate betrayal of *what we see for ourselves* to be the good and the right. The first offers a reason for compassion toward mankind (and sometimes an understandable impatience with the timetable of God's creation!). The second is the basis for a passionate prophetic or "social gospel" demand for social righteousness, added to our redemptive Christian concern with community as in itself a good. The third is of "ascetical" importance in terms of humility and repentance, and of tremendous ethical bearing in personal religion. Given this third cause, none of us can escape his own personal responsibility for evil by merely pleading psychobiology or "social conditioning" as an excuse! Over and beyond all hereditary and environmental explanations of human sin, individual and social, there is the *personal* or "moral" reason for it.

⚙ HOW SIN IS SOCIAL   It is necessary on the other hand, as Temple knew, to avoid treating sin unrealistically as purely or merely personal. It does have its social dimension. If a drunken driver whose car has a defective steering gear crashes, the "moralistic" personal-religionists blame it on his self-indulgence. The "mechanistic" causationists blame it on the steering gear. Both may be right in part. But the significant observation is this: *even if the driver were sober as a judge,* an accident would be bound to happen sooner or later.

Moralism trivializes and subjectivizes morality's scope and problems, and it would be moralistic to see sin solely as a personal fault, without facing its contextual, social sources. Temple was never a moralistic Christian of the sort who says, "If individuals would just do the right thing, the social system would be all right." He knew that systems—whether little steering gears or great national economies and governments—have to be right as well as the motives of people within them.

We might explain his position this way. St. Chrysostom once said that the essence of sin lies in the confusion of means and ends. We sin when we turn what are only means into ends in themselves. This has always been a good rule-of-thumb in ethical

analysis. It applies to social policies as well as to personal behavior. Sociologists speak of pathologies or social ills being due
to "the substitution of instrumental for terminal values," but
this is just a jawbreaker way of saying what St. Chrysostom said
long ago.

Applying this principle to systems as well as to motives, let us
look at our economic problem. The private-profit system of
laissez-faire capitalism was explained by Adam Smith on the
highly dynamic theory that private profit is a strong incentive
to industry and production, and that the motive of private gain
is only the means, while an over-all gain in the standard of living
of the commonwealth is the end to be served. (It is sheer ignorance which treats the "profit system" as solely consecrated
to greed, just as the theory of "automatic harmony" between
private and public interest may be sheer naïveté among the
system's defenders.) Temple argued that a time comes when,
under the free-market supply-and-demand way of determining
prices, the actual production of wealth becomes so plenteous that
it results in "overproduction." At this point various "rationaliz-
ing" devices are resorted to—price-rigging and monopoly and
production control—in order to reduce the supply and thus raise
prices and widen the profit margin. The *means* (profit) is being
served at the expense of the *end*. This is social sin. A good
example may be seen in the American farm policy of artificial
scarcity, under which warehouses bulge with unused butter and
grain, and farmers are paid not to plant crops. This policy is,
therefore, sinful—social sin; it reverses means and ends.

The same principle of sin-analysis can be applied to personal
systems as to social systems. For example, a patient suffering
from satyriasis or nymphomania has, for unconscious reasons,
made sex an end in itself instead of a means to love and affection and maturity. The patient's psychic system is disordered,
not merely his motives. Depth therapy is needed to *reorganize the
structure* of the personality, and all the moralistic appeal in the
world to the patient's love or duty or honor or self-control or
ambition or prudence won't change anything. Sin is *disorder*, as
well as a wrong disposition of the will! Systems as well as sentiments have to be changed, and to forget this is to be moralistic.

Such moralism is the characteristic fault of personal, soul-saving, "private" religion. [127] Temple never made this mistake, although his conservative critics would have preferred that he had.

A kind of footnote is called for here. Temple, like Boethius of old, was a great believer in the "apparent good." In a strange way people may often *do* evil but they always seek good. "That any man," he said, "ever chose evil, knowing it to be evil for him, is to me quite incredible. He may say, under an impulse of defiance, 'Evil, be thou my good,' but his pursuit of it is then due to the fact that he has adopted it as his good and not because it is evil. To desire evil for its own sake is impossible!" [15] It is a salutary and sobering thing, a good corrective for the self-righteous, to remember that just as finite human beings cannot be perfectly good, neither can they be perfectly evil. We share in the "solidarity of goodness," growing through the lovingness of others—as well as in the "solidarity of sin," being pulled down by the sin of others. And in this way we see *both* sides of our finitude and moral imperfection. We cannot be anything but partial in either sin or righteousness. There *is* good in the worst of us, as the old saying goes, as well as evil in the best of us. "It was not crime or vice that sent Christ to the Cross; it was respectability and religious stagnation and compromise." [16]

❄ THE GOOD OF EVIL Temple realized that we cannot think of "sin" and "evil" as the same thing. Evil is a broader category which includes sin. "Evil," he said, "is of three main kinds—Error, Suffering and Sin, and to a very great extent the two former are due to the last." [17] He meant that there is *intellectual* evil (error, including both ignorance and bad reasoning), *emotional* evil (suffering, both mental and physical), and *moral* evil (sin, both as self-centeredness and the actual faults it leads to). An honest mistake, or something under the heading of "invincible ignorance," would be an example of error; no sin is involved. An earthquake, or crop-ruining rains, or cancer, would be examples of suffering; no sin is involved. Such "pure" and non-sinful evils are "cosmic" evil.

Still, as he said, there is often a lot of human perversity mixed up in many so-called cosmic or "natural" evils. Disease-dealing radiation from nuclear bomb tests would be a case; or a farm drought due to selfish denuding of the top soil for quick crops; or ruthlessly selling off the trees for lumber. Some moral evils (sins) are personal, like burglary; some are corporate, like wars or unemployment. Even if we agree to hold men responsible for their own disobedience or sins, how are we to account for the *cosmic* evils—unchosen error and suffering? How could they exist in a world created and governed by a loving and all-powerful God?

Temple's answer was much like the "good-of-evil" doctrine of Harvard's Josiah Royce at the turn of the century. In *Mens Creatrix, Christus Veritas,* and *Nature, Man and God*—all three of his major theoretical works—Temple surveyed and rejected the three traditional attempts to explain *im*personal evil. One of these is that we are such limited creatures that we don't know what is good; if we did, we would find that what seems to us to be evil is actually good. This, he said, is a pathetic *argumentum ad ignorantia* which wipes out all human moral judgment and perception. By inference it subverts moral concern as futile. Another explanation is that evil is only the absence of good, that evil is the not-good—as St. Augustine once argued. To this Temple replied that giving it another name, making evil negative rather than positive, changes nothing. [128] It leaves us with the same problem, and is therefore no solution at all. [129]

Again, he rejected the third theory that evil exists because God cannot help it. On this theory, it is argued that He did not create it and cannot destroy it; He can only hold it in check. This "finite God" explanation, Temple thought, sets up a rival god (the Devil) at the expense of monotheism and the unconditional being of God. It seemed to him that this kind of Persian dualism about a cosmic struggle between good and evil deities entails chaos rather than order and predictability, and flies in the face of both scientific and common sense. What, then, was Temple's answer?

All depends, he thought, on setting up the problem the right way. When we set it up in the common fashion as a contradiction between the fact of evil and the love of an omnipotent God, we make two questionable assumptions: (1) that if God is almighty He is able to do what He wishes—which ignores the possibility that He might will to set aside or suspend what He wishes (self-limitation), and (2) that if God is good He will make men perfectly happy. This latter is a kind of hedonistic notion, which ignores the possibility that God has higher (better) values than pleasure in prospect for human beings, and it also neglects Temple's big point, the creativity of struggle and suffering. [130] Our success in finding answers usually hangs on asking the right question to start with. The correct question is not, "What is the source of evil?" It is, "What is the *good* of evil?"

We are dealing, he said, not with the problem of evil but with the problem of the good of evil. "If you take all the evil out of the world, you will remove the possibility of the best thing in life . . . moral victory." [18] Just as our mental powers are raised by having to solve problems and *think*, so it is with our moral or spiritual powers. [131] Socrates is better than a pig, however well tended it might be. The goal of human life is "the widest possible fellowship," and the way to grow from selfishness into fellowship is through struggle and suffering. They provide "the indispensable conditions of fortitude and the most potent stimulus and bond of sympathy." Temple added, mournfully, "If we were not so self-centered we should find in joy as strong a stimulus to sympathy as in pain and sorrow; it is certain that in fact we do not find it so." [19] This explanation, he thought, preserves the validity of man's ethical discernment, it recognizes the reality of evil, and saves Christ's victory on the Cross from being a victory over an illusion only. Most of all, it retains the sovereignty of God, the rule of Love, and respects the validity of human experience with evil.

⚙ ETERNAL LIFE Temple believed in personal survival after death. He was convinced that the future shape of civilization depends on how men believe about two questions—a personal God and eternal life for persons. The development of personality is, he believed, a permanent achievement: God is not playing games. The main outlines of his view of eternal life were set forth substantially in the Drew Lecture for 1921 in *The Idea of Immortality in Relation to Religion and Ethics.* [132] The core of it is: "Man is not immortal of nature or right; but he is capable of immortality and there is offered to him resurrection from the dead and life eternal if he will receive it from God, and on God's terms." [20]

He held, first, that "immortality" is a Greek and pagan idea, not Christian. There is nothing in the Bible about human beings having "immortal souls," whether pre-existent or not, making the "question of the hereafter" simply one of heaven or hell. The New Testament doctrine, he said, was *resurrection.* While Temple found no single, consistent doctrine of eternal life in the New Testament, he did find a prevailing belief that God only is immortal. Along with this went the faith that man enjoys eternal life as a loving gift of God, and that it is by becoming one with Christ that we are raised with Him in His Resurrection to eternal fellowship with the Father. This is his first point: that eternal life is not something given in human nature as such, but gained for us by Christ. Eternal life, then, as Temple saw it, is a gift and not a right. It is the prize for which Christians run the race of life. The Stoics taught indifference to death, Temple noted, but the Gospel taught victory over it. Yet the victory is guaranteed by God's love *for* us, and not *by* us through our goodness. If it depended on our kind or measure of love, we would be lost. And it comes about not as something calculated as profit or gain on a rewards and punishment basis, but as something discovered to be inherent in God's creative love.

Only God's love is absolute enough to encompass eternal consequences. Temple understood quite clearly that *we are not saved by our faith in God, but by His faith in us.* He pointed out, incidentally, that Plato reasoned falsely in the Phaedo by assuming, Greek-like, that a "soul" (or, to use St. Paul's better word for it, a *soma* or *person*) is immortal and that the disease of the soul, injustice, could not cause its decay. Temple pointed out that there is, after all, another logical alternative to hell or heaven. The person could end in annihilation—decay, nothingness. He showed that there are, as a matter of fact, many places in the New Testament where the alternatives posed are either eternal life in Christ or annihilation, and not heaven or hell. (In most New Testament passages this is the issue posed, the "good news" being that all *could* be saved by accepting Christ as their Savior. In some places, although not the majority, the "good news" is that all *are* saved or *have been* saved. Compare Philippians 3:11, "If possible I may attain the resurrection" to I Corinthians 15:18, "That God may be everything to everyone.")

It was the eventual dominance of pagan immortality over biblical resurrection, even within Christendom itself, which led to the popular idea, as in Dante and Milton, of the choice between eternal joy or everlasting torment. Given the pagan "immortality" idea, the Christians of the "dark ages" misconstrued a verse like Matthew 18:18, "thrown into the eternal fire," to mean that the "lost" burn eternally when in fact it was the *fire* that burned eternally, not those in it. Gehenna was a dump fire outside the Jerusalem city walls, burning constantly, as is usually the case with such refuse heaps, while *the things in it are consumed*. (None of this, of course, has anything to do with the physical body being somehow raised with the person. Temple did not entertain any idea of physical resurrection. He was a believer in cremation for urban-social reasons, and his body was burned at his own request.) [133]

Temple dropped any and all ideas of hell. He declared that "such conceptions could not permanently survive in the minds of people who read the gospels. Steadily the conviction has gained ground that the God and Father of our Lord Jesus Christ cannot be conceived as inflicting on any soul that He has made unending torment." [21] This left him with heaven only, as a certainty of faith.

❀ FOR SOME OR ALL?   But what about the question of annihilation? Temple admired the logical structure of the medieval theology, still taught by the Roman Church. "Universal immortality is assumed; for those who are beyond pardon there is Hell; for those who are pardonable, Purgatory; for those whose pardon

is accomplished, Paradise. And alongside of these, for the unawakened soul, there is Limbo." [22] He said in a jocular way that
he saw certain "administrative difficulties" in all of this except
for the idea of Purgatory. Can we be sure a baby is unawakened
and ineligible? How can we say who or what is unpardonable?
He regarded it all as unreal, however watertight logically, for
"how can there be Paradise for any while there is Hell . . . for
some?" No. "Each supposedly damned soul was born into the
world as a mother's child; and Paradise there cannot be for her
if her child is in such a Hell."

This declaration of faith left him in something of a quandary
theologically, although more a doctrinal than an ethical one.
In his discussions of it he always admitted it was a "bewildering
subject" and "the kind of problem which peculiarly belongs to
the eternal world, and is therefore not likely to be open to complete solution here." [23] In his lectures to students in London in
1909 he had asserted his conviction that the purpose of God and
the uniqueness of every soul (person) make eternal life a necessary
corollary. He contended, "It is impossible that God should allow
the universe to be impoverished" by the loss of a soul, and that
God's love won't allow the destruction of what He has created.
"The love of God is the basis of our hope of immortality." [24]

This way of talking is obviously close to universalism—the
belief that all will be saved. Yet he continued to feel a dilemma
in the question. Baron von Hügel had convinced him that it
pulls the rug from under morals if we deny that there are "abiding consequences" from evil or sinful deeds, and this we do by
getting rid of hell. [134] Temple used to remind his hearers that
even Kant resorted to immortality as a necessary compensation
for the sacrifices that moral principles entail. At the same time
Temple repudiated any appeal to fear in support of morality:
"Fear is the most self-centered of all emotions, and the use of it
as a constant moral appeal can only make us more self-centered,
and therefore it must defeat the very object it is desired to attain." [25]

More important, however, is the seeming dilemma between
God's all powerful, victorious love, on the one hand, and on
the other, the freedom of man—his radical freedom, if he
chooses—to say No finally and irreversibly to God's offer of fel-

lowship. Temple was drawn by the kind of conviction that F. D. Maurice held about the universality of God's society, of His all-inclusive family under Christ's headship. In the theology of Maurice, eternal life is not selective or a merely contingent offer. He had no place for outcasts or second-class citizens in the universe. When it came down to it, Temple was not only unable to accept a hell; he could not imagine, for the same reason, that God's love will not in the end triumph in every person's life, "even Judas Iscariot's." [135] He could not accept the logical weakness of all damnation doctrine, that it ignores human creatureliness and makes a *man's* will absolute and final, equal in power to God's love.

He allowed for what was, in effect, Purgatory, as a midpassage after this life and before heaven, for those who die indifferent and unrepentant. There, he thought, the pulling power of God's love will go on until it triumphs. "Eternity cannot be too long for our finite spirits to advance in knowledge of the infinite God." [26] He was not, however, as confident on this count as he was about most things in his theology. In *Nature, Man and God* he offered what he called "a slender hope of a solution"; and the hope was based on that same paradox of love with which, as we have seen, he solved the question of the tension between human freedom and divine grace. As with freedom and grace, he reasoned that the tension between man's freedom and God's ultimate victory over his soul will "in the end" be resolved in God's favor, because "the grace of God will win its way with every human heart."

God's victory will be finally won either on earth or in the hereafter. Just as every man is a child of God, so is every man already "in" eternal life. Talk about "preparing to meet your Maker" is entirely beside the mark. Eternity is the Eternal Now —what St. Augustine called the everlasting here and now— whether in this world or the next. We have all met Him, with a Yea or Nay. And in this creative, constant contest of human wills and divine love, "all that we could contribute of our own would be the resistance of our self-will. It is just this which love breaks down, and in doing so it does not over-ride our freedom, but rather calls it into exercise." [27]

VII

Worship and Sacraments

Temple's conviction was crystal clear that "religious faith does not consist in supposing that there is a God; it consists in personal trust in God rising to personal fellowship with God." [1] Perhaps we can say that this was what his whole understanding of prayer and worship came down to—continuous companionship with God.

It is a view of worship which carries an electrifying test of a Christian's vocation in life. It means, in effect, that a Christian is one who is practicing (whether consciously or not) the presence of God while he does what he does or makes what he makes, either for his living, or as an avocation. It means being able to answer Yes to such questions as: Can I pray while I am working? Can I visualize Christ busy at my side, working with me? Can I claim that my work is for God's greater glory? It should be obvious that on this basis there are a lot of things—from arson to zealotry—which, when followed by alleged Christians, reveal a lack of faith, and therefore of worship. There are some things we cannot work at no matter how much belief we profess, or how many services we may attend.

❂ Worship Is Action "Worship" is the main term. It includes *conduct* as well as prayer. It covers not only our participation in the sacraments, in liturgical and devotional disciplines, and other such "religious" things. Christianly speaking, it covers everything. As Temple said, "Worship includes all life, and [those] moments spent in concentrated worship, whether 'in Church' or elsewhere, are the focussing points of the sustaining and directing energy of the worshipper's whole life." [2] He told a group of clergy at Washington's College of Preachers in 1936, "The heart of moral improvement, the heart of moral progress, therefore also of social progress, and the amelioration of this world's bitter condition, is always to be found in worship." [3]

First of all, let it be clear that Temple was not holding out for an activism in which "building the Kingdom" is substituted for a deliberate and regular practice of prayer. For one thing he knew of no reason to think men could build the Kingdom. They are God's co-workers and agents as *He* builds it, and beyond that, of their own, they can only prevent it, not build it. The Benedictine maxim *laborare est orare* is not good enough unless, as St. Benedict intended, a part of the work is prayer. "It is mere humbug to say that we will serve God by our conduct but cannot find time for prayer and worship." A Christian, by formal prayer, focuses and highlights the active worship in the rest of his life. Temple looked at the question from a theological point of view: "People are always thinking that conduct is supremely important, and that because prayer helps it, therefore prayer is good. That is true as far as it goes; still truer is it to say that worship is of supreme importance and conduct tests it. Conduct tests how much of yourself was in the worship you gave to God." [4] He often used the term "moralism" to mean not only trivial morals but also the mistaken idea that "being good" is the point of the Christian life. "I mean the notion that a man is to aim primarily at being good, the love of God being a kind of sauce (ingredients unknown, and perhaps better not to ask) which may be added." [5]

There is nothing in this to comfort the practitioners of piosity and religiosity. We might say that his formula actually theologizes and baptizes activism! He was always of the firm opinion that prayer without action is superstition, just as action without prayer is presumption. Worship is really the same as Christian vocation, which includes both conduct and the devotions of authentic piety. In this broad sense of worship he could declare, facing the German military invasion in 1940, "This world can be saved from political chaos and collapse by one thing only, and that is worship." [6] We worship God with all we are and all we have and do, as well as in "acts of worship" at Church or elsewhere.

The supreme, essential form of "concentrated worship" or formal worship is *adoration*. [136] But what of the other forms? In his opinion, if listed in their descending order of spiritual value, they would be praise, thanksgiving, confession, intercession and petition. Taking the last first, petition or asking-prayer, we shall be able to see how he regarded the others, too.

❀ WHAT PRAYER IS NOT In a brief, pointed treatment of Jesus' teaching about prayer, Temple summarized it all. [137] Taking the liberty of further reducing his own brief points, we find that he had four things to say: (1) God is perfect love and wisdom, and there is no need to try to bring Him to a better mind by asking Him to be more loving than He would otherwise be, or bringing to His attention what would otherwise escape it; (2) we *may* not want what is truly good for us—we have to trust God in prayer; (3) we must persevere when our prayer seems ignored or unanswered; (4) the essential act of prayer is bending our wills to God's, not His to ours.

God has no need of us to tell Him anything. The divine mind includes everything. Nor is there any need to persuade or entice Him into doing for us what He might not do if we left Him to His own devices and His own unsupported motives. The divine love includes all. And to imagine that by petition we could alter His purpose would be blasphemous. What is actually the case is, in fact, to the contrary: we do not always know *our own* good. "Your father knows what you need before you ask him" (Matthew 6:8). Indeed, in petition, we run the risk of getting what we ask for rather than what we would like. "As we pray for an increase of strength or virtue, let us remember that the answer is likely to take the form of opportunity to exercise it, like the lady who prayed for patience and was provided with an ill-tempered cook." [7] If, for example, we asked and received deliverance from a besetting temptation, it might only induce moral flabbiness and a lack of watchfulness over ourselves. The beefsteak yearned for by a typhoid patient would kill him.

The petition in the prayer of St. Chrysostom in the Prayer Book would much better read *"heed* our requests" than "fulfill" —as it does at present. God knows, and we must trust Him. And for these reasons the man of faith will persist in prayer in spite of disappointment. This perseverance is what is urged on us in the parables of the Importunate Friend (Luke 13:22-30) and the Unjust Judge (Luke 18:1-8), which are almost hilariously inapposite in that God certainly would not give us what we want just to be rid of our nagging! *Nor does He need to test our faith in Him.* He knows perfectly well what it is worth. Faith's essence, as distinguished from that of belief, is trust.

Faced on all sides with religiosity and the demand by people for "spontaneous" and "free" expression of their own inner life, Temple retorted, "Well, I dare say that is what we should all like our religion to be, but it is not what the Christian religion is. The Christian religion is not the expression of our spiritual aspirations; it is the expression of God's revelation to Israel through Jesus Christ, to which we have to make response." [8] Prayer is a true discipline, and not for our entertainment. We have to remind some people of this when they complain that corporate worship is too dull or repetitious or lacking in novelty. Temple found in his own practice ("prayer life," as some say) that since as humans we only encounter God directly in the Incarnation of Christ's human form and address, we will do well in prayer to keep His figure before our inner vision. Then you should pray to God, "as you see Him there." [9] Yet he was not a mystic in the non-theological, non-Pauline sense in which the term is often used by retreat missioners. He warned against the "alluring peril of mysticism, according to which a man may have direct experience of immediate communion with the infinite and eternal God. That is not so; and any experience taken to be this is wrongly interpreted. Only the Son has direct communion with the Father." [10] He took the author of the Fourth Gospel (John 1:18) at his word.

✹ MAGIC Magic aims at our control of God, prayer aims at God's control of us. The heart of the business of prayer is submitting our lives to God's will, not the reverse. It is trying by the conscious practice of His presence to do what He wants, to serve Him and His redemptive love. Petitioning prayers, both the straight, narcissistic give-me, give-me kind and the more "altruistic" form of intercessory prayer, are too commonly self-centered, having our needs or our friends' needs at the center of attention, rather than keeping God there. [138] When the sons of Zebedee, James and John, asked Jesus, "Teacher, we want you to do for us whatever we ask of you" (Mark 10:35), His answer was of the sort that the divine love always must return: Are you able to share my sacrifice?

Petition, then, according to Temple, is the most immature and dangerous form of prayer. In his opinion, the Christian prototype and model is Christ's prayer in the Garden of Gethsemane, "Not my will but thine be done" (Luke 22:42). At the same time he was understanding about human fright and frailty. Even Christ, there in the garden, first said to God, "If thou art willing, remove this cup from me." But the point is that our Lord said "if" when He asked, and closed His petition with an obedient request to do the Father's will, not His own. It was with this *obedient* concept of prayer in mind that Temple always recommended: (a) no prayers for victory in wartime, (b) many prayers for the enemy. [139] He argued that Christian men on opposite sides of a battle can pray together in perfect unity, if they pray as they should!

There is both human sympathy, mixed with the kind of humor Temple loved, and a warning, in Randolph Crump Miller's remark: "It is not possible to pray without desire, and those who profess to do so often end with the absurdity of the girl who prayed, 'Dear Lord, I want nothing for myself, but please send my mother a son-in-law.'" [11] Desire may persist, of course, even when we refrain from asking. Temple knew and pondered the spirit of Archbishop Fénelon's classic instruction: "To pray is to desire; but it is to desire what God would have us desire." In all the debate over the efficacy of prayer, whether it works

and how, Temple as a man of faith took only an academic and
analytical interest. Of the two theories of prayer's efficacy, the
psychological and the theological, he was not in the least put
off by the former. To the thesis that prayer's effect is auto-
suggestion and subjective, something that helps people to crystal-
lize their thinking and aspirations, he replied, "Of course, and
what is wrong with that?" It is one way, perhaps a good way, of
describing what happens.[12] But, he added, whatever mental
mechanism it employs, prayer is a genuine communion with a
personal God, and this opens up our lives to grace or the power
and illumination of God's love. He held, this is to say, an objective view of prayer's virtue or effect. Certainly this is the classical view—and it was Temple's.

✿ SACRAMENTATION   The central act of worship for Temple,
as it has always been in the liturgical and devotional tradition
of Catholic piety, was the Eucharist. His understanding of it calls
for a sharp examination. Because sacramentalism loomed so large
in his view of things ("The Sacramental Universe"), we need to
grasp his dynamic conception of the sacramental principle itself.
To him the sacramental process is the dialectic of spirit and
matter. He spoke often of "the ethical utilization of a material
object for a spiritual end," and called a sacrament "the embodiment of spiritual things." He could see only two ways of regarding the relation between matter and spirit: the one of Hindu
Maya with its despair about spirit's control of matter and its
consequent dismissal of the material as illusory; the other of
Christianity and dialectical materialism in which the working
principle is that we are not to ignore matter but to use it.[13]

To give this dialectical view of sacramental philosophy its
proper theological setting, as Temple saw it, we cannot do
better than quote a basic statement with which he prefaced his
interpretation of the oblationary (offering) meaning of the
Eucharist.

"We usually think of the Holy Communion in association
only with God's act in Redemption; we must also think of it in

connexion with His act in Creation. Then the power that guides and sustains us will be indeed the Holy Spirit proceeding from the Father and the Son." [14] As a dialectical unity of spirit and matter, Holy Communion is a ritual expression of the redemption of the world and of mankind effected by the unity of divinity and humanity in the Incarnation. That is a cosmic dialectic, indeed! But the Sacrament is also a ritual expression of the continuous *process* of creation, which is also a dialectic of the material and spiritual. In the work of the Creator Spirit ordering all things to the divine purpose, "spirit arises within and as part of [the] material, and expresses its spirituality, not by ignoring but by controlling it." [15] Creation, Incarnation, Communion—all are dialectical, all are sacramental.

Temple was sure that the way to spiritual values is not around and in spite of material things but through and by means of them. He thought Christianity's strength to be in "its claim to be the most avowedly materialist" of all religions, and that its central doctrine (the Incarnation) commits us to "belief in the ultimate significance of the historical process, and in the reality of matter and its place in the divine scheme." Said he: "Its own most central saying is: 'The Word was made flesh,' where the last term was, no doubt, chosen because of its specially materialistic association." [16] With common sense and modern science he held that matter precedes human mind and spirit (not, of course, the divine mind and spirit). "Our starting point is therefore closer to Materialism than to Idealism. It is indeed closely allied to that Dialectical Materialism which Marx and Lenin adopted as the philosophical basis of Communism." But because of the fundamental theological difference between Marxism and Christianity, "our method might fitly be named Dialectical Realism." [17] [140]

On this basis we may speak of the formal sacraments of the Church—Baptism, Eucharist, Orders, and so on—and of "sacramentals," which would be farms and tractors, factories and sculptors' marble, spinning wheels and mass-production assembly lines, books and bread and wine! The Creator Spirit, or Creator Mind, works in and through and upon all things to shape them to love's use and quality. *Creation is sacramentalism.* [141] And the supreme sacrament is the Incarnation.

All of this is, of course, a Christianity miles apart from the pietism or religious idealism which separates "spiritual" concerns from, for example, economic concerns. With the Marxists, Temple realized that idealism as a philosophy is "dead as a doornail" in the same way that the old gross materialism of Mach and others is dead. The *spiritualizers* are always with us, spreading a Persian-Gnostic dualism in which things temporal are evil, the body is "the prison of the soul," and social questions are either un-religious or ir-religious! The issue between sacramentalist materialism and spiritualist idealism is profound. Idealism lurks behind all forms of the demand that "religion should mind its own business." Sacramentalism is the drive behind all demands for social action and economic justice.

☯ THE SACRIFICE Another way of expressing Temple's view of the Eucharist, besides calling it materialist, would be to say it was *sacrificialist*. He was sensitive to the first step in eucharistic worship, the oblationary part, which is the thankful offering of all our material and spiritual resources to God under the signs or symbols of bread and wine. These symbols are themselves material things which, by their divine employment, represent how the *sacramentality* of all material things is being realized in the world process. Temple, be it noted, never held to the Latin doctrine of "the Sacrifice of the Mass," meaning a re-enactment of Christ's sacrifice on the Cross. That was done for us, once and for all. His sacrifice could only be remembered, memorialized.

But, as Temple understood it, the Eucharist is forward-looking ("teleological" and "eschatological") as well as retrospective. It is a sacrifice in the positive sense of something presumed to be acceptable and therefore offered on God's table to be transformed, made holy (*sacer*, holy; *facere*, to make) for divine use. It means, of course, that the things we offer "in" the bread and wine—our economic and moral assets—have to be worthy of being offered. These things include raw materials, industrial structures, political institutions, tools and capital, cultural and spiritual resources—everything—for "All things come of thee, O Lord." Christians making their sacrifice in the Eucharist are engaged in a very revolutionary, deadly serious rite, not a pretty ceremony. The communion comes after the sacrifice and bears the quality of the sacrifice, such as it is. If the offering is not at least free of private and social sin as much as we know it *could* be, we eat and drink damnation unto ourselves. We cannot offer God lives and possessions *inexcusably* tainted with exploitation, dishonesty, self-indulgence, suffering, and greed.

"In the Holy Communion service," said Temple, "we take the bread and wine—man's industrial and commercial life in symbol—and offer it to God; because we have offered it to Him, He gives it back to us as the means of nurturing us, not in our animal nature alone, but *as agents of His purpose,* limbs of a body responsive to His will; and as we receive it back from Him *we share it with one another* in true fellowship [142] . . . If there is to be a Christian civilization, there must be a body of Christians dedicated to God and His Kingdom in a manner of which the Holy Communion, so regarded, is the picture, and for which it offers the spiritual strength." [18]

All of this says, in summary, that (1) we bring to God's table our material and spiritual wealth, under the representative symbols of bread and wine; (2) we thus express our spiritual purpose (redemptive, creative agentry) through material vehicles—*sacraments giving body to the spirit;* (3) these things are God's gifts now mixed with human labor (bread, not just wheat; wine, not just grapes; automobiles, not just mineral deposits); (4) alms are collected as representing the motive of charity or love, yet the *oblations* of all we are and all we have, not the alms, are the primary thing in eucharistic action; (5) we do it as our Lord directed, in memory of His own saving self-oblation; (6) we receive it back in shared fellowship, a redemptive communion in His Body—the company of the faithful; (7) and finally we go back out into the world again, we go forth "in the name of the Lord," empowered or en-graced to carry out our redemptive vocation of working to spread God's Kingdom, and so to return again and again to God's table with more and more sin worked out of the things we offer.

✿ VIRTUAL PRESENCE As to the question, about what *happens* when the offering is received and en-Spirited, after the Invocation of the Holy Spirit (*epiklesis*), Temple worshipped by a definitely Real-Presence faith. He did not agree with the radical, Protestant-sect notion that the eucharistic feast is purely a memorial of Christ's sacrifice—without any sacrifice by the participants themselves, and without any divine response.

By the Real Presence, however, he did not mean the Roman Catholic theory of "transubstantiation," in which the unseen "substance" becomes Christ's actual body and blood while the seen and felt "accidents" of crumbs and red liquid remain the same. [143] Nor did he mean the Lutheran idea of "consubstantiation," in which it is believed that a divine substance of Christ's body and blood somehow enters in and coheres alongside the natural substances. The logical opposite of these late medieval theories is the radical Protestant doctrine of receptionism, the belief that the bread and wine are not actually the body and blood but only subjectively so—for the believing recipient— not objectively or "really" present in the elements themselves. Temple settled for a Real Presence doctrine known as "virtualism"—sometimes called convaluation or transvaluation. (By "present" he understood *accessible* or "apprehensible.")

In this view Christ's presence is virtual but not local. There is no question of the divine residing alongside the natural or material substance in some kind of concomitance. No substantial change takes place in the elements, but there is a difference in their power or virtue or effect. They are invested with Christ's grace—i.e., the power or effect of love, just as calico is always calico but when it is arranged in the Stars and Stripes or the Union Jack, its virtue is decidedly different. [144] Temple was in complete agreement with St. Thomas Aquinas' repudiation of the notion that Christ's body is locally there in the sacrament —the popular piety of "The Prisoner in the Tabernacle." [19] He thought that "language which implies a local presence of Christ ought to be scrupulously avoided." [20] The main thing was the sacramental effect or "virtue" of the elements. "The 'Real Presence' in the Eucharist is a fact, but it is not unique. The Word of God is everywhere present and active. The Bread and Wine have a symbolic meaning before they are consecrated—they are the gift of God rendered serviceable by the labor of man." [21] Little is gained anyway by a fine-pointed debate over the "how" of the eucharistic presence. Temple was pleased to abide by the statement of the Doctrinal Commission, which he chaired: "Many Anglicans would point to the fact that their Church does not require them to hold any particular theory, and . . . they find it quite unnecessary to do so." [22]

One qualifying consideration was emphasized in Temple's theology of the Eucharist. It is a delusion, he insisted, to suppose that we receive eternal life by receiving the consecrated meal. As he remarked pointedly, "The flesh does not profit at all, if it be only flesh, and even though it be the flesh of the Son of man." [23] And for another thing, "What Christ has done for us avails for us so far as through the surrender of our wills to Him He also does it *in* us. We must not come before the Father offering Him as our sin-offering and not offering ourselves." [24]

🏵 TWO MEMBERSHIP RITES About the other "Sacrament of the Gospel," Baptism, Temple did not write much. We have already seen how he regarded it as a symbolic act of *membership* rather than of salvation or regeneration. On somewhat Maurician theological grounds, he believed that Christ as Man (all mankind) has revealed that we not only might be, but are, children of God; and that by His sacrificial life and death He loosed in the world that power which will bring all men to Him in a conscious fellowship or new creation, the new beginning. We are already Christ's when brought to the font, and in Baptism Christ receives us into the Church—the fellowship of faithful believers who *know* they are His children, and who seek to bring that same good news to all the world. In His Incarnation or Atonement our Lord "turned the tide," He won the victory for us. The Church's work is to bring men to acknowledge their true status and surrender their lives to Him in whom they actually live and move and have their being, even if they know it not.

By Baptism we are enlisted in the forces of the Christian army of co-workers with God in His process of creation.

In Baptism, he said, the Church acknowledges that we are the children of God; in the Confirmation rite we acknowledge it for ourselves. These two sacraments are ritual marks of two stages of Christian growth. And since there are many ways by which the baptized may then or later acknowledge their debt to Christ, in personally responsible terms, Temple gave Confirmation—as many quite recent theologians have been doing—a fairly subordinate and *pro forma* place in the scheme of things. Thus on the question whether those who are baptized but unconfirmed could share in Holy Communion, he was quite clear that Confirmation was a discipline for *Anglican Church people only*. He once told Canon Baker, when he approved of giving Holy Communion to a dying Methodist who had asked for it, that "the rubric at the end of the confirmation service must be interpreted as applying [only] to the Church of England." [25]

Of the other "sacraments of the Church" besides Confirmation —orders, matrimony, unction, and penance—he had little to say, except for orders. To that subject and the question of the Church, we turn next.

Part II

ECUMENICAL THEOLOGY

✵ ✵ ✵

VIII

Anglicanism and Orders

Both within the life of the Church of England itself and in ecumenical circles as he worked to heal the divisions of Christendom, Temple had one pivotal principle: the duty and privilege of seeing to it that the *mediating vocation* of the Anglican Communion was fulfilled. For as he understood it, his Church is both Catholic and Evangelical in a measure not found elsewhere, even though church people in all parts of Christendom have always known that both traditions have their rightful place. [145] Although they sometimes forget it, Christians in one church tradition or another know that the differences between them are not absolute. None of these traditions, when true to itself, is blind to the virtues in either the Protestant or Catholic heritages. (Temple felt that the liberal tradition, so-called, is not distinctive as such, for it properly enters into all of them as a permeating leaven. Liberal theology, he said, is the result of the meeting of religious experience with all the other phases of life's experience. [146])

⚙ CATHOLIC AND PROTESTANT In the Catholic genius he saw concern primarily for order. He regarded structure and law as the core principle of the Roman, or Latin, ingredient in the Christian life. This concern is usually expressed in terms of a focus on creed and ministry and even, on its worst side, in a canonical legalism. Authority is the prime factor and the individual's part is to be obedient. The creed is used as the Church's defense against disastrous speculation (learned from bitter experience) and while its authority for the individual may

101

not be expressly absolute, any questions asked can hardly be more than academic. Its ministry, a three-fold one of bishops, priests and deacons, has authority because it is the primitive and persistent structure of the Church's internal ministration. This whole order is treasured as the guarantee of the corporate life of Christian people, a society or fellowship indwelt by the Holy Spirit. The Christian's life is never, therefore, an individual or private business; it is the life of a member of a *body*—an emphasis which is familiar to all readers of St. Paul's epistles.

This high premium on order is expressed in hierarchy, of course, but it also appears in sacramental worship. For Catholics the sacraments are activities of the Church, of the mystical Body of Christ. The Church acts corporately and individuals benefit only as participating members, as in the meal of fellowship. And another feature of the Catholic genius is its approach to God as *transcendent,* the Most High, calling for abasement and adoration. Temple thought that this side of Christian worship has been "more potently upheld by Rome than by any other part of Christendom," and that it is, after all, only a God who is altogether above us who can bind us together in unity.[1] For if we put our faith in a God whom we fully understand, He will then be made over in our own image, and our own images differ too much and too pettily.

On the other side, the Evangelical tradition appeared to Temple to put freedom, rather than order, first in the spiritual life. Freedom is obviously as essential and necessary as order; for if order is maintained in such a way as to shelve or undermine the individual's responsibility (which is his personality), genuine religion dies. "Every soul that God has made is welcome as a child in his Father's home, and there is no need for elaborate organization either of ecclesiastical hierarchy or dignified worship in order that the child of God can speak to his Father and enter into the most intimate communion." [2]

Along with this principle there has been, in Temple's opinion, more Evangelical concern for social righteousness than can be seen historically in the Catholic tradition of the English Church. He recognized, however, that in recent times the High Church party of the Anglican Communion has shown more interest in social progress than have the Evangelicals. Rather shrewdly, a sociologist would say, he put this Catholic concern down to the fact that all "post-modern" social reforms move increasingly in the collectivist direction, which consequently appeals more to the Catholic sense of being members of the one Body than to the Evangelicals' historic emphasis on the individual.[3] Nevertheless, on a backward look over one hundred and fifty years, the Evangelicals had outdone the Catholics in such triumphs as abolition of the slave trade, and the opium scandal, factory control and labor leadership. The *totally* evangelical—the nonconformist Free Churches—have led all the rest in spite of what he regarded as their sub-Christian Puritanism.

In tension with Catholic transcendentalism, the Evangelicals seemed to Temple to emphasize the divine immanence—God's closeness, His presence directly in each person's life, and in the course of history. This tendency, while it loses the power to unite men before God's majesty, nevertheless better encourages the love of God pleaded for in the New Testament.

The dangers of Catholicism, to be seen plainly enough on the record, he listed as (1) rigidity, (2) lack of sympathy, (3) legalism, and—especially in its interpretation of sacramental rites—(4) magic. The dangers of Evangelicalism, he said, are: (1) disintegration or sectarian atomization, (2) one-sidedness at the expense of the total Christian heritage, (3) Pelagianism or spiritual self-sufficiency. Expressed in these negative forms, it was Temple's belief that Anglicanism offers Christian people their best hope of keeping all such faults to a minimum. They are, of course, only distortions of sound principles, but *corruptio optimi pessima.* At the same time he cautioned Anglicans, who are eager to offer The Book of Common Prayer as a *via media* in worship, that it will help only if they remember that the book is for *common* prayer. It is not a library covering the devotional life; it needs to be supplemented by individual, spiritual practice. He further warned them to remember that the book itself is a product of the Church's life—not *vice-versa!*

✸ THE BRIDGE CHURCH Temple saw it as Anglicanism's special task to be a "bridge-church"—to hold both of the great traditions together in a living fellowship. Painful as the tension between them sometimes is, their vocation is to hold before the world something of what the full Christian heritage may be. This Anglicanism can do because it is something infinitely more than the geographical location its name might suggest. Other churches and communions, including now the younger churches of Asia and Africa, have their own gifts to bring to the treasury of the Universal Church. But the Catholic-Protestant bridge is Anglicanism's "destiny which providence, through the processes of history, has marked out for her." [4] He never claimed she was a model for other churches, only that she had a special gift of historic value to bring. He was as pluralistic about the Christian Church as he was about politics and society. Let there be variety within unity. "Reunion, when it comes, will not come by absorption (though Rome impenitently clings to that vain hope)." [5]

He was certain that Anglicanism is "solidly Catholic" in doctrine and in the affirmations of its continuity in time and unity in space, preserved in the creeds and sacraments. Equally are we "in the fullest sense heirs of the great spiritual movement known as the Reformation," with its stress on immediate personal access to God, free of any priestly mediation which acts as a monopoly of approach to the holy.[6] He also always stressed the Protestant "genius for freedom" in the Anglican Communion. This is why it is a free federation of episcopal churches throughout the British Commonwealth and beyond it in America, China, the Philippines and Japan, rather than a monolithic structure with a single center of authority. As the Encyclical of the 1930 Lambeth Conference put it, it is "a commonwealth of churches without a central constitution; it is a federation without a federal government."

Along with its structural freedom goes its personal freedom. [147] Temple many times quoted Henry Scott Holland's comparison of the Anglican "you-may" and the Roman "you-must." He thought that Anglicanism offers the full wealth of the

Catholic heritage, yet (Protestantly) invites men "to come and take their full share, but leaving them always in the last resort to decide" in personal responsibility.[7] To those critics who claim that this refusal to join issues and decide them one way or the other amounts to a confession that Anglicans prefer peace to truth, he always answered that it would be more adequate to the facts to say that Anglicans have been taught by experience how nearly always peace *is* the best way to truth. The exclusive this-or-that-only method cut across Temple's principle of coherence; he was certain that it obscures truth and closes our eyes to it. "Let individuals or groups within the body contend vehemently for the truth as they see it; that is their contribution to the life of the body; but let them not rend or break the body itself, and let the body rejoice in them." [8]

Consistently with this, he did not denounce party-men. He was able to accept those who joined Anglo-Catholic and Evangelical groups. He thought that every Christian should study the issues and make up his own mind. Then it may be that "he will develop his religious life best by associating with others to whom the truth has come in a somewhat similar way; so parties arise, and I think it desirable that parties should arise; but it is indispensable that we should be free from the spirit of partisanship, for that means the spirit which regards members of other parties within the Church as in a sense antagonistic. Then if I am a Catholic, the Evangelicals are my antagonists. But the real enemies of any real Christian are the world, the flesh, and the devil." [9]

His charges and sermons were filled with appeals to Anglicans to strengthen the bonds of unity. He asked them to be grateful for their own rich heritage, and then take their strong faith in their own order and liturgy to the other churches, trying at the same time to see the values inherent in the traditions of their separated brethren.[10] In scrutinizing the *parti pris* arguments on either side of the Catholic-Protestant debate, he usually discovered that he could endorse their affirmations but had to discredit their negations.

This is a tricky principle to follow, and not always very rewarding in the short run. Newspapers never carry headlines saying, "Unanimity in the Church," even when, quite commonly, it is achieved; but they are always ready with "Crisis in the Church." (Devoted pastoral work, miracles of grace in the changing of lives, deep fellowship experiences—these are not "copy.") At the same time the desire to escape the discomforts of "pluralism" in order to enjoy the false comfort of a too-narrow "unity" must be sternly repressed. Variety is the key to creativity. Loyalty to the Anglican Communion, he insisted, means accepting the double Catholic-Evangelical ethos and wanting, furthermore, to *continue* it. Trying to be loyal to *one rather than the other* is disloyalty to Anglicanism, for the Church has always bridged the gulf ("or sat on the hedge, if you like") and no one phase can claim loyalty exclusively of the other.

Non-Anglicans, he knew by experience, like to tease Churchmen or even bullyrag them for trying to hold together what *they* (the non-Anglicans) presume are incompatible principles. Temple was inclined to look at Anglican pluralism as a typical English phenomenon, and so in a way it is. Nobody knew better than he, however, that Anglican Churches in other parts of the world are no mere imitation of the English Church, and that a Pan-Anglican Congress shows far more variety both culturally and theologically than the English alone could possibly produce. The policy, or method, of searching for right theory or practice by means of inclusive rather than exclusive logic is no more peculiarly English than was his own personal theological "encirclement." It has its merits, even though it continues to be the despair of the systematizers—whom Kierkegaard feared beyond all others.

⚙ THE BACKWARD LOOK   He took pride in the non-doctrinaire, non-legalistic character of Anglicanism—in its minimum of those confessional formularies which try to spell out the creeds in minute detail, and its relative lack of canonical rules and regulations. The prefaces to the prayer book, the Catechism, the Thirty-nine Articles, he contended, were on a modest scale compared to the pronunciamentos of Lutheran, Calvinist and Roman Churches. With their criteria of Scripture and primitive practice the English Reformers sought the spiritual welfare of England, not some special line of doctrine or worship. Although "neither we nor any other Church," Temple said, can claim to be free from the sin of sometimes putting something other than Christ first, and although we cannot pretend to be all the Universal Church is called to be and do—still, the Anglican Communion is in a good position to represent its own character in the wider forum. [148] In no other part of the Christian Church, he felt, was there *more* of the complex of inherited qualities formed by the Church's absorption of Jewish morality, Greek intellectualism, and Roman order.

Looked at in historical perspective, it seemed to Temple that the Reformation had cut off the southern European Church from Teutonic local autonomy and consequently it ended in papal centralization. By the same token it had deprived the northern Church of the Latin sense of order, leaving the field to regional and congregational localism—which ended up in the infinite "divisiveness" of American Protestantism. In its own way and temper, Anglicanism has tried to keep these geniuses together— sometimes, admittedly, without much equilibrium and often only alongside each other rather than really combined. At the Reformation, most obviously, the purpose had been to shape a Church which in faith and order was not a new one but the old Church reformed—the same, age-old Church in its ministry and services, especially the Holy Communion. To those Englishmen who had decided to stay in the Roman fold the Church declared that not the reformed Anglican Church but "Rome itself was the defaulter, leaving the standard of primitive purity and allowing superstitious accretions to become attached to the faith of the Gospels." [11] Appeal to the Bible was the purifier.

The papal power had been inspired by a good motive, although mixed with worldly ambitions. It had wanted to bind all of Europe together in the unity of obedience to God; but it tried to reach a spiritual end by unspiritual means, and the results were disastrous. At a non-institutional level, the magnificent unification of thought constructed by St. Thomas Aquinas has never been equalled before or since, yet its very completeness fettered the minds of later generations. Looking back at it,

Temple thought that the confluence of medieval feudalism's breakdown and the Reformation's revolt also, unfortunately, brought about a surge of nationalism. Nationalism, as the political side of the revolt against a "mummifying" central religious authority, was by no means an unmixed blessing. It not only fragmented the *res publica Christiana,* it also resulted in "territorial" establishments of religion. The Calvinists tried to erect theocracies (rule by the Church). On the other hand, the Lutherans subordinated religion to State sovereignty and the princes, under the rubric of the "divine right of kings" which was an essentially Protestant doctrine and not a medieval one.

All three Reformation traits entered into the Anglican character—appeal to Scripture, national establishment, and the right of private judgment. [149] We have seen how Temple qualified his view of the authority of Scripture with the principles of critical integrity, and the strong reservations he had about private judgment with its danger of becoming self-centered— even though he put personal freedom at the top of his value scheme. In the same way he put careful conditions on national churches.

His own loyalty to the English Establishment was fully enough tested in the Life and Liberty Movement, but he made it clear that the Church could accept such a partnership only on terms which allow her to pursue her proper business. And the Church would keep on with it, as far as he was concerned, only as long as the partnership allowed an opportunity for the Gospel's influence not otherwise available. In any case, he rejoiced in the steady and inevitable spread of un-established Anglicanism throughout the world—in Scotland, America, South Africa, Wales and Ireland, China and Japan—both within and without the Commonwealth itself.

First and last, however, Temple reminded himself and others that the irenic policy of Anglicanism is not to be treated as a peace-at-any-price policy. Rather, peace among sincere Christians is the first condition for learning fuller truth about the Prince of Peace and what He wants of us. As a *style* of Christian discipline it is admittedly beset by difficulties of its own. Nevertheless, he was sure that it is too easy merely to grasp at aspects of the truth one by one, just as it is too easy to cultivate the virtues of Christian ethics one by one, ignoring others meanwhile. The Anglican family is not always strong on points where others are, and as a communion it is still learning how to fulfill its bridge function. Yet the Christians within the fellowship know that it is moving steadily toward greater unity, and that this may well be its greatest service to Christendom as a whole.

✿ A HERITAGE The notion of the Christian *heritage* is central to Temple's faith. He always felt a grateful assurance of our receiving something that has been *given* to us—God Himself in Christ, His love in grace, the Scriptures, the lives of the saints and the insights of the great doctors, the Church and sacraments. For this reason his tendency was less and less to look upon the demands of Christian living and church unity as matters which require us to contrive new sources and solutions, and more and more, instead, to try to receive or rediscover them. He felt, for example, that where church Order (and by this he meant the three-fold ministry) is not accepted as something given *to* us instead of a thing to be decided upon *by* us, there is apt to be a similar reluctance to accept the revelation in Christ and fellowship with God as things given.

The great Reformers, as he believed, acknowledged only one half of their inheritance. They accepted the givenness of the Church's Bible but not of its Order. Temple even suggested that this non-acceptance is a form of Pelagianism which, in spite of Luther's and Calvin's tortured efforts, has grown up in some branches of Protestantism to a degree that could not happen in churches of the historic Order.[12]

Temple's view was that the earliest records show the Church as a body of Christ's disciples with the Apostolate as its focus of authority and administration. The primitive Church was not "an undifferentiated fellowship" which elected to give delegated powers to a ministry *it* had appointed. On the contrary, the Apostles were *Christ's* commissioned order, charged to "feed His sheep." It was they who took steps to perpetuate that ministry, and it has descended by their successors through the centuries to our own times. [150] "So when I consecrate a godly and well-learned man to the office and work of a Bishop in the Church of God, I do not act as a representative of the Church, if by that is meant the whole number of contemporary Christians; but I do act as the ministerial instrument of Christ in His Body the Church. The authority by which I act is His, transmitted to me through His Apostles and those to whom they committed it; I hold it neither from the Church nor apart from the Church, but from Christ in the Church." [13]

❀ AUTHORITY This authority to consecrate and ordain witnesses and servants, he said, testifies to the continuity of the fellowship in Christ; and every priest thus ordained, in celebrating the Holy Communion, acts not only for the congregation present there, not only for the whole of the present-day Church, but as an instrument of the *whole Body of all time*. Even if only "two or three are gathered together" the actual congregation is the entire Communion of Saints in time and space. Like the Incarnation, the celebration is the eternal in the midst of time. He willingly allowed the possibility of sincerely holding this faith without expressing it in the apostolic (episcopal) ministry; but he insisted nevertheless that those who have received it will not give it up—nor, on the other hand, do anything to make it hard for others to share in it.

He held no mechanical or "tactile" theory of succession in which the passage of valid episcopal order depends on unbroken consecration of bishops from one to another over the centuries from earliest times. He doubted, as well he might, that any such "chain" ever maintained itself intact. The claim of the papists that certain of the Anglican bishops were not in this mechanical pipe-line succession, and the attempt of some Anglican historians to prove that they *were,* he looked upon with wry amusement. It is the authority of Christ in His Body the Church, and the intention of the Church to maintain the continuity, and order, that validates it. He protested the twisting of "succession" (which has in fact been the way the Church followed in passing on the apostolic commission) into *transmission*—a late idea which falsifies succession.

Furthermore—a point of considerable importance for Episcopalians in their ecumenical role—Temple was quite positive that, in episcopal ordination, what is conferred upon ministers is not the *power* to make sacraments a rite which could not otherwise be genuinely sacramental. What is conferred is the authority to do so.[14] This authority can only be rightly administered by those who have the whole Church's commission to do so, and the apostolic episcopacy is the right order to provide it. The *potestas* (authority) as used in the ordination service, he said, is without "any authoritative interpretation," and until the Reformation there was never any need to distinguish between power and authority because they always went together. Now that Christendom is so divided, it is vital to insist that charismatic power may be received through means which are defective in the authority of their commission—as all non-episcopal ministries *are*. The age-long claim that ministration "must" be by a priest has always meant *should*, not "can only be." [15] In his Paddock Lectures at The General Theological Seminary in New York, in 1915, Temple spoke of non-episcopal orders as "irregular" rather than invalid, quoting Pusey of the Tractarians: "We have never denied that God may make His own sacraments efficacious even when irregularly administered."

It must be obvious, then, that Temple believed the episcopacy to be needed for the well-being and right condition of the Church (*bene esse*), but that it is not absolutely and exclusively necessary to its very existence (*esse*). Its absence from the non-episcopal sections of the Church does not invalidate their ministries and sacraments. [151] Again and again he declared against assertions that only the sacraments of episcopally ordained ministers (whether bishops or presbyters) are valid.

He often had to deal with arguments from some of his fellow Churchmen that non-episcopal churches have no real sacraments. He always countered with the warning that to hold any such thing is to fall victim to the peril of all strong sacramental doctrine—its liability to magical notions. He also called it an untenable and unintelligible claim, as well as magical.[16] The Anglican Churches' adherence to episcopal ordination is therefore a question of loyalty to right order and definitely not a hubristic, disdainful claim that other ministries are "invalid" or of none effect. On this equable ground he once told the Convocation of Canterbury that preachers from non-episcopal bodies might be invited to preach at the Church's choir offices (Morning and Evening Prayer, which are not priestly ministrations) but not at services of Holy Communion. At a Eucharist, he decided, a minister as preacher would be tantamount to "indifferentism," or acting as if a vital principle needed no consistent defense.

"To me it would seem shocking presumption," he said, "to question the reality of the Sacraments administered, for example, in the Presbyterian Church of Scotland or the Lutheran Church of Germany. As Christian disciples, the members of those bodies belong to the soul of the Catholic Church; by baptism they are admitted to membership in its body . . . They are, as their fruits have shown, parts and organs of the Universal Church." [17] And again: "I am convinced that the Anglican Communion is right to maintain its insistence on the Historic Episcopate, but I am equally convinced that Anglicans think far too much—not necessarily too highly, but assuredly too often and too long—of that same Episcopate. It would be better for us if we could take it for granted and give our undistracted thought to other matters." [18]

Speaking for himself, Temple was happy to believe that some day the Church would confer Holy Orders upon women. He once wrote (1916) to a priest's wife that "as at present advised" he would like to see women ordained but would have no part in a big push for it. Desirable as it would be in itself, the effect might be (probably would be) to put back the reunion of Christendom—and reunion is more important.[19] (If he ever changed his mind, or was otherwise "advised," it is not recorded; Iremonger says he never changed.) In the meanwhile he gave vigorous support to the role of deaconesses in the life of the Church—he preferred, instead of calling them "female deacons," to call them "women ministers" because theirs is an *ordained* ministry, too. [152] He pointed out that the Church recognizes lay Baptism in emergencies, although this sacrament like the others, is properly administered only by the bishop or by him "to whom the bishop may entrust it." Temple then added that *there is no difference in principle as to lay celebration of the Eucharist!* But while in a highly ordered Church all such lay ministrations are limited to emergency conditions, the requirement of ordination (meaning both Order and ordering) is of the *bene esse* only.

❀ HIGH AND LOW   On churchmanship questions he had little to say and took little interest. His writings and addresses are significantly bare of statements or arguments on such matters. He was at home in all kinds of parishes and took his part in "high" and "low" services alike, although his own personal preference was for the simpler prayer book forms. It was because of his eagerness to see Anglo-Catholics better provided for that he defended prayer book revisions (as in the 1928 proposals), and it was also one of his reasons for working so hard for the Establishment's freedom from civil control in liturgical matters.

However, he opposed, without seeking to forbid, non-communicating communions, a High Church practice which has not been so much defended since his day. He regarded the practice as a betrayal of the Catholic-Evangelical balance. He said to a rural deanery meeting, "Whilst I can see no kind of objection to the presence of communicants at a celebration of the Holy Communion who do not make their communion on that particular occasion, I do think it is quite plainly disloyal to the whole spirit, as well as the specific regulations, of the Church of England, to hold a celebration of the Holy Communion at which no opportunity is given for any but the priest to communicate, or at which the communion of the congregation is in any way discouraged." [20] In Temple's opinion this un-Anglican practice exactly defines "the Mass" which the Reformation had rightly and deliberately stopped in order to return to an earlier, more congregational communion. In the same address he pointed to the service of Benediction as another betrayal of the balance, explaining that reverence in places where the Blessed Sacrament is reserved is entirely consistent with Anglican traditions, but "organized devotions" are not: "That is the right place at which to draw the line."

If we were to reduce Temple's views of the Universal Church and Anglicanism to their simplest terms, to put an ecclesiastical label on him, it would have to be "Church-Christian." Using Ernst Troeltsch's classification of Christianity into the church and sect types, Temple was inclusive rather than exclusive, and minimal in his demands for the sake of a wider fellowship. He had no sectarian liking for strict definition at the cost of narrowing and hardening fellowship. His was a non-legalistic and non-doctrinaire search for a range of fellowship which can include the erring neighbor as well as the righteous brother. No better illustration of his attitude can be found than his words to rebellious and skeptical young people in the years of the Great Depression. He wanted to find a way to bring them into the Church as a group of disciples who were not yet ready to say the creeds. After all, Simon and Andrew, and the brothers James and John had not been ready either, when they left all and followed Jesus. "Perhaps," he suggested, "there should be established an associate membership of the Church." [21]

IX

Reunion and Rome

In his sermon in the Cathedral Church of St. Giles, at the opening service of the Edinburgh Conference on Faith and Order in 1937, Temple said both sorrowfully and hopefully: "I speak as a member of one of those Churches which still maintain barriers against completeness of union at the Table of the Lord. I believe from my whole heart that we of that tradition are trustees for an element of the truth concerning the nature of the Church which requires that exclusiveness *as a general rule,* until this element of the truth be incorporated with others into *a fuller and worthier conception* of the Church than any of us hold today. But I know that our division at this point is *the greatest of all scandals in the face of the world.*" [1] This, he said, is a cause for deep penitence, but under the pain of it we may try all the harder to get rid of the hindrances to unity.

⚙ FAITH FIRST, THEN ORDER For a man who hated that party strife against which St. Paul warned the Churchmen of Corinth (I Corinthians 3:4-9), to speak in this fashion of the pain of separation was altogether sincere with him. As a pluralist who believed that creativity comes out of variety-in-unity and that we are led to deeper insights by the encounter between differences, he could not abide to see a fellowship of faith in one Lord and God broken by *beliefs* about interpretive questions which might arise within the circle of that faith. At a diocesan conference in Manchester when he was bishop there, he put very plain words to his conviction on that score. "In regard to the matter of Revision [of the Prayer Book] I find myself quite unable to agree with the proposition that has been advanced that, as a foundation of the Church, faith and order stand on a level. Faith seems to be perfectly indispensable and about that there must be an agreement on the vital points, before union and communion are possible. But that we should agree about any necessary order in the Church for maintaining that seems to me, at any rate, less important and, I am inclined to think, not essential at all." [2] Here, surely, the Protestant side of him was speaking in full voice.

The natural and legitimate desire to think through the shape or pattern of the fellowship of faith can bemuse us into for-getting Christ's call to oneness in Him, if it is put first or wrongly conceived on its own grounds. In this connection Temple liked to quote Father Waggett [153] who once told him, "Do not think of the unity of the Church as like that of a box, which is defined by its boundaries, so that you are either inside or outside; think of it as like the unity of a ray of light, about which you know where it shines brightest, but cannot tell where it shades off into complete darkness." [3]

There was nothing special about his ecumenical theology. What was special was the personal force and weight he brought to it. In terms of formulae the basis of his approach lay in the Chicago-Lambeth Quadrilateral, a four-point statement of the essentials of unity first drawn up by Anglicans in the American Church and then adopted by Lambeth. It contained what he was convinced are the marks of authentic Anglicanism as well as of the wider Church: (1) the Bible as the norm of faith, (2) the Apostles' and Nicene creeds, (3) the "dominical" sacraments of Baptism and the Supper of the Lord, (4) the historic (yet adaptable) episcopate.

He also followed a somewhat fuller statement drawn up by Anglican and Free Church leaders in May, 1922, which offered a minimal consensus. It could be summarized as an agreement that (1) the Church requires a ministry of both Word and Sacraments; (2) it has, under the authority of Christ the Head, maintained a ministry since the Apostles' days—as a ministry of the whole Church, not of any part of it; (3) it must be con-ferred by the Church in ordination, by representative bishops "who ought to be accepted" as the Church's authority; and (4) with its episcopacy the united Church should preserve the presbyterial and congregational principles as parts in its constitution and structure, taking care not to disown or discredit the non-episcopal ministries it supersedes.[4]

⚙ THE POT AND THE KETTLE Temple's dialectical method was bound to draw him into the ecumenical process. His whole mode of approach was one that could thrive only, or at least thrive best, when differences cried out for resolution. It also made him an ideal chairman for conferences on unity. He not only recognized the vitality of differences in cultural outlook and habit, and tried to make use of them—he actually welcomed them. As far as the European sector of the Church unity problem was concerned, his reading of history had convinced him that northern Protestantism needs the Roman instinct for order to keep it from "fissiparous sectarianism," while Rome needs the northern love of liberty to prevent hardening of the arteries in the fellowship. The practical West, he would add, needs the East's philosophy and mysticism, while the East needs the ethical concern of the West to save it from metaphysical unworldliness and brooding stagnation.[5]

He was never one to assume a man was wrong merely because he disagreed with him. He knew that nobody falls into an error unless it contains an attraction of some kind. "At least," he used to say of encounters with those who held another view, "let us first learn what he fears that he may lose by accepting our interpretation in place of his own." [6] In an address to an inter-denominational gathering in Ireland in 1935, he quoted Ruskin on social issues, as a warning which fits theological issues too: Ruskin observed that "many of our troubles arise from the fact that the wise of one class habitually contemplate the foolish of the other." [7]

He always contended that the sin of disunion is shared by all and therefore the pot is usually calling the kettle black, because if any division exists anywhere, it makes *all* Christian bodies schismatic, cut apart. [154] But wide as this tragic truth is, he still declared (without the least false humility) that a heavier burden of guilt lies on those who have kept the historic order *"and failed to commend it"* than on those who broke away for conscience's sake.[8] Nor was it false piety on his part to remind himself and others from time to time that "the way to the reunion of Christendom does not lie through committee-rooms" as much as through personal union with the Lord and by the strength of the unity of the Father and the Son described in St. John 17.[9]

At the same time he was not going to minimize the reality and the enormity of the differences to be resolved, by entering into pseudo-unity and pseudo-communion. His importance to the ecumenical movement was in no small part due to the fact that his own Anglican convictions were firm and his loyalty to them unassailable. Too much was at stake to allow the use of jerry-built households of "homogenized" faith. He was not the kind of immature "ecumaniac" for whom nothing else matters—who falsifies reality for quick "unity's" sake. Any purely "spiritual" unity, without objective and material expression sacramentally, is not good enough for Christian purpose. Yet *en passant* there are countless ways to express brotherhood while we search for its organic realization, without, as he put it, having to "give away for this purpose the only means we have for expressing and realizing organic union itself." [10]

Just as we commit a sin by treating a means as if it were the end, so it is sinful to reverse the perversion and use ends as if they were means! At ecumenical gatherings he always candidly affirmed the Lambeth Conference declaration that Anglicans *as a general rule* should receive Holy Communion at the hands of priests (i.e., episcopally ordained ministers), except when they are "cut off" from their ministrations. He himself willingly adhered to that decision. He was happy, on the other hand, that the bishops of both the York and Canterbury Convocations (with the full knowledge but not formal concurrence of the Lower Houses) had approved opening Anglican Eucharists to reception by all comers at inter-church meetings. And this decision, too, he followed.

✸ SOUTH INDIA During the sometimes heated debates in the Convocations and Church Assembly over whether the Church of England should enter a limited inter-communion agreement with the Church of South India, which during the Second World War was forming out of the Anglican, Presbyterian, Congregational and Methodist Churches, Temple put some of his theories into rather battle-drawn practice. He took up the cudgels in support of South India both before and after he was Primate of the whole Church. Keen as he was for federations and councils of churches, he knew they were not of themselves enough to "restore the circulation" of the Christian fellowship. Some means and measure of *communion* must be found. He found it in South India.

At first it was protested that he who had always been careful to warn Christians that inter-communion is the end of the reunion process and not the means was now betraying his own principle. To this he replied that the Church of South India Scheme of Union provided a genuine organic unity or communion, even though limited, and that a careful eye to genuine unity as the only basis for communion does not mean complete agreement or uniformity. For example, the Anglican concordat with the Old Catholics (the Bonn Agreement, 1932) had quite specifically provided that it did "not require from either communion the acceptance of all doctrinal opinion, sacramental devotion, or liturgical practice characteristic of the other." [11] This has become nearly a fixed formula of all such concordats: the Church of England's with the Church of Sweden, for example, and the American Episcopal Church's with the Philippine Independent Church, and the Spanish Reformed and Lusitanian Churches. It has been the principle running through discussions of the English Church held with the Churches of Norway, Denmark and Finland.

Eric Mascall, one of the "younger theologians" who were about then deciding that Temple was theologically behind the times, wrote a pamphlet to show that Temple and Archbishop Garbett were guilty of speaking "with one voice to Rome and with another to the Protestants of South India." The Church had, he argued, "a duty to save them from themselves." [12] To Temple it was clear that "restricted inter-communion" was, in fact, only making sure that Anglicans do not impose on others terms of union more stringent than those obtaining between the Anglican churches themselves. When it was complained that the Scheme failed to spell out what the nature, powers and authority of the bishops of South India would be, he replied that it limited ordination to bishops, which is all the Anglican churches do (as a look at the Preface to the Ordinal shows) and without any "particular interpretation." As to the objection that there were elements of the Presbyterian and Congregational order in the Scheme, he appealed to the primitive Christian polity as a precedent for combining a council of presbyters and a congregational meeting with a constitutional episcopacy.

What moved him most was his certainty that the "irregular" ministries (non-episcopal) are in any case blessed and owned by the Spirit. They are effective, Temple asserted, in their own spheres. But as a matter of reunion procedure, or strategy, he thought that Anglicans cannot recognize them, in order to bring about Christian inter-communion, until they have made "an operative decision to unite in a way that ends the irregularity." *Then* Anglicans ought to recognize them "during a period of transition" until the new order is settled and all ministers have been episcopally ordained.[13] And in the Church of South India, as its subsequent history has shown, he correctly discovered exactly that promise and purpose.

The fact that South India's basis was one of church unity without theological and liturgical uniformity bothered him not at all. It was, so to speak, acting out his own method and principles. To some of the High Church party who were troubled and resentful, he replied, with perhaps a touch of asperity, "In one of my convocation speeches, I said that many of our troubles seem to me to be the drawing of negative conclusions from positive premises. In this debate, I seem to detect the frequent recourse to a kindred fallacy, the confusion of contradictories with contraries. (Sorry! 'Once a don, always a don.' But one must think as one can and not another way.) By this fallacy, non-acceptance is treated as repudiation." [14] Temple was ready to rely on the Holy Spirit as the catalytic.

❄ THE CHURCH AND THE TRINITY   His own guiding rule was that Christian fellowship aims at a unity of harmony, not of uniformity. The Church, ideally, is nearer a symphony than a chorus singing in complete unison. St. Paul's analogy of "many members, one Head" and St. John's "many branches, one vine" provide the principle. Temple knew perfectly well that the Church started out with differences such as the ones between Peter and Paul (Galatians 2:11), and between John Mark and Paul and Barnabas (Acts 15:36-41). Set Aristotle aside as he might on philosophical grounds, he knew perfectly well that the Stagirite's concept of differentiated unity is as essential to the fellowship of the Church as it is to the Trinitarian version of monotheism.

As a matter of fact, Temple often drew a parallel between the Church and the Trinity. It was, of course, to the effect that the unity God seeks in His Church is of the very same sort which is eternally characteristic of the triune God. The invariable habit of the thoughtless is to assume at once that only by uniformity can unity be expressed. Temple, like Church leaders today, was often faced with bitter objections to statements drawn up by various ecumenical commissions or councils of churches, for example on social questions, on the ground that they had no right to speak for the member-churches or *their* members. To reply that such statements are only addressed *to* the churches is perfectly correct but hard to bear, if their social or theological content is unwelcome. [155]

Temple's ecumenical activity was motivated by prudential as well as theological considerations. He appreciated that the imponderable trends of history are all on the side of unity and interdependence, everywhere at every level of life. The momentum of the "collectivist" process seemed obvious to him. He thought most men (but certainly not *all*) were happy to ride the "wave of the future." He could see that Communism and Fascism have a strong appeal because "there is a widespread hunger for unity, and it is by satisfying this that the new political religions have gained their hold upon men." [15] In his providential or process theology, as we have seen, Temple assigned to the emergence of community, to its deepening and widening development at all levels of human existence, a kind of A-1 priority on God's creation-agenda. The realization of unity and community is the realization of the divine will, of God's purpose, and the fact that "all the tendencies of our time are toward unity" must be seen in that theological context.[16]

History, in this era, he believed, is against individualism, and on the side of socialization. The instruments and institutions of modern society are by their nature unfavorable to claims of unique interest and isolationism. As Temple read the signs of the times, "collectivism" or structured common interest is the order of the day in everything from mass-production in industry, and federalism in national and international politics, to the ecumenical movement itself in religion. It was with this perspective, among others, that Temple saw in the Church unity program the great new religious fact of our era.

✿ PHYSICIAN, HEAL THYSELF   Yet he was never forgetful of the maxim of the 1937 Oxford Conference on Life and Work: "A divided church cannot heal a divided world." Nor can the Church stand in judgment over the world's economic and political and racial divisions while it continues to maintain its own lines of separation. *Una sancta* only in theory, only belies itself as a theory. As things stand now, he saw, the Church is as much a part of the disease as of the cure. "Physician, heal thyself!"

And just as the Church's disunity is its Achilles heel in its desire to witness to the social order, so it is a fatal flaw in its witness to the non-Christian peoples and cultures of the world. Only the whole Gospel carried by the whole Church to the whole world can fully satisfy its Lord's demands and the world's doubts. As early as 1914 he had written that only a "Catholic Church," meaning a united Church, could challenge bellicose national sovereignty in defense of the world's peace.[17] By this he meant that the ecumenical effort had to be aimed at a far wider unity than that of Western Protestantism.

Before his death, there had already been serious ecumenical

discussions with Eastern Orthodox churchmen in various study commissions and conferences. In the following period, 1945-1956, several patriarchates became members of the World Council of Churches, reaching back across the great East-West schism. But the other great schism—between Rome and the rest of Western Christendom—still loomed like a black cloud. Temple was never one to run to cover or to ignore a problem, hoping that it would go away. Nor was he immobilized by what he called Rome's "impenitent" and stubborn way of hanging on to the "vain hope" that unity will be restored to the Church by the absorption of all fragments into the Roman fragment.

◉ ROME   He habitually took time and thought at ecumenical gatherings to express his regret that representatives of Rome were not present. (They did send observers to the first meeting of the World Council in Amsterdam in 1948, and subsequently observers have appeared with increasing frequency at certain special gatherings and Central Committee meetings.) At Edinburgh in 1937 he said, "We deeply lament the absence from this collaboration of the great Church of Rome—the Church which more than any other has known how to speak to the nations so that the nations hear." [18]

Shortly after the First World War, when he was a Canon of Westminster, he said to a reporter from the London *Daily Telegraph*, "Personally, I think reunion with Rome is so far off that it need not trouble us just now; there are other things to do; but I would certainly refrain from anything which made ultimate reunion more difficult. [156] And so I hold fast to my Catholic doctrines." [19] This he always did in his own witness; and he always encouraged his own Church to act on the same principle. He said, "I wish the Church to hold her dogmas, because I would do nothing to widen the gulf which separates us from the other great Churches, the Roman and the Eastern. The greatest political aim of humanity, in my opinion, is a super-state, [157] and that can only come about through a Church universal." [20]

An Italian friend of Temple's, editor of a magazine in Italy (and not a Roman Catholic), had argued that if a church persists for any considerable time it must have something essential to the religion of Christ. When Temple challenged him to say what was essential in the Roman Church, he replied at once, "the Papacy." Telling about it later, Temple explained, "I was surprised for a moment, but I saw presently what he meant. The desire of the world is for peace, universal harmony. Can that ever be achieved by a disunited Christendom?" [21]

Just as communists and socialists quarrel more bitterly with each other than with non-Marxists, so Catholics, Protestants and Orthodox quarrel with each other—as if they had more fear and dislike of each other than of pagans and unbelievers. The distance between them often appears to be greater than the gulf between Christians and non-Christians! But Temple, by method and in spirit, refused to fall into such fierce polemics. "The difference between Catholic and Protestant is very small," he said, "compared with the difference between Christian and non-Christian." [22] He was impatient with those who "complacently" look upon the Papacy as based on nothing but priestly ambition and popular superstition. He called that attitude "the popular English error" and an "old libel." [158] "And this piece of ignorance and stupidity," he warned, "has a practical enough result, in that it helps to perpetuate the disunion of Christendom and therefore its impotence." [23]

When we pray for "the whole state of Christ's Church," in the Eucharist, according to Temple, we are praying alike and together for Rome, the Eastern Orthodox bodies, the Reformation churches, and the "sectaries"—the liberal Protestant bodies —for all of them. It is, admittedly, very trying to deal with the attitude shown by the Romanists, as when they take the line that the "basic difficulty" at Protestant ecumenical gatherings is the false assumption that such churches are parts of the true Church of Christ. But this is not of itself enough to release non-Romans from their Christian obligation to draw the Romans into fuller participation.

He had no illusions about Rome's historic intransigence. He knew that "the whole ethos" of Romanism and Anglicanism is "radically different." Of his obviously fuller commitment to cooperation with Protestants, he said simply that we move as and where we can, and the Protestant Christians are thus far more open to the spirit of reunion—perhaps because their greater guilt makes them humble and hungrier for unity. Nor was he willing to be held back by the angry reactions of High Churchmen, since the sort of people who are actually drawn in the Roman direction are not, he thought, of too much use to the Anglican Communion.

The Romanists, for their part, were never cold to Temple. Several of their spokesmen had publicly welcomed and praised *The Pilgrim* when he edited it. He was, as we saw earlier, occasionally asked to address theologically-oriented Roman Catholic groups, such as the Aquinas Society and the Thomas More Society, on such stock-in-trade topics as the philosophy of law and of nature. He had personally encouraged an Anglican-Protestant-Roman inquiry into Natural Law in which one or two Roman Catholic theologians occasionally took part. In the Second World War there was a serious attempt to bring Roman Catholics and Protestants together in a program of common social action and Christian witness on social questions—but the Romans decided, after some discussion, to pull out of the "united Christian front." Even so, they got their feet wet or, if not quite that much was accomplished, at least they had tested the water.

Temple's friendship with Cardinal Hinsley, the Roman Catholic Archbishop of Westminster, was a well-known and widely valued one. He kept in close correspondence with the Roman hierarchy as well as with the Free Church leaders. And let it be added that his efforts to keep the Romeward lines of communication open were attacked time after time by militant and intransigeant ("black") Protestants—within and without the Church of England—as attempts "to sell the pass" to the enemy! When he wrote to the Pope (Pius XII) in October, 1943, to express sympathy because of the confinements and embarrassments the Papacy had to endure under the German occupation of Rome, there were mutterings in the purlieus of Protestantism. On Good Friday, in 1944, he sent another message to Pius and a prayer, that the "whole fellowship of Christ's disciples may be so guided by the Holy Ghost that we may together declare the Christian principles for ordering human life." Again, there was a great uproar, organized public protests, demonstrations by pressure groups, and dark, paranoid accusations of "secret negotiations."

If and when Temple's hope is realized and the Romans join the quest for unity, as the Second Vatican Council encourages us to hope, the pluralistic and multi-unitive temper which Temple championed will undergo its fullest and most vital test. The one-true-party line in politics and the one-true-church principle in theology—indeed, all monistic conceptions—threaten to impose what he thought of as uniformity, instead of unity. It is not easy to defend his dialectical or coherent method against so many monists on the one side, and against as many on the other side who are content with their separations or who, as social conservatives, oppose church unity because it is part of the "collectivist" trend. They fear exactly what Temple, with critical reservations, welcomed as sure to come in the creative process toward fuller fellowship.

Temple's own ultimate expectation was that "every existing Communion should die in order to rise again into something more splendid than itself." [24] This is the dialectical principle of the unity of opposites which, in synthesis, die in themselves to rise again at a higher level. His understanding of the dialectic of creation and development was part and parcel of the resurrection principle, whereby Churches as well as persons may die unto self in order to be raised in a new creation.

X

The Church Is Mission

The ecumenical movement, according to Temple, is a confluence of three major streams of Christian vitality: the International Missionary movement, the Life and Work movement, and the Faith and Order movement. He put them in that order. When he was enthroned in St. Augustine's marble chair at Canterbury in the middle of the Second World War, his sermon dwelt on the fierce tensions between the world's power centers, then locked in devastating war, over against which he posited the growing, world-wide fellowship of the churches as a possible countervailing force. [159] This fellowship, he said, which is "the great new fact of our era," is a result of the missionary enterprise of the preceding one hundred and fifty years.

It was first begun and carried on by means of gospel preaching and with individual soul-saving as its aim. There was very little conscious purpose of arriving at corporate results in the way of either religious or social institutions. Perhaps the Roman Catholic missions sparked by the counter-Reformation had more corporate goals in mind than the pietistic missions which made the first Protestant beginnings in the eighteenth century. But in any case a century without major wars, from the end of the Napoleonic conflicts in 1815 to the First World War in 1914, combined with the new modern communications and rapid transport, has brought it about that the Gospel is now preached in every independent country of the world except Afghanistan, Bhutan, and Outer Mongolia. [160]

Temple's awareness of the importance of Christian missions was matured by his experience in Jerusalem in 1928, as a Church of England delegate to an international missionary conference. There were fifty countries represented—including many of the younger churches of Asia and Africa. This meeting seems to have started him on a course of thinking not about "missions" only, but about the far more basic concept of *mission*. As he saw it, it was the latter which provided "missions" with their conceptual context—overseas missions in particular were in his opinion only one phase of the total concept. What follows is an attempt to describe his thought about *mission*. It comes, briefly, to considerations under five heads: its nature, method, motive, goal, and strategy.

✦ THE NATURE OF MISSION   "To be a Christian is to be a missionary." [1] Christianity is evangelism; it is missionary activity. Christianity in Temple's theology does not *have* missions, it *is* a mission. Evangelism is not what the Church does, it is what it is. For the individual Christian, the only question is, What kind of a missionary is he? "We have got to say that wherever a Christian lives at all, he must be a missionary, a good one or a bad one; by his life, by his witness, he is drawing men to Christ or sending them away from Him, because he is the representative of Christ among them. To *be* a Christian is to be a missionary." [2] But Temple was prepared to put this perception in imperative as well as indicative terms. He said, "Every Christian is a missionary or he isn't truly or deeply a Christian." [3]

He was influenced by Bishop Azariah's practice in South India of having those who had just been baptized recite, "Woe is me if I preach not the Gospel." The proof is in the pudding. For example, the Christian Bartoks of North Sumatra living under Japanese occupation and cut off from the supply of clergy, nevertheless increased their numbers from 400,000 to 600,000. Why? Because their rule was, "No Day Without a Word for Christ." For reasons like this, Temple made his starting point on the subject of mission a proposition in the indicative mood: Christianity is a mission and Christians are missionaries.

❧ THE METHOD OF MISSION The Christian contagion
spreads, as all contagions do, from person to person. For good or
ill the method of mission is interpersonal; it is experiential
through relationship. It is not propositional through arguments.
Bishop Fulton J. Sheen is credited with a wise saying, "Win an
argument and lose a convert."

When God sought to win men into His fellowship, He did not
send a set of proposals or counterpropositions; nor did He send
up any trial balloons. Indeed, He came in Person and met man
face to face, acting out what He had to tell him. The central
place held by fellowship in Temple's theology led him inevitably
to emphasize the dynamics of relationship in evangelism. Christian outreach in this respect is exactly like Church life within
the household of faith. Not doctrine but actions are the tools
of conversion.

"It is," said Temple, "of the utmost importance to notice that
our Lord did not take steps to provide for the fellowship of his
disciples an exact record in terms fixed by Himself, or the principles which were to guide them. But He left in the world a
fellowship of people who had been companions, who had come
under His influence, who had begun to understand His work
and person, who became His interpreters to the world." [4]

In many different ways Temple pounded on this point: that
the you-have-to-show-me temper of the modern world, its pragmatism, is such that the Gospel's pulling power is in its demonstration, not primarily in its proclamation. He spoke of the
"rather frightening fact" that the Church as a whole is the most
potent evangelist—for good or ill.[5] He knew that it is all very
well to *claim* that the Christian faith "offers a principle of integration" to a divided and frightened world; but only if we "live
by it" and thus "commend it to others" by our own example,
paradigmatically, are they apt to begin "entering upon a glori-
ous inheritance." [6]

It would be false logic and imprudence, however, to conclude
from this that Temple minimized or belittled thinking as distinguished from doing—or believing as distinguished from behaving. On the contrary, he always contended that people are

all of a piece, and that what they think influences what they do just as what they do (or don't do) exposes what they think.

In a broadcast on the National Day of Prayer in 1942, speaking of the outrages in countries over-run by Nazi armies (such as genocide in the extermination of the Jews), he pointed out that they are not simply wicked men doing what they know is wrong. The trouble was that many Nazis believed it was right to do these things! And then he made a theologically important point: *a false belief is worse than any wrong action, because it leads to innumerable wrong actions.* "How often we hear the old silly saying that it does not matter what a man believes, and that this is a private matter between a man and his Maker." The German belief in Germany's supremacy is a false *belief* and to "worship a false god is the worst thing a man can do—far worse than deliberate atheism" or neglect of the heavenly Father.[7]

Incidentally, his view of conversion was definitely one of gradualism or growth; it was not apocalyptic, but progressive, as was his view of the coming of the Kingdom. Of the reality and authenticity of sudden conversions, characteristic (for example) of some forms of Methodist evangelism, he raised no skeptical questions. But his own experience and observations, as well as his basic theological method, pointed instead to a conception of conversion as a process rather than an event. Indeed, he said quite precisely, "Conversion is a progressive process. The beginning is to admit the Lord to our lives at all. But when that is done there are many doors still to be opened."[8] He listed some of the doors that have to be opened: patriotism, citizenship, housing, unemployment, education—hardly the pious abstractions usually dealt with in "devotional" treatises!

⚙ THE MOTIVE OF MISSION   If what we believe shapes what we do, an important question is raised about Christian missionary outreach. What do we believe we are taking to non-Christians? Is it a joyful truth and fellowship we want to make known to others? Or are we engaged in a do-or-die, sink-or-swim, last-chance rescue mission? Temple declared emphatically that if you have the faith "you cannot keep it to yourself because of what it is"; and he added, "not passing it on proves that you haven't got it." [9]

Nowhere in his thought, however, is there any evidence that he shared the fierce, almost frantic urgency with which many pietistic, soul-salvation missionaries from Western Protestantism went out to the "heathen" in the eighteenth and nineteenth centuries. They were altruistically driven to "save" those who would be "lost" if they died before they "heard the Word" and accepted Christ as their Savior. That "rescue mission," or crisis view, was certainly not the mission principle that possessed and moved Temple. [161]

Although his frequent struggles—maybe "twistings" would be a better word—with the question of the universality of salvation left certain points unresolved at the level of logic, he always stood by his basic conviction that God's love finally embraces all and loses none. Of St. Paul's two analogies (Galatians 4:1-7), he preferred the one that describes men as God's children under tutelage to the one that says that they are not His children until He "adopts" them. In Temple's theology, all human beings are already members of God's family; and there are no favorite sons. They stand in need of salvation, not from eternal damnation but from spiritual darkness.

This, of course, makes the Church's mission one of sharing a truth and a fellowship, not a rescue operation with a boom-or-bust ultimatum. What he called "the divine constraint of Christian missions," in his address to the Student Volunteer meeting in Indianapolis in 1935, was the pressure of God's love to share with all sorts and conditions of men their *knowledge* of that love made manifest in Christ. That God's love is eternal, unshakeable, and all-embracing is presupposed; there is no hint that it is in any way a contingent offer. Only a man's believing response to God's love is uncertain, not that love itself.

In the construction of his theology of mission, Temple was positive that (a) what the world is struggling toward is a one-world civilization, and (b) Christianity provides the only religious unifier that can fulfil that purpose. Any attempt to bring mankind together by combining "the common elements" in all religions into some kind of confederation of faiths will not work, he warned. If, he said, we took spokesmen for the world's religions to Geneva (today we would say United Nations, New York) and told them "they shall not be let out until they have agreed upon their formula," they would come out with something like "everybody should be good"—and still mean different things by "good."

No common standard can be found, according to Temple, unless (1) there is a God who is the Father of all, and (2) He has made His will and purpose known. "Our claim for the Gospel is precisely that it declares this Father of all mankind and that in it He has disclosed His character and purpose." [10] If we are told by cultural relativists that Christianity may suit Europeans but animism suits Africans better, there are two things to be said in reply. First, Christianity is not a European faith in origin or in its history. Second, if the Gospel is true, the question is not whether it suits us but whether we suit it—we English, we Arabians, we Burmese, we Bantu.

"Truth is truth wherever you go." If a Tibetan business man said that "two plus two equals four" is too rigid to suit the oriental temperament, we would, Temple declared, have every right to say, "Temperament be blowed. Two and two make four." And by the same token—if you believe in the Gospel—anybody anywhere who conducts life on any basis other than the Gospel's is making a fundamental mistake. He is building his house on sand. "The Gospel is true for all if it is true at all." [11]

This will be sure to strike a great many people as being absolutistic and even naive about the relativity of religious ideas from one culture to another. It would certainly not fit with the outlook of a man like Arnold Toynbee who has aligned himself against St. Augustine (and Temple) with Symmachus, the fourth-century Roman pagan. Said Symmachus, of knowing either God or His absolute purpose, "The heart of so great a mystery can never be revealed by following one road only." Toynbee believes he has found in Temple—"in spite of the inevitable bias and limitations of an hereditary Christian standpoint"—a theologian who comes at least comfortingly close to his own pantheonic point of view.[12] Like many a sophisticated modern, Toynbee holds that all of the "higher religions" (Hinduism, Judaism, Islam, Buddhism) have some of the truth, and none of them all of it. In his *Study of History* he quotes Temple's *Readings in St. John's Gospel*: "All that is noble in the non-Christian systems of thought or conduct is the work of Christ upon them and in them. There is only one divine light; and each has only a few rays of that light, which needs all the wisdom of all traditions to manifest the entire compass of the spectrum" (I. 10).

To grasp the difference between Temple's and Toynbee's positions is important to modern Christianity's understanding of its task. Temple could agree with Toynbee that any person or church claiming to have a monopoly of the divine light would be guilty of *hubris,* and that denying all truth to other religions would be blasphemy. But while Toynbee holds, in effect, that the revelation of God in and through Jesus Christ is on a par with what He has revealed in Socrates or Gautama Buddha, as part of the symphonic whole, Temple sees in Christ the very Truth incarnate, *Christus veritas.*

God is in Christ, only imperfectly and partially understood by the Christians themselves, yet not on a level with any other figure known to man. Temple agreed with Toynbee that other religions have insights to contribute and that Christians can learn more of Christ by their help. He did not agree with Karl Barth's wholesale repudiation of the "data of natural theology," declared by Barth to be irrelevant to faith. Yet it is Christ that all men need to know. Temple was a man of Christian faith precisely at the point where it *is* different from the other higher religions.

It may well be that the really decisive issue for Christians in what Temple called the "post-modern" world is joined at a point beyond ecumenical problems. The ecumenical challenge arises *within* Christendom, the "Christian West." But now, in the jet and space age of United Nations diplomacy and global power politics, the encounter of one Christian denomination with another seems to present a problem almost "old hat" compared to the encounter of Christianity with the non-Christian religions. Temple was only beginning to see dimly the outlines

of this challenge when he died. [162] He said more than once
that missionaries are "thinking ahead of the world about problems vitally affecting the world." [13] In 1938, Hendrik Kraemer
wrote, for the International Missionary Council, a study of the
inter-religion problem—as distinct from the inter-church problem or the "inter-faith" problem (Jewish-Catholic-Protestant).
Temple wrote a foreword for it in which he prophesied that
Kraemer's analysis would "supply the principles of missionary
policy for our generation." [14]

Kraemer, in his analysis, suggested that cultural relativism—
a perfectly legitimate and proper principle for an honest modern
man—is now raising the problem of religious certainty as "the
ultimate problem." It was that certainty that Temple had. Temple, then, was unlike Toynbee and Ernst Troeltsch. Troeltsch
refused to concede that Christ is the ultimate and exclusive
truth, but he claimed for Him a so-called "relative absolute-
ness." True, Temple held that our human apprehension (which
is never *com*prehension) of Christ is only relative, but he was
positive in his faith that He whom we relatively apprehend is
absolute.

His sure and realistic sense of social forces led him to agree
quickly with Kraemer's warning that the non-Christian religions
are not free-floating "systems" but tenacious parts of the sinews
of complex civilizations and social structures. They are not just
abstract "religions" without a culture context. Consequently
they cannot be displaced in popular sentiment by a strategy of
counter-religious influence only. Indirect Christian influence—
Christianity as mission—through non-theological factors of politics, economics, and technology is what is called for now, not
the old style, direct appeal of Christian "missions." The Gospel
will be either spread or buried by social-ideological changes.
Christians must not, said Kraemer, try to argue it out theologically: they must try to make it attractive in the "clear and per-
severing witness of words *and acts*"; and they must build living
Christian communities all over the pagan world—paradigms of
fellowship in Christ. Let them rely on the witness of such demonstrations, and trust to God as Lord of history.[15]

⚙ THE GOAL OF MISSION   Already, under such heads as the Kingdom, the Church, Personality, and the Sacraments, we have explained how Temple understood the *goal* of Christian mission. What more needs to be said about it? Its goal can be nothing less than, nothing other than, God's purpose to make all things one in conscious and willing response to His love—"to appease the hunger of the heart of Christ." [16] And to make "all things one" means *all* things: not only church unity but economic and social unity—in short, to contend against class systems, racial barriers, political discrimination, ideological sectarianism, national tribalism. For example, Temple hazarded the thought that a converted Africa and India may yet bring to bear an influence to "complete the work of making England into a province of the Kingdom of God." [17]

At the Jerusalem meeting the tension between the Gospel and economic imperialism (both coming from the West) was uppermost in everybody's mind. How, it was asked, shall the standard of Christ win Chinese and Indonesians under the moral shadow of Standard Oil and Shell? The revolutions in those countries since 1948 (history's quite predictable answer to the question) show how easy it is for the younger nations and younger churches, both, when trying to throw off the shackles of the European powers, to escape one Western evil (colonialism) only to take on another (nationalism).

In his address to the conference, Temple argued that of the two extremes, it would be better for China to have many denominations, all international, than a United Chinese Church which was only national. Frances Wei of Central China College said that the Chinese had to have "unity" among themselves whatever their connections abroad, through religion or anything else. R. H. Tawney, who supported Temple's view, said, "All you Orientals seem determined to go the European way to hell." [18] [163]

The goal of Christian mission in overseas witness was stated in Kraemer's *Christian Message* in rather exact terms for the period just before and following the Second World War, but changes in the world picture have already outmoded it in many respects. For example, in spite of Kraemer's concern for the ministry of the laity, which Temple shared, he nowhere recognizes what a difference it makes now that Christian clergy abroad are numerically insignificant compared to the *laymen* who fly back and forth over the world and spread into every corner. The development of non-religious forms of mission, such as the American Peace Corps, adds a fresh "non-theological" factor in many places. In 1926, Temple mourned the failure of Christians in the Atlantic community to make it clear that "the Church stands for the universal brotherhood of all nations and all races." [19] Since then the global drive of evangelical Communism as a non-theistic "religion" poses questions Temple may have appreciated in principle but certainly not in full practical force.

Decades later the image of Christianity is hardly any clearer to the peoples of the world—not even in the "Christian" cultures. Temple used to tell a tale about an officer, who, at the end of the First World War, grew so excited about Woodrow Wilson's proposals for a League of Nations that he accidentally knocked over a glass at dinner. First he said, "Damn," and then apologized to a chaplain at the table. "Sorry, Padre. What I mean is, I can't stick all this blather about human brotherhood." Temple's comment was that this was typical: the chaplain was supposed to be shocked at hearing "damn" but not at hearing the Gospel sneered at in a blasphemy about brotherhood.

Nevertheless, the League of Nations, which Temple defended so stoutly, has learned its lessons, died and risen again in the United Nations with greater realism and far wider participation. As a matter of fact, it represents a far more inclusive "meeting" at the secular level than the World Council of Churches does even within the narrow range of the Christian religion! What abides is Temple's assurance that the Church's task is primarily to be itself—the people of God, the household of faith, the Body of Christ. Only when the Church *is* the Church can it win the world to itself.[20] As with persons, so with the Church: self-realization is the prerequisite to winning friends and influencing people.

⚙ THE STRATEGY OF MISSION   Temple never took it upon himself to tell those who were at work in the Christian mission, at home or overseas, how to do their job. For one thing, he was never a missionary himself, in the popular sense—his work was in settled churches. For another, he knew the danger of the theologian trying to play the technician's role. Most of all, however, he identified "mission" with the whole range of Christ's witness anywhere with anyone, regardless of the place or person carrying on the evangelism. (He used the word "evangelism" as freely as a Free Churchman would.) But of two practical truths he was certain, and never ceased to say so: (1) the Gospel to be intelligible and attractive has to be offered in terms of its social bearing, and (2) its influence and spread depends on the laity, not on the clergy.

The strategy of mission is social witness, social action, social theology. "The social witness of the Church," he said, "is thus at one and the same time a preparation for the full gospel and a consequence of it." [21] The "social gospel," as Liberal Protestants in America might have said (he never used the phrase), is "an indispensable preliminary to effective evangelism"; and yet quite apart from that fact, "it is a primary obligation even though no evangelism should follow." Fundamentally the Christian witness is in loving obedience to God's love, and "like the message of the prophets, involved direct intervention in the political sphere—not indeed in the region of ways and means, but in that of principles." [22]

What he urged was an evangelism (whether at home or abroad is a secondary consideration) *in depth,* eager to be as intensive as it is extensive. It was a vertical mission, not merely horizontal— a presentation of the Christian faith which carried it down into the social fabric of human affairs, without sailing off over their heads on some pseudo-eschatological clouds.

Temple lectured on *Evangelism in Our Times* to clergy and ministers (i.e., Free Church) in Bristol in 1940, and in 1943, and delivered his Beckly Social Service Lecture, *Social Witness and Evangelism,* little more than a year before his death. These two documents have almost no equal as brilliant and contemporary statements of what evangelism is or must learn to be. He underlined the fact that nowadays men fight, bleed, and die over *social* issues. The ideological problems of corporate existence raised by science and technology have the center of the stage. The Gospel seeks to meet and speak to men where they are, and therefore its light must illuminate the social question in this era as it did the "personal fate" questions of an earlier time. Temple's plea was that the call to *individual* evangelism is not likely to have a wide appeal unless it is prefaced by evidence of social concern and ability to effect social changes. If men have come to neglect the question of their personal destiny, it will only be through the prophetic social passion of the biblical faith that they will be led back to a renewed belief in the need for individual conversion and dedication. The essential Gospel does not change.

A fair summary of his thesis could run as follows: (1) some challenges to the Church are dominant over others from era to era; (2) renewed evangelism is the dominant thing in this era; (3) the core of evangelism is a call to men to respond to God's love as He showed it, in sacrificial and redemptive *action;* (4) the setting for today's evangelism is the sickness of society in need of the Christian remedy; (5) the Church's approach to social questions should emphasize that fellowship is both the answer to the world's hunger and the goal of the Gospel; (6) all situations and proposals are to be tested by their help or their hindrance to fellowship; (7) *economic* community or sharing is the real test of fellowship; (8) the age group from 14 to 20 is the most important one for the new evangelism to reach. [164]

In this strategy, he looked to the laity as the key. We have seen how he taught that the laity are the Church's chief ministers to the world, as the clergy are Christ's ministers to the Church. "It is impossible for the clergy and ministers alone to preach the Gospel to detached multitudes." The clergy minister to the ministers, so to speak, by supplying the Word and Sacraments to those whose ministry is Work and Witness in the world. The laity are the Church in the world, not called to "do church work" but to *be* the Church in the world where the Gospel and secular society intersect. The Christian layman is *out there;* he knows

by daily experience what the facts are to which the Gospel must
be interpreted relevantly. Furthermore, people in our modern
culture look with suspicion or a "mental block" upon the
clergy who, in secular eyes, are religious professionals with a
vested interest. Those inside the fellowship know better, but
"the man outside feels differently, and to him the lay witness is
most effective," said Temple.[23]

"It is quite impossible," he believed, "to leave the responsibility of Christian witness in respect of most practical problems to
the clergy. [165] They have not the requisite knowledge; but
besides this, they have an outlook which is specialized in an
irrelevant direction. None the less they have a real function in
this connection; it is not to formulate policies, but to stimulate
in the laity a sense of responsibility and remind them of the
claims of their Christian faith in the various departments of life.
But the actual leavening of the world's lump with the energies
of the Kingdom of Heaven must be done by laymen." [24]

Temple knew perfectly well that this puts the question, an
explosive one, straight to the laymen. The layman, he held,
must make his Christianity effective in politics, business, social
policies, and "he must be a Churchman . . . before he is a
citizen." [25] And this, he said, the layman has to do by bringing
his resources and concerns to God in the sacrifice of the Eucharist. In no other way, we might say, can the Gospel get from the
pulpit and pew to the pavement. There are bottlenecks in both
pulpit and pew—to say nothing of the "sales resistance" on the
pavement. But the pews, the laity, are the fulcrum in the leverage
of the Gospel in the world.

One of the greatest difficulties, in a world of religious illiteracy
and secular separation of the Church and society, is that the
theological address meets no echo—there is no cultural resonance
for it. The modern mind provides none of the vital chords of
response. "We have to speak," said Temple, "to people who attach very little meaning to the word 'sin' and none at all to the
word 'redemption.' It is not that they understand what we mean
by these words and reject it; they do not attach any real meaning
to the words at all . . . the whole conception is alien from the
modern outlook." [26]

Enough has been said of Temple's views on grace and sin. But by way of transition to the final section of this book— Temple's social teachings—we might do well to pause here to spell out his concept of "redemption." This will give us some idea of how little redemption is understood by the modern world, and possibly even by those within the Church itself.

When he thought or spoke of the redeeming of the world by our Lord Jesus Christ, Temple did not mean transcending or eliminating it. He didn't mean escaping from it or by-passing it. To all other-worldly religions, Christianity declares that God, who made the world, sees it is good, loves it so much that He gave his only begotten Son to redeem it. As we have seen, Temple understood the sin or selfishness of the world to be both a wrong disposition of the will *and a disorder*. Sin is a structural as well as a volitional fault. Therefore, redemption for him meant rescue from, or conquest of, social disorder as well as personal selfishness. To "redeem" is to *re-order:* to put first things first—God, not man; neighbor, not self; fellowship, not private interest; ends, not means. It means rightly ordering all these things. It means putting persons right within themselves—in their own lives—but also putting their relationships with others right. Relationship is society.

Redemption, in short, is personal and social. To live the good life we have to get right with ourselves, as the psychologists and psychiatrists keep telling us. But the title of Temple's Gifford Lectures, *Nature, Man and God,* points to the complexus here. Besides getting right with ourselves, we also have to get right with God, and with man, and with nature (i.e., the physical and material order).

A helpful way to put this might be to say that Christian redemption is, exactly, the business of getting things right. Soul salvationists and pietistic Christians speak of "getting right" with God, but, unlike Temple and his social theology, they do not give much thought to getting right with man or with nature. If and when they ever think of getting right with others, of relationship, they think of it in purely individualistic one-to-one terms. Some pietistic sects—especially the "communistic" ones— have a strong in-group feeling, it is true, but this gives them only a distorted, because narrowed, conception of the social or corporate dimensions of their discipleship. Because this is the way so many Christians think about redemption, is it any wonder that if non-Christians can put any meaning at all in the term (other than a pawn-broker's or a bail bondsman's), they take their cue from the pietists and dismiss it as a socially indifferent, self-regarding insurance program for some other world than this?

In Temple's theology then, God is understood to be seeking the redemption of the world rather than the extrication of souls "up out of it." According to his process principle, God is progressively reordering the world—that is, reordering history which is the social and cultural process—by the principles of personality and fellowship. In his theological scheme of redemption the task of subjective or internal reordering ("getting right" with oneself) is accomplished in and by means of reordering *relationships*. And the three primary relations of men, in the order of human growth, are (1) to nature, (2) to man, (3) to God. In the order of their theological importance they are God, man, and nature.

Men are God's creatures. They grow up into personality in fellowship, in relationships. They are not *isolates* who can exist or grow by and unto themselves. There is no place for individualism in the Christian doctrine of man. Neither are they *agglomerates* who have no reality or integrity of their own. Radical collectivism of the kind expressed by a Fascist ideologue, who said "people have no meaning or value apart from their citizenship," always horrified Temple. On the Christian view, as he understood it, men are *associates* by their created nature. We may demand respect for the individual person's "integrity" (as a *person*, not as an individual!) but only because the individual's life is *integrated* with the lives of his neighbors—the family of God.

This associate, this person who is an individual-in-community, said Temple, is conditioned and shaped and moulded by the three primary relationships of life. Taking them in their theological order, we may say: (1) our relationship to God is the peculiar business of what is commonly called *religion;* (2) our relationship to man, to our neighbor, is *politics;* and (3) our relationship to nature—to the material creation—is *economics.* All three of these—religion, politics and economics—go together to make up a single, coherent pattern, the Christian scheme of *redemption.* Such a schematic way of painting the picture of God's mighty redemption, so obviously a biblical and prophetic picture, can help the naive or purblind to see what an enormous difference there is between "religion" and Christianity.

It is possible, then, to structure the total pattern of redemptive activity in a diagram something like the one below. Man is dependently related, for his full personal development and status to three given realities:

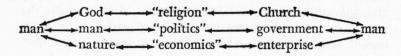

His relationship to God, called religion, finds its necessary embodiment or sacramentation in the Church. His relationship to his fellows, called politics (or social organization), is structured under law in various governmentally supervised ways. His sacramental relationship to nature, the source of his food, shelter, fuel, clothing and tools, called economics, is arranged in various forms of private and public enterprise.

God's concern is that men should "get right," redeem or reorder their relations, on all three levels of His creative process. And all of these relationships and activities are for the sake of persons, not vice-versa. When any religion, or political or economic institution, tries to become an end in itself, using persons as means to its own ends, that is structural sin. They are here, rather, for the more abundant life of man.

"It is a great mistake," said Temple in a 1940 series of B.B.C. talks that brought war-scared people up sharp, "to suppose that God is only, or even chiefly concerned with religion." [27] To most non-Christians as well as to the masses of theologically misled and uncultivated Christians, such a statement seems odd and senseless. But Temple's method of theologizing life and its adventures encircled the concept of redemption and, speaking

Christianly, put religion coherently in its proper place along with politics and economics. He insisted that failure to order our lives as Christianly as possible in any one of these three basic phases of life simply cuts out or cuts down our gains in the others—that they all three go together in one complexus.

Here is an evangelism that makes sense to intelligent and anti-religious people, who suffer with the world's suffering and reject any world view that passes it by, or passes it off, as temporary. It is holy worldliness, or worldly holiness. It is prophetic. God's redemption of the world, it declares, is a process of re-ordering or re-structuring life's relationships. It involves us as His co-workers in political and economic change as much as religious change. Temple thought about redemption not as a "religious" man but as a Christian man.

Part III

SOCIAL THEOLOGY

✻ ✻ ✻

XI

Morals and Natural Order

Having no extensive or specially written treatment of ethics from Temple's pen, it is necessary to cull out his views on the subject from many settings. Of a theoretical kind, there is a fairly full discussion in the heart of his *Nature, Man and God*.[1] His practical use of ethical principles is seen in his discussions—often quite incidental to broader topics—of questions of conscience having to do with law observance, lying, gambling, war, citizenship, sex, and certain motives such as love, fear and self-interest. Behind everything he said and thought there was a sort of keystone syllogism, theological in kind: he set it out as early as 1904 in a paper, *The Province of Science,* which he read to the Oxford Junior Scientific Society. The major premise was that the world must be consonant with the requirements of mind. The minor premise was that mind is not only cognitive—it is moral or purposive. His primary conclusion was: we cannot accept any account of the world which does not encompass its morality.

Our wisest course will be first to examine his view of moral values, their nature and claims. At bottom he made two assertions about value: (1) that the good or right is something objective, not merely subjective, a case of "what's one man's meat is another man's poison"; and (2) that goodness is, as lawyers might say, a personal quality, not "real"—that is, that moral worth comes from the fact that things are valued by somebody; it is not located in the actions or things themselves. He also made two assertions about obligation: (1) that it is a social matter, rather than individual—meaningless in isolation and meaningful only in relationship; and (2) that right and wrong are relative, not absolute—all depending upon the circumstances.

It has been quite apparent all along that Temple's primary or

determinative interest was in the pre-ethical, in the faith foundations for what we think and do. All questions of good or evil and
right or wrong have to be set in a theological frame of reference
to start with, before they can have any meaning or importance.
It is because of God's love that Temple *cares* whether a thing is
right or wrong. It is because of God's Kingdom that he *works* for
the good and against the evil. It is because of God's creative
process and sovereignty that he *expects* the right and good to be
effective. It is because of man's agentry ("vocation") in God's
redemption of the world that right is *urgent*. Without this pre-
ethical theology, as he saw it, there was no point in any moral
concern beyond enlightened self-interest and merely trying to
"get along" in calculated comfort.

⚙ THE GOOD IS OBJECTIVE The good is what God sees it
to be, ultimately, not as man sees it. Only on a naturalistic, non-
theological basis could it be supposed that the universe is indifferent to moral value. All questions as to what is good are settled
positively by the loving will of the Almighty, and theologically
speaking, man's moral task is therefore not to determine the good
but to discover it. [166] Our human recognition of the good, and
our human decisions as to the right, are at best always imperfect.
But the objective truth of the matter, the actual moral quality at
stake, is an issue already settled in the mind of God. The only
alternatives open to us are success or failure in trying to do what
is the right thing, for righteousness is of God. It is not ours to
determine the truth, only to decide what we judge it to be.

Many years ago at Oxford an old limerick went the rounds:

> There was a young man who said, God
> Must find it exceedingly odd
>   That that juniper tree
>   Simply ceases to be,
> When there's nobody out in the quad.

The limerick's purpose was to lampoon the subjective theory that
if nobody hears a tree fall in the forest there is no sound; if
nobody sees a rabbit run there is no motion; an untasted per-

simmon is not sour, and the like. A companion limerick was
written (some said by Father Knox of Campion Hall) bringing
out the point from the reverse perspective:

> Dear Sir, Your astonishment's odd.
> Someone's always about in the quad,
> > And that juniper tree
> > Never ceases to be
> Since observed by, yours faithfully, God.

Temple's point was that the reality is there whether men perceive it or not, and in the same way values are there whether men
appreciate them or not. God is always "out in the quad," seeing
all and evaluating all. If it were not for its theological basis,
Temple's view of ethics and value would be (like those of most
non-theological philosophers) essentially subjective.

He said he could not attach "any meaning whatsoever" to a
statement by G. E. Moore, the Cambridge philosopher, that
beauty (which like good is a form of value) could exist whether
or not it was appreciated by any mind—divine, angelic, or human. Said Temple, almost in the vein of recent linguistic analysis
by Oxford philosophers, "The word 'good' as so used seems to me
to be a noise and nothing else." [2] His reason for saying so was, of
course, his belief in the omnifacience of God's will; he could
not suggest that either angels or humans determine or assign the
actual worth of things. His objective view was objective for a
theological reason—nothing else; he was always fully aware of
the wide variety and relativity of human appreciation. Without a
theological foundation there would be no reason for thinking of
values as anything but purely subjective.

This theological objectivity of Temple's ethics is not only opposed to the notion that things are good or evil according to
the way people happen to regard them. By logical implication it
also opposes any idea that civil and common law in human
society, enacted by kings or congresses, or hallowed by custom,
can determine the right and the wrong. This view, often called
"legal positivism," cannot be accommodated to a theological view
of ethics. The civil power may manage, if it is wise, to *incorporate*
the right in the law, but it does not *create* the right by doing
so. As prayer is the business of finding out what God wants, not

what we want, so morals is the attempt to learn what God's will is—not man's.

But can a man find out? Temple thought so. In the first place, he simplified the question by lumping the "good" and the "right" together, contrary to the practice of a lot of philosophers. He was clear in his own mind that the good is whatever is right in the circumstances, and the right is whatever is good in the circumstances. [167] He also held that the insight or ability to discover what is moral is a natural and a human ability; and that to be "good" men do not have to be religious. He asserted, to the contrary and with strong emphasis, that "the moral judgment is quite absolutely independent of religion." [3]

The ability to make value judgments, to judge the worth and desirability of anything, is reached in men as their development from animal life to human mind goes forward: in short, as their critical faculty matures. Here Temple is saying what we have all observed—that very often non-religious people have a higher, more dedicated sense of obligation and justice than many self-professed Christians or, for that matter, religious believers of any faith. It is a *human* capacity, deepening as personality matures.

Indeed, Temple thought our developing human ethical insight has been a prime factor in the progress of religion itself. He argued that it has been man's moral criticism of his own ideas of God—"thinking that the God he is worshipping is acting in a way that he cannot justify"—which has brought about important doctrinal changes. The common example of this is found in the shift in the Atonement theory, from the ancient notion that Christ died to pay off the Devil or satisfy God's wrath, to a position more consonant with the divine love. "Religion," he said, "must commend itself to the moral sense, and therefore we cannot claim that the moral sense is dependent upon our creed." [4]

However, not only have men's doctrinal ideas grown with their ethical insights, according to Temple's process-theology; their moral understanding has grown, too. As he saw it, the growth is two-fold. First, it grows in content—the line of development being from the negative (prohibitions and do-nots) to the positive (affirmations and do's); from "Thou shalt not covet" to "Love thy neighbor as thyself." Second, it grows in extent—the line of progress being from tribal to universal obligation, from purely local or kinship loyalties and concerns to wider and wider fellowship in class, international and inter-racial terms.

Then arises the question whether revelation illuminates the search for the right and the good—whether it adds anything to the light of human reason. Temple's reply boils down to a fairly simple one: Yes, God in Christ reveals that love is the highest good and the supreme law or standard, as reason alone could not. This is not to say that revelation provides rules of conduct for *specific situations* in any fuller measure or in more certain terms than reason does. What Christ's life and death reveal, as Love incarnate, what they show us, is the "law" by which we are to live—the law of love. This is what St. Paul meant by saying in Romans 13:9-10 that all laws are included in one, "You shall love your neighbor as yourself," because "love is the fulfilling of the law." [168]

It is important in this connection to remember that the Holy Spirit does not legislate. Treating God's "general" revelation in His natural creation, or His "special" revelation in the Bible, as if it were *torah*—statutes of fixed conduct—twists the spirit into a letter that kills. And again, while our human capacity for seeing the good exists apart from religion, the ability to do the good we see is another thing altogether. Temple said, quite wisely, "I do not find that the recognition of a duty is of great assistance to its performance." [5] In his opinion the thing that Christian experience and faith supply is not the *what* of morality but the *how*. Faith adds a powerful and empowering motive force to a man's limited natural capacity for doing the right. That power is the "grace" that comes from the Cross—from the Christian's sobering knowledge that sin has cost God so much—and from his consequent caring, his *minding* that evil is loose and must be opposed.

☼ THE GOOD IS PERSONAL In the second place, Temple claimed that moral value or goodness is something that depends on persons for its actuality. "The only good or evil I know is the good or evil of persons . . . [and] I know of no way of proving *a priori* that anything is good or evil; we must go to our moral judgments." [6] To be good for anything a thing must be good to, or for, somebody. There is no such thing as "good" apart from persons. Temple's was a stoutly personalist view of morality, as we might expect. Value of any kind—whether goodness, or truth, or beauty—depends on somebody valuing something. It exists in nothing all by itself. Ice cream isn't good. What makes it good is that somebody likes it. He would have meekly but confidently bowed to Dorothy Emmet's opinion that his ethics were "too exclusively" personalist.[7] An appreciating mind or intelligence, either God's or man's, is needed to make things good. Some person has to evaluate it, has to put worth into it—not "find some good in it," as we commonly say.

Just as Temple said that revelation depends on an appreciating mind, so he said that value depends on the appreciating mind.[8] Good is a predicate, not a substantive. In that Temple's personalism was of a theological and biblical kind, the Person who is the true evaluator and worth-giver is God. Human appreciation varies in depth and consistency, and if the worth of a thing were solely a matter of human appreciation it would have no permanence or rational coherence.

The value God gives to a thing is always according to the contribution it makes to love and personal integrity, and therefore what is required of the conscientious person will change from one set of circumstances to another. The goodness of a thing, or its rightness, is not intrinsic, is not *in* the thing itself. It is not "real" and may not be "reified." A great deal of Christian thinking in the past has tried to reify goodness: not attributing value *to* things but purportedly finding it *in* them—as if their value (the rightness of an action, such as truth-telling, for example) were intrinsic or inherent in them. But value is like your name, not like your nose. It is what people call a thing; it isn't really part of them.

Temple looked at value as personal, and being personal it could not be real. He saw any action as right and anything as good only when and because they served some personal need, some human or divine interest. So-called spiritual and cultural values are "higher" than material values only as, if, and when they meet human needs and enhance human personality. If any action or thing were without personal bearing altogether, either good or bad, it would be morally indifferent. We must remember, however, that theologically regarded, nothing is morally indifferent because God's purpose covers everything.

Human persons with their imperfect insights sometimes find it quite impossible to see any value at all in a particular act or thing. But, in Christian ethics the authority or value-giver is a Person who is all-knowing and all-loving, God Himself, and therefore everything has its moral significance.

Having thus strongly emphasized that good and right are extrinsic and personal, not intrinsic or real, it is important to indicate with equal emphasis that in Temple's theology there is after all one intrinsic, inherently valid, and "real" good—personality itself. It is by and for the sake of persons that everything else is judged to be good or evil. Love (when genuine and unperverted) which is always for and between persons (not between things) is therefore the supreme good and the norm or standard by which to judge whether an action is right or wrong. God is good in Himself. And He has created men in His image, i.e., personal as He is personal, so that they, too, are intrinsically valuable in that respect.

It was this belief which lay at the bottom of Temple's passionately democratic politics. He judged all political programs "according as men do or do not believe that personality in man has a status [value] independent of all earthly associations and allegiances because of its kinship with the personality of God." [9] Only personality is precious in itself and an end in itself. Only love is always good and right—only hate and indifference always evil and wrong. And the theological way of putting it is to say that the true value of human persons is what they are worth to God—which value judgment He made clear in the sacrifice of Christ on the Cross.

❀ OBLIGATION IS SOCIAL   Just as Temple's principle of personality led him to an extrinsic conception of moral value, his principle of fellowship led him to a social view of obligation. At one time he went so far as to state it with radical and exaggerated bluntness: "The isolated individual may be wise or foolish; he cannot be moral or immoral. The Atheistic Debauchee upon a Desert Island is not liable to moral censure. [169] It is, then, our membership in society that makes us capable of morality, and it is consciousness of that membership that endows us with a moral sense." [10]

The exaggeration in this illustration is more apparent than real. Temple was using it to establish an area of agreement with those who might not share his theological premises but could share his conclusion about the social nature of ethics. "If some catastrophe," he said, "swept all conscious beings out of existence with the exception of a single man, would he still be under any sort of obligation? Not to other men for, *ex hypothesi,* there are none; nor to God, for He, too, as a conscious being, is excluded by the hypothesis. Can he be under obligation to himself? . . . Duty is a term never strictly applied to the isolated individual." [11]

For the man whose view of life is godless (Temple is saying) obligation, and therefore morality in general, is a social phe-nomenon—meaningless apart from human relations. As Temple put it, "So far as I can see there is no obligation to self. Obliga-tion is the relation that exists between one conscious being and another." [12] In his own theological framework, of course, Temple found the sanction for sociality in the will of God and the nature of creation itself. Furthermore, the theological view entails the presence of another Person always, even if there is only one lone human person on a desert island. Theologically under-stood, nobody is ever alone. Therefore Temple could not take seriously any hypothesis which included only one personality, and only a *human* one at that. Nevertheless, he held firmly that both theists and atheists recognize that obligation is social—mo-rality is relational.

In a kind of un-psychological way Temple understood the psychological factor in ethics. He knew that in practice nobody is more ethical than his motives require. And because love was his *summum bonum,* Temple was very positive that if fear rather than love is the motive of conduct, all genuine morality will be undone. Fear is a self-centered emotion, and therefore essentially sinful. The appeal to it, as in ordinary prudential morality, only makes us more self-centered—defeating the very purpose morality seeks to serve! [13] Only love can break us out of this vicious circle.

Sometimes Temple seems to have made a distinction in kind between love and justice—the former being a higher principle, the latter lower or lesser. In his discussion of how these two virtues (dispositions or motives) are related, he was inclined to say that love works through, or makes use of, justice. This is in keeping with the classical tradition in which love is a "theological" virtue, along with faith and hope, while justice is only a "cardinal" virtue, like prudence, temperance and fortitude.

Thus classified and treated as discrete virtues, the moral theologians have often engaged in long and complicated discussions of the relation between love and justice, and of their supposed conflicts in some cases. An example of "perplexed conscience" dealing with the love-justice struggle would be a mother whose love urges her to give her crying baby enough milk to stop its hunger, while her sense of justice commands her to leave it still hungry in order to give some to a neighbor's child, starving to death. [170]

Actually the social virtue of justice is love's rival or antagonist, or its policeman, only when it is natural (eros) love, i.e., self-regarding, preferential love. But love is its own policeman if it is Christian or agape love, for theological love is always aware of its obligations to go out to all neighbors however many there are, not just to friends or a single beloved. The "conflicted" mother is not torn between love and justice at all! She is being forced to choose between one kind of love, passionate, beloved-love, and another kind of love, dispassionate neighbor-love. "It is axiomatic," said Temple, "that Love should be the predominant Christian impulse, and that the primary form of Love in social organization is Justice." [14] Another way of putting this Christianly would be to say that justice is love distributed or shared between many neighbors. Love's task is a simple one when only one neighbor stands before us; but in social fellowship there are many neighbors. Justice is love facing this complexus, facing multiple and sometimes even conflicting claims.

Temple tended to use "love" when dealing with one-to-one relationships, as in romance and marriage, and "justice" when it came to many-to-many relationships—as between corporations and unions, or between one nation and another. [171] On this basis he often spoke of our loving an employer but not a company, and of nation-states being able to serve justice but not love. Yet he fully realized that justice and love are one and the same, and therefore he could say, "Love, in fact, finds its primary expression in Justice." [15]

❂ OBLIGATION IS RELATIVE   The other thing about obligation in Temple's analysis is that *what* we are obliged to do is only relative, but the obligation to *do* it is absolute. Our obligations are always relative but *our obligation to be obliged* is absolute. This he found to be true not only in ordinary morality but in Christian ethics, too. Just how much we are obliged in conscience to give to (let us say) the Red Cross or a political party will vary relatively, depending on many factors. The right thing to do is always a situational decision, but if and as any obligation is discerned, we are obliged to fulfill it absolutely—not relatively. The *what* varies, but not the *must*. "Universal obligation attaches not to particular judgments of conscience but to conscientiousness. What acts are right may depend on circumstances . . . But there is an absolute obligation to will whatever may on each occasion be right." [16] The sense of obligation (Kant's "oughtness") is one of the dynamics of progress, as the sense of goodness is. The two together make up man's morality. When we study human cultures and their history we discover that two things are generally true about morality. One is that the sense of obligation, or oughtness, is universal. The other is that the sense of goodness is only local.

All men feel obliged, but the objects of it vary from one society to another. To a degree they vary from one person to another, even within the same culture group. Temple was sure that the two things are not mutually dependent; that the sense of "I ought" is not always tied to "I ought to do what everybody else does." The latter, customary morality, is the most immature and primitive kind of ethics; and conventionalism is the form it takes in more sophisticated societies. But mature and creative morality dares to go beyond mere averages and accepted norms. It does not account for the conscience which defies social averages.

"Luther's declaration before the Diet of Worms," said Temple with a touch of irony, "has not the appearance of an overwhelming impulse to conform to social context." [17]

What is true of oughtness and goodness in natural morals is true also in Christian ethics. Temple saw no difference. [172] The sense of oughtness is, theologically, the Holy Spirit.[18] The Spirit transcends *torah*, reaches past fixed and rigid codes and statutory morality. The New Testament's adventure beyond the law is made by grace, by the Spirit. As St. Paul said over and over again, righteousness does not come by the works of the Law but by the Spirit. We are not "justified" (accounted as if righteous) by the Law but by faith. It isn't in laws that love fulfills itself, but in the freedom to go far beyond any law's demands, in seeking the neighbor's good.

Indeed, as Temple looked at it no rule of conduct or behavior could be followed always without subverting love. "There are," he said, "no moral laws that are absolute except the law to love one's neighbor as oneself." [19] Nor is there any principle "that can be made entirely binding and universal, except the law to love our neighbors as ourselves." [173] Love is not a formula; it cannot be put in a mathematical equation or a statutory regulation. Like faith, morals are a matter of decision, not of conclusion—of a leap of commitment, not of proof.

For example, consider the prohibition of murder. In the first place, it is not killing that is forbidden. If we want, we can say that murder is *always* wrong. But by definition murder is wrongful killing. It does not cover such things as justifiable homicide, military killing, or capital punishment. Therefore to say that murder is always wrong only says tautologically that wrongful killing is wrong. On the question of divorce Temple ran afoul of the old guard in the Mothers' Union because he opposed their condemnation of all divorces as such and their refusal to accept any divorced persons into membership. Being a theologian, he understood that spiritual sins are worse than carnal sins, the sexual sin "is not the only sort of sin nor the worst," and that pride (not lust) is the root sin.[20] (He believed the Church must hold the line against remarrying divorced persons, for the sake of the ideal, but should not exclude them from the Church's fellowship and sacraments.) About birth control he held, on the same principle, that "there can only be a highest way for each pair in their own circumstances."

And so with lying: Temple said ethics "parts company with common sense and common conscience" if it accepts Kant's conclusion that it is always wrong to lie. [174] He refused to agree that he "must not lie in order to send [a would-be murderer] down a wrong road and so save the victim." 21

When Temple says that what makes a lie evil is its breaking faith with another person, he goes to the heart of the matter.22 Theologically speaking, if a lie does not serve love it is evil and wrong. There is no such thing as a morally indifferent falsehood, because truth is owed to God and His ordered, purposive creation. If the world is only by accident a combination or pattern of things, there is no good reason not to lie about reality unless the liar is held back because it somehow threatens his self-interest or might hurt somebody else—and he *happens* to care. Without faith in God as Creator there is no ultimate reason why a man should not turn his back on what he knows to be the truth, feeling quite free to "kid" himself and others that the earth is flat, if it happens to suit his interests.

Let Temple speak for himself: "People sometimes become confused by this recognition that the rightness of most acts is relative and not absolute; but this does not mean that the rightness is in any way doubtful. To take Plato's example, the third [ring] finger is both short and long—short in relation to the second and long in relation to the fourth [little finger]. But in relation to the fourth it really is long. The general principle is that relative terms are absolute in the appropriate relations. To kill is right, if at all, relatively and not absolutely; that is, it can only be right in special circumstances. But in these circumstances it is absolutely right.

"It is doubtful if any act is right 'in itself.' Every act is a link in a chain of causes and effects. It cannot be said that it is wrong to take away a man's possessions against his will, for that would condemn all taxation—or the removal of a revolver from a homicidal maniac; neither of these is stealing—which is always wrong; though high authority has held that a starving man should steal a loaf rather than die of hunger, [175] because life is of more

value than property and should be chosen first for preservation
if both cannot be preserved together.

"The rightness of an act, then, nearly always and perhaps always, depends on the way in which that act is related to circumstances; [176] this is what is meant by calling it relatively right;
but this does not in the least imply that it is only doubtfully
right. It may be, in those circumstances, certainly and absolutely
right." [23]

What moral theologians call conflicts of conscience, when two
principles clash in actual situations, Temple analysed in terms of
tragedy. One big reason why no rule or principle of conduct can
be absolutely right is because it may violate or prevent another
one, due to the finite and relative wisdom and power of even
the best of men. There simply *are* times when truth-telling violates the law of love, Kant notwithstanding. Temple was im-
pressed by Hegel's thesis in his *Aesthetic,* that melodrama is not
tragic. Melodramas deal with the conflict of good with evil, but
that is not tragic even if the villain destroys the hero. Failure
and innocent suffering are commonplace features of evil.

True tragedy entails a conflict of one good with another, right
against right. "Whenever the recognition of one right involves
the violation of another, we have the material of tragedy." [24]
Hegel's example was Antigone, torn between loyalty to family
affection and a desire to bury her brother Polynike's body, and
her loyalty to King Creon's city-state and its law that traitors
must lie carrion. Temple's example was Othello, pulled in one
direction by friendship-loyalty to the lying Iago and husband-
loyalty to the innocent Desdemona. The reasons for moral relativism run deep.

This approach was brought into full play in 1940, during the
Second World War, when Temple defended the war effort
against pacifist criticisms. His defense was not something newly
"cooked up" to justify what he had to support because of his
high office. In his addresses in Oxford a decade earlier (1931) he
had taken the same view, and before that in 1914.[25] Late in 1923
he wrote, "An act cannot, strictly speaking, be wrong in itself,
apart from motive and consequence. [177] So isolated it is a mere
physical act devoid of moral value." [26] (Here he is speaking of
"human acts," so-called in moral theology; that is, things done

freely and knowingly. Theologically regarded, an action is wrong if its effect is unloving, because in that case God judges it so, yet no guilt attaches to it if the agent is ignorant of its unloving consequences or is innocent of unloving motives.)

For Temple, of course, the goodness or badness of an action lies in personality—in the agent's motive and its effect on others. He therefore set three criteria by which to value or judge any act: (1) the character expressed in it, (2) the principle involved, (3) the resulting consequences. [178] He applied this relative ethic and its three tests to gambling: the upshot being that while gambling is not inherently and absolutely evil, it is still *almost always* wrong. He reasoned that even when its motive is good (the character expressed), it still remains that its principle is wrong (avarice, and the irrationality of distributing income by chance rather than by reason and purposive will). And its consequences are either immediately or remotely bad (gambling contributes to such social evils as family neglect, racketeering, the something-for-nothing mentality). Like a lie, which is wrong because it falsifies reality (God's reality), a gamble is wrong because it spurns cause-and-effect (God's order). Neither of them is good or rightfully used unless by circumstances love is truly served.

"Particular acts," he said "derive their value from their capacity to promote or hinder the best relations between people, the relationship which must express their personality." And, he added, "All particular commands or prohibitions derive their value from their tendency to promote or to hinder the relationship of love on the widest possible scale; and all value judgments, in the last resort, are forms of this." Therefore, in the pursuit of ethical success, he said, "I want to suggest that the thing that really helps is to get quite clear which things are means to ends, and which are ends in themselves," because to be morally clear-sighted "we must settle what is the thing we are aiming at, which we want for itself alone." [27] That thing-in-itself (the theological version of Kant's *ding-an-sich*), that highest good, is love. Only love is an end in itself, intrinsically good—just as its opposite, malice, is the only intrinsic evil. This is the conclusion of all *theological* relativism in morals. [179]

If the key to sound morals is the separation of means and ends, subordinating the former to the latter, how go about it? As we have seen, Temple like Chrysostom found the essence of sin to lie in the *disorderly* relation or confusion of the two. This, of course, is the point in St. Thomas Aquinas' calling sin *inordinatio*. A part of the answer is Temple's insistence on love as the controlling norm and final end, applied socially in the form of justice. The other part of his answer was that "natural order" is a guide. His love and respect for the Christian past caused him to take a good, hopeful look at the Natural Law concept of medieval Catholic theology. And he did this even though he declared his "inability to accept the Thomist scheme as an assured starting point" for Christian social ethics.

He was clear that the "natural law" (usually capitalized) in the classical, Stoic-Christian tradition is not the "natural law" of the sciences. Filial piety, or respect for parents, for example, is not the same kind of "natural law" as the law of gravitation in physics or of diminishing returns in economics. Some so-called laws are not really laws of either necessity or morality. Supply-and-demand is an example, Temple thought. Supply and demand in the commodity market stand in no physically or mechanically necessary relation. Fair men can refuse to take advantage of a customer's (or merchant's) necessities. Only laws based on logic and mathematics are really laws: you can't distribute wealth not produced, or indefinitely carry on a business at a loss. But, urged Temple, we sometimes can and *must* ignore "supply and demand"! [28]

The *moral* natural law of classical ethics and theology is not to be confused with the *physical* natural law of science. [180] The former's role in the classical tradition has been to indicate "the proper function of a human activity." Here Temple was, of course, thinking in the same teleological way about means and ends ("true purposes") that Aristotle and the scholastics had employed. As to how to decipher these natural laws—supposedly established in the very nature of man and of existence—Temple, like the classicists before him, thought there are two keys: (a) to see what is "generally accepted" among men as the standard, and (b) to use human reason to figure out the proper function of things. [181]

He argued, as an illustration, that the "Natural" Law (or Order) of economics is that goods are produced to satisfy human needs, and that therefore finance exists for the sake of production and production for the sake of consumption: money's true end is real wealth, and real wealth's end is use. If bankers control industrialists, or industrialists control the volume of goods—especially if for profit's sake they *reduce* the volume they could turn out—then ends have been subordinated to means. And that is disorder, inordinate, sinful.

Our purpose here is only to bring out the fact that Temple's normal practice was to speak of the "Natural Order" when he reasoned along these lines—rather than using the more traditional "Natural Law." He sometimes used these phrases as if they were interchangeable. A careful look at what he said tends to suggest that he preferred "order" to "law" because of his fundamental reservation about law's role in human morality. [182] And more than this it is significant that he nowhere spoke as a modern Roman Catholic theologian would, about the "natural laws discoverable by human reason" being "given in the nature of things" (*de rerum natura*), nor does he speak of them as being permanent and universal.

Natural *order*, according to a rational, love-measured view of purpose and function—so much Temple could accept. But we have seen his reasons for holding a relativistic ethic, which could not very easily fit the Roman "Natural Law" idea that nature provides universally valid prohibitions of such things as artificial birth control and sterilization. As a matter of fact, he said as much. He thought that "the old conception of Natural Law" has lost its appeal because it tried to fix forever a "special relation to a feudal and peasant society." [29]

The notion of social function or order which he thought to be at the heart of the old Natural Law needs revising and reviving. He believed, he said, that there is "an order of the world and of life in which men and women and their various activities have their place. It is a natural order, in the sense that it gives a proper place to each person and function according to the best service which can be given to the whole." This idea was Plato's justice, and for Christians it is "a divinely appointed order because God is Creator of the world; but it can be in very large measure ascertained without any conscious reference to God." [30] And he thought that if it were not for human sinfulness, men would "almost automatically" establish a social order according to the natural order. [183]

Only along this line, he felt, could Christian ethics make a practically effective critique of the family or the State or the economic system. The principle of order teamed with the principle of freedom would provide the needed balance of the conservative and radical tempers. "Freedom is a finer thing than order, but order is more indispensable than freedom." [31] It was an inquiry of this kind that he tried, without success, to have explored by an ecumenical team of scholars, including Roman Catholics.

Temple's interest was in theological morals, or moral theology. The datum line of his thought was that God's is the appreciating intelligence which gives moral values their ultimate validity. His self-revelation in Christ gives men, at their relative level of living, the norm or measuring standard of right and wrong— the love shown on the Cross. Good is what it is because of God. As Temple once remarked, Plato started out to describe the world as under "the Idea of the Good," but he ended by seeing it as the providence of "the mind of Zeus." It is only personal deity that sanctions morality.

He could easily have written Jean-Paul Sartre's essay, *Existentialism,* for him. In this essay Sartre says, lugubriously, "The existentialist finds it very troublesome that God does not exist, because with Him disappears all possibility of finding values in an intelligible world; nor can there be any *a priori* good, because there is no infinite and perfect consciousness to think it . . . I am very much vexed that it should be so." [32]

XII

Society and Church

A personalist theology like Temple's is also inescapably a socialist theology—using both words without capitals. (Temple was
neither a doctrinaire Personalist nor a doctrinaire Socialist.)
He conceived of personality as a "dialectical" phenomenon of the
individual-in-community, and it was this which he believed to
be the goal of redemption and of history's creative process. He
thought of it as a process moving towards the fullest possible development of individual personality in the widest and deepest
possible fellowship.

From the perspective of his faith in the reality and ultimate
realization of God's family, he looked upon all human divisions
as Christianly or theologically negligible. The religious divisions
("neither Jew nor Gentile"), the cultural ("Greek nor barbarian"),
class ("bond nor free"), even sexual ("male nor female"), are all
forms of backwardness obscuring the truth that all are "one man
in Christ Jesus." It is only as men grow in capacity for neighbor-
concern—through the slow pressures of natural altruism or the
quicker effects of grace—that their fellowship can deepen. This
means, he said, that even though rights and duties, broadly
speaking, are correlative terms, it will only be as men transfer
the emphasis from rights to duties that their community life will
achieve democracy. And it was Temple's conviction that democracy is the political approximation of the Kingdom.[1]

Temple followed Aquinas who followed Aristotle who said
that man is a *zoon politikon,* a social being. He held that man
is "naturally and incurably social" and "this social nature of man
is fundamental to his being." [2] By this he meant to claim that
man *is* a social being, indicatively; not only that he *should* be,
imperatively. Man's social being is a theological truth; it is a

part of both creation doctrine and redemption doctrine. Church and society, therefore, are not to be related as good and evil, for society is something good, "capable of becoming completely good." [3]

In such a theology it is necessary to insist, in and out of season, on the distinction between personality and individuality. "Of course every person is an individual; but his individuality is what marks him off from others; it is a principle of division; whereas personality is social, and only in his social relationships can a man be a person." [4] Temple's personalism compelled him at all times to balance together his precious principles of freedom and fellowship, and their balance resulted in his conviction that "the inherent value of the human person" is what gives history itself its meaning.[5]

It is not, however, the individual that counts, but the individual-in-community, i.e., the person. [184] For Temple the individual apart from society is as much an unreal abstraction as society would be apart from the individuals who make it up. As we have seen, he believed society transforms the individual into a person, and for this reason he regarded all withdrawal from society with suspicion. He therefore gave first place to the Christian vocation for civic life, even though he allowed a place also for the monastic life as a special vocation. But in no case could his principles provide a Christian vocation for the hermitage or eremitic practice—which, although like the monastic in its withdrawal from society, lacks even the limited community of the monastery.[6]

❀ COMMUNITY AND STATE   Society, then, is one of the orders of creation, a part of God's own providence. This is why Temple told the Malvern Conference, "All the great political questions of our day are primarily theological." [7] In the order of being, so to speak, community comes before government or any other social institution. All institutions are derivative functions of community.

This basic principle is of the most vital importance to any

relationship-theology, especially in our modern era when government in the form of the State has acquired so much more power and importance than any other agency of the community. In the primitive stages of society there were very important forms of government, such as the nuclear family, the clan, the tribe, or the manorial authorities of the medieval feudal order. But in modern times, with the State so powerful and its authority so extensive, people too easily commit the *sin* of confusing means and ends. They are prone to treat the State as if it were society itself, or to think of the State as the end and society as the means! "That identification is," he said, "the one great [political] heresy." [8] This is precisely the structural disorder, or sin, of totalitarianism: it is the doctrine of the omnicompetent State, the Fascist dogma.

The State is in truth only one among several agencies of society. The blasphemy of treating the State as an end in itself was for Temple symbolized by Machiavelli (in *The Prince*) and Cesare Borgia. The school, the Church, the family, the factory, the shop and market, the studio and playing field—these other agencies of society have their claim and place, too; and it is a mark of evil when they begin to be used by the State rather than served by it. Over and over again he pointed out the peril of forgetting that "the State exists for the citizens, not the citizens for the State." [9] When society shapes the State and controls it, all is well; when the State controls and moulds society, swallowing up all of society's other agencies, things are going wrong. When Temple wrote his *Citizen and Churchman* in 1940, that was the practical difference between England and the United States on the one hand, and Germany or Russia or Italy on the other. [185]

❀ DEMOCRACY   And in this dialectic of the person and society Temple saw democracy to be the political key. He had three simple but searching tests for an authentic social democracy: it has (1) concern for justice to individuals, (2) regard for minorities, (3) respect for personal conscience. He tended to make the third the most decisive. A democratic society, he thought, "rests on concern for individual personality," and "its real inspiration is always to be found in the belief that every personality is sacred." This belief, he was sure, is "definitely a Christian product." [10] [186]

He had no use for *limited* democracies, as in the Greek city-states where citizenship was something for the free but not the enslaved; and he was equally opposed to merely formal democracy in which anything is justified if it gets a majority vote, no matter how it ignores or transgresses the integrity of individuals and minority groups. [187] Very candidly he said, "The legal omni-competence of the King-in-Parliament is nothing more than the non-existence of any other legal authority exercising legal control over the Sovereign. The supremacy is real in legal theory, and for legal purposes; it is not an empirical fact, and *only under an inconceivable despotism could it become one.*" [11] [188]

A democracy, then, "to be Christian must be a democracy of persons, not of individuals." [12] It is not just an impersonal affair of statistics and an honest count at the polls. Democracies are interpersonal fellowships—and Temple never hesitated to employ such theological categories when he discussed politics, merely out of fear that the secular ears of men (in and out of the Church) might "hear" something supposedly sentimental or unrealistic in their overtones. He frequently harked back to the attempt of the French Revolution to juggle Liberty, Equality and Fraternity, explaining that, from the viewpoint of a personalist theology, it should not be surprising that an overweening zeal for equality smothered fraternity and judicially murdered freedom. He saw the same thing, he thought, happening in Soviet Russia.[13] Communism lets economic democracy (equality) hinder freedom; capitalism lets political democracy (liberty) hinder equality. And in the first case fraternity is sectarianized, in the second it is ignored.

Society being *given,* in Temple's creationist theology, not chosen or devised, men cannot be said to have contracted with each other to form community out of their privacy. Community is already *there* in the human condition. And the Kingdom-community to come is the redemption of natural community, not the introduction of a new dimension in human life. Apart from community, membership one with another, men are sub-human —not merely sub-Christian. [189] And this natural sociality, Temple thought, is to be governed by four primary or axiomatic social principles to which he was committed all of his life: (1) the necessity of liberty for the person, who is created *imago Dei,* (2) the reality of brotherhood or fellowship, (3) the duty of neighbor-service, and (4) the power of voluntary sacrifice.[14] These principles are the threads that run through all of his theologizing about society.

⚙ THE SOURCE OF THE STATE In the history of political thought there are alternative theories about the origin of the State.[15] (They were also used sometimes to account for the starting of society itself.) One theory holds that human nature is social, that society is therefore natural and inevitable, and that the State—government in one form or another—naturally or logically emerges in society. Aristotle and Plato held this view. This natural theory is expressed theologically as "creationist"— that is, that God made it a part of the original order and nature of things. This is what St. Paul meant, evidently, by saying that the governing authority is ordained of God (Romans 13:1-7). In Temple's theology the State is a combination of the divine right of civil authority (not kings) and popular will.[16]

The other kind of theory is *contractual.* It starts from either the individualistic postulate that men are fundamentally self-contained or from the more social postulate of the anarchists that only community—not government—is a natural and given fact about human existence. In either case it is contended that government came into being as a strictly human invention—that men were compelled to adopt it out of enlightened self-interest, that somewhere along the way men made a prudential decision to sacrifice a little of their self-sufficiency for the sake of security in common law and order. In European thought the idea is, of course, usually associated with Hobbes (*Leviathan*) and Rousseau (*Le Contrat Social*). [190]

Temple's most complete discussion of the different theories of the State is in the second chapter of his Scott Holland Memorial Lectures, *Christianity and the State*. (The first lectureship in the series, just preceding Temple's, was Tawney's *Religion and the Rise of Capitalism*.) He noted that while Christian political theory has tended to be creationist or naturalist in orthodox Church circles, in liberal sectarian circles it has been contractual. Whether it is the classical orthodoxy of Catholics or the Reformation orthodoxy of the Protestants, orthodoxy in either case tends to treat government as God's creation—a divine order—and *a good thing*. On the other hand, liberal Christianity tends to treat government as man's device—a human ordinance—and either a *bad* thing or at best a necessary evil.

The great Church establishments of Lutheranism, Calvinism and Anglicanism, being orthodox in their view of the State, have found it possible to enter into a Church-State partnership. The sectarian and "free" churches, on the other hand, always struggle for separation—a doctrine which has won its way with the most success in America, and in the Communist countries since the Second World War. Like Plato, the orthodox theologians have tended to look upon the State as a good thing unhappily subject to corruption, while the sectarians see it as a bad thing which at most has its uses in a "fallen" world. Liberal Protestants typically feel, as nineteenth-century capitalists did, that "the best government is the least government." Socialists, like orthodox Christians, give government a positive and constructive role in society.

⚙ THE WORK OF THE STATE   By an irony of intellectual history, Karl Marx is much closer to Plato, St. Paul, St. Augustine, Thomas Aquinas, Martin Luther, John Calvin, and Richard Hooker than are John Milton or Thomas Jefferson! And Temple stood in the great tradition.[17] The State in his view is more than a policeman, it "does not and cannot stop short at the maintenance of order," because its function is to build up and enhance the lives of citizens by positive *construction*, not only by protection from internal or external dangers. There was never any doubt, for example, that *William Temple stood on the side of the Welfare State.*

This positive or affirmative way of looking at government appeals to both conservatives and radicals. Temple thought that conservatives lean toward making government the trustee of historical continuities but are slow to inaugurate policy changes, while radicals look to government to be a *spokesman,* generally responsive to popular demands and with a strong sense of obligation in the present. Temple's desire was to keep these two roles of the positive State in balance and tension—neither wholly conservative nor wholly radical. But whether we are conservatives or radicals, we are, he was sure, bound to remember that government, good and necessary as it is, is *not* the community but its servant. He preferred Plato's Good Man to Aristotle's Good Citizen (and Plato to Aristotle) precisely for a theological reason, that "the individual is immortal and the State is not; that is the fundamental conviction which must always distinguish Christian politics from secular politics." [18] He reasoned that if a man is a child of God then the State exists to serve an end beyond itself; and since "the higher spiritual interests are only realized through the free activity of personality, the end of the State is freedom." [19]

We have seen that Temple set law not *against* love but rather *before* it, as a precursor and trail-blazer. The democratic State's regulations as set forth in law are necessary for the common welfare, for justice's sake. He had no sympathy for either rigid legalism or its opposite, antinomianism. Even in its most primitive form, the *lex talionis,* law said only *one* eye for an eye, *one* tooth for a tooth. It set a limit to pre-legal savagery, which often wants to kill in return for a minor tort!

Theologically, he set limits to the powers of law. He was ready to acknowledge that good law tries both (a) to check the evil act, and (b) to convert the evil will. On the latter count law has some effect, most certainly. [191] But it has not enough effect, nor is it quick enough. Love does it faster, fuller. Before the judge at law we fear only what he will do to us. Before our father—

whether heavenly or earthly—we fear what we will do to him. Only love drives straight at the evil will.

At the same time, Temple prized law as he did order because it is an aid to self-discipline, and self-discipline is the indispensable basis of fellowship.[20] The Gospel, as he understood it, does not abrogate law as such—only particular codes, such as the *Torah*. The Gospel builds on law, and he thought the law's precedence to the Gospel to be "part of the providential ordering of history . . . We know in our own lives that we need the coercive control of law as well as the uplifting appeal of the Gospel." [21]

By the same logic he always refused to set love over against power. [192] Love opposes hate and indifference; and for love's sake, when justice requires it, power is to be used. "You are very near a definition of the Kingdom of God when you come to the expression, 'power subordinate to love.' " [22] True to his value theory, he refused to treat power as either good or evil. Like all compromise, the purpose of power is to assist the development of the ideal in the actual. "This seems to be alike the great principle of Christianity and of statesmanship: wherever you see Power, call on it for service." [23]

Thus in the field of contracts and promises: "If I am honest, I shall pay my debts by free choice; but if I am dishonest, I shall still pay my debts for fear of the inconveniences that follow my refusal to do so. There is then nothing morally good about my action; but the right act is done." [24] Temple believed "that the method of the State is so to order life with sanctions and penalties, that the lower motives in men's souls are enlisted in support of that conduct which the higher motives prompt." [25] He liked to quote a remark by A. L. Smith, Master of Balliol: "Personally, I *prefer* to purchase my railway ticket, but doubtless the presence of a ticket inspector has often clinched the matter!" [26] It was by means of the team of law and love (or grace, if you prefer) that Temple saw civilization being furthered, and the strategy of the Christian with his Kingdom-goal is to cooperate with all others who have the same convictions about policy and action, even though they do not share the Christian faith-foundation.

⚙ RIGHTS AND DUTIES   Temple conceded no absolute or unconditioned sovereignty to the State, either in its relations to its
citizens or to other states. Like all classical theologians he held
to the maxim *conscientia semper sequenda est.* True to his conception of freedom as a moral and spiritual attainment, he insisted that *political* liberty is not "freedom to do as I please but
freedom to do as I ought." [27] But this rule—that we are always
to follow our consciences if need be, in spite of orders from
State, Church, or any other authority—is to protect as well as
reinforce the citizen's obligation. On its part, the State's obligation is to respect the citizen's integrity; it "may not claim the
subservience of his conscience." [28] By democratic legislation the
State may impose penalties for violations of its laws, but it is
none the less as much the citizen's obligation to obey his conscience, even if the law is broken, as it is the State's to impose
the penalty. But if the State fails to keep its laws to a wise
minimum, it is failing in its task.

If the principle of the supremacy of conscience is accepted,
there will always be the possibility of civil disobedience and
sedition. If citizens are faced with tyranny or totalitarian pretensions, said Temple, "there is no sedition in disturbing a government of this kind." He followed Aquinas' opinion that in such
cases it is the tyrant that is guilty of sedition.[29] The theory of
absolute sovereignty has no place in any *theological* view of the
State. (Like others in Western civilization, Temple was genuinely
indignant to discover in 1914, and again in 1939, that Germans
took seriously Treitschke's and Hegel's dictum that power only is
what holds the State together, and the State is the highest good
that exists.)

What is true of the State's relations to its citizens is true of its
relations to other states. They are as subject to moral principle
as individuals. Sometimes when people protest against something
a government has done, they say that what is morally wrong cannot be politically right. This is a common maxim of pacifists.
Temple was ready to agree, but only if it meant that it is politically wrong for the State to do what is morally wrong for the
State to do! Too often, however, the maxim means that what it

is wrong for an individual to do is also wrong for a government to do, "and this," he said, "is completely untrue." [30] Private persons are correctly denied the right to exact tribute of their neighbors, but a State may levy taxes; sales of land at gun's point are immoral, but governments may exercise eminent domain; vendettas are wrong, but wars may be justified. We are increasingly troubled in conscience about capital punishment by the State (Temple was entirely certain it was wrong); however, there is no serious debate about the evil of private executions or killings in retaliation.

It is true that morals are usually more complex in social than in private relations. Even so, it seemed perfectly plain to Temple that states are subject to moral obligations in both internal and external relations. If it were not so, the anarchic theory of absolute sovereignty could not be challenged. But having said as much, one is faced with the grim fact that community within nations has dangerously far outstripped the growth of community between nations. The One World concept is still only a gleam in a moral man's eye. "Within the nation, unity (broadly speaking) is given; the problem is to foster independence; among the nations, independence is given and the problem is to foster unity." [31]

However, even though every effort must be made to overcome the time lag in the growth of international community, we must, he warned, avoid any basis for it which discredits or detracts from patriotic loyalty. Love of one's country he called "the best actual achievement of the principle of fellowship to date." [32] He saw precisely this danger in the Communist effort to unite men across national frontiers on a basis of working-class interest, which he called a retrograde loyalty because a nation's unity is far richer than any class unity. [193] "The values won in the nationalist phase of history must not be lost as we consciously and definitely enter on the international." [33]

⚙ CHURCH AND STATE   Those who claim that Church and State should be completely separated got little support from Temple. He not only felt that they could not be separated, because both have the welfare of their people as their business and are therefore bound to meet, but he further believed that in any case they *ought* not to be divorced. Obviously it was his *Church* convictions, as distinguished from a sect view of the Body of Christ, which disposed him to favor alignment of Church and civil authority. As we have seen, he not only believed that all men are in reality in Christ; he claimed also that Christ's Kingdom is working through government. In his theology both Church and State are "divine orders" (to use the Lutheran term). [194] As institutions they should, he thought, cooperate even at the price of some compromise. But they should never merge: no theocracies or Church States.

He held that the State's proper function is not to regulate the churches but to give them free scope and to uphold the rules laid down by religious associations (as the State must regard them). On the other hand, the Church is to admonish the State: it is Lambeth's duty, he said, to remind Westminster that Westminster is responsible to God. But that does not mean that Westminster is responsible to Lambeth. For example, he favored something like the French system of licensing and performing marriages. "I should most strongly favour a complete separation of the civil aspects from the religious aspects of marriage by requiring that all marriages should be authorized under the State by some civic ceremony, and only subsequently solemnized in the Church in the case of those people who mean by marriage what the Church means by it." [34] [195]

Temple's militant role in the Life and Liberty Movement, and the protests he made when Parliament turned down the Prayer Book revision, brought to light some of his reservations about the Church Establishment. He knew that in England there would never again be, in the foreseeable future, a situation similar to that of the Reformation when Parliament's members were all churchmen. It was in that day an assembly of churchmen representing churchmen, although on a civic and not an ecclesiastical basis. Toleration has by now turned it into an assembly of every kind of believer and non-believer. [196] Only a very qualified kind of Church-State partnership is just or sensible in such circumstances. But short of actual distortion and disruption of the Church's own business by the State, the partnership was worth keeping. "I believe it is good for the State to be (so to speak) affiliated to the Divine Society; and so far as Establishment means this, it is altogether wholesome." To drive the point home he added, "Even if the citizens were all atheists, [the glory of God and the welfare of the people] is still the true goal of the State." [35]

As a model of the arrangement he believed to be essential, he said, "Only if the Church of England can win for itself, or the State is willing to confer upon it, such freedom in spiritual matters as is enjoyed by the Established Presbyterian Church in Scotland" is the Establishment in England right. If not, "then the sooner the Establishment is ended, the better." [36] Here, as in so many things, he formed his opinions in historical perspective. In Scotland the Calvinistic reformation established the King as head of the Kirk, but vested its government ecclesiastically in an Assembly, not in Parliament. It was a happy contrivance of civil support and spiritual autonomy. (Twenty years after Temple's death, in 1962, the William Temple Association recommended that instead of appointing bishops on nomination by the Prime Minister to the Crown they should be elected by the Church, through the provincial synod.)

In England it so happened (accidentally, not as something essential to the Reformation) that Lutheran influence encouraged an Erastian arrangement. The secular officials ruled the roost, by putting the Church under civil rule by Parliament, lock, stock, and barrel. Legally, Parliament governed in matters of faith and worship as well as in the temporalities. Once the members ceased to be Churchmen, this kind of establishment became an absurdity. It was from this point of view that Temple worked so hard for the creation of the Church Assembly (Enabling Act, 1918) and said, after the Prayer Book fiasco, "The Church must act through its own organs, and leave the State to do what it thinks right" about the Establishment.[37] For, he said, "it is no concern of the Church. We have a divine commission; we exist as a divine creation. If the earthly State likes to associate itself with us, let it." [38] And Parliament's interference with the Church's worship was one of the features of the Establishment he found "to be in the proper sense intolerable." [39] Let the Church be the Church. [197]

Throughout his analysis of the Church-State problem he related the two as distinct but coordinate functions with mutual duties. The State stands for justice, the Church for love; let the Church therefore be more concerned with justice, which is love at work. The State stands for man's material and physical welfare. Let the Church be more concerned, sacramentally, with the material needs of society. The State is particular and local, the Church is universal. Let the Church, therefore, show her broad loyalty to mankind by helping the State to transcend tribalism and localism. The State is a natural grouping, the Church a "supernatural" (spiritual) grouping. Let the Church, therefore, for the redemption of the world not reject or bypass its natural orders.

❦ LOYALTIES Temple's extensive treatment of politics, for which he made no claim of completeness, was framed in a certain scheme, or typology, of relationships and loyalties in human society.

On one occasion, in Chicago, he even offered a brief outline of it.[40] A capsule description here will help to explain why he thought the class-loyalty of Marxism was not rich enough, and why he was skeptical of the super-national sentiments of so many communists and pacifists. In the starkest terms, he had three classes or categories of relationships in which he believed that men lived their lives: communities, associations, fellowships.

What he called "communities" are the natural, or given, relationships into which we are born. We come into them by coming into the world. [198] The various sub-communities in this category are of two kinds: family, locality. There are, indeed, many family or kinship groupings; modern civilization is characterized by the nuclear or immediate filiation of parents and offspring. By localities he meant everything in area from the village and town to the nation—and the wider their extent, he held, the greater their claim on us. (He could hardly have more deliberately reversed the usual flow of feeling!) These communities are "group egoisms" based on contiguity and blood (none the less real because we are in them by accident) and some measure of common tradition and interest. They are marked by their *comfortability*.

The "associations" are groupings of voluntary membership, or *chosen*. They include such things as labor unions, employer federations, universities, group insurance plans, fraternal organizations. At the international level the League of Nations was one, as the United Nations is today. Associations are purposive and deliberately formed interest-groups which the members join in order to gain something—higher wages or more profits or greater security, for example. They are marked by their *profitability*.

The third type of grouping is the "fellowship"—a devotional rather than natural or prudential affiliation. It is neither given nor chosen. In a sense these groups choose their members and are not chosen by them. Some person or purpose calls out a loyalty and commitment from those who thus become members, often at the cost of great sacrifice of convenience, substance, and even of life. In Temple's view the pre-eminent fellowship is Christ's Church, of course. An example of a political nature would be the Communist party, which often has utterly devoted and even sacrificial members. There are also brotherhoods of a non-religious, non-political *raison d'être* which appear now and then in human society—groups dedicated to "racial purity" or family feuds, or the like. [199]

It is apparent that communities depend upon the loyalty of their members, even to the point of self-sacrifice, and they exact it *with or without compulsion,* as in conscription and warfare for the State. Associations rely on each one of the members' loyalty to his own immediate or long-run interests—they are based on enlightened self-interest. Fellowships depend on their members' loyalty to something or somebody beyond the group—

they are empowered by commitment to a "good" that is higher than the group itself: for example, God and His Kingdom beyond the Church.

In Temple's scheme of relationship there is a descending order of loyalties required by Christian ethics. The first and highest loyalty is to God and His Kingdom: only to this loyalty can we give an absolute surrender of our lives—no other can be preferred to it. "The question is not—Shall I do my duty as a Christian or as a citizen? The question is, What is my duty as a Christian citizen?" For the Christian citizen "there can be no conflict of ultimate loyalties: ultimate loyalty is due to Christ alone." [41]

Second on his priority list is the loyalty we owe to our natural groupings—and as among them, the wider the community the more loyalty we owe it. On this basis, as Temple always insisted, the nation-state has the fullest claim, while provinces, towns, and families are subordinate. Yet any and all such community-loyalties are limited by the prior loyalty, to God and His purposes. [200]

Third on the list are the associations. They are still further limited by the loyalties above them on the scale; they are always limited by the interests of fellowship and community. (On the lowest rung of the ladder he put loyalty to the single neighbor —whose interests are to be measured on a level with one's own.)

For the Christian, who measures obligation theologically, the problem of membership in such groups is to think through their policies as Christianly as possible, and then try to win the other members to the Christian "line." But, Temple said, in every case the Christian must either abide by the membership's decisions or withdraw from the group. [42] Questions of conscience about membership are searching and frequent for Christians. Their lives are more complicated than the un-theologically oriented can ever imagine. Issues arise in embarrassing and often harrowing forms—especially in the areas of economic, political and foreign relationships, to which we must now turn.

XIII

Socialism and Ideology

Before he was well settled in as an undergraduate at Oxford, Temple discovered that the very foundations of his social order were on fire on two levels—moral and technical. It was declared to be (1) undesirable because of its inequities and cruelties, and also (2) unworkable because of its structural and systemic faults. His early Tory resistance to this radical viewpoint soon collapsed, and he began to find the familiar banner in parades of the unemployed and socialists somewhat to his own taste: "Damn your charity; we want justice." [1] When he went as a missioner to parts of London like Bermondsey, far removed from the comfortable atmosphere of the Fulham and Lambeth Palaces, he began to see what was meant in Disraeli's phrase, "We are still two nations." [2]

In particular, Temple learned that "Karl Marx will continue to be a great force, because he first expressed with insight and passion the supreme importance of the economic factor in politics and the close connection between economics and ethics." Armed with his own fairly solid knowledge of history, he realized that these principles "are commonplaces today; but they were novelties when Marx first insisted on them, and he deserves in full measure the credit due to a pioneer." [3]

Yet Temple was never for long a socialist in any sense acceptable to secular socialists. (The term does not even appear in the index of Iremonger's biography.) There is a wide range of Marxist views, including many "revisionist" positions and nearly as wide a variety of "sects" as Christianity can boast, but very few of even the right-wing Fabian socialists would allow Temple to use their label. As a matter of fact his quarrel with capitalism was fundamentally moral and theological, and he was always prepared to plead that, despite its evils in its present form, it "has

179

certainly given to the mass of the people a higher standard of life—a larger enjoyment of material goods—than any previous system." [201] He would sometimes say that our present system, although not anti-Christian, is un-Christian, by which he meant *sub*-Christian. "In countless ways it is marked by the influences of Christianity upon it. Let anyone who doubts that compare it with the civilizations of those countries which have hardly been touched by Christian influence." [5]

At the end of his life he said, "Socialism is a vague term, and in some sense we are committed to Socialism already"—meaning that the necessities of social planning and managed economy have brought about a pattern which old William Gladstone would have called socialistic.[6] In the same spirit, in 1926, he was saying, "We are all Socialists now." [7]

The ideological polarity of Socialism *vs.* Capitalism was to him a case of Scylla and Charybdis. As we have seen, he attacked every such antithesis with his encircling method of synthesis. He was quick to agree that the socialist position was one that a serious Christian might embrace. On the question of socialization of the means of production, either for or against, "a perfectly good Christian may hold either view. There is nothing in the Gospel to say what is to be held as to the economic system." [8]

The course of his opinion about socialism seems to have followed a three-stage development, once his schoolboy Tory assumptions were gone. The first stage is seen in 1908 at a Pan-Anglican Congress in London where he met John Malcom Forbes Ludlow. Ludlow was then eighty-seven years old and the only survivor of the famous trio of Christian Socialists, Frederick Denison Maurice, Charles Kingsley, and himself. The Congress decided that capitalism is immoral; and Temple, declaring for nationalization of industry, urged his fellow Churchmen to see that practically, as well as theologically, "the Christian is called to assent to great steps in the direction of collectivism." [9] That same year he wrote in *The Economic Review* that the Gospels "taught nothing less than evolutionary socialism . . . the alternatives stand before us—Socialism or Heresy; we are involved in one or the other." [10] That alleged dilemma he quickly forsook. On his 1910 Australian tour he said flatly, "Competition neither can nor ought to be eliminated; we should aim at a society co-operative in principle and competitive in detail." [11]

In 1912, however, he was willing to allow it was "a matter which seems to me indifferent from the point of view of general principles" whether State ownership or State control of privately owned capital is adopted in a *Christian* society, when we try to think "what a Christian society would look like." [12] But for here and now he favored the former. He joined the Labour Party as a Christian Socialist, not a Marxian. Then by 1927 he was at his second stage of opinion, saying that "free enterprise, conducted in a spirit of public service, will serve the public better than an industry under a centralized control." [13] He was still talking about the world we have now, not about the ideal of the King-dom. In this second stage he clearly favored private ownership under public control—much closer to the Aristotelian and scholastic principle of *noblesse oblige* or "stewardship" than the Platonic and patristic communism he favored in his first stage. His third and last stage was a pluralistic one, favoring the use of both principles, private and public. It was a policy under which both ownership and control could be either public or private as conditions might suggest. Our problem, he said, is "to get the best out of both." [14] No either-or.

At no point along the road did he ever lose sight of the central importance of a theological orientation. The fact of first con-sideration in his estimate of Marxism was its non-theistic doctrine of man and society, contrasted to a Christian culture's primary faith that men are children of God. His theological position chal-lenged *every* ideology across the board, not just the Marxist brand. "The fundamental political question of today is a theolog-ical question: for it is the question whether the individual man or woman exists for class [Communism], State [Fascism], or the racial community [Nazism], or whether on the other hand each in-dividual has, through relationship with God, a status and worth altogether independent of any earthly associations." [15]

To show how seriously he took Communism, he warned that "If you cut out the religious and spiritual background of human nature, then I do not think there is a direct answer to the Com-munistic philosophy or any ground of real resistance to it." [16]

His "anthropological" quarrel with Communism is, of course, a matter of pre-political Christian principle which he applied to all forms of Marxian socialism. [202] He was sure that no other humanistic view of men and society, no other non-theistic man-centered outlook, has the coherence and vitality of the Marxian version.

He never made the superficial error of lumping Communism and Fascism together. It was clear to him that Fascism is "less congruous with a Christian outlook. For the avowed aim of Communism is a part of the hope of Christians." [17] He said of Communism that it was "the only theory which I personally regard as seriously formidable . . . There is so vast an amount of truth in it; it is so impossible to doubt that our moral standards are very largely framed, without our being aware of the fact until we have studied it, by the organization, and particularly the economic organization, of the life in which we live, that it seems possible at first to argue that all moral conceptions are simply derived from economic forces, and that by reorganizing the economic forces and those akin to them we shall reorganize people's moral conceptions and regenerate them. Moreover it is entirely true that by reorganization of this kind one could do a great deal toward the regeneration of character." [18]

In this carefully phrased statement we have an early (1912) sample of Temple's belief in the reality of economic determinism. He construed the eighth and ninth books of Plato's *Republic* as an exposition of that doctrine.[19] As we have seen, his determinism was not of the mechanistic variety which, in effect, makes automatons of man. Nor, for that matter, is Marxism's. He had no patience with what the Marxists call "vulgar sociology" and "historical formalism." [203] Nevertheless, during the Second World War he was still saying that "more potent than school, or even than home, as a moral influence, is the whole structure of society, and especially its economic structure." [20] Yet, in opposition to those who absolutize the economic interpretation of history and make it into a strait jacket dogma, he simply asked: "What is there peculiar about the economic, social or political organization of Palestine in the first centuries B.C. and A.D., which accounts for the life of Christ? . . . [for] unless this theory will account for the genesis of Christianity itself, it is obviously unable to account for the human history which, from that day to this, has come under Christian influence." [21]

He was entirely consistent with this in asserting his theology of Christian materialism. "Christianity, whatever else it does, certainly does full justice—and, I think, alone among religions does full justice—to the physical and material. It is, indeed, its materialism which is the stumbling block to many who aim at holding purely spiritual views of life." [22] [204] He had no use for the kind of "ultra-spiritual" doctrine that St. Paul had to contend with in Corinth, which minimizes or degrades material and physical things.[23]

Temple never accepted the notion of "detachment" from worldly things which is often read into St. Paul's remarks in I Corinthians 7. To the contrary, he always insisted on the importance of material goods, both as an aid to personality development and as a means of expressing neighbor-love. Allowing for the validity of special vocations to voluntary poverty, Temple was positive that poverty is not the normal or constructive principle to be employed by Christians. We need wealth in order to do love and justice, for they require material expression or sacramentation. It was St. Francis' vocation to embrace poverty, and it was Pope Innocent's to recognize and approve his order; but if Innocent III had joined the Franciscans, "it would have been a stark dereliction of duty." [24] [205]

Temple's economic determinism did not necessarily entail any *liking* for economic influence. Like the Marxists (who usually won't admit it because of their distaste for moralism) Temple had moral objections to the economic determination of personality and policy. He was convinced that, while many socialists take "a too narrowly economic view" of life and values,[25] no honest apologist for capitalism would deny the force of economic factors. "It was not some Socialist fanatic, but that prince of orthodox economists, Marshall, who said that the two strongest influences in forming the moral character of citizens are the religious beliefs in which they are trained and the economic system in which they grow." [26] And in so far as the capitalist system relies for its functioning upon selfish motives he acknowledged its realism about sin, but he denounced its complacency about it. In his theological analysis "the trouble is not wealth; it is sin—which is the perquisite of no class, and (incidentally) besets us who are ecclesiastical officials as much as others." [27]

Sin is the dynamic of the profit motive, inspiring class consciousness and status seeking. Yet it is a human, not a class phenomenon, and Temple was sure, therefore, that class struggle as such would never help. [206] When class war is added to class feeling one evil has compounded another. "Communism seeks to create by force a world of mutual cooperation, believing that those who grow up in such a world will be freed from acquisitiveness and self-concern. But the effect will only be to direct those motives upon other objects than wealth, such as honour and influence. And the initial trust in force, which is always an appeal to self-concern, will stimulate the sentiment it aims at destroying." [28] The voluntary communism of the primitive Church supplied us with the norm and standard, but it "is as different from what is ordinarily called communism as anything can be; it is, indeed, its polar opposite." [29] Temple often pointed out that it was Adam Smith who first underlined the class-war as a fact, "And when Marx and Engels proclaimed it as a duty, they were only doing what Adam Smith and his followers had done with other facts." [30] He meant that Adam Smith had called selfishness a duty (which, theologically regarded, is carrying coals to Newcastle), while Marx called class brotherhood a duty in overcoming selfishness, and that he (Temple) found class loyalty too narrow and yet morally superior to self-seeking.

Temple changed "Workers of the world, unite!" to *"Peoples of the world, unite!"* He agreed with St. Ambrose—"a great officer of State as well as a Bishop"—that common use is natural and that usurpation and avarice caused private property. For this reason almsgiving is an act of justice rather than of mercy. [207] But he held with Ambrose and Augustine that the law of private property, when properly qualified, is a constructive form of realism about human selfishness. [31] Frequently he followed a usage of the English Distributists (e.g., G. K. Chesterton), i.e., the observation that every argument for private property is an argument for its widest possible distribution.

We have seen that Temple's sacramentalism was "a dialectical realism," and that he once thought of calling his Gifford Lectures *A Study in Dialectical Realism* because of the strong appeal of Marx, Engels and Lenin in the modern world. Few modern Christian philosophers have seemed able or willing to acknowledge, as he did, how clearly akin Christianity and Marxism are on that score.[32] Nevertheless, he had no high opinion of the Marxists' grasp of the facts and complexity of history. He was convinced that Marx "was not a profound or an accurate thinker," but one who combined moral passion "with a social philosophy which was much too simple for the facts"—even though intelligible in principle and *apparently* balanced. To show its inadequacy, Temple thought, it is only necessary to point out that "a vital part of the Marxian doctrine is that economic development must follow a certain course, which as a matter of fact it has not followed." [33] [208]

But while he had no confidence in the Marxian use of history's data, he felt a kinship with its concern for history. He knew that his true antagonists—common in "religious" circles—are the idealists, the spiritualizers and the trancendentalists; in short, all forms of pietistic other-worldliness. "The Christian understanding of history has much closer affinities with the Marxist view [which regards history as belonging to the essence of existence] than with the interpretations of Christianity in terms of idealistic thought which were lately prevalent." [34]

His dialectical method was another thing that brought him close to Marxian analysis. He himself employed the Marxian dialectical principle. For example, he argued that the human intellect works constantly against, but yet because of, contradiction. "Contradiction is what it cannot think; and yet contradiction is what makes it think." This, he thought, is the key to what he called "the logic of civilization" whereby we can see a change from (1) primitive or savage communism, denying individual values, to (2) a stage of human society in which men are aware of and jealous for the individual, and then a new shift to (3) a new and different corporate interest, when it is realized that the competition and unique interests of individualism endanger both the community and too many individuals as well.

Temple said that, under the impact of science and technology with their inherent principle of organization and coordination, we are in these times at the point of a shift from private back to public or corporate interest. The old "tribal" identity or solidarity now rises to a higher level of development. "Consequently a new tendency toward centrality appears, under the names of Socialism and Collectivism, which aims at state control precisely for the sake of individual freedom. This tendency will probably develop, with subordinate oscillations, for five or ten centuries, until it is found to "contradict" some interest which it exists to safeguard, and so will again be thrown back by a new individualism." [35]

The basic things to grasp here are Temple's characteristic rejection of the either-or, and his use of his encircling method. He championed economic pluralism, a mixed economy including both public and private enterprise. His hope was that social policy would be shaped by a tough-minded pragmatism rather than by any doctrinaire predetermination of the Left or Right. He preferred the harmony of different parts to straight unison, whether in economics, choral music, theology, or anything else. "Our task must be to do justice to the truth of capitalism, as well as the truth of socialism," for we do not want "one cast-iron system." [36] "To put it shortly, we have talked in a doctrinaire fashion about socialism and individualism long enough; it is time to try to get the best out of both. The question now is not, Shall we be Socialists or shall we be individualists? but, How socialist and how individualist shall we be?" [37] The greatest futility for him was the intractable polarization of principle which comes so easily to die-hards of Left and Right. Given current usage, it was entirely misleading, therefore, of the Earl of Selborne to say, when Temple died, that he had been a "politically advanced socialist." [38]

At the same time, his "pragmatism" was not a repudiation of principles or of rational theory. "A false belief is worse than any wrong action because it leads to innumerable wrong actions." [39] As a theologian he was increasingly dissatisfied with the piecemeal approach to Christian social concern that had been followed at the C.O.P.E.C. meeting in Birmingham back in 1924, where only specific social problems were considered. One of his primary

interests at the Malvern meeting in 1941 was to start working out
a view of "the whole order of existing society in the light of the
intrinsically right relation of the various functions of society—
financial, productive, distributive, cultural, spiritual—to one
another." [40] He was always impatient with the anti-intellectuals,
the vulgarists, and their pseudo-practical contempt for unitive and
coherent thought. He inveighed constantly against all "autono-
mies" by which anarchic and idolatrous claims of independence
from other interests are made, such as "business is business," or
"art for art's sake," or "virtue is its own reward," or Machiavelli's
"the State is its own judge." He sought the subordination and
integration of activities to one purpose—God's Kingdom. This
was the true conspectus for life and it was a conspectus "primarily theological, not primarily political or even sociological." [41]

Planning, then, social planning, is needed in the modern world
of steadily increasing interdependence. There is no real choice
between planning and not-planning; only between good and
bad planning. "We can so plan for efficiency as to destroy freedom; Fascism does this. Or we can so plan for freedom that we
lack efficiency. Our aim must be to plan efficiently for the
maximum of freedom." [42] In short, as a typical result of his
dialectic, he was saying that in a technical civilization we can
preserve freedom *only by planning for it*—and his desire was to
make it the very first thing on the social planning agenda.

He thought the English were poor at bureaucracy, and since
"the bane of our democracy is the red-tape of the clerical departments," it should be kept to a minimum as a necessary evil. In
1926 he said that the "real objection" to Socialism is that "no
person or body of persons" is wise enough to run so complicated
a machine as a modern economy. For this reason he favored free
enterprise, moved by a spirit of public service, to a centralized
economic control.[43] He later corrected that second-stage opinion,
modifying it in the direction of planning authority. But he never
forsook it entirely.

Only government can guarantee these various purposes in the
social order. As we have seen, he had a positive view of the State's
function—with no negative "bourgeois" feelings toward it. It has,
he was sure for theological reasons, a more constructive rule than

mere police power. It is wrong to see the State as only the up-
holder of order, for "order" inevitably develops from merely
preventing riots or attacks to deciding, for example, that cut-
throat competition is another form of cutting throats! [44] He was
close to both Plato and Marx in this respect, and much closer to
the realities of modern society than the lunatic "liberal" Right,
who are always wanting to "return" to the minimal government
of the nineteenth century. And Temple's belief held firm that
in a politically democratic society it is possible to move along
the lines of his pluralistic process. "To the process Tories and
Liberals and Socialists must each contribute as much as the
criticism of the others allows to pass. The only people who increase the danger are the Diehards and Revolutionaries—who
create, and largely depend for existence upon, one another." [45]

Ideologically, he was non-utopian—yet pro-utopian, not anti-
utopian. As a social realist he did not discount the time factor or
the unevenness of development in the social process. The Kingdom, theologically regarded, he said, makes our task one of "preparing the way for something outside history altogether—the
perfected Kingdom of God. In that work of preparation we have
to make rough places plain; but as soon as we do this, places
previously plain are found to have become rough." [46] God's
creation is an uneven thing by human standards and human demands. Nor when the Kingdom itself comes in its best conceivable
approximation on earth (our goal), will it be a perfect social
structure, transcending our human and historical relativities. It
will be a *moral* achievement—a spiritual victory, for we are not
to forget that *it is a moral, not a hedonistic goal.*

"Still city and country life with all their manifold pursuits, but
no leading into captivity and no complaining in our streets; still
sorrow, but no bitterness; still failure but no oppression; still
thoughtless luxury, no grinding destitution; still priest and
people, but both alike unitedly presenting before the Eternal
Father the one increasing sacrifice of their own lives in body
broken and blood outpoured; still Church and world, yet both
together celebrating unintermittently the one Divine Service,
which is the Service of mankind." [47]

XIV

Economic Reconstruction (1)

Being non-doctrinaire and merely "muddling through" are not the same thing. Englishmen have too often lost sight of the difference, admittedly—so much so that England and Muddling Through are associated in many minds. Temple was no muddler. If he had been, there would have been less complaint in conservative circles. He was a gradualist and a pragmatist, avoiding all arbitrary blue-print, pre-packaged theories about social policy, but at the same time he had quite sharply drawn ideas about policy, no matter how tentative and exploratory they were.

The rule of law was precious to him; and lawful goals, like Rome, are not built in a day. Nor are the delays of the law always used merely to excuse complacency about tardy justice. Such delays may be unwelcome yet tolerable brakes on justice, when seen in the balance of good perspective. After one of Temple's attacks on the immoralities of business, it was charged in counterattack that his own hands were not clean, that the properties of the Ecclesiatical Commissioners included slums and brothels. Temple insisted on a full investigation, and the charges were substantiated. In spite of his disgust and chagrin he gave no order for their sale, because the civil laws of tenure and occupancy protected the slum conditions and the prostitution. Their sale would probably only make things worse. Change the law, he said. We are all responsible for that.

The process of translating principles into programs is as serious as fixing upon the principles in the first place. The choice of means no less than the choice of ends is an exacting matter, freighted with remote and uncertain consequences. For the Christian the application of faith's imperatives is a continuing problem, never ending, never set. This is especially true of social applications, and nowhere more than in economic policy. "No degree of personal piety," said Temple, "and no amount of theological learning will enable a man in the smallest degree to pronounce a competent judgment upon the probable actual effects of any economic action." [1] Nor can we be any more confident of our wisdom in choosing the political means which, like economic means, are necessary to the ends we have chosen! "The Gospel does not give us any help in determining what political methods are likely to lead to the [economic] result we want in any given situation." [2] As a matter of fact, in questions of means rather than ends, "The Christian as such has no more reliable judgment than an atheist." [3]

⚙ PRINCIPLES AND PROGRAMS   Nevertheless, principles require programs. To preach principles in the abstract, without being committed to actualizing them in a definite program, is in fact to be quite unprincipled! As spiritual purposes have to be materialized or embodied, principles have to be concretized or embodied. Both processes of enbodiment are forms of sacramentation. To the question, "Do you believe in faith or in organization?" Temple replied, "Do I believe in my eyes or in my ears? Why not both?" [4] In a personal letter to his friend John Stocks, when Temple was ordained, he said of the faith-versus-works controversy that "anyone who is not interested in 'good works' is *pro tanto* anti-Christ," and the same thing applies to his spirit and to his principles. They all have to *work*. Faith works, spirit matters, principle practices.

Yet even though Temple recognized the authority of technical competence and the need to be humble before expert know-how when choosing ways and means, he knew that we are not excused from responsibility for choosing means of some kind. Talk is cheap. We have to see to it that the policies adopted "conform to and do not ignore or defy right principles." [5] The community's vocation of justice is served through many agencies besides the State. This justice is distributive as well as corrective (penal), and in a democracy the Christian citizen through his influence and franchise is the judge of social principles and also of practical programs.

We need, Temple warned, to keep in mind the difference between the individual Christian and the Church. The Church's task, he thought, is solely in the realm of principle. The Church has "not only the right but the duty" to lay down the principles to govern the whole broad range of social life—even "the conduct of great corporations of people—trade unions, employers' federations, national States and the like—and to exert its influence not only upon the way in which men and women behave in society, but upon the structure of society itself." [6] When it comes to translating the Church's principles into practical or programmatic terms, *that* is the vocation of members of the Church in their role as Christian citizens. Their obligation is to join with others, both Christians and non-Christians, in social-action groups and at the polls, to further the implementation of the Church's principles. (Many non-Christians, he pointed out, will have very much the same aims for their own reasons.) Individual Christians may seriously and reasonably disagree about the best programs. But as Christians they may not disagree about the principles themselves.

"I am convinced," Temple wrote in 1940, "that one reason why the Church has counted for comparatively little in the public affairs of recent times is that its spokesmen have talked a great deal too much about love and not nearly enough about justice." [7] It is too easy, and unimpressive, to talk in generalities. Love is only effective in its works, as the Cross demonstrated. To talk of love without translating it into working principles or practical programs is to imprison it and make it of none effect. Propositions of any kind have to be converted into their operational terms: who does what under which circumstances. Otherwise they are morally ineffective and cognitively meaningless. [209]

It is only when Christian principles are thus sacramented that they seem to some to endanger the *status quo*, stirring up cries of protest against the Church's "interference" in temporal affairs. Just the same, said Temple, the Church by its own declarations of principle, and through the practical action of its members, "is bound to 'interfere' because it is by vocation the agent of God's purpose, outside the scope of which no human interest or activity can fall." [8] Therefore "the Church cannot, without betraying its own trust, omit criticism of the economic order, or fail to urge such action as may be prompted by that criticism." [9]

The problem is to balance expertness and democratic control, getting the best out of both. "We need experts," Temple said, "but their function is to persuade public opinion, not to decide what shall be done; the expert in office is a public menace." (In 1941, the armies of Hirohito, Mussolini, and Hitler gave a dramatic reason for being jealous of losing democracy.) He continued, "I dispute the view that the opinion of 'experts' is alone of value; that notion heads straight for Fascism; democracy is government by public opinion, that is, the opinion of those who are not experts . . . My elder brother is something of an expert on sewage; he would rightly treat me as he formerly did in the schoolroom, if I claimed on theological grounds to correct his technical proposals with regard to a drainage system." [10] Even so, the Church's business is to hold in principle that health takes precedence over economy in such matters.

In opening the Malvern Conference Temple directed attention to the task of converting principles into practice. How, for example, is a company director going to "love" an employee or a customer; how is one State to "love" another? "We lack," he said, "what one school of Greek moralists called the 'middle axioms' —those subordinate maxims which connect the ultimate principles with the complexities of the actual historical situations in which action has to be taken." [11] [210] That was Malvern's work as he saw it, to "supply what among the ancients were called 'middle axioms'—maxims for conduct which mediate between fundamental principles and the tangle of particular problems." [12]

⚙ OPPOSITION He knew perfectly well that he risked trouble with those whose toes might get stepped on. But he also knew that in this "fallen" (struggling) world our only choice is between the kind of troubles we get into because we *don't* put our principles into practice and those we get into because we do! [13] He preferred, as a Christian, the second kind of troubles. The cry that he was aiding and abetting controversy only amused him, when it didn't sadden. Nothing could be, as he said, more controversial than the Word of God, which declares that man is not the center of reality, and puts God and neighbor before self. The Church is supremely controversial in itself, and its respectability in most people's eyes is a sad commentary on its cultural captivity!

Controversy is the growing edge of the creative process, arising inevitably wherever men are engaged in creative, new activity. Because the Church is not engaged enough in controversy, Temple realized, it is commonly regarded with indifference as somehow off in a side eddy of the main stream, irrelevant to human struggles and aspirations. People always quarrel with each other about the things that really matter; no debate means no interest. At Malvern there were divisions: the conservatism of Eliot and others; the Social Credit forces; people like Sidney Dark, editor of the *Church Times,* who held out for a straight socialist policy; Ruth Kenyon's "Christian Corporatism," and Sir Richard Acland's strong plea for common ownership. It was the kind of friendly friction which Temple was confident would give off light. And the setting is not to be forgotten: as the Allied nations fought back at the Axis powers, lovers of democracy were discussing what it was they were fighting for. The language and promises of democracy could be heard everywhere, and men like Temple were determined that *economic* democracy was to be part of the fuller democracy they would win—they were not going to be satisfied any more with only the political side of it.

A National Churchmen's Defense Committee was formed to break down Temple's influence and discredit Malvern. What the Committee lacked in substance and effect it made up in accusations. He was charged with "gravely imperilling the cause of unity among churchmen." They said that his impenitent and "persistent intervention in political affairs" was an attempt "to use the Church for political ends." And, true to form, they declared piously, "We believe that the duty of the Church is not the preaching of a planned economy but the spiritual regeneration of the multitudes so long neglected, and now again being tragically frustrated by the preoccupation of so many of the Church's leaders with social and economic questions, to the side-tracking of the work of the evangelist." [14] That is, of course, the theme song of pietism everywhere.

One member of the Committee, also a leader in the F.B.I. (Federation of British Industries, like the American N.A.M.), re-minded Temple of the Gospel's call, "Seek ye first the Kingdom of God and His righteousness," without showing any sign of understanding that the Kingdom has to do with the present world and with human society, or that the word for righteousness in the Greek text of the gospels means *justice*. (It means more than justice, but it starts with it.)

One thing which perhaps especially annoyed and even fright-ened conservatives was Malvern's urgent call to "cell" activity in the churches, and Temple's approval of it. Even though they were to be formed "upon the basis of common prayer, study and service," the very word carried a picture of Communists boring from within like a fifth column, since the cells were not only for prayer—which pietists always naively assume is "safe"—but for the discussion of the Christian way of life in society.

There is no doubt that Temple and his associates meant busi-ness and were ready to get down to it. Indeed, *business* was pre-cisely their focus. They were looking for the means and methods to the Kingdom-goals of Christian living, and it was clear to them that the whole economic sphere is concerned with means. Man does not, however, live by bread alone. [211] Temple there-fore pounded constantly on the theme that business is not to be judged primarily by efficiency as measured in costs or output, but by whether or not it fosters the real ends of life (joy, peace, brotherhood) for the greatest number of people.[15]

As we have seen, he was sure that economic factors, not only possessions but the economic system itself and its moral standards, are the most influential of all things in the shaping of character. It does no good to call upon men to have loving neighbor-con-cern if their economy is based on self-interest and self-seeking. Indeed, "the impotence of moral advice" always emerges in the face of "perpetual suggestion" from social structures. "It must be remembered that when exhortation and suggestion are at variance, suggestion always wins." [16] [212]

In the preceding chapter we saw how it was Professor Marshall, not Karl Marx, who convinced Temple of the moulding and decisive importance of economics. This was an early form of "the sociology of knowledge" and of the social psychology of later analysts like Karl Mannheim. It is logical to expect that the profit system in vogue will influence character in an un-Christian direction. "And that is precisely what it is doing," said Temple.[17] He urged men to begin to "transform industry from an opponent of Christian influence to an ally." [18] As it is now, things are in the saddle and ride men, but what makes it wrong is not the material things themselves but the putting of last things first and first things last.

"It is clear," said Temple, "that, in the natural order of things, God's order, the object of all industry is the supply of men's wants; in the language of the economist, the consumer is the person whose interest should be supreme in determining the whole process; for his sake goods are produced; and finance comes in as the servant of production. But in our world, goods are produced, not primarily to satisfy the consumer but to enrich the producer. The profit-motive predominates over the service-motive; and this inversion of all that is right has gone so far that now finance controls production instead of production controlling finance, and the consumer, for whose benefit alone production really goes on at all, becomes no more than an indispensable condition of successful business enterprise." [19]

Temple took the reality of sin and self-centeredness too seriously to suppose that profit-seeking entrepreneurs can be relied upon to control themselves. They are often not enlightened enough even for enlightened self-interest. Social control is needed; the only questions about it being how much and in what way. What he called "the new prominence of the State" in our era of history is, he believed, the answer to how we will have to "meet the stark necessity for corporate planning in the economic sphere." [20] The issue is not planning *versus* no planning, but good *versus* bad planning. [213]

❀ A PATTERN OF APPROACH   The Malvern Conference was in some measure a result of Temple's influence, but it also exerted a considerable influence on him. His most succinct treatise in this area was his Penguin book, *Christianity and Social Order*. He prepared the call to Malvern and formulated the Conference findings. Later he chaired the work of a follow-up Committee created by the Conference (including business men, economists, and theologians) and wrote up its report. All of this taken together seems to have given his thought a rather definite structure. In 1940 Bishop Bell of Chichester wrote for Penguin Books (then burgeoning as a new wartime departure in paperbacks) a popular treatment of the political problems of war and government, *Christianity and World Order*.[21]

Temple's Penguin was a kind of companion volume on Christianity and the *internal* social life of the nations, dealing primarily with economic questions. His approach was worked out on five levels. (1) First of all, the source, aim, and norm of everything is love, "for the aim of a Christian social order is the fullest possible development of individual personality in the widest and deepest possible fellowship." [22] This has already been spelled out for us in thorough theological detail. (2) From this norm or standard certain "fundamental principles" come, which Temple divided into primary and derivative. (a) The primary are two basic theological loyalties: i) to God and His purpose, and ii) to man in his dignity, tragedy and destiny. (b) The derivatives are three theological guidelines: i) freedom, ii) fellowship, iii) service. [214] We have also reviewed the meaning with which he invested these principles. On such a foundation he constructed the analysis described in this chapter and the next.

(3) Following his fundamental principles, Temple set out six "objectives" by way of "middle axioms" for a Christian social philosophy. They are: (a) decent and roomy enough housing for all; (b) basic education until eighteen; (c) a secure income adequate to the first objective; (d) everyone to have a voice in control of the enterprise that employs him; (e) a five-day work week and annual vacations with pay; (f) civil liberties of worship, speech, assembly and association. It was to find some such objectives as

these that he called Malvern's meeting. These goals had much in common, naturally, with the report of the economic section of the 1937 Oxford Conference on Life and Work. The main text of the Malvern findings was published as "The Archbishop's Resolution," to which was added Acland's amendment on abolition of private property in capital goods. Temple then urged them upon the critical attention of all, not as the last word on the subject but as a "starting point" for a discussion that must be carried through. The Industrial Christian Fellowship bulletin, *The Malvern Torch,* records that discussion pro and con.

Next (4), in his approach there is a level of concern with means, properly open to non-experts. Temple realized that even given such objectives as the six listed above, the problem of how to order the economy still remains. What structures and policies are to be the means? Without going into the technical details of how to carry them out, he offered six program proposals of his own, consistent with Malvern's findings but going beyond them, to a much more practical level—to the level where proposals of any kind take their real shape, and where nobody can suspect the proposer of trying to avoid being pinned down to the actual meaning of what he proposes.[23]

Whereas, he said, every Christian ought to endorse the norm of love, the five fundamental principles, and the six objectives, these six program proposals he offered only as "suggestions for criticism." They are what he honestly thought should be done and he put them forward as his own personal contribution to the debate about post-war aims. In the face of sometimes vicious protest he was encouraged to do this by various people, among them the economists Pigou and John Maynard Keynes, and his friend, the economic historian, R. H. Tawney. As Temple himself put it, you "cannot get much attention for or discussion of fundamental principles until you can also show people how you think they would work out; and it is only by indicating the specific lines of action that you can claim attention to principles themselves." [24]

Before looking at his program proposals, however, we should recall how two decades of economic security were quickly and revealingly brought to an end by the First World War, to be followed by the Great Depression and the Second World War. This was the background of Temple's thought. In the twenties and thirties there was widespread unemployment of both labor and capital, fluctuating in its extent but victimizing millions. They spoke of "starvation in the midst of plenty" because the system was allowed to run down and come to a halt. This happened even though it was obvious that all the M-factors of prosperity (men, managers, materials, machines, markets—all of the "real" or material requirements) were available, except the sixth M(money). The strong full body could not function, in one figure of speech, because the blood didn't circulate. The business cycle had its recurring phases of prosperity and depression almost as if it were a "natural" phenomenon beyond human control, and there were champions of "free enterprise" who talked darkly of the evils of "interfering with nature" when planning and control were suggested. They even denounced the "pump priming" policies of the British and American governments, whereby purchasing power was poured into the business system from outside through direct relief and public-works jobs. As in treating a Christian Science patient, the system's defenders wanted it to get well, but without either medicine or surgery. (This obstructionism ended, of course, once the threat of Fascism took aggressive military form.)

Temple was sure the war's end would usher in social changes and that the Church should be ready for new days and new ways. He frequently repeated his charge that the system had reversed the "natural" (i.e., logical) order by making consumption depend upon production and production depend upon finance. People were hungry because they had no work, and they had no work because prospects seemed poor for financial profit. He knew something was wrong if people were ill-fed, ill-clothed, ill-housed, and still, in spite of all this crying need, there was no "market" to motivate the business system. The result of trusting to the profit-motive, he said, has been the absurd phenomenon of actual stagnation in the midst of potential prosperity. When full employment and full production were realized immediately, once the system was threatened *by enemies from without,* the artificiality of the depression was exposed to plain view. It showed that depressions could be planned and controlled away, and Temple and men like him were going to see to it that henceforward they would be. What could be done to protect the nation's citizens from invasion could be done to protect them from hunger and cold and the shame of uselessness.

"We must," he said, "begin to organize our industry with the supply of need as the primary aim and the making of profits as entirely incidental. This is a return to the 'natural order' as it exists in the mind of the Creator; but of course it is a reversal of the order natural to the selfishness of men! The Church cannot say how it is to be done; but it is called to say that it must be done." [25]

Within that broad purpose he made, on the fifth level of his approach, six programmatic suggestions: (1) subordination of profits, (2) withering capital investment, (3) employment ownership and control, (4) a socialized monetary system, (5) mutual export trade, and (6) the social use of land. In that order (which was his order, too) we shall briefly examine them in the following chapter. [215]

XV

Economic Reconstruction (2)

His *First Proposal* was for the subordination of private profits. He did not call for their elimination. He was willing to allow private capital a remunerative but not a speculative reward: there has to be both a ceiling and a floor on it. What he wanted was to make profit only one of the factors in enterprise, and to drop it back to a secondary place, putting first things first. His firm opinion was that "there is no harm in the profit motive . . . it is the predominance of the profit motive—the fact that it comes first in the determination of so much of our economic and industrial activity—that is a great evil." [1] [216] Incidentally, Temple was never in the school that favors abrupt expropriation of privately owned capital, not even in his early Oxford days as an out-and-out Socialist. On the other hand, as we shall very shortly see, he did not favor a policy of *buying* them out either.

How did he propose to go about the policy of subordinating profit to other considerations? His answer was to adopt a system of income distribution in business based essentially on the policy of paying into five different and constant reserve funds all profits over "a maximum rate of dividends." This he proposed as the system to be followed in all incorporated enterprises (which are the most important ones in our modern business structure). Their shareholders could rigidly be limited in what they take out of such enterprises, since they enjoy limited liability. [217] This policy, he reminded a B.B.C. audience, "was keenly advocated by the early Christian Socialists when Joint Stock Companies were beginning to be formed. It would have saved the world much evil if their warning had been heeded." [2] In short, he started with a fixed limit on profit distribution to private shareholders. *Temple wanted as much profit as possible, but he intended to use it in a corporate rather than a private way.* He proposed to put as much as possible of the company's income, after payment of costs, into corporate profit, to be distributed between the five reserve funds—all of which would be for common-interest purposes. Those reserves were:

(1) An equalization fund to maintain wages and salaries in bad times. This was to be used to supplement payments for labor, either managerial or manual, if the market falls off or if, for any reason, prices drop enough to endanger the profit margin and reduce labor costs. Labor in this context means the total human contribution, whether of the company's "workers" or their supervisors and administrators. (Salaried people work or labor as hard as wage earners.) In capitalism the owners hire their brains as well as their brawn; and, as employees, managers should share in the fund's protection. (The same principle had been pioneered before Temple's time. In America the Columbia Conserve Company had used it, for example. It lies behind all "elevator" or cost-of-living clauses in labor-management contracts, such as the one between General Motors and the auto-workers' union. It is embodied in a guaranteed annual wage arrangement between the meat packers' union and the Hormel Company in Austin, Minnesota.)

(2) An equalization fund to maintain dividends in bad times. After all, if and as long as any enterprise is using capital borrowed from investors—who are "outsiders" in the sense that they do not give of their own lives by personal participation in the company's struggles and successes—their interests, like the workers' and managers', should be safeguarded against reverses. Some sort of insurance is owing to them.

(3) A sinking fund to amortize or retire the capital debt of the enterprise. With this device a company could slowly and steadily buy out the "money lenders" (investors) involved in its affairs, so that increasingly and finally it would be owned as well as operated by its working personnel. The purpose here is unmistakably revolutionary. Yet it is not violent nor confiscatory revolution, and it works out gradually. The end in view, obviously, is to eliminate the "capitalists" and vest the ownership in the hands of the workers and managers; in short, to reduce the

interest-groups from the usual three to the two active ones only —rather like a producers' cooperative. Temple quoted Paulsen's classic work on Christian ethics: " 'If any will not work neither let him eat' is only another way of saying 'Thou shalt not steal.' " [3] Nevertheless, as long as *borrowed* capital is used, it must be rewarded just as *owned* capital is, with a share of the profits. (This sinking fund was one part of Temple's total scheme for eliminating private capital: the other part will be described in the next chapter, as his second major proposal.)

(4) An extension fund with which to increase the capital equipment of the enterprise. This is a sound principle already employed in orthodox, capitalist business. Enterprise must grow, and to do so there must be a fund from which to purchase additional tools and plant. This fund, incidentally, is not for capital renewal or replacement. That is already taken care of, along with overhead, taxes, and the like. Obsolescence is a fixed operating cost in all sound cost accounts, regardless of whether they are used in a capitalist or socialist system. The issue here has nothing to do with efficiency or sound management and business methods; only with the status and treatment of *private* ownership's claims against enterprise.

(5) A civic development fund. Temple called it the "public service fund." In his view of things, business enterprises must cease to be private in the much too common sense of being selfish. Too many companies concentrate on their own interests in a "business-is-business" spirit, taking no care for the social milieu in which they operate. Their indirect (and usually grudging) contribution to the community by way of taxation is not good enough. Where local political forces can be dominated or intimidated by the financial power of callous business leaders, the people's health and their scenic surroundings are often ruined by pollution of air and water, without a care for civic values. Whole areas are sometimes victimized by indifference even to little things like smoke-abatement devices in mill furnaces. Strip mining (to offer one example) has scarified scenic treasures, making everything ugly for those who live and produce there, while the profits go to owners who are safe and happy in far distant residential areas carefully zoned to protect them. Civic pride and public service should be a responsibility not only of

government but of business itself. It often is, already, with the better type business, but Temple wanted to make the responsibility one of law and economic provision, not leaving it to taxes and the personal taste of company directors. He wanted society to abandon the principle of the "irreducible minimum" in this matter, as in others, and adopt "the maximum attainable."

So much, then, for Temple's method of subordinating profits to other things. First in his audit were such aims as security of income, elimination of lenders in favor of workers and managers, and civic improvement. His five other proposals were equally specific and "operational" in their terms.

⚙ INVESTMENT AND OWNERSHIP   Temple was unwilling to rely upon only one device for subordinating profit—namely, by limiting the profit account and distributing income to other more important funds. He was also determined to eliminate payment of private (in the sense of individual) profits to "outside" investors. His goal was to turn it all into corporate profits, to be distributed to those who personally engaged in giving themselves in the enterprise. He was sure that the elimination of private profit-seeking would contribute to the subordination of profit-seeking as such. And to this end he made a further proposal, his *Second Proposal,* which was for withering-capital investment.

Temple, true to his prophetic practice of applying old and tried principles to new conditions, called for a modern equivalent of the ancient laws of Jubilee and the Sabbatical Year, in the Mosaic and Deuteronomic law. They forbade the purchase and title of land in perpetuity because it belongs to God, the only true landlord, and is granted by Him to His people for their use only. Temple was all for applying the same principle to capital in our industrial economy, now that it is the primary material factor of production, as it was once applied to land in an agrarian economy. "All things come of Thee, O Lord, and of Thine own have we given Thee." Every seventh or sabbatical year whatever had been given over as security for loans had to be returned; every jubilee, or seven times seven years, the slate was wiped clean of the debts themselves. No final alienation of anyone's share of the divine patrimonium was possible.

There must, said Temple, be a similar limit to the levies of money-lenders on the enterprise and labor of others. Twenty years earlier his friend R. H. ("Harry") Tawney, in Chapter VII of his *Acquisitive Society,* had examined the implications of limiting the returns paid on invested capital. "Above all we should seek to end the right to bequeath from generation to generation power to levy private taxes on industry in the form of dividends, thereby placing on industry a burden disproportionate to the benefits received and maintaining a distinct 'shareholding' class in the community." [4] Temple wanted to be sure that "no one, by investing capital alone, can become possessed of a *permanent* and salable right to levy a tax upon the enterprise together with a voice in the control of it. Thus the grip of profit-seeking capital upon industry will be loosened." [5]

The present system of lending and interest-taking, he thought, falls under the condemnation of usury. Indeed, it is worse even than usurious interest, high though that is, since usury has *some* limit to it. But in the private investment system, as now practiced, there is no theoretical limit to the payment which can be taken for the use of money lent to an enterprise. It can go on as a levy *ad infinitum,* and does! Investors or their inheritors have been known to receive back in dividends (loan charges) ten, twenty, thirty times as much as the principal sum invested (lent). The Catholic economic doctrine of the Just Price is logically accompanied by the Prohibition of Usury, as Temple saw it, for there must be a just and fair price for the use of money as there is for consumer goods or for land and its use (rent). [218]

To meet this protest, Harold Laski many years ago proposed what he called "wasting bond investment," whereby investors would receive interest or dividends in gradually diminished amounts proportionate to the principle until all claims are gone. J. L. Benevenisti, the Italian economist, made the same recommendation, and called it "time bond" investment. They were aware, as Temple was, that at five per cent compound interest a loan doubles itself in fourteen years. Sir Josiah Stamp more conservatively proposed to put an end to the interest-dividend exaction by adoption of Rignano's method, by which death duties (inheritance taxes) would be light at the first transfer, heavy at the second, and annihilating at the third. [219]

As in the case of his *First Proposal* for the subordination of profit, in this withering-capital policy Temple's purpose was the gradual but complete elimination of the "capitalist" (investor) from any given enterprise—although, as we have seen, *not* from the system as a whole. He made this proposal in keeping with his announced aim of getting rid of investment for speculation and replacing it with investment for the sake of things produced by the enterprise (goods and services) without ulterior purpose. He was prepared to discuss other methods: "Such may take the form of debentures and be repayable at a certain date; or invested capital may lose a proportion of its value each year until it is extinguished; or the inheritance of it may be curtailed by drastic death duties." [6]

Of these three devices he found the first not genuinely a form of investment at all but much nearer a simple lending transaction, and the third too slow and traumatic. He therefore preferred the second, which he called "withering capital." As for the transition to the new capital-investment policy, he proposed that the State should take over our existing securities on a redemption basis, or that private enterprises voluntarily convert their existing shares into debentures repayable at a certain date when the money could then be reinvested. [220]

Temple's idea was that the value of securities should not be reduced until "the interest paid on any investment is equal to the sum invested," and then it should go down by x amount annually "until the claim of the investor to interest or dividends was extinguished." [7] His notion of how fast this should be done (although such technical actuarial questions were for experts) may be seen in his deliberate shift from a soft to a hard formula. In 1940, he said that shares should lose x per cent of their capital value every year until they are gone, after bearing interest for a period of fifty years. But in 1942 he felt, more radically, that as soon as the interest paid totalled the principal invested, the reductions of face value should begin at once.

Assuming that the interest is five per cent annually, and the annual reduction is ten per cent, on his first (1940) basis a $100 share after fifty years will have brought in $250, or two and a half times its original amount. Being reduced to $90 in its fifty-first year, it would only earn $4.40 in interest or dividends, and so on year after year. When the sixtieth year is reached the share will be worthless and $22.50 in income will have been paid for the withering period. Thus a total return of $272.50 will have been received in sixty years, for the $100 invested.

With the same assumptions as to interest rate, principal, and the percentage of annual value reduction, Temple's second (1942) suggestion allows a total return of only $122.50 after thirty years. For in twenty years the dividends would equal the principal (there being no use here of compound interest). It would then start to wither, and in ten years earn a total of $22.50. A few seconds with a pencil will show that over and above returning the principal the first scheme pays an average of $2.88 per year for its use, and the second scheme only $0.75. Whatever huge profits might be made by the enterprise and paid out in wages, salaries, security benefits, and corporate capital gains, it is clear that investors for income would have no chance to make a killing! (Its similarity to certain forms of insurance endowment contract, already in use, will be apparent.)

One of the first things to arise is the hoary old counter-question, "What is to become of the widows and orphans who depend upon income from investments?" Temple's answer was that contributory social security benefits will be their primary resource, although the limited yield of private investments could augment that income. As far as savings for retirement are concerned, insurance funds of all kinds, the enhanced earnings projected in his system, and corporate retirement plans will suffice. [221] What comes off at one end goes on at the other. Lord Teviot, a leading banker, asked him: "When the dividends of the enormous Church investments in land, mines and house property have reached the original outlay, would the Archbishop be in favor of the capital involved being cancelled?" [8] Ignoring the distortion of his proposal, Temple replied: "I have considered how these changes would affect charitable societies and the like which hold stock as the endowment for their work. Of course I have! How could an Ecclesiastical Commissioner do otherwise? I think they must be prepared for some considerable financial loss." [9] [222]

The conservative weekly *Truth* ran an article about Temple's "shocking ignorance." *The Economist* hedged by saying, without mentioning Temple's name or suggesting that it applied to him, that "comments of churchmen should be properly informed." It did not, however, take issue on any question of fact. *Truth's* editorial came up to par by literalizing the Parable of Talents (finding its meaning within its field of image) as if it were meant to say that people should invest money and demand the utmost in return, usuriously. It accused Temple of implying, therefore, that the Parable is "pernicious nonsense," and that he wanted "some kind of communist world." [10] The use of epithets in social debate, instead of descriptive terms, has changed very little in the past twenty years.

✿ LABOR AND SOCIAL CONTROL The third of Temple's economic suggestions, his *Third Proposal,* was for industrial or economic democracy. He expected and wanted that some of the war-time controls on enterprise would be lifted, once the fighting ended. But not all, and certainly not the principle of control itself. He was convinced that if "equality of sacrifice" was a sound principle when the nation is at war against an alien power, "equality of interest and control" should obtain in the war against unemployment and poverty. His guiding principle was that personal rights are more important than property rights, and that power cannot go to property—it has to go to people.

In both America and England during the Second World War the nations, as true natural communities, had united all classes and parties in the direction and control of wealth production. It was industrial democracy in a measure, and for a while. There were price-controls and management-labor-public boards in the planning and administering of the nation's resources and manufacturing. They were called "industrial councils" at the upper and broader levels of inter-industrial policy-making, "working committees" in the local concerns. There was no question about the full participation of both labor and management with public authorities. Temple wanted to make that policy permanent. He insisted, "Every citizen should have a voice in the conduct of the business or industry which is carried on by means of his labour." [11]

This meant that labor unions were to cease being conflict organizations or bargaining agencies, as in the trade-union and capitalist conception, and become partners or participants in the economy's ownership, control, and profits. (He would have approved the profit-sharing agreement between American Motors and the United Auto Workers.) His notion of economic democracy called for a just distribution of the economic powers as well as the political powers of society. He was sure that no society, in terms of initiatives and controls, could continue very long to be democratic in the political sector and not in the economic (England's problem), any more than the reverse could continue (as in Russia). Democracy is either advancing or retreating.

In concrete terms, Temple called for wealth production under the multipartite direction of labor, management, private capital (if and as much as it takes part), and the public consumers. [223] (His economic pluralism generally favored private enterprise in the small-scale yardstick and innovative fields, cooperative or corporately owned enterprise in light industries and most heavy industries, and State-owned and managed enterprises in such vital industries as public transport and some of the basic commodities like coal and oil. The focus of his proposals for reconstruction was on the cooperatives.)

Temple's fear of bureaucracy caused him to favor what he called "functional and regional devolution," aimed at putting the planning and controlling of all industries in the hands of their own personnel, and to hold down all central or government coordination of controls (Americans would say Federal) to a minimum. Rather like the Guild Socialists and the system now in Yugoslavia, he wanted a national economic council to legislate industry's own affairs, subject to Parliamentary (Congressional) veto, and local councils to administer production policies. He was convinced that state socialism (communism) is inherently a centralized bureaucracy, and therefore undesirable.

In making his plea for economic democracy, Temple always tied it to his proposals for withering-capital investment, because they were aimed at eliminating the outside investor and vesting ownership of an enterprise in the workers and managers whose labor of head and hand carry it on. "The contribution of labor must, equally with capital, and with still fuller right, carry a title to representation on the board of directors. The investor gets his interest; the workman his wages. There is no reason why the former should also get control and the latter not. It is on the whole more reasonable that labor should hire capital than that capital should hire labor, because capitalism can exist without capitalists but labor cannot exist without laborers." [12] To this he added that there should nevertheless be representation for those who invest their money without taking part in the labor, "*so long as* the concern is making any use of investments earning interest."

Temple's aim was to make this last proviso good for no longer than is necessary. He wanted the "so long as" to be as short as possible. Like the Malvern Report, Temple was inclined "to leave open what might be the most vital question whether or not private ownership of industrial capital is to survive." [13]

The purpose of his plan was to minimize outside ownership, maximize inside or corporate ownership. (How to distribute it between the people in the industry he left to management experts and democratic choice.) But he laid great stress on the *personalist* principle that people are more important than property, and that what creates property or proprietary rights in wealth is the mixing of the person with the material things. His personalist-sacramental theology set him dead against the classical, capitalist notion that labor is a commodity, to be bought and sold and paid for by the impersonal working of supply and demand in a "free market"—as if it were a mere *thing* like the other factors in production. Even *if* profit and rent should be fixed in that way, he said, we cannot fix wages (or salaries) impersonally because labor, whether manual or managerial, is always personal. People are subjects, not objects. [224]

On this basis Temple sought to vest both ownership and control in the persons who carry on a business, "mixing" themselves with it, squeezing out all impersonal money-lenders as much and as fast as possible. He was convinced that the active employees would have all the brains, skill, and brawn needed. Enterprise as he saw it needs all the capital it can get, but it does not need "capitalists." [225]

We have, he thought, allowed the industrial system too often to treat wage-earners "as only part of the *means* of production." This he deplored. He proposed to put all business on a "profit-sharing" basis; for if property ownership is good for personality, "then it must be good for all persons to own property," and a condition in which so many do not own any at all calls for correction.[14] There are too many people "for whom the bottom is liable to fall out of life through no action of their own," due to an economic system over which they exert no control nor any real knowledge as to its condition.[15]

Nobody wants to return to the feudalism of the Middle Ages, but in that system people at least enjoyed some basic security. The principles of enfeoffment saw to it that a peasant could not be alienated from the land, which was the basic means of production. Prophetically, Temple wanted to bring the feudal principle up to date, replacing the contract basis of labor with a status basis. He was determined that labor should cease to be a factor and become a partner, ending its existence as a bargaining-from-outside force, to become integrated in the ownership structure itself.

❀ MONEY AND CREDIT   Temple's *Fourth Proposal* was for the socialization of money, taking it out of private hands entirely. The heart of the proposal is "social creation of credit." [16] It is important, therefore, to grasp his concept of money in general and credit in particular.

Money, Temple explained, circulates in two forms: credit and currency. Currency may be either in coins or in certificates (bills). Credit instruments are of different kinds: bank drafts (or checks), IOU's, discount papers, bills of exchange, bank overdrafts. But the important thing to grasp about money (the sixth M, *supra*) in our modern, high-energy, high-productivity economy is that the total volume of currency is less than one-tenth of the money in circulation. All the rest of it, nearly all, is credit. Since money is the life-blood of the economic system—circulating or carrying values from the point of production to the point of consumption—credit, therefore, is the key to prosperity and capital

growth. [226] "No scheme of publicly organized production can
be satisfactory apart from national control of credit." [17] It
seemed to Temple absurd and ridiculous that even in wartime,
"when the nation needs credit for carrying out its purpose it
should borrow that credit from one section of itself and pay
interest on it." [18]

Money serves in two ways. It is first of all a medium of exchange or common tender which obviates the need of directly
bartering one real economic good or service for another. But it
is also a storehouse of value, representing saved labor and production which can be spent (exchanged for somebody else's
labor) at one's own convenience. Because of its great instrumental importance, therefore, even though it is only a symbol
or token, money tends for many people to become valuable in
itself.

Temple felt that Thomas Aquinas was right to insist that
money is only an instrument or means to wealth, not wealth itself; it is artificial wealth, not the true end or real wealth of economic activity. So far has this sin of confusing means and ends
gone, in a money-centered (pecuniocentric) culture, that the con-
tainer of the official standard weights of gold and silver in the
vaults of the Bank of England is called the Pyx! It contains the
most widely acknowledged "reserved sacrament" of our society.

In fact, of course, the precious metal base upon which bills are
supposedly circulated by the banks is disappearing. America has
been "off" the gold standard for a long time, and England's
sterling support is little more substantial. But even so, the
amount of money in the form of certificates and bills—though
the piles of it in the teller's cage may seem vast to a poor man—
is so small that it means nothing in the monetary system compared to the credit in circulation. "For the greater part of our
business is carried on by means of credit." [19] But of even greater
significance than the relative unimportance of currency compared to credit is the fact that most of the credit itself is in the
form of bank loans or overdrafts. Most checks are drawn on loans
made by the banks themselves, not on deposits, and most of the
loans represent no deposits at all, by anybody.

In the sixteenth and seventeenth centuries goldsmiths and
silversmiths in England and the Low Countries accepted deposits

of precious specie for safekeeping, allowing their owners to write notes of withdrawal on them to others. These were the first bank cheques. After a while the opportunities of commercial and industrial expansion began to outstrip the supply of precious metal available for "financing" the cheques drawn, and the smiths started giving depositors permission to write notes for more gold and silver than they actually had to pay out. It was usually a good risk because note-holders would ordinarily not ask all at the same time for the actual metal itself ("a bank run"), and also because the new economy (merchant capitalism) was growing in a dynamic and aggressive way.

It has been centuries since the Western economy was willing to restrict its rate of growth to the amount of new capital it could buy with money saved out of previous production. Most of the money used for capital growth and ventures is supplied by the banking system. However, most of this money is based not on deposits or savings, but on the potential capacity of society to produce real wealth equivalent in value to the loans—to the hypothecated money.

So: most of our money is credit-money, and most of the credit-money is money *ex nihilo*. The man in the street may suppose that what banks lend is what has been entrusted to them for safekeeping, that behind every loan is a deposit. But not so. [227] To use the language of William Patterson, when the Bank of England was founded in 1694, "The bank hath benefit of interest on all monies which it creates out of nothing." All banks, especially the commercial banks and underwriting houses, carry on this "Dutch finance." [228] The meaning of this, Temple said, is that credit-money, the life-blood of our common economic activity, is in the hands of private profit-seekers (banks are private enterprises), and it represents nothing they have earned or saved or acquired in any other way. What gives our money its value and integrity is the capacity of the whole community's labor and brains to produce *real* wealth to offset it. It is in fact *social* credit, said Temple, and should be socially, not privately controlled. And the terms and conditions for sound economic borrowing by producers should not be set by the non-moral, supply-and-demand system of profiting from scarcity. The Just

Price for money is what it costs to produce it, as in the case of real wealth. [229]

There is a shrewd old saying in verse:

> God out of naught creates us and hence
> Demands our love, Creation's recompense.
> The banks create from naught with equal zest,
> And in return ask only interest.

Temple was sure that we ought not to be repaying to banks what it is not theirs to lend. He pointed out that for three hundred years now no government has allowed private citizens to mint money in the form of currency, and declared that we have "reached a stage where the private manufacture of credit is become an anachronism." [20] His was no crank attack on banks, like Father Coughlin's. "We all have reason," he argued, "to be grateful for the public spirit and integrity with which our banking system has been administered. There would not be a proverbial phrase 'as safe as the Bank of England' if its management had not been so conspicuously sound." [21] Nevertheless, private credit-creation must go.

First of all, "The State must resume the issue and cancellation of every kind of money." [22] In his view this did not entail the abolition of banks; quite the contrary. Their function—their proper function—as the bookkeeping agencies of enterprise and exchange is a vital and necessary one, and he wanted to convert them from profit-making into public-service institutions. "I cannot see why anything more should be paid for the service than the actual administrative cost, which a very high authority has told me is perhaps one-eighth of one per cent." [23] The bookkeeping of the banks is a service that should be remunerative, i.e., cover the rent, salaries, and materiel involved; but it should not be speculative or contingent. He was advised that on this basis interest charges should be 0.12%, not 3 to 5%. So be it. [230] Whether they should be "owned or worked by the State or should be Public Utility Corporations is open to question." He added, "My own preference is for the latter wherever the method can be followed." But in any case, if the first five M's of *real* wealth and *real* demand are available, there need never be a lack of the sixth—the artificial monetary token.

"It may be that there are other and better ways of attaining our object. But our object is clear: it is to reverse the reversal of the natural order, which is characteristic of our phase of civilization; the natural order is that consumption should control production and production should utilize finance." [24]

☀ TRADE AND PRICES Temple's *Fifth Proposal* was for international mutual-export trade. He could see ahead to the trend toward regional and even broader markets. He knew that such recent programs as preferential trade agreements and economic unions (like the European Common Market) were sure to come. [231] To bring an end as soon as possible to economic nationalism was as important to him as ending the national sovereignty of the past era. He hoped that "federal union" would grow by development out of common economic and collective security interests, rather than by being contrived or imposed. "It is quite unreasonable and contrary to Natural Order to make political and economic frontiers identical." [25]

To bring this *Fifth Proposal* about, "commerce must become avowedly an exchange of goods for mutual advantage, in which all search for what is called a favorable balance of trade is repudiated." It seemed logically obvious to him that "the pursuit by every nation of a favorable balance of trade is inevitably a source of conflict; for if the balance is favourable to one it must be unfavourable to another." [26]

Past and present national tariff policies aiming at a favorable balance and the "protection" of domestic businesses have been based on what Temple believed to be both a fallacy and a specially evil feature of the capitalist past. The favorable balance doctrine seemed to him both immoral and imprudent. For it is not only "an attempt to gain advantage at a loss to others" (what St. Paul called the mind of the flesh), it is also actually a policy which loses real wealth for the sake of money—and for the power it gives over others. Of the favorable balance he said, "Why so called it is hard to see; for the phrase means giving something for nothing, not getting something for nothing. It is possible only by the export of capital, i.e., involving the other nation in debt." [27]

The mercantilist traders and adventurers of the seventeenth century were interested in gold and silver specie, not in capital or consumer goods. They ignored the teaching that money is properly only a means to wealth and must not be sought in order to gain power over others. A "successful" trader nation was therefore the one that managed to ship abroad more goods than it imported in return, so that the "unsuccessful" nation had to make up the difference by handing over bullion or by giving some of its capital away. [232] This is, of course, a nutshell definition of imperialism. And it is structural sin because it has turned a means, money, into an end.

As an interim measure Temple proposed that the nations adopt a policy of imposing tariffs on imports, but that they were to be calculated to raise the price of such imports only to the level they would cost if produced at home—and no more. He was for neither Free Trade nor Protection. [233] This, he hoped, would prevent the undercutting of home industries operating on decent standards, and also raise standards in lands where labor is cheap and exploited. He called this an "interim" policy because he looked forward to the time when matters of commercial policy, as well as migration and communications, would no longer be decided by national governments but by an international authority.[28] [234] "There is obviously no middle way between International Anarchy . . . and some form of Federation."

⚙ LAND AND USE   The *Sixth* (and last) of the economic proposals on Temple's agenda was the socialization of land: a policy of "occupying ownership." Going back to something he had said about the ownership of shares (his *Second Proposal*), we should recall how he was influenced by the ancient Israelitic law prohibiting the purchase of land in perpetuity. This was a point he made frequently and sharply, even though he realized that land has taken a place to the rearward as far as economic importance is concerned.

"There are four requisites for life which are given by the bounty of God—air, light, land and water. These exist before man's labor is expended upon them, and upon air and light man can do nothing except to spoil them. I suppose if it were possible to have established property rights in air, somebody would have done it before now, and then he would demand of us that we should pay him if we wanted to breathe what he called *his* air. Well, it couldn't be done, so it hasn't been done. But it could be done with land, and it has been done with land: and, as it seems to me, we have been far too tender towards the claims that have been made by the owners of land and of water as compared with the interests of the public." [29] [235]

Having said this much, he added that "we come back to the great Christian principle, that the right which attaches to ownership is a right of administration, but should never be a right to exclusive use. That is a principle deep and constant in the old Christian tradition about property, but we have so largely forgotten that property is, in its own nature and of necessity, a social institution and a social fact, that we have ignored the rights of society over against the rights of those to whom it entrusts ownership, and we must redress the balance." [30]

He never lost sight of the principle in the English common law that the land belongs to the King as representing the whole community. [236] This means that "so-called landowners hold the use of the land but not absolute dominion over it." [31] This principle is a part of the American Constitution, in the rule of eminent domain. "What we in these days call private property in land," Temple reminded his readers, "was not recognized as such in the Old Testament. The land was held in trust by stewards as the property of the Lord and had to be administered accordingly." [32]

In all of this there are three basic points to be grasped: (1) The only property right is one of administration: ownership or title is not exclusively or perpetually private. In moral theology it is said that no human rights are perfect. (2) Men hold their

wealth by "stewardship"—it is God's by right, not theirs. [237]
(3) The claims of the community come first, not those of the
individual. Temple on this basis proposed a policy of occupying
ownership. He had in mind, among other things, the abuse or
injustice of unearned increments in land values. Landowners
can and commonly do hold out land, not using it productively
or serviceably, until the adjacent properties have been developed
and en-valued by the human enterprises of others—somebody
else's tears, sweat, toil. Then they reap the benefits in higher sales
value. [238]

As a remedy Temple proposed three things. First, there should
be a gradual (and compensated) transfer of all land in cities to
society, "for there is little service, if any, that the owner of
urban sites can render which cannot be as well or better rendered
by the public authority." [239] He added: "There is no reason
why we should pay certain citizens large sums of money for
merely owning the land on which our cities are built." [33] Second,
as to rural lands, he proposed to leave them in private hands on
a sort of leasehold basis, their continued possession depending
on their satisfying minimum standards of productive use. This
occupying private ownership of *rural* land he thought would
give the best results—better than nationalization. And in any
case, "It should be illegal for an owner, as distinct from a pur-
chaser, to mortgage or to burden it with debt except by license
from the Minister of Agriculture." [34]

A striking example of his shrewdness is seen in Temple's proposal about land taxes; namely, that they should be according
to use. At present if an owner improves the soil, builds good
buildings, and the like, he is penalized by a higher land or
property tax. If he lets it lie unimproved, his tax is low. Temple
proposed to reverse this, rewarding rather than penalizing the
good user. And he had a very effective device to guarantee that
neither the landholder nor the community would be taken in by
false evaluation. "The owner," said Temple, "should be called
upon to value the land himself, the State having the power to
purchase it at the figure named or levy a tax upon it, as may
seem more expedient in each case." [35]

❋ CONCLUSION   George Orwell in *The Lion and the Unicorn,* a wartime book not as famous as *Nineteen Eighty-four* or *Animal Farm,* insisted that England can only be saved by Englishmen, not by imitation Russians. It was not the least of Temple's qualities that he was so essentially English, and that what he proposed as new departures were so English. Churchill was half American and loved histrionics. Lloyd George was a Celt with the usual virtues and defects. Temple was, *par excellence,* English.

He made no dogmatic or absolutistic claims for his practical proposals. He did mean to see that there was no pussyfooting about his own views! "If all these proposals were adopted, a great transformation of our social and economic structure would result. Yet this would involve no breach of continuity. It would be transformation by adaptation, not by destruction. Moreover, this method of approach to the whole problem has the advantage that the various suggestions can be adopted separately and in varying degrees of completeness. No violent revolution is involved; no rigid system would be imposed." [36]

After his controversial address to the Bank Officers' Guild (February 4, 1943), the *New Statesman and Nation* commented: "In addressing a trade union audience the Archbishop might seem to begin with a number of handicaps; Rugby, Balliol, a Double First, President of the Oxford Union, Fellow of Queen's College, Headmaster of Repton; born in an episcopal palace— he has, in fact, spent a large part of his life in episcopal palaces —his only parochial experience four years at St James, Piccadilly; what art, it might be asked, could enable a man with so abundant a lack of first-hand experience of bread-and-butter problems and such a very prosperous and secluded background to hold his audience in the hollow of his hand for a solid hour? He has not a single rhetorical trick; only an occasional touch of humour. The answer is that people do respond to knowledge and sincerity, to precision and lucidity of statement, and to the force of reason. It restores faith in the power of reason to see an audience moved by it." [37]

XVI

War and the Sanctity of Life

Temple took the view that there is a place for pacifists in society, and he thanked God for their witness. He also thanked God that there are not too many of them! Just as a few Christians are called or have a "vocation" to withdraw from civil society to become nuns or monks, so he thought some may be called in conscience to withdraw from civic responsibility for the national defense. The chosen vocation of the pacifist is to witness to the radical, dangerous, and sacrificial demands of love. And since in this "fallen" world we all have to live by compromise, their witness is vital because it keeps *what we are compromising* vividly before us. They are, indeed, confronting us with the thing —the *only* thing—that Christians can fight for. Vocational pacifism is therefore legitimate and even precious to us all.

Each citizen must decide for himself ("and he is not infallible") whether he can conscientiously kill or be killed for his country. [240] But if he decides to be a conscientious objector, he "must not complain if the State treats him as a criminal; it treated his Master so." [1] In the Second World War, remembering how some of his conscientious objector friends (for example, Stephen Hobhouse) had been mistreated in the First War, he held the line of government policy firmly in their favor. Percy Hartill—Archdeacon of Stoke and a leading pacifist—testified that, although Temple was "the strongest theological opponent of pacifism he was tremendously loved and respected in pacifist circles." [2] With another pacifist, Canon Raven of Christ's College, Cambridge, he wrote a joint statement (1943) in which they agreed that war is organized and deliberate sin. "All war is the devil's work." [3] And for his own part Temple scornfully repudiated the charge that pacifists are trying to evade suffering and danger.

❂ THE PACIFISTS' CASE He could not agree with Raven, who argued that war is never a lesser evil, and he tried (probably without much effect) to argue that a Christian pacifist has more in common with a Christian warrior than with a non-Christian pacifist. He was ready to agree that we cannot fight for Christianity, but Raven would not agree with him that we *may* fight for a civilization in which the Gospel is at least being given a chance. "No positive good," Temple said, "can be done by force; that is true. But evil can be checked and held back by force." [4] It is not power itself that is evil, but the motive with which men use it that may be evil: "There is only one strong argument against the use of force; it is that none of us are (sic) good enough to use it without moral deterioration." [5]

Temple went on the assumption that the most to be claimed for our civilization, as against the goal of the Axis powers, was that our society is at least Christian "in a rudimentary sense." [6] He minced no words: "The British pacifist at this moment is not merely taking no part; he is weakening the British capacity to fight and so far is increasing Hitler's chance of victory. He may be right to do this; but let us—and let him—face the fact that he is doing this." [7]

Christians in the nuclear age may now question with Canon Raven whether war is the lesser of two evils. The global delivery potential of the new military technology and its weapons of mass extermination have so altered war as a means to good ends, in a nihilistic way, that the issue must at least be re-examined. But present-day "nuclear pacifists" are really following Temple's relativist principle—only now they are having to weigh a different set of evils, radically different from the relatively mild weapons that were weighed in Temple's ethical scales. [241] Had Temple lived to see our weapons of mass extermination, he might well have joined forces with the war resisters; but it would have been on grounds of relative and pragmatic judgment and not because of any pacifist claim that force and violence, as such, are inherently and intrinsically evil.

❀ THE JUST WAR Temple's ethical relativism insured that he would take his stand with traditional Christian ethics and moral theology. In short, he accepted the Just War doctrine. He did *not* accept the Crusade or Holy War; he saw, as Lincoln did, that in war men are tempted to *use* God, whereas they ignore Him in peace. Under this principle Christians could conscientiously fight or give military service if they had honestly assured themselves that (1) a legitimate government was conducting the war, (2) all other methods of settling the dispute at stake had failed or were impracticable, and (3) enough good could be gained to outweigh the evils of war, so that the end would justify the means. On this ground he concluded that England's end in both the great wars with Germany and her allies (1914 and 1939) was good enough to justify the evil means. "It is the spirit of resentment, not the act of resistance, that our Lord condemns." [8] [242]

To those who narrowed down the moral issue to the sheer question of taking life, he replied that life, physiological life, is not sacrosanct. This notion, Temple said, is Hindu or Buddhist, not Christian. The martyrs were not wrong, nor are heroes who risk their own lives to take or defend the lives of others. It is not necessarily wrong to give or take life—all depends on the circumstances. He held that *"as compared with some other things, the loss of life is a small evil; and if so, then, as compared with some other things, the taking of life is a small injury."* [9]

Quite correctly he pointed out that the Sixth Commandment was never meant as a prohibition of war, and that it says "Thou shalt do no murder"—i.e., no unlawful killing, as the Prayer Book version is careful to render it—not "Thou shalt not kill." It is, he said, not animal or physical life that is sacrosanct or sacred absolutely, but *personality.* [243] "Be not afraid of them that kill the body, and after that they have nothing that they can do" (Luke 12:4). And if the loss of life is not the greatest injury to suffer, it is not the greatest to inflict. To enslave the mind or spirit is worse. "Taking life should be the last resort; but justice is more sacred than life." [10]

In his discussion in *Is Christ Divided?* Temple contended that the pacifists' call to the nation to submit to aggression, whether against itself or against a neighbor-nation, rather than use an evil means of defense like war, is a false personification of the nation. "It is vain to ask of nations, such as they are, that they love one another." [11] For groups "the way of love lies through justice." [12] [244] (Once in discussion with Temple some pacifist students committed themselves to this social version of Ruskin's "pathetic fallacy." They told him that England should in Christian sacrifice prefer the interests of other countries to her own. Temple asked them if they were prepared, then, to tell a union committee it should prefer the company's interest to the workers'. They were not, of course. Temple applied his "conditional justification of war" to inter-class conflict as well as to inter-national conflict—as many anti-union and conservative patriots would not.[13])

While it is entirely Christian for any individual to sacrifice his own welfare out of sacrificial love for others, Temple would add that such love is a personal act and not appropriate to a national community of diverse and separate interests. Only if a nation were united in the decision to surrender to an aggressor, so that it was a truly voluntary sacrifice, and not imposed on some by others, could it be right to submit to an unjust aggression. (Here, presumably, is a case in which his reservations about the principle of formal or majority democracy might be set aside.)

Justice is a matter of distributing love lovingly, among *all* whose freedom and security are at stake, and in aggression by force and violence this has almost always called for a war of defense rather than submission. (It does not, he thought, call for wars of aggression.) In 1939, it was not a question of showing love to the Germans, but to Germans, Poles, Czechs and French all at once! And furthermore, said Temple, we should not be immobilized when we face up honestly to the fact that no nation ever goes to war entirely guiltless, either of past wrongs or present selfishness. [245] If a house is burning with a child trapped inside, we cannot wait until we have purged ourselves of a desire for glory or gain before we rush in.

While he admitted all natural communities (such as the na-

tion) "are animated by a measure of corporate egoism more intense than that which animates the component members or
individuals," he refused to admit that this is a necessary trait
of all societies. In any case it is one which must be acted *with*
rather than *in spite of*.[14] He was willing to concede to the pacifists that "there is urgent need for fresh examination of the limits
of political obligation." The developments since Hiroshima and
Nagasaki would certainly have intensified his grounds for a
review.[15] It is more the business of the State to serve its citizens
than theirs to serve the State, for they have an eternal destiny
and the State has not.

❂ WAR AND PEACE   War is a moral evil, not a cosmic one.
While inhumane, it is yet human. Temple had no patience with
the fatalism lurking behind such phrases as "war broke out," as
if it were a dreadful disease that befalls us through no fault of
our own, and as if it were an irrational interruption of peace
which requires to be ended so that peace can resume its normal
course. Peace, he said, is not the absence of war but the presence
of justice. It is not "natural" to selfish men and has to be *made:*
hence "Blessed are the peacemakers," not the peaceful—for
nothing is worse than to cry "Peace, Peace" when there is no
peace.[16] Peace in the sense of the absence of war may be sought
most earnestly by, for example, financiers and commercial interests which are entirely unmoved by the ideal of fellowship.
Compared to certain goals and motives, some wars might be
nobler than some kinds of peace.[17]

No. Theologically, said Temple, war is a divine judgment on
us. God doesn't *send* war to punish us for our war-inducing
selfishness and fear, but He has endowed His creative process with
a kind of Law of Harvest of which the prophets spoke, under
which what men sow—individually or collectively—that do they
reap. God doesn't manipulate history unpredictably by whim or
anger, but he *judges* it through the operation of His own cause
and effect in the moral order. Intrigue and faction and exploitation and indifference bring on war; and the fact that they do is

evidence that love is the principle of the moral order. The Christian theology of war is that the sovereignty of love means judgment as well as consolation, and that it promises the ultimate doom of all that stands in its way.[18]

In 1914 when people charged that the World War was proof of the bankruptcy of Christianity, Temple replied that, on the contrary, it was evidence of new vitality and an advance in Christian insight. It showed that Europe was rediscovering that if nations were Christian there would be no war! This, he said, had been forgotten since Constantine. What was breaking down, he pointed out, was a civilization which was not Christian—and therefore one that was vulnerable to attack by either moral and/or military forces. The whole point about the spread of communism was that it had a moral vacuum to fill.

The only true victory, according to his understanding, is the victory of love by the method of the Cross. "The 'non-resistance' to evil which is enjoined upon us that we may be the true children of the heavenly Father is no mere amiability which accepts an injury rather than face unpleasantness. It is the method of active love." But until love has no need any more to distribute itself through justice, and no reason to calculate and share its benefits, there may be need of force for the neighbor's sake and for constructive self-defense. When men said that Christians are impractical dreamers because of their law of love, Temple replied, "If so, Christ was a deluded fanatic and his religion a fraud." And if they said that "you can't change human nature" (an ancient postulate of every kind of reaction), he replied, "No, but God can. Christ was born and rose again and sent the Holy Spirit to do that very thing." [19]

✸ WAR AND PRAYER In debates with both pacifists and jingo patriots, Temple often bewildered his antagonists by insisting that "it is the simple fact that Christians who are sincere in their loyalty to Christ are united across all divisions." [20] To the pacifist, waging war against a fellow Christian or any child of God was morally impossible; to the jingo, an enemy could not be a Christian and was regarded as at least sub-human. Neither view, in Temple's opinion, took full enough account of the tragic relativity of human understanding, or of every man's obligation to do the right as he is given to see it.

When Christians were scoffed at for praying against each other, English Christians against German Christians, and so on, he met the issue head-on by saying, "It is a test of our discipleship in prayer whether a patriotic German Christian could join us in our prayer." [21] In taking this line he was, of course, simply building his "Gethsemane" principle—that authentic prayer aims at our being done with as God wants, not at God doing for us what we want. And this he called the prayer of a brave man, not of a coward. It is the prayer of a man ready to give his life rather than anxious to save it. In war we are to test our prayer by the pattern (Lord's) prayer, praying not for our glory, but the hallowing of God's name; not for the success or even the preservation of our country, but for the coming of His Kingdom; not for the fulfillment of our hopes, but for the doing of His will.

"But prayer for our victory is prayer for the enemy's defeat; we must desire that; it is, as I believe, our duty to fight for precisely that; but because here satisfaction to us means frustration of purpose to other of God's children, we must not in His presence assume the function of judge." [22] Perhaps "advocate" would have been a better metaphor. Temple's point was that when we are in conscience bound to push a cause, we still know we may be wrong and that only God truly knows: therefore we may and must plead our case with other men. We can only humbly and hopefully lay it out before Him. Before that Judge, unlike all others, there is no argument.

When various people (including Archbishop Garbett) reasoned with apparent logic that if you are not convinced of the justice of your cause you can't ask God to back it nor fight for it yourself, but if you are convinced you must so pray and fight, Temple's reply was that they simply misconceived the nature of prayer. It is not, he insisted, a way to enlighten God or win Him over to the side of justice! Further, they were forgetting the difference between God's judgment and that of a human court. We are not, he pointed out, to suppose that a war is a puppet show danced and dangled by God—at the end of which He gives the victory to the just cause and defeat to the wrong. History is not a puppet show, with God always guaranteeing the certain triumph of righteousness. Instead, alas, the fact of human freedom often entails innocent suffering and the frequent victories of might over right. Christians in war, he said, are called to "the hardest of all tasks; to fight without hatred, to resist without bitterness, and in the end, if God grant it, to triumph without vindictiveness." [23]

❂ BEYOND THE NATION   In Temple's sweep-view of history one of the post-modern world's traits is the trend toward trans-national community. He saw the medieval era of European life dominated by the great experiment of a trans-national, imperial integration of society—both civilly and ecclesiastically—in Emperor and Pope on the Roman model. Local lords and bishops were not all-powerful in their own domains, but answerable to an authority from outside which could intervene anywhere between any king and his subjects, if they needed help. The feudal structure started to decay about 1300 A.D. and its collapse was complete by 1500 A.D. Then the modern period of nationalism started, and now it, too, is coming (dialectically) to its close.[24]

For all his realistic appreciation of the nation-state, Temple felt it was at bottom atomistic and ultimately doomed. It has become too great a limitation and restriction of fellowship and unity. After the First World War he looked at the League of Nations as marking "the end of this horrible idolatry of the State into which Christendom slipped with the decline of the Middle Ages." [25] *Corruptio optimi pessima:* the corruption of the best is worst. Nationalism is now becoming, in its turn, the greatest threat to democracy. It is increasingly driven to try to be the omnipotent State, and that is democracy's Achilles' heel. Nationalism has helped democracy in the past; now it may kill it.[26] When the first steps toward a wider community faltered (the League's eclipse by the Second World War) he began at once to add his voice to the appeal for the United Nations, in rebuff to cynics and isolationists and jingoes everywhere.

The problem for Christian statesmanship, indeed for statesmanship of every kind, is to find how the corporate egoism of nations can be subordinated to the welfare of the family of mankind. Temple reduced the strategic essentials to three. First, "Every nation should abandon its claim to be judge in its own cause." Let Security Councils and international courts administer a rule of law! Second, since fear is the chief source of danger, the competition in arms must be ended. "It is not more wicked to kill men with a big gun than with a small gun," but knowledge that rival nations are expanding their weaponry creates panic, and especially (this was in 1935) all private trade in arms must stop. [246] Third, the principle of collective security must be accepted, for as Maxim Litvinov was then saying, peace in a technical era is indivisible.

Here we can see that he was appealing to the "Social Contract" motive, to prudential sacrifice of unilateral power for the sake of security, even though his theological conviction was that the nations *are* a family in "natural fact." And if individuals are to be defended by and must defend their nations ("patriotic loyalty"), so single nations are to be defended by and must defend the world-community ("a collective security").[27] And he foresaw not only political integration but economic, too. The same forces will sooner or later weld economies together, as in such common market treaties as have already developed in Europe, beginning but certainly not ending with them—stretching even across the Atlantic! [28]

He was no great admirer of Tennyson's poetry, yet every English schoolboy was required to know it. And he often recalled how in *Locksley Hall* Tennyson had prophetically (as early as 1842!) foreseen the "Parliament of Man, the Federation of the world"—coming as a frightened retreat from aviation and the horror of battles between the "air navies" of the nations. [247] Temple lived to see these horrors, and civilization's first tentative gestures of self-defense. He knew that "dominating all other concerns today is the supreme issue of Peace or War." [29]

XVII

Postscript

In the same way that Matthew Arnold always insisted that literature's task is to be a criticism of life, Temple applied the equivalent rule to theology, too, and cut his cloth accordingly. Like Joseph Butler, Richard Hooker, and F. D. Maurice, he was a "constructive" theologian more than a "biblical," "historical," or "systematic" theologian, concerned to represent his Christian heritage by speaking *to* the questions and conditions of modern times. He mournfully observed that, in his own language, too many theologians spend blameless lives giving correct answers to questions no one wants to ask. His sympathies were plainly with Mr. Ordinary Jones, and he never forgot a college student's remark about Bishop Gore (whom Temple loved and admired), "I could see his mind was an awfully jolly merry-go-round, but it never stopped where I was so I could get on."

Possessed as he was by an unceasing drive to interpret the Christian faith widely, relevantly, and persuasively, it was perhaps inevitable that he would be concerned with social theology. He went farther and deeper in cutting new paths of social idealism than other theologians. At a time when organized labor was still struggling for its right to exist, and before it had reached its somewhat complacent present role of political, vested interest, Temple saw it as a social "front" and strode out on its firing line. An examination of the *Dictionary of National Biography* for the decade of the Second World War and its aftermath shows no distinguished Nonconformist linked with Labour; but, says the editor, "there is by contrast the outstanding and beloved example of William Temple, the first Archbishop to have been a member of the Labour Party." [1]

It has been said that if Canterbury were an elective office,

Temple would never have been chosen by the clergy because too many were, even at that late date, of the kind found in Anthony Trollope's novels. But even so, the people of England would have brought him in. It was not that he was contentious or merely *avant garde;* we shall see how he avoided both those positions like the plague. He had no impulse of the sort seen in the American social-gospel leader Walter Rauschenbusch, who, before preaching, asked himself what it was "they would least like to hear." [2] Temple felt that "to become bitter in controversy is more heretical than to espouse with sincerity and charity the most devastating theological opinions." [3] As a kind of God-intoxicated humanist he was bound to be humble; but his humility never corroded into false modesty. Temple himself once said, "The humility which consists of being a great deal occupied about yourself, and saying you are of little worth, is not Christian humility." [4]

Therefore, in "theologizing" he never hesitated to put ancient faith in modern dress. At the same time his inventiveness did not break him off from the going, recognizable norms. Students of Temple cannot help being struck, for example, by the close parallels of his life and thought and Canon Oliver Quick's— another expositor. They were born at the same time, studied together at Oxford, were both "non-party" men, maintained a lifelong friendship. Temple wrote a memorial preface for Quick's *The Gospel of the Modern World* in 1944, the year they both died. (This Temple-Quick accord has no recognition in Iremonger.)

Dean Iremonger's biography is superb, a mine of information; our debt to him is immeasurable, as it is to Mrs. Temple who supplied source material and advice in every way. There are, nevertheless, curious lacunae in his work, some of which I have at least partially supplied in the Biographical Sketch in this book. Take, for example, the absence of any reference by Iremonger to Temple's visits to Scotland, or to his I.C.F. missions after Malvern. We have reason to be grateful also to Canon Baker for his two collections of Temple materials, and to Canon Warner for his brief (sometimes too terse) readings.

Dorothy Emmet, the philosopher, once said that Temple

never appeared to be "very seriously puzzled." Yet only a cursory study of his writings is enough to call her remark into question. For example, there was his lifelong indecision, and pulling and hauling, about the universalism-damnation question. He could be puzzled, all right, but not shaken. With us all, he experienced perplexity about some problems raised by his faith, yet it was not about the faith itself. He wrestled with some things intuitively (i.e., pre-consciously), letting them simmer and, later, as in lecturing, discovered that he had "root convictions" he was only then fully aware of, products of the thinking that "goes on behind the scenes." [5] And always, whether in debate with himself or others, his sense of humor held. Sir Julian Huxley has remembered him most for his laughter, when he was an undergraduate at Queen's and Temple a don; laughter "in the grand manner and on the largest scale, earth-shaking laughter that shook the laugher too," and again near the end of Temple's life when his laughter was "a vivifying tonic" to a war aims committee huddled in a basement in one of the worst of the daylight air raids.[6]

Years ago Walter Marshall Horton called Temple a "centrist," meaning he was not a traditionalist or modernist or neo-orthodox, no more than he was "high" or "low" in church doctrine.[7] His was an openness *cum* classical teaching much like that of John and Donald Baillie, Oliver Quick, George Tyrrell and Baron von Hügel. They all transcended the latter-day camps and fashions, none of which will survive as critical classicism will. Temple cannot be easily categoried. In quite recent years (say, since 1960) most of us have lost interest in neat doctrinaire labels anyway, as much in theology and philosophy as in politics. We are more eclectic, as Temple was, both in method and results. While he was a Christian Socialist (a title not much used anymore), he was not a socialist in the style of secular socialism nor a Christian in the manner or posture of conventional churchiness. Nor did *he* ever use any of these labels. Theological differences between Bishop Paget of Oxford and Archbishop Davidson affected the former's refusal to ordain Temple and the latter's willingness; yet it was that same Temple who chaired the English Church's commission appointed to remove or reduce such differences!

Because of his "dialectical" method, consecrated to the annulment of either-or reductions of understanding, it follows that we find no clearly marked "periods" or "stages" in Temple's development. Some commentators try to simplify his thought with that device, but close scrutiny discredits it. Patterns of "from idealism to realism," "modernism to classicism," "metaphysics to empiricism," "socialism to pragmatism," suggest certain developmental emphases, but they remain essentially lazy-minded epithets and verbal conveniences. Through all of such characterizations there run, in fact, his abiding core categories of theology—the immanence of the transcendant, the centrality of the Incarnate Lord, the dynamics of creation as process, a personalist view of value, the primacy of relationship, social redemption.

His first concern was with what Americans speak of as "the communication of the Gospel" in contemporary, intelligible terms and thought-forms. A century ago F. D. Maurice said that the modern world was shaping the kind of man to whom the Gospel could not be preached, an insight more recently expressed with effect by Dietrich Bonhoeffer. Temple knew that the heart of Christian ministry is effective communication and contagion, verbally and actively, and that the post-modern era, as he called it, is doubling or multiplying the problem seen by Maurice. ("The bewilderment of our epoch is due to the fact that the period hitherto called Modern, as distinct from Ancient or Medieval, is manifestly coming to its end."[8]) It was this concern with evangelism and "apologetic" which colored all of his work. As Paul Tillich says, on behalf of his own version of the method of correlation, apologetics is an "omnipresent element and not a special section" of theology.[9] So Temple saw it. He addressed his witness to all men straight across the board. Hence Bishop Kirk could say of Temple's *Nature, Man and God* that the first part was for philosophers, the second for theologians, and the third for "the simplest layman." Kirk described it in these terms, even though he realized that in the important lines of thought it opened up it "stands in a class of its own in modern theological literature." [10]

All of this Temple carried on without any of the posturings of a pseudo or forced-draught modernity. He only threw out the bathwater, not the baby. One American Congregationalist said of him that his Incarnation-focussed theology "is not very distinctive" but "rather conventional." [11] To these complaints Temple boldly pled guilty; he looked at the pivotal, historic faith in the Incarnation—the Christological keystone—as precisely distinctive of Christianity, and always urged that theology try to be as "conventional" in that way as possible. A writer in *Essays in Anglican Self-Criticism* (1958) says: "By the 1930's, the younger theologians were turning decisively away from the idealist philosophy of religion which underlay Liberal Catholicism, and as William Temple, the most eminent of the Liberal Catholics, noted, the future lay with a theology that would subject the assumptions of Liberal Catholicism to the most radical criticism in the name of a new grasp of revelation." [12] He referred, of course, to the so-called "recovery of the Bible" movement. Temple, not without reason, feared a leaning toward arbitrary biblicism and Continental pietism in some of the young men under German influence, yet it was his own devastating critique of idealism in the Gifford Lectures of 1932-34 that started the shift.

Lest young men in the middle of the second half of the twentieth century suppose that their problems differ too much from those of the middle of the first half, they need only recall that when Temple opened a discussion with the younger theologians in the Anglican journal *Theology* on the eve of World War II, he described the struggles of his generation on three scores that fit things for Christian theology, fifty years later: (1) a struggle against the Victorian agnostics who wanted to keep Christian ethics and forget Christian doctrine, (2) a struggle against Rationalist ideas of automatic progress, and (3) a struggle to help men filled with anxiety because the old nineteenth century security was crumbling away in the First World War and its aftermath.[13] Each of these phenomena finds its place prominently in the contemporary scene.

Whether he succeeded entirely or not, Temple's tremendous attempt to construct a social theology was an important intellectual labor, all the more viable because it was not academic but hammered out in the midst of affairs. There are many points he neglected, being only one man of a certain time and place.

Theologically, he offered little on the doctrine of the Holy Spirit, even though he called it "the clue to the chief of our modern difficulties" (God's mode in history), as Christians face skeptics.[14] On the social agenda he completely ignored social biology and the population problem. Nevertheless, Temple constructed a contemporary theology in the three main areas which give this "portrait" its major divisions—expository, ecumenical and social. If the ecumenical section seemed shorter, it is no less important than the others. He did less theorizing on that score but acted fully, labored abundantly. And what he did do was the fruit of his fuller theorizing about the Christian faith in its doctrinal and social dimensions.

Biographical Sketch

In 1840, the Society for Promoting Christian Knowledge published a little book called *How William Temple Rose in the World: A Tale for Working Men*. This William Temple, a purely imaginary figure created for the purposes of Victorian moralism, rose by being a "good" workingman who knew his place and humbly stayed in it, thereby winning a decent home —better, or at least neater, than his father's. He was that paragon of nineteenth-century individualism—a "self-made" man. The William Temple of real life had no such pretensions. He would have echoed Franklin Roosevelt's remark in his First Inaugural Address, "It is literally true that the 'self-supportive' man or woman is as extinct as the man of the Stone Age. Without the help of thousands of others, any one of us would die." [1] Temple was too humble to claim any such thing for himself, and too realistic to conceive of such a silly proposition about anybody else. As we shall see, his understanding of man was, on the contrary, a highly social and interdependent view of human life and personality.

William Temple was born October 15, 1881, in the Bishop's Palace in Exeter. When he died on October 26, 1944, in a Kentish watering place called Westgate-on-Sea, Allied Forces had broken through the Siegfried Line and invaded Germany. These are the natal and mortal dates of the most renowned Primate in the Church of England since the English Revolution. It was the life span of sixty-three years for a man whose role in the Church was unique and influential beyond any equal, in spite of the hope-shattering brevity of only two years as Archbishop of Canterbury. [1] As an editorial in *Christianity and Crisis* put it, "The man, the hour, and the office stood in a creative relation to each other in a way we are not likely to see again in this generation." [2]

Looking at his life, it may be hard to resist rancor—not to sneer at, or at least minimize, his accomplishments. A sympathetic Methodist writer, E. H. Jeffs, said that a "son of an Archbishop of Canterbury" faces "an unspoken prejudice against the unduly rapid rise of a cleric born to the purple." [3] For those who have suffered serious privations and reverses, doubts or indecision, it is morally and psychologically tempting to "explain him away." The material, intellectual, and spiritual resources open to him were not unique, of course; but others who enjoyed them made no such use as he did. Still, he was privileged. Even Dean Iremonger, a friend-biographer, recognizes that "the note of tragedy was missing from Temple's life." [4] Albert Mansbridge, another friend and co-worker in Temple's Oxford days, tells how he and Canon Barnett wished that they could get him "into a spot," because in "facing and overcoming" it he would be an even stronger man.[5] But his strength and stature in any case were never in question.

"History is prologue," it says on the steps of the Archives Building in Washington. We might, therefore, more fully appreciate Temple's life and thought if we were to take a look at his ancestry and inheritance. [2] None of his biographies thus far published has had much to say on this score, and Temple himself seems to have had no taste for genealogy—only for family anecdotes, and then only if they amused.

✿ His Grandfathers   His paternal great-great-grandfather was William Temple, a merchant in Allerdean, near Berwyck-on-Tweed, England's northernmost town on the Scottish border where the river flows into the North Sea. He was twice mayor of the town (1750 and 1754). His wife was also North Country, Miss Ann Stowe of Northumberland, a family connection of Sir Francis Blake of Twizel Castle.

The merchant's son was William Johnstone Temple. In his "teens" he studied at the University of Edinburgh, where he became a fast friend of Boswell, Samuel Johnson's later companion and biographer. The record shows that young Temple opposed Boswell in politics, being described as a "Whig and water drinker." Boswell's father was a Whig, too, a rigid Presbyterian Whig; but the young Boswell wore a white cockade and defiantly prayed for King James. (One story says that his uncle finally gave him a shilling to pray for King George and he did so, arousing Sam Johnson, when he heard of it years later, to remark that "Whigs of all ages are made in the same way.") Like Boswell's, Temple's family was of the rising middle class, not of the landed gentry or aristocracy. It was only later, with William Temple's inheritance through his mother from the Lascelles and the Howards, that the Temple line took on aristocratic weight enough to satisfy any Tory.

Mayor Temple back in Allerdean fell on hard times, apparently, and had to bow to bankruptcy. Nevertheless, in 1758, his son managed to be made an exhibitioner with financial aid at Trinity Hall, Cambridge, and then a scholar in 1759. There he formed another literary friendship with Thomas Gray the poet, and it was through this friendship that he came to know Horace Walpole, Thomas Wharton, and others. When he came down from Cambridge to live in London, he roomed for a while with Boswell in the Inner Temple Lane and soon, with the others, attended upon Dr. Johnson at the Mitre Tavern in Fleet Street. His chief claim to fame was his companionship with the three literati, Thomas Gray, Oliver Goldsmith, and Samuel Johnson —and, of course, Boswell. Boswell's first book, published when he was only seventeen (1757), consisted of letters written to young Temple, whose pseudonym was "Atticus."

After some further study, and second thoughts, William Johnstone Temple was ordained by the Bishop of Exeter. (His own grandson was later to be Bishop of Exeter, then of London, and then Archbishop of Canterbury, and father of our Archbishop, William.) He was promptly launched on a typical eighteenth-century clerical career by the Viscount of Lisburne, Wilmot Vaughn, who gave him a living (but a skimpy one) in the pleasant rectory of Mamhead, in the Exeter diocese. We don't know much more about his history. He had financial troubles in 1768 "by reason of Mr. Frederick Stowe" with whom he got involved because his wife was somehow related to him. A letter he wrote at the time said he "contemplated separation from his wife." That unhappy but entirely canonical development appears not to have come about, even though a year earlier, in 1767, he had been in great distress "through filial piety" (due to the same or possibly another deal with his wife's uncle) and "desired a chaplaincy abroad." According to the *Dictionary of National Biography*, neither the emigration nor the separation materialized as a solution of his difficulties.

In 1774, he published a work entitled *An Essay on the Clergy, their Studies, Recreations, Decline of Influence,* which was much admired by his Bishop, Keppel of Exeter. Keppel thereupon made Temple his chaplain, possibly to pad the family budget, and also promised him encouragingly "the best living in the diocese of Exeter, the present incumbent being eighty-six." In 1775, the Bishop paid off on his promise, and Temple got the parish at Gluvias near Falmouth. The literary critic lived there happily ever after. He and his incompatible wife had two sons, each of whom was a man of note in his day. The first was Francis, who became an admiral in the Navy. The second was Octavius, who entered the Army, and whose son was the 95th Archbishop of Canterbury—whose grandson was the 98th. [3] The Temples, by the way, are the only father-son pair ever to ascend to the chair of St. Augustine. (The nearest thing to it: Randall Davidson was Archibald Tait's son-in-law.)

Octavius, 1784-1834, seems to have been a more colorful personality than his father or his son. He was more like his grandson, Archbishop William. He became a Major in the Fourth Foot, then a sub-inspector of militia in the Ionian Islands of the Mediterranean. His wife was Dorcas, daughter of a Richard Carveth of Cornwall, who traced her descent from Guy de Beauchamp, second earl of Warwick through the Les Despensers. Her father was a stern and upright Cornishman who allowed no smugglers' cave on his estate, nor any cockfighting. He opposed Dorcas' marriage because he objected to soldiers coming into the family, but they went ahead without his blessing.[6] Major Octavius traced his descent through his mother from Richard Grenville, third Duke of Buckingham and Chandos.

But whatever the past had been, their own circumstances were at best only plain and modest financially; and for a while Dorcas and Octavius lived on a farm in the West country, in Devonshire, near a little place called Culmstock. There they started their family of, ultimately, fifteen children. The Major interested himself in Poor Law Reform and land re-distribution, typical "radical" enterprises of the day. "He burnt with indignation at the state of the poor, and persecuted the Devon farmers into giving them allotments." By this he only succeeded in offending the intense conservatism of his West country neighbors. "Had he remained at Culmstock, it is practically certain that he would never have lived down the terrible prejudice his conduct was bound to create." [7]

But the Major never put his survival value to the test in Culmstock. Instead, he went out with his growing family to the Mediterranean, where his inspectorship led to the post of Resident on Santa Maura (Leucadia), a strategic island off the Greek peninsula—known in legend as "Ithaca." It was here that Frederick, "our" William Temple's father, was born in 1821, the thirteenth child and youngest survivor of fifteen.

In 1830, Octavius resigned his Army commission and returned to Devon. But in 1833, he accepted the governorship of Sierra Leone, a British colony on the West Coast of Africa, now an independent nation. He died there in 1834, after less than a year, and Dorcas returned with her children to Devon. [4]

One cannot help suspecting that if more were known of Octavius, his likeness to William his grandson would be strengthened. Snell says, "Major Temple was a short thickset man, and Frederick, in growing up, promised to resemble him." [8] Actually, Frederick became a tall man, though burly, whereas William in the next generation, like the Major, was short and thickset. They may well have been alike in temperament, too.

❁ HIS FATHER Frederick Temple's dates, 1821-1902, almost correspond with Queen Victoria's. He was born two years later than she and outlived her by one year. He celebrated her Diamond Jubilee in 1897. His was a Victorian life and career. In

August, before his death, he officiated at the coronation of King Edward VII and received the collar of the Victorian Order. Devon, where he grew up with his many brothers and sisters after their return from Africa, was the country where his grandfather William Johnstone Temple had had his livings. At that time, it included both Cornwall and Devonshire, and only later was Truro carved from it. It was where Octavius and Dorcas had married, and where, later, their son Frederick returned as Bishop. It was hard to make ends meet, but Dorcas managed, even though, as her son said later, he knew ("it was the thing that pinched me most") what it was "to wear patched clothes and patched shoes." [9] She started him on his early training in mathematics and got him into Blundell's School in Tiverton as a scholar. He won a leaving scholarship and, with an anonymous gift of fifty pounds, went off to Balliol College at Oxford on a "sink or swim" basis. His reward for winning a Double First in classics and mathematics was to be made a lecturer in logic and mathematics and then a Fellow of Balliol. In 1845, he was elected Junior Dean. Meanwhile he studied for Holy Orders, following in his grandfather's steps—although at Oxford instead of Cambridge.

His tutors were Robert Scott, partner with Liddell in the famous lexicon; Archibald Tait, later his immediate predecessor in the See of Canterbury; Benjamin Jowett, the classical scholar, only four years his senior; and W. G. Ward, the Tractarian who led off the trek of Newman and several other contemporaries to Rome. Although he himself never cared to "swim the Tiber," he voted against Ward's censure and degradation. A Tory as an undergraduate, he thought himself into the Liberal position as a graduate scholar, and stayed in it from then on. (An example of his liberality: he once spoke in the House of Lords favoring the opening of churchyards to non-conformist burials!) He was ordained by Bishop Samuel Wilberforce in 1846-47.

An expert in education, he left Oxford for ten years' service in a government post in Whitehall, during which he wrote several important reform measures. His friend Tait had left Oxford to be Headmaster at Rugby; and in 1857 Frederick Temple's leadership was recognized by his being elected to take Tait's place when Tait became Dean of Carlisle. (He had a brief in-

terim period as Principal of Kneller Hall.) He followed Tait
again, when he went to Canterbury. In 1869 Gladstone offered
him the deanery of Durham; but when he turned it down, he
was offered the bishopric of Exeter and accepted. He was going
back home, but with a difference! A storm of opposition to his
appointment arose because he had contributed an essay on
education to the controversial "modernist" symposium, *Essays
and Reviews*. The Earl of Shaftesbury and Dr. Pusey led the
fight against his consecration. His friends urged him to make a
formal declaration of orthodoxy, but he refused to do so until
after his consecration; then he withdrew his essay from further
editions. (It is doubtful that his son William would ever have
followed such a course of even partial retreat.)

In 1876, while Bishop of Exeter, he married Beatrice Blanche
Lascelles, whose grandfather on her father's side was the Earl of
Harewood; on her mother's side, the Howards, the Earl of
Carlisle was her grandfather, and a daughter of the Duke of
Devonshire her grandmother. Her brother, William Temple's
uncle, was ambassador to Russia and to Germany. Although
William was never like the Lascelles, "so tall they have to walk
in the gutter," nevertheless he began life with all the advantages
that come with a family inheritance of English privilege. William's relationship with his mother may be seen in a story told
by Beverley Tucker, former Bishop of Ohio who, as a fellow
student of William's at Oxford, went down for a weekend at
Fulham. The future Archbishop got into some sort of an argument with her in the Hall, but after a decent interval she closed
it by going up the stairs (down the balustrade of which he slid
on a teatray as a small boy), saying, "You know more than I do,
William, but I know best."

In a minor incident he anticipated his son's interest in America, although Frederick Temple never visited her shores. Having
been translated to the London diocese in 1884, he agreed with
Senator G. F. Hall of Massachusetts that the Bradford Manu-
script, incorrectly called "The Log of the *Mayflower*," should be
in the possession of the United States, and he offered to hand it
over from the Fulham Palace Library. (His successor, Mandel
Creighton, made the actual transfer.) In the year of his translation from Exeter to London, he delivered the Bampton Lectures

on religion and science, a combination of forward-looking thinking and ecclesiastical leadership of the sort his son was to possess in such abundance. His charges to the clergy show some social and apologetic concern; one was on the Church's relation to the London poor, and another on the growth of skepticism. But the dramatic and democratic leadership in the dock strike of 1889 was the ex-Anglican's, Cardinal Manning's, not Frederick Temple's. In 1896, Lord Salisbury nominated him for Canterbury, and in 1897 he was enthroned. He lived for five years as Primate of all England.

Frederick was not the genial and polished person his son was, just as he was not as radical in his social outlook. This may be the old, old story of the "socially insecure" compared to the radicalism of "to the manner born." Archbishop Benson wrote in his diary, in 1891, after hearing Temple speak in the House of Lords: "It is painful, very painful, to see the Lords always so unappreciative of the Bishop of London—the strongest man, nearly, in the House, the clearest, the highest toned, the most deeply sympathetic, the clearest in principle—yet because his voice is a little harsh, and his accent a little provincial (though of what province it is hard to say) and his figure square, and his hair a little rough, and because all this sets off the idea of his independence, he is not listened to at all by the cold, kindly, worldly wise, gallant, landowning powers." [10] Only some of this would have applied to William—the "independence" certainly, the clarity, and so on. But he was not harsh nor rough, nor provincial. And there was no mere coldness among the "landowning powers" toward him; their feelings were often a lot warmer than that! There was a world of difference between his father's temporizing in the dock strike in 1889, and William Temple's role in the coal strike in 1926.

✿ HIS OWN LIFE William was the second of Frederick's two children, both born in the Palace at Exeter. The first son to arrive was Frederick Charles, January, 1879; William was the second, two years later. His father had not married until after five years of the episcopate, and was nearly sixty years old when he was born; and his mother, though young compared to her husband, was already thirty-five.

The fullest account of his childhood and youth, but by no means a detailed one, is Dean Iremonger's. It is based on his gleanings, chiefly from letters Temple had exchanged with his parents and his brother. Some of his friends from school days at Rugby have supplied bits of reminiscence, especially R. H. ("Harry") Tawney of the London School of Economics, the Labour Party's platform consultant; Sir Frank Fletcher, headmaster of Charterhouse, who taught him at Rugby; H. H. ("Harry") Hardy, headmaster of Shrewsbury; J. L. Paton, headmaster of Manchester Grammar School; A. F. L. ("Lionel") Smith, rector of Edinburgh Academy; John Stocks, vice-chancellor of Liverpool University. Unlike so many of these early schoolmates, Temple returned as a master to school life for only a short time (in the headmastership of Repton, 1910-1914). Friends he made at later stages, such as his Oxford contemporary E. J. ("Jimmy") Palmer, Bishop of Bombay, and from the Repton days, D. C. Somervell (the abridger of Toynbee's *The Study of History*), have helped to fill out the story.

His capacity for lifelong friendships appeared first with Ellen Langdon, the Devon woman who took over as "Nana" in his nursery days. She stayed with him, when practicable, until his marriage in 1916, after which he visited her with loving regularity and frequency until her death many years later in a nursing home for the blind in St. Albans. In her will, she left him nearly all her life's savings. So with Edith Maskell, his governess. Before he was four years old his father went from Exeter to Fulham Palace as Bishop of London, and there young William lived until he was fifteen years old. Then in 1896 his father was enthroned at Canterbury and Lambeth became his home. While still in Fulham, he had "married" himself with full liturgical invention to Agnes Fisher, daughter of the then Vicar of Fulham and Rural Dean of Middlesex. Much of his play and pageantry showed that he already leaned to ecclesiastical roles. It was a taste inevitably fed by watching and listening to his father. One of his lower-school friends at Colet Court in Hammersmith in London was P. T. B. ("Tubby") Clayton of later

Toc-H fame. There he started learning Greek from John Sankey who was ultimately to occupy the woolsack as England's Lord Chancellor. [5] William, running true to his personal pattern, was more than fifty marks ahead of the nearest competitor in the final examinations when he finished at Colet Court in 1894.

As a boy his life was full: of music—mainly on the piano and organ but with one poor try on the oboe (a complaint from the archbishop put a stop to the French Horn), and hearing choral anthems and Saturday Pops [6]; of seaside and country holidays; visits to the Crystal Palace with Nana; comedies (even *Charley's Aunt*) and drama; Thames boat races watched from the roof of the Palace in Fulham Road; school affairs; the usual childhood illnesses; matter-of-course and usually joyful church-going.

He started to find himself at Rugby where, forty-five years earlier, his father had been Headmaster. He entered in the Fall of 1894. There he began friendships with some of his beloved schoolmates, especially the trio of Harry Hardy, Harry Tawney and Lionel Smith, which lasted through Oxford and life. In later years he was to describe Rugby's "ethos" as one of loyalty to Thomas and Matthew Arnold's ideals; he proudly contrasted its "justice for the stupid" (his father's maxim) to the brilliant individualism-cum-indolence of Eton. In a way, William at Rugby proved to be more like the "good" kind of Etonian, because for all of his devotion to the corporate principle of Form living he himself reached the Sixth Form at the earliest permissible age, fifteen and a half. There he remained, studying hard and profitably, until he went up to Oxford in 1900.

During the Rugby period he wrote daily to his mother, and every Sunday to his father. [7] His brother, who had reached Rugby before him, volunteered for the Boer War while William was still in school. This was perhaps his earliest personal experience with matters of dramatic social significance. At Rugby, his mind got going: his contemporaries have remembered that he cut corners on linguistic and grammatical details because they seemed, as Iremonger puts it, "comparatively trivial when the whole world of thought and action lay before him." [11] He was never a "pure" scholar. In Sandford's *Life* of his father, we find William being chided for impudent parodies of Aristophanes'

Frogs and for transliteral Greek gibberish such as βαϑ ϑαϑ ("bad dad"). But on Sunday afternoons, while others played, he read until chapel bells rang. On holidays in the Lake Country, while others fished, he read Kant's *Critique of Pure Reason*.

He had more than the usual catalogue of childhood illnesses to handicap him. When only two, he had his first attack of the gout that finally brought about his early death. (He used a special gout boot for years.) He was always stout, and came to wear a seventeen-and-a-half collar! He had to wear false teeth and glasses; he suffered chronically from both lumbago and hay fever. A cataract in his right eye, from childhood, had ended sight in it altogether by the time he left London for Manchester. This may account for his remarkable visual memory, for he had to read all of his life at a steady, deliberate pace—he could always "see" the page in memory and quote its number and lines accurately. His wife said he read in "the page-as-a-whole" manner. He was a life-long abstainer from both alcohol and tobacco, yet at no time did he intrude his discipline upon others. Occasionally, in his later years, he spoke for temperance—but never for prohibition.

The only sport that survived his youthful efforts and carried over into adult years, yet only sporadic at that, was tennis. In Rugby football his main part was to lean his weight on the backs of his linesmen; small boys tried to avoid playing against School House for fear he would roll on them. In later life he tried, and dropped, other sports. As he admitted, "The reason I gave up golf was that I began to wonder why I should care whether the ball went into the hole or not. It generally didn't. Well, once you begin to question, the game is ruined. You have got to take it mystically, or not at all; for it is an end in itself." [12] And in *Christian Faith and Life* (p. 14), discussing the essence of personality as choice or purpose, he said, "The billiard ball only goes in where you push it. That is the most humiliating fact in my experience; but it is true. If I could only suppose that it had a will of its own, I should be much happier."

In the school debating society he had a fluency that pointed toward his successes later in the Oxford Union Debating Society. His command of language can be seen in his use of "meiosis" (a

Greek-rooted term for minimizing, like "litotes" in rhetoric) to describe a report on his limited Rugby football capabilities. At this time he acquired his lifelong devotion to the philosophical theology of Robert Browning's poetry, and to the prophetic passion of Shelley's. It was poetry and drama that he loved most. Later he read some novels: he thought Dostoievski's *Brothers Karamazov* the greatest ever written, and he even read an occasional detective story. (Interestingly, his favorite writers were women: Angela Thirkell, Dorothy Sayers, Ann Bridge—but add John Buchan.) He thought of them as a game: the pleasure consists in being beaten. If you spot the guilty one before the end, it spoils your pleasure. But Browning and Shakespeare were the constants, other literature the variables. His lifelong distaste for Puritanism left him cold to Milton, warm toward the Greeks. He always rejoiced in George Bernard Shaw—quoted his plays with gusto, but not so Chesterton, and never H. G. Wells whose secularistic deism was unattractive. These were things he learned at Rugby.

E. V. Knox has described him in those days as "A boy called Billy Temple, who was much more like Billy Bunter . . . he was stout; he was good-natured; he was 'raggable'; he had that queer high laugh that went on so long and never left him; he was full of stories that he found at least as good as his hearers did. But from the start he had a sort of quiet purpose that was recognized. It earned some respect: grudging, I suppose; for boys admire prospective athletes and soldiers, not embryo theologians." [13] He finished at Rugby third of the twenty-two on the Upper Bench; the Headmaster wrote to his father, "I think *anything* is possible to him."

❁ OXFORD   At Balliol he took Oxford seriously, and Oxford took him seriously. But it was never a merely solemn or humorless regard on either side. As a "freshman" he admired and queried (Sir) William Beveridge, later to be head of the London School of Economics and architect of a "cradle to grave" welfare proposal for the English Welfare State following the Second

World War. In 1902 he took a First in classics and in 1904 another in Greats (literature and humanities). [8] His election to
the presidency of the Oxford Union was a university, not just
a college honor. Others who were there then have said he was a
calm, unexcitable figure in Oxford affairs. (Worry was never a
part of his response to life; later in Manchester, he used to tell
the younger clergy that the chief cause of feebleness is anxiety.)
He could always stand up in any gathering, not only stating an
issue cogently but laying out the pros and cons so clearly that
people came to terms across their differences. This developed in
time into what he called his "little parlour trick" of bringing
about a consensus in many contentious theological, ecumenical
and social-policy conferences.[9]

When he took his degree in 1904, he was offered about thirty
different positions, chiefly academic. Unsurprisingly, he chose to
accept a post as Fellow and Lecturer in philosophy at Queen's
College which he held for six years. His friend, Bernard Streeter,
was shortly to become Provost there. He was one of the Six
Tutors' Campaign of the Cataline Club of "leftish" dons who
agitated for the introduction of a program of social studies at
Oxford, which finally materialized in the now celebrated "P.P.E."
or degree in philosophy, politics and economics. Canon Cyril
Hudson of St. Albans, who later became a contributor to English
Christian Sociology, knew Temple then and was struck (as were
most of the "young bloods" among his fellow Oxonians) by his
"odd interest" in workingmen and social justice. Edward Caird,
the neo-Hegelian Master of Balliol, to whose memory he dedicated his Gifford Lectures in 1934, influenced him greatly as an
undergraduate; but in the long run, the personal influence was
stronger—through Caird's social idealism, not his philosophical
idealism. At least he won him to not only tolerating but to
actually *using* differences. (It was Newman who had first used
"liberal" as an epithet—but his influence was understandably
not great in Oxford.)

In this period he immersed himself in the classical and English
philosophers. He made a special study of St. Thomas Aquinas.
He did his vacation reading in Italy, Austria, the Low Countries. Twice he took leaves to study in Germany, especially at

Jena (where "Harry" Tawney joined him), to sit under Wendt especially, but also Eucken, Harnack and Simmel. [10] He tried for the Ellerton Theological Essay Prize and, let it be of note in his normally successful career, he lost it to somebody else. As an undergraduate he had read his first public theological paper, on the doctrine of the Atonement, to the Bible Reading Society.

Problems of political analysis held his attention, especially the State. The Incarnation became and remained central in his theological outlook. He seldom waited after dinner to dawdle with the others in the Senior Common Room. (They shook their heads ruefully, saying, "He has gone to the good.") He preferred to rush off to a socialist meeting or to plan some work for the University missions to London's poor. The latter had been started earlier, one by Canon Barnett and T. H. Green, and one by Benjamin Jowett at Toynbee Hall. It was at this time that he and Tawney and Albert Mansbridge worked so hard to build up the Worker's Educational Association ("W.E.A."). He became president in 1908 and stayed in that office for sixteen years—not resigning until three years after he had assumed the duties of Bishop of Manchester. In worker's education he was carrying on the flag for Frederick Denison Maurice, the mid-nineteenth century theologian and Christian Socialist. Like Maurice, Temple wanted to challenge both "the unsocial Christians" and "the unchristian Socialists." [14] He soon saw, with Holland and Gore, that the problem was to re-inspire social idealists with a sense of the Gospel's relevance in a time when the Evangelicals were preoccupied with individual salvation, and the Tractarians with patristic theology. At the Pan-Anglican Congress in London, 1908, which obviously reflected the influence of the legatees of Maurice and Kingsley—the Guild of St. Matthew, the Christian Social Union, and the Church Socialist League—Temple declared for nationalization and said (predictively), "The Christian is called to assent to great steps in the direction of collectivism." [15] (The Congress concluded that "capitalism" was both immoral and unmoral.)

If we may say that temperamentally the reactionary does not *want* social change, the conservative does not *expect* it, the liberal only *hopes* for it, cautiously, and the radical *expects* it and looks forward to it, then in such a typology Temple was all his life a radical.

During the First World War (shades of the Red Menace and McCarthyism) Temple's name, because of the W.E.A. and his professed Socialist convictions, went on the C.I.D.'s list (like the F.B.I.'s) of dangerous and suspicious characters. Helping the workers to help themselves was his answer to the social-service paternalism of the University Mission. At the Matlock Conference of the S.C.M. in 1909, he opened a discussion which produced *Discipleship and the Social Problem,* a landmark of social concern in English Christianity. He obviously regarded social service, by itself, as too "liberal"—in the definition that a political liberal is "a conservative with a tender conscience." His leadership in the W.E.A. was always on the side of education tailored to workers, not merely lectures transplanted from the university to the workers' hall. He often told a tale about the University Extension sending a young man to a Welsh mining village where a miner told him, "Young Man, I've no quarrel with you, for you're doing your best; but them as sent you 'ere ought to be 'ung." [16]

In this same period he began to develop his passion for ecumenical effort: he went in 1910 as an S.C.M. steward to the Edinburgh meeting of the International Missionary Conference, and afterwards at John R. Mott's invitation toured Australia as an S.C.M. lecturer.[11]

❀ ORDINATION The story of Temple's ordination has lost nothing in the telling. The fully developed tale makes him out so heterodox, if not actually heretical, that his decision to ask for ordination might seem almost dishonest. The true story is considerably less dramatic and in it the issues were less sharply drawn. Dean Iremonger deserves great credit for the balance and matter-of-factness with which he tells it.[17] His version rests soundly on the actual correspondence between the principals involved. In a few words it amounted to this: since early boyhood Temple had meant to enter Holy Orders; but in 1906, Francis Paget, the Bishop of Oxford, decided that he could not ordain him because Temple had acknowledged he was only "inclined, very tentatively," to accept the Virgin Birth and the Bodily Resurrection. The news of this set-back reached Temple while he was visiting his uncle in the British Embassy in Berlin. After a careful and mutually respectful exchange of letters with Paget, over a nearly three-year period, Randall Davidson, who had succeeded Temple's father at Canterbury, decided to be less cautious than Paget and ordained him Deacon, in December, 1908, and Priest, in December, 1909. [12] It taught Temple that when fundamentalism crops up in the Anglican Church, it takes the creedal rather than the biblical form. As to the latter form, he explained later in *Foundations* (p. x) that his father had taught him "to reverence the Bible; but from him I learnt, too, to use my wits in reading it."

Temple explained that he somewhat more confidently believed in the "Bodily" Resurrection than in the Virgin Birth. Even at this early stage he had begun to distinguish between "faith" (trust and commitment) and "belief" (propositional assent), and to put faith first. To his brother he wrote, "I am, however, convinced that the Church needs very radical reform, and I may perhaps help on that better outside." But later that same summer, he was saying to his brother, "Probably it is better not to try a movement outside the Church, but inside it. If the Church turns one out, one must go on outside." This, of course, was the kind of thinking he did later in the discussions about disestablishment, when he took the position that the Church must do what her mission requires, letting the State, if it chooses, disown her, but never voluntarily breaking away *before the issue is drawn*. In any case, in time the Virgin Birth doctrine ceased to trouble him at all, one way or the other, and his "Bodily Resurrection" was never imaginably a matter of gross levitation. [13] When Temple had hauled his immense girth to the top of Great Gable in the Lakes District in 1929, on a climb with Tawney, Geoffrey Bell, and Sir William Fyfe, he mopped his brow and said, "Thank God, I do *not* believe in the resurrection of the flesh!" And before he left Oxford he finished his first book, *The Faith and*

Modern Thought, which by its perception and skill should have fully reassured the most phrase-bound, formula-reciting cleric in the world!

◉ THE SCHOOLMASTER On his way out to Australia in 1910, he received and accepted a call as headmaster of Repton School in Derbyshire, an ancient foundation refounded in 1557—ten years before Rugby. He gave up his role as an Oxford philosopher and, continuing to be a "collar-and-tie parson," became a schoolmaster—but with some doubts about his fitting into the job. The doubts were fairly soon borne out. Psychologists are free to speculate that he was "father fixated" and trying to reproduce old Frederick's lifeline: Balliol, donship, fresh theological ground-breaking, headmastering—and certainly the pattern proceeded later on: diocesan, archdiocesan, primate. He did not stay long enough to see even one Form through from start to finish. His lack of vocation for school work was not so much a dislike for it as too much liking for other things on a grander and wider scale. He could not be enclosed or so sharply focused. While his father at Rugby had been "a beast, but a just beast," William Temple was popular, a laughing Head whom the boys called Billy. Yet he was unable to keep at it for more than a third of the time his father gave—in Frederick's case, it was a dozen years. At the time he went to Repton, Archbishop Davidson made him one of his chaplains and that role he kept until 1921 when he went to Manchester; but his headmastership he surrendered within four years (1914). He had hoped to democratize at least one "public" school, but he soon confessed it was an unrealistic goal. And with the hope gone, his devotion went, too. He came to speak of public schools as "those large private institutions called public schools."

During the Repton period, Temple was moving in a more orthodox direction, through the friendship and influence of Charles Gore (by then Bishop of Oxford). It has been said that Gore was certain about the creed but struggled with doubt about God's love, while Temple was certain of God's love but struggled with doubts about the creed. Others who influenced him were Father Kelley, S.S.M., and the lay Roman Catholic theologian, Baron von Hügel. None of his Anglican contemporaries interested in philosophical theology were Evangelicals or High Churchmen—F. R. Tennant, C. C. J. Webb, O. C. Quick, A. E. Taylor, and W. R. Matthews—except that Taylor, like Temple, leaned in the moderate Gore direction. Temple wrote *two* of the essays in *Foundations,* restating doctrine in modern, scientifically oriented terms. One was on "The Divinity of Christ" and the other on "The Church." He also wrote the epilogue for the authors, the "Seven Oxford Men."

At no time did he ever fear the *odium theologicum.* Ronald Knox, who went over to Rome, attacked *Foundations,* said its hero was "a man named Jones," a decent fellow but not a really devout man—a questioner for whom they were trying to reduce the faith to a minimum in order to keep Jones in the fold. Temple replied that he was *not* a theological doctor trying to see how much Jones could swallow and keep down. He said, "I am Jones himself asking what there is to eat." Years later, in a "Reply" in Kenneth Ingram's *Youth Looks at Religion,* he seriously proposed an "associate membership" in the Church for those who cannot conscientiously recite the creeds!

Harold Begbie, the "Gentleman with a Duster," quoted Temple in 1922, "A man comes to me for adult baptism . . . He might say to me, 'It would be immoral to assert that I believe what I have not examined, and to examine this doctrine so thoroughly as to give an answer not immoral would take a lifetime. Am I to remain outside the Church until then?' Here I think, the Church can take a step which would widen its influence enormously. No man ought to be shut out of Christ's Church who has the love of God and the love of humanity in his heart . . . What I should like to see would be a particular and individual recital of the Beatitudes." [18] This quotation serves to show that Temple was, in Ernst Troeltsch's typology, a "church" rather than a "sect" Christian.

In private these authors called themselves the "Holy Lunch" party, because their collaboration was super-prandial. His *Repton School Sermons,* published in his last years there, show how thoroughly "Incarnational" his whole theological outlook had become. In his second year (1911) his social-personalistic view of man was crystallized in *The Nature of Personality*—another one of the core elements in his theology. When he left Repton he felt drawn to the principalship of St. John's College, Agra, in India, but fortunately Archbishop Davidson practically forbade him to deprive his home Church of his strong "in" with the Labour Movement. [14] He was offered a Canonry at Westminster Abbey, but the offer had to be withdrawn to everybody's embarrassment because he had not yet been ordained for the required six years. Yet already he had, to quote Archbishop Ramsey's account, moved forward "from being a wistful seeker after orthodoxy to being one of its supreme exponents." [19]

⚙ A LONDON RECTOR His next step was not along his father's path. Whereas Frederick Temple never had a parish, William left Repton to become Rector of St. James's, Piccadilly, in London's West End. He kept his hand in education by his chairmanship of the Education Section of the British Association for the Advancement of Science. St. James's, like Repton, was a four-year stint. Pastoral care was not his natural bent. It may be doubted that he often sought out persons for individual counsel and comfort. St. James's, being central, required many kinds of ministration—such as marrying Percy Dearmer in August, 1916—but such services are not "pastoral" in the literal sense. It was often said, "The emotional and the intimate are not his element." In any case he was not idle; as he had neglected the Common Room at Queen's, so here he withdrew from a clerical club ("The Brotherhood") because it spent too much time in friendly small talk.

It was his great preaching that won him the appointment. His powers of speech were a natural gift, like William Pitt's: clear, concise, progressive reasoning; very English in all absence of histrionics and purple passages—quite unlike the Lambeth Conference sermon of an American bishop, described by one acidulous English prelate as "impressive oratory of fluent incoherence." He loved to tell about an American advertisement showing a truculent man shaking his fist in the reader's face and saying, "I can make you an effective speaker." He was a democrat, but not a demagogue. While at St. James's he was made honorary Chaplain to the King, an honor he shared with his friend G. A. ("Woodbine Willy") Studdert-Kennedy, and kept until he surrendered it and his other chaplaincy (the one to the Archbishop) after his consecration as Bishop of Manchester in 1921. His mother, who had kept house for him at Repton and then accompanied him to London, died in April, 1915. (His "Nana," Ellen Langdon, still faithful, stayed with him until his marriage.) In May, even though the *Lusitania* had been sunk by a German submarine with thousands of passengers drowned, he sailed the Atlantic to give the Paddock Lectures at the General Theological Seminary in New York City (*Church and Nation*). But he returned to his war-bound home immediately they were delivered.

About this time he met Frances Anson. He was chairman of the Westminster branch of the Christian Social Union; she was its secretary. With her intense social concern, matching his, her superb talent for hospitality and friendliness, her attractive and vivacious personality, she was everything he could want. They were married in June, 1916, by the Archbishop, at St. James's. No children ever came to them—still another reversal of fortune, dwarfing an occasional minor loss such as the Ellerton prize. She was a cousin of Bishop Richard Dyke of Bombay and of Sir Richard Acland, the M.P., who as a Christian Socialist in the Second World War wrote *Unser Kampf* and gave away his estates to the government. It was this same Acland whose amendment favoring common ownership involved Temple in a furor at the Malvern Conference in 1941. Typical of Temple, his engagement present to Frances was a set of fresh copies of all his books published to date, now numbering ten, including two privately printed. The night before his wedding he sat up late in the St. James's rectory finishing a major philosophical work, *Mens Creatrix*. On their honeymoon in the Porlock Valley, for only ten days, he read Browning aloud in the evenings, they walked and napped in the daylight, and she got her first test of helping him to struggle with lumbago and hay fever. But in spite of these trials they laughed together, and laughed together from then on over big and little things. [15]

It was at this time that he made his first sortie into journalism, as editor and a regular contributor to *The Challenge,* 1915-1918. C. B. Mortlock first (1914) tried editing it—a new venture in weekly Christian papers. Temple was a contributor of funds (he bought a large part of the shares) as well as of articles. When Mortlock quit in 1915, Temple took over. The enterprise was too ambitious: an attempt to be "Church of England" in a layman's language, urging the "ministry of the laity," trying to deal with religious and political problems and foreign affairs by Christian social principles—it tried to break too much fresh ground. Since it was not a party organ nor a family paper, it fell between two stools. The pressures of the War created almost unbeatable obstacles. Temple's sharp editorials against the mounting English hatred of Germans ("Huns") and his espousal of the "radical" doctrine of equality of sacrifice—for every citizen "a soldier's wage, a soldier's ration, and a soldier's discipline"—were too much for a class-discriminating society, even in the sacrificial mood of wartime.

Nevertheless, Temple's editorials for nearly four years made it clear to the whole of Britain that here was a Churchman to be reckoned with, neither an orthodox obscurantist nor a Colonel Blimp type whose notion of the ministry centered on "the squires in the shires and the spinsters in the spas."

At a Convocation, in 1918, he announced that he had joined the Labour Party, in a debate over what was described in Dean Inge's diary as "a wild-cat socialistic resolution by Canon Garbett and W. Temple," although they were only advocating a living wage, unemployment insurance and collective bargaining—all accepted policies today.[20] Some years later, Henson, Inge's companion in opposition to the Christian Socialism of the "Gore-Temple Axis," called it "shallow Georgian optimism." They, in return, held that Henson's confidence in business to work out the issues of labor relations justly without need of unions was Victorian optimism. To use a phrase of Maisie Ward's, they were always prepared to combine re-surrection and in-surrection! In

1942, in a letter to Dean Matthews after the Malvern Conference, Henson said plainly, "I dislike his (Temple's) judgment, dislike his company, and dissent from his reading of ecclesiastical duty," [21] yet in a handsome way, he subsequently acknowledged that Temple had been the most distinguished Archbishop of the thirty-two in Canterbury since the Reformation.[22] In the same letter, Henson regretted that the War had caused a "new intimacy with the Americans" because they are definitely lower than our own people in the two respects of sexual morality and civic quality," and concluded: "I think I am more apprehensive of moral damage from America than of economic and political damage from Russia."

William Temple was obviously *not* in the tradition that made of the Establishment a "religious" framework for the Conservative Party at prayer! Indeed, it was the company surrounding him on *The Challenge* (G. E. Newsome, Maude Royden, Tissington Tatlow, Leslie Hunter, Spencer Leeson) who helped a lot to spark the Life and Liberty Movement; although the paper had the reputation, falsely, of being the Movement's organ, its Christian social thought was most certainly a catalytic in the movement's development.

Besides editing a series of *Papers for War-Time* (Oxford University Press, 1915-1916), based on a set of non-pacifist principles to which he was unwaveringly faithful all his life, he made one other, somewhat more successful editorial venture. This was *The Pilgrim* ("A Review of Christian Politics and Religion"), a quarterly idea-journal rather than a weekly of news and comment. Mr. R. G. Longman of Longman's, Green and Company, brought the suggestion to him; it was not the other way around. It ran from October, 1920, through July, 1927, with editorial essays by Temple and papers by all of the outstanding lay and clerical leaders of the post-war era: Streeter, Gore, Barry, Peter Green, A. J. Carlyle, Henry Scott Holland, Tawney, Mozley, Pym, Zimmern, A. E. Taylor, the Knoxes, Webb, Collingwood, Bevan, Garbett, Quick, Storr—a host of them, a roster of the Church's post-war potential. Not everybody was in sympathy: Inge, the Dean of St. Paul's, declared himself to be too much a believer in "Whiggery" (political individualism) to like *The Pilgrim*.

There were plenty of others, less candid. A careful scrutiny of Temple's editorial essays in *The Pilgrim* discovers the germ, and often the actual form, of things to appear later in his books. His prophetic powers were by then quite manifest. He came to believe of the radical's role and the prophet's, "His appeal is not to a new principle, but to a new application of an old principle, so that he often presents himself as urging a return to the better ways of past generations. Few radical reformers can hope for great success who are unable to present themselves with perfect honesty as the only true conservatives." [23]

He took hold as editor in 1920, the year after the Enabling Act ended the Life and Liberty story. He stayed with it throughout his life, as Canon at Westminster and most of his episcopacy in Manchester. Like *The Challenge,* it died because not enough Churchmen were enough concerned with Christian social witness and action to keep it alive. There were too many Whigs!

⚙ LIFE AND LIBERTY   The Life and Liberty Movement was a watershed in Temple's history. He had first "played ball" with a more or less official effort to adjust the Church's thought and ways to meet the new crisis in society precipitated by the First World War. As Canon Scott Holland said bluntly, the Church is in a bad way because it "has been allowed to lose its grip on the real facts, so that the big affairs of the world go on their way as if it were not there." [24]

In 1916 the Bishops chose twelve men, of whom Temple was one, to propose a plan—with "seventy others also" added later —for a National Mission of Repentance and Hope. It was a mission to *the nation,* not a nation-wide "mission" of the usual sort. But it never got off the ground. Sectarian churchmanship, officialitis, conservatism—these things prevented repentance and killed hope, i.e., hopeful reliance on *the Church* itself. Temple worked night and day, up and down the country, confronting the Church with its weakness and pleading its case with the people; to no avail. It was a bitter pill for him, and eye-opener. The one positive gain was a unanimous report of the Archbishops' Commission on Church and State, advocating a new and genuine measure of legislative autonomy for the Church: Lord Selborne was its chairman, Temple its youngest member. But the report began to "sit quiescent in the archives" almost at once—except that Temple was not going to let it die (and soon made his purpose clear). Under the confident urgings of his friends, perhaps especially of H.R.L. ("Dick") Sheppard of St. Martin-in-the-Fields, he sparked and skippered a new and vigorous, single-minded effort at reform-from-within-under-pressure-from-without. Sheppard called it a "ginger" group in the Church, and this one got results—not the least of which was Temple's national fame and prominence.

The Church was without any real initiative in the conduct of its own affairs, having to depend upon Parliament in an Erastian fashion that Temple hated. Army chaplains reported the contempt of the common man for the Church and its remoteness. The Church simply had no economic or cultural leadership. A "conspirator" group of about forty, meeting in St. Martin's in 1917, saw in Temple the leader so badly needed. [16] Churchmen, Catholic and Evangelical alike, trusted and respected him. Some of the group wanted to meet the sneers of Britain's increasingly socialist working people by at least wiping out the radical differences in salaries, whereby, for example, $20,000 might go to a pastor ministering to fewer than a thousand souls while others with twenty thousand souls in their parishes might receive only $1,000. (Their idea of a common treasury and a basic stipend, incidentally, continued to crop up in later manifestos like *Men, Money and the Ministry* and *Putting Our House in Order*, with which Temple from first to last aligned himself.) Having no real choice, nor wanting any, Temple resigned from St. James's—dropping in salary from $10,000 in the pounds sterling of those days to about $3,500, his new wife and marriage notwithstanding. He plainly said that he was determined to win self-management for the Church "even at the cost of disestablishment," although he was sure that "establishment counts for a great deal as a national profession of faith, and may count for more in this direction in the future." [25]

Temple was the Movement's mind and muscles. "That," commented *The Church Times,* "is its present strength, it may be its future weakness." Temple's task was to keep in harness both those who were sure freedom could be won without disestablishment and those who were equally sure it could not be. He hoped the former were right, but he couldn't be certain. [17] The Life and Liberty campaign was a non-party one: it had the support of all but the openly Erastian, whose view of Church-State "unity" is rather like the ancient Arian theology which claimed the Father and the Son to be one in the Godhead but nevertheless "subordinated" the Son to the Father!

It was not Church reform as an end but as a means that motivated Temple. "The end," testifies Dean Iremonger, who as Secretary took a strong part in it, "was that the Church should be able, through a cleansing of its life, to preach the Gospel to the nation with a clear conscience." The only limitation lay in Sheppard's slogan, "No Gaiters." Ecclesiastics below the rank of Bishop might be members, but "gaitered" clergy of any rank were excluded from the councils of the Movement. Hensley Henson, Dean of Durham, a Protestant and an Erastian, saw Gore's hand hidden in Temple's glove; on the other hand, extreme (not representative) Anglo-Catholics held off because they could not count on Temple to favor their special interests.

A vast throng attended the opening public meeting of Life and Liberty in the great Queen's Hall, London, and an overflow, chaired by Cyril Garbett, sat in the small hall. Henry Scott Holland said prayers for the leaders before they took the stage. Temple's speech that night, July 16, 1917, is still remembered by a few survivors with the same emotion, the same excitement and elation, that they felt when they heard it.

"Come out of your safety and comfort," he said. "Listen to the voice of the wind as it sweeps over the world, and stand where you may be caught in its onward rush." It caught on contagiously. The Dean of Durham was the only Nay voter on the resolution. [18] It urged the Archbishop to find out "without delay, and make known to the Church at large, whether and on what terms Parliament is prepared to give freedom to the Church in the sense of full power to manage its own life." Temple, Garbett (who followed Temple in the primacy of York, in 1942), and Albert Mansbridge, took the resolution to Archbishop David-son.

Little or nothing seemed to be of promise in the interview, and when the Archbishop promised to go into the matter of Church freedom "with reasonable speed" they knew they had to revolt. They did. They set out to do something about the recommendation of the Selborne Commission—autonomy for the Church. To the plea of the "obstructionists" that they should wait until the War ended and those at the Front came home, Temple replied that the Trade Union Congress and Labour Party were not "waiting," nor were the teachers with their new Education Bill; neither would the Church. He hurled himself into action. Up and down the country's length he went again, speaking and conferring from Land's End to John o'Groat's. It was a killing pace, combined with his editing of *The Challenge* (in railway carriages) and his continued work for Worker's Education. Mrs. Temple found a little house for them in West Kensington, London. He even arranged to celebrate Holy Communion weekly at the nearby church, St. Mary Abbots, where his former Queen's student, Cyril Hudson, on the staff there, taught him to don the "high church" vestments. [19] Briefly he thought of volunteering for the Forces but Gore and Davidson talked him into sticking to the home front.

By the Fall of 1918, after about a year's hectic effort, the Church's leaders agreed to push Parliament for a Church Assembly in which the Church could legislate its own affairs. Temple fought hard and successfully to open Assembly seats to women, a battle against the kind of reactionary second-class-membership spirit which still prevails in the General Convention of the American Church. He also successfully defended the "Baptismal franchise" (Confirmation not required for voters) in choosing delegates to the Assembly, and here he trod on Bishop Gore's toes! [20] Again, Henson's hand was the only one of the Church's leaders to go up against the vote to have the Archbishop present an enabling act to Parliament. (By this time Henson was Bishop of Hereford). Life and Liberty's main work was done. In the Assembly it had won the Church a place for free lawmakers, if not yet for free prophets, through the Enabling

Act of November, 1918. University College, Durham, asked Temple to come there as Master, and Balliol asked him back as Chaplain and philosopher. He turned them both down. Hoping to read more fully in classical theology, rather than in philosophy, he accepted a canonry at Westminster Abbey. It was, by the way, his third offer of a canonry at the Abbey in six years. By then he definitely preferred the Church road to the University road for himself, but he kept trying in *The Pilgrim* to maintain a happy combination of the Church's Christian witness, the University's rational inquiry, and the Labour Movement's passion for social justice.

❧ MANCHESTER, C.O.P.E.C., AND THE COAL STRIKE

Only sixteen months later, Lloyd George asked Temple to follow Bishop Knox in the Diocese of Manchester. Davidson, at Canterbury, and Lang, at York, urged him to have his name sent to the King. So did Dean Ryle and Bishop Gore. On January 25, 1921, William Temple was consecrated in York Minster. "Dick" Sheppard preached the sermon.

Knox had been a militant Protestant, and Manchester, in the heart of Lancashire, was notoriously Conservative; but Temple was neither. What better evidence could there be of his winsome nature and "catholic" temper than Manchester's immediate and unchanging love of him and pride in his episcopacy among them? And in Mrs. Temple, whose work as a Justice of the Peace ("J.P.") set a goal for many a competent Englishwoman. In much the same way that the parish of St. James's had never complained that he "neglected" it or failed to "stick to his knitting," so the Diocese of Manchester only gloried in his leadership both there and at large. And, in fact, in spite of his own lack of interest in administration as such, his natural tidiness and efficiency gave his Diocese, and later his Primatial Sees, better than average oversight anyway. One Lancastrian observed that Temple had "a natural inability to do anything badly." [26] Another comment was that he was a poor money-raiser but a good (economical) money-spender.

For example, he managed to do what the Diocese wanted and his predecessor did not. He made two workable jurisdictions by separating Blackburn. He showed the common touch by keeping on year after year with Knox's Blackpool Mission, preaching on the seaside sands in the midst of hordes of Bank Holiday trippers and bathers. Once he confirmed five night club dancing girls just before they sailed off to an engagement in New York. At this time, Harold Begbie spoke of the "significant fact of his happiness," calling him "a man whose centre must be cloudlessly serene, and who finds life definitely good." He also described him as "this fair-haired, fresh-faced and boylike Bishop of Manchester, smiling at us behind his spectacles, the square head very upright, the broad shoulders well back, the whole short stocky figure like a rock." [27]

Furthermore, just as he had, as Rector of St. James's, written *Studies in the Spirit and Truth of Christianity* and then *Church and Nation,* and as he had finished *Mens Creatrix* when he married and shortly afterward produced his *Issues of Faith* and his *Plato and Christianity,* so he marked his entrance upon the episcopate by producing in the first year at Manchester his *Life of Bishop Percival* and the S.C.M. lectures, *The Universality of Christ.*

A surprisingly wide range of life and thought in the modern churches, including the ecumenical Conference on Life and Work, got its start in the Conference on Politics, Economics, and Citizenship ("COPEC") in Birmingham in 1924. Its direct origin lay in a small group called the Collegium. This was sparked by Malcolm Spencer who later headed the Christian Social Council, an ecumenical study program for which Canon V. A. Demant once did research. The Collegium with a center in St. George's Square, London, was a non-denominational enterprise or fellowship. Temple liked to say that the Church is the only cooperative society which exists for the benefit of non-members. They sought to bring Christian social analysts together for prayer and study. Temple was chairman. Only one book was produced, *Competition,* to which Temple contributed a share. "COPEC" was first suggested by the Collegium in 1919 when Temple was still a Canon at the Abbey. With Bishop Gore as its Chairman, the Interdenominational Conference of Social Service Unions formally set up "COPEC." Temple was chairman of the Conference, Hugh Martin headed the executive committee, Canon Raven and Lucy Gardner were secretaries. Four years were spent in preparation before the Conference opened, with Temple presiding. It had produced, beforehand, twelve volumes of Christian social analysis of every aspect of society: cultural, economic, political.

Fifteen hundred delegates were there, eighty of them foreign participants from European and Asian lands; messages were read from the King and Ramsay MacDonald, the Labour Prime Minister, and from two ex-premiers, Baldwin and Asquith. Temple's part in it made him a man now doubly marked in the eyes of England, and of people abroad.

The Conference's social probes and findings were of the first order, but of even more lasting consequence was its permanent imprint on the budding ecumenical movement. It proclaimed that a common concern for social witness was the most vital basis for Church unity; that when churches work together, they can pray and think together. Temple symbolized this, eighteen years later, by his leadership role in the Oxford Life and Work meeting ("Church, Community and State") in the Summer of 1937. It was followed by his similar role in the Edinburgh Conference on Faith and Order. And from the two was born the World Council of Churches of which he was the Provisional Committee's first chairman as well as first president of the British Council of Churches.

There is a kind of irony in Temple's going to Manchester with his social views. Manchester is the name that sticks to the whole *laissez-faire* school of capitalist individualism against which Temple constantly fought, both in theory and practice. He had as strong convictions about its evils as any Marxist of his time, although on different, Christian grounds. The "Manchester School" held that "competition is the life of trade," an oversimple, pre-corporative notion: Temple had some reservations! It also held to the idea that "the best government is the least government," a negative and bourgeois view of the State which Temple, with St. Paul and St. Augustine, as well as with Plato and Marx, sharply repudiated. The Anti-Corn Law League of 1839 in Manchester had dedicated the city's name and fame to the hatred of all "government interference" in business, welfare, education—in anything but national defense. Temple, on the contrary, reversed the charges: he complained that business, by its failures and injustices, was interfering with the work of both Church and State! [21]

If the Manchester cotton magnates had any lingering hope that the Bishop would prove to be a "safe" man, it was rudely dispelled during the coal "stoppage" following the General Strike in 1926. The General Strike lasted only a few days. Called in sympathy for the Miner's Federation, it was soon called off in sympathy for the general public and concern for the public order and welfare. Temple happened to be at Aix, on the Continent, being treated for his chronic attacks of gout. But the coal strike was another, deeper-going matter, and it brought him into direct conflict with Conservatives from the Prime Minister (Stanley Baldwin) down.

Speaking of it in retrospect, in *Christianity and Social Order,* he said, "It is commonly assumed that Religion is one department of life, like Art or Science, and that it is playing the part of a busybody when it lays down principles for the guidance of other departments, whether Art and Science or Business and Politics. When a group of Bishops attempted to bring Government, coal-owners and coal miners together in a solution of the disastrous Coal Strike of 1926, Mr. Baldwin, then Prime Minister, asked how the Bishops would like it if he referred to the Iron and Steel Federation the revision of the Athanasian Creed, and this was acclaimed as a legitimate score." Temple heatedly repudiated any pietistic divorce of Christian duty and social concerns.

For seven years England's coal industry, because of its economic ills, had been on and off strike, limping along with government subsidies and controls, torn by owner-miner antagonisms. In 1919, a Royal (Sankey) Commission recommended nationalization, which the owners naturally opposed. In 1926, another Royal (Samuel) Commission urged only partial nationalization, but even this was bitterly rejected by the mine and collieries owners. (In the end, twenty-years later, Lord Sankey's whole-hog proposal was adopted anyway!) The brief but dramatic General Strike of the T.U.C. (like America's A.F.L.— C.I.O.) did nothing to ease the tension. The government seemed to do nothing on the excuse that first the miners and owners had to agree, which seemed not likely as things had gone. For this reason P.T.R. Kirk of the Industrial Christian Fellowship formed a group of Churchmen, including the Free Churches, to mediate. As a member of the committee, Temple joined a deputation to see the Prime Minister, to explain that they had concessions from the miners but none from the owners, and wanted the government to take some initiative. Baldwin refused. Temple, in an open letter to Baldwin, made public knowledge of the essential facts. Furious, Baldwin and others said that by their interference the Churchmen were only prolonging the conflict. Nothing aroused Temple more than the suggestion that the "Church" was "interfering" in something "not the Church's business" where social issues were at stake. [22]

At no point, it should be noted, did the Church mediators enter upon technical grounds. They took no side, for example, in the debate over whether a State subsidy or a loan should be used to "prime the pump" of the coal markets. They were only willing to go as far as to sound out owners and government on substituting a loan for a subsidy since Baldwin was adamantly opposed to the latter. Temple wrote to his wife: "But Litchfield [Kempthorne] agreed with me that while the Church, acting for good will, may pass on technical proposals to promote it, it is quite another thing for the Church to take the field saying some technical proposal (e.g., a loan) is certainly the righteous line of action." [23]

"Our religion and our office required of us," he wrote later to *The London Times,* "that we should do anything which lay in our power to bring them, in a literal sense, to reason." [28] To him this meant that his responsibility was to see if possible that the settlement was not only economically sound in itself, but reached with the minimum of bitterness or resentment and the maximum of good will. The whole episode was a big step forward, of course, in the ultimate semi-socialism of Britain following the Second World War. A year later his own political views were published in *Essays on Christian Politics;* and in the height of the Spanish Civil War he had already begun to voice opposition to "the Totalitarian State, whether Communist or Fascist."

One other affair brought Temple into tension with the secular powers; that was the refusal of Parliament to grant the Church the right by law to carry on its worship with the revised Prayer Book of 1928. It is a sad story in any perspective. The Church Assembly, brought into being by the Enabling Act following the Life and Liberty campaign and the Selborne Commission's report, had never justified Temple's hopes, to say nothing of the demands of others far to his left in the matter. He had claimed that, once the Assembly was created, [24] three reforms were urgent: a form of worship with more latitude and more catholicity, for different liturgical tastes; ecclesiastical courts with genuine moral as well as legal power; and a voice for the laity in the choosing of clergy for their parishes, regardless of whether the stipends came from advowsons or out of the funds of the Ecclesiastical Commissioners.

Here, only ten years after its opening, on the very first score of urgent reform, the Assembly's lack of genuine independence was made more than manifest in the Prayer Book defeat.

For twenty years official and unofficial committees had worked to put together a revision of the 1662 book which would be theologically, liturgically, and historically sound. Temple himself had labored on the proposals as they reached the Bishops, and, in his eyes, their final form was rightly inclusive. As he saw it, the Anglican genius is to be inclusive, not middle-of-the-road; he was himself a dialectical combiner of different values, not a compromiser nor an "in-betweener." [25]

Old Bishop Knox fought the Revised Book; the heavily Protestant people of Temple's own diocese resented it. Yet his defense of it at the Manchester Diocesan Conference in 1927, backed by Canon Peter Green and others, resulted in a favorable vote of better than two to one. His address was published under the title, *A Plea For The New Prayer Book*. By June, alas, Parliament had killed it legally.

Ramsay MacDonald, the Prime Minister and an elder in the

Presbyterian Kirk of Scotland, expressed his embarrassment at being in the position of having to deny to Church people the right to worship as they themselves thought fit. One bishop in the House of Lords said, with meaningful glances in Nonconformist directions, that it was all due to "machinations of the Protestant underworld."

What were they to do? Temple wrote, "I fear there will be less defiance in the Archbishop's utterance than I should wish for." And so it proved. Temple himself gave no comfort to those who said, "I told you so," pressing afresh for disestablishment. He had moved a long way from the opinion he held in 1913, when he "did not believe there was any means of release from our difficulties except by way of disestablishment." Nevertheless, he declared in the Church Assembly after the Prayer Book defeat, "The price of disestablishment would not be too great to pay" if needed after all to gain and keep the Church's freedom. The following July the Bishops somewhat defiantly declared that by the *jus liturgicum* any bishop might properly permit by his ordinary powers the use of the illegal Book in churches—not a quite straightforward bid for freedom, yet at least mild revolt. Temple himself left word, for example, that his funeral was to be according to the Revision, and so it was done at Canterbury in 1944.

⚙ YORK AND CHRISTIAN UNITY Stanley Baldwin, Temple's antagonist in the Coal Strike in 1926, nominated him with good grace three years later to King George for the northern primacy, the Province of York. [26] Cosmo Gordon Lang had been translated from York to Canterbury, following Davidson's retirement (one Scot after another), just as Temple would later be translated after Lang's resignation. *Eboracum* had a new "Ebor" just when its mining and industrial dioceses (e.g., Newcastle, Durham and Sheffield) were in near social chaos and needed a spiritual leader of his stamp. That Baldwin would go through with it, as Churchill had to do in 1942, is enough evidence of Temple's stature in people's eyes. He was indeed the only "People's Archbishop" (to use Sidney Dark's title), in the sense of a popular ecclesiastic, in hundreds of years. [27]

His thirteen-year Archepiscopate in the "North Country," 1929 to 1942, was his longest service in any one post. Only once did he find the broad mass of people dubious or disappointed in him, and that was when he joined forces with Baldwin to oppose the contemplated marriage of King Edward VIII to the American commoner, Mrs. Wallis Warfield Simpson, a twice divorced woman, thus causing the King's abdication in the same year as his accession. (Said Temple, "The harm was not in falling in love with another man's wife, but in not stopping the relationship when it began to go that way.") His leadership, his theology, and his social "radicalism" came to their mature development in the York days. And it was also in this period that he reached his stature in the ecumenical movement.

In this York period he was a world figure. He chaired the Council of the British Broadcasting Company, when radio was young. He was sworn in as a member of England's Privy Council. He preached at the Disarmament Conference at Geneva in 1932, a whole-souled advocate of the League of Nations. In his sermon he directly challenged the popular view that Germany's was the sole guilt in 1914, as set into a clause of the Versailles Treaty: "We have to ask not only who dropped the match but who strewed the ground with gunpowder." (According to G. K. A. Bell, in his book on Randall Davidson, Temple tried to get the Archbishop, his "second father," to sign a statement confessing England's share of war guilt, but Davidson refused.)[29] He took the chair at the Lambeth Conference of Anglican Bishops (1932). He continued preaching University missions (e.g. Oxford, 1931, and Dublin, 1934), delivered the Gifford Lectures at Glasgow, revisited the United States for the Student Volunteer Movement and to lecture in various American universities. A Wesleyan critic, who prized preaching and thought that bishops and archbishops "have no very brilliant record in the matter," believed Temple to be "the ablest preacher that has filled either of the provincial thrones." At the same time, his energies were equal to both the demands of his diocese and his obligations as the Metropolitan of his Province. When he left York in 1942, he had visited 424 of its 457 parishes, some more than once. Unlike most other incumbents, the Temples knew everybody in and about Bishopsthorpe, and were welcome visitors in most homes there. In addition to his own provincial responsibilities, Lang's illness of several years saddled him with the duties of both Primates. Men in secular walks of life, whether professed Christians or not, drew his interest and sympathy because—as he explained in his Lenten book *Citizen and Churchman*—"Worldly cynicism is less nauseating than pious humbug." [30]

And with all this, he still produced another dozen volumes in addition to papers in journals, magazine articles, and chapters in important *symposia,* including *Contemporary British Philosophy, Doctrine in the Church of England, Men Without Work,* and *Revelation.*

In a dozen years he produced a dozen books. The Gifford Lectures, *Nature, Man and God* (one volume of 530 pages) were alone a prodigious achievement. Temple is the only archbishop who ever delivered them, and we must regret that Dean Iremonger's detailed biography not only omits any circumstantial account of their preparation and delivery but fails even to mention the sojourns in the University of Glasgow, and the visits with Sir Robert Rait, Principal and Vice-Chancellor. [28] They were written in trains and hotels, in snatches of a free hour at home in Bishopsthorpe on York's river Ouse (in their beloved garden, when the weather was right), or in his London lodgings in the Lollards Tower at Lambeth, or half-hours at bedtime. It is an interesting study to determine by careful scrutiny how much of these lectures consist of passages from earlier publications, not only such philotheological works as *Mens Creatrix* and *Christus Veritas,* but other books and articles, now woven into a new construction, revised, rephrased, and polished with amazing continuity. They were written *as he gave them,* beginning in November, 1932, and ending in March, 1934. (Inevitably his ecclesiastical, social, and ecumenical leadership kept him from being the detailed scholar some of his contemporaries were: Kenneth Kirk, A. E. Taylor, Oliver Quick, as examples.)

Christian Faith and Life, which had eleven printings in his lifetime, was published from a shorthand report of his addresses in 1931 at the Oxford University mission. It was usually thought to have been the most effective of his popular, apologetic presentations of the Christian faith to students. As a philosopher-theologian he knew perfectly well that faith is not to be had by any simple exercise of reason. There is the neo-classic and unprecedented story of his faltering and retreating in embarrassment, at a loss for words (almost an unheard of thing) because it suddenly occurred to him, addressing a student gathering at Swanick, that in all of his life he had never really felt any doubt of God's existence or love; and therefore to "advise" the true doubter was for him presumptuous! His sympathy for intellectually honest doubt was unbounded.

As with his catch-as-catch-can work on the Gifford Lectures, so it was with his *Readings in St. John's Gospel* (two volumes of 412 pages). The Fourth Gospel was part of the warp and weft of his mind. This book may seem a *tour de force* of biblical scholarship, and it is often attacked on grounds of technical critical learning. Even so, its meditative thinking probably came easier than other things he wrote out of the hurly-burly of his life. There is much truth in John Bennett's remark that Temple "receives publicity for everything except the thing that he is most concerned about—personal religion." [31] People have said—Reinhold Niebuhr, for one—that the *Readings* combined the devotional and scholarly in a new way, and some even thought them the best devotional treatise by an Anglican since William Law's *Serious Call.* "With St. John," he said, "I am at home." He always believed Browning's *Death in the Desert* to be the best commentary on the Fourth Gospel. His defense of its historicity, when this was not the reigning view, puts him very close to contemporary scholarship. [29]

Early in the twenties, some uneasiness over the inclusiveness ("lack of agreement") in the Church had brought into being a Doctrinal Commission of all stripes of opinion, to explore doctrinal differences and how they might be minimized. Started on its work in 1922, under the Bishop of Oxford (Burge), the Commission finished and reported in 1938. Temple succeeded Burge in the chair in 1925 and remained fourteen years to the end. Its report, *Doctrine in the Church of England,* is not of uniform quality and in some ways is surprisingly oversimple. Yet it has the virtue and value of being the only study of its kind, a corporate inquiry into "Anglicanism." It gave no comfort to those who wanted a "rule of faith" with which to measure orthodoxy. As the title put it, the Commission described the doctrine "in," not *of* the Church. A group of irritated Norfolk laymen wrote that "a higher standard of honesty was expected among businessmen," to which Temple replied that if honesty means "saying what you think when you haven't taken the trouble to think much," then they may be right. But he believed honesty meant a serious effort to study and think through various sides of the truth, and on that view the report was at least honest. (Perhaps this is the highest claim we can make for nonconfessional Anglicanism: in any case, Temple's distrust of code law and doctrinaire dogma was such that the report caused him no disappointment.)

"Ecumenics" were in the forefront of his attention those days. He was aware of the tragedy in Anthony Trollope's remark, "The Apostle of Christianity and the infidel can meet without the chance of a quarrel; but it is never safe to bring together two men who differ about a saint or a surplice." [32] He worked for Christian unity on all fronts: in evangelism and missions, [30] life and work, faith and order. In his case it went back to his S. C. M. stewardship in Edinburgh in 1910, and his tour of Australia. In 1928, he and Tawney, eager to fall in with J. H. Oldham's and John R. Mott's plans for an ecumenical conference in Jerusalem, went out there to the Missionary Conference. In 1927, the Church Assembly had agreed that the Church of England should take part in the Lausanne meeting on Faith and Order; and Temple, still at Manchester, was one of those nominated. There he worked with Brent, Archbishop Söderblom, Garvie, Deissman, Gore, Headlam, the older leaders; and he learned the ropes wherewith to link their spirit with the vigor of younger "ecumenists" coming along. In 1929, he was Chairman of the Christian Unity committee of the 1930 Lambeth Conference. For all of this he felt he had a Johannine charter, what he thought was "perhaps the most sacred passage even in the four Gospels," the Great High Priestly Prayer in Chapter 17: "Holy Father, keep them in thy name which thou hast given me, *that they may be one, even as we are."* It is a cause for some regret that Temple never took time, perhaps could not do so because of his "existential" involvement in it, to write as extensively on the theory of ecumenics as on other phases of contemporary constructive theology. But perhaps his active contribution, as a doer of the word, was of greater value to Christendom: in any case, what he *did* about it obviously acted out the whole of his theological point of view.

His labor and *travel* for Faith and Order, accompanied by his wife, or described in letters to her, is typical of all his ecumenical efforts. In 1929, at Maloja in the Engadine, foot of the Italian Alps, he was elected to succeed the American Bishop Charles Brent on the continuation committee. This strategic and vital post he held for the next fifteen years, in the *decisive* fifteen years before the World Council of Churches started. In 1930, he went to Murren, near Interlaken at the foot of the Jungfrau, for a committee meeting. It took him to Hertenstein on Lake Lucerne in 1934; Fano on the west coast of Denmark in the North Sea in 1935; to Clarens on Lake Geneva, near Montreux, in 1936, and again in 1938. (The settings of these meetings suggest something more pleasant than hard work, it will be observed.) And, of course, he chaired the Conference on Faith and Order in Edinburgh in the summer of 1937, where as a student in 1910 he had shown conference members to their seats. After he died, the *Christian Century* (Nov. 8, 1944) chortled editorially about the last night of the Conference, when, as a typical gesture of geniality and fraternity, he laid aside his clerical garb of gaiters and apron to preside at the closing session in a light gray suit and a blue tie! [31]

So with his ecumenical concern in other areas. Two weeks before the Edinburgh meeting opened he had attended the Oxford Conference, on "Church, Community and State." (He did not get to the first one, the Stockholm meeting on Life and Work in 1925, nor the Madras meeting in 1937.) Already he had contributed papers to a preparation volume, *Christian Faith and the Common Life.* The first, yet not so faint, signs of totalitarianism (then especially fascism) and of scientific humanism, portending one-party states and nuclear militarism, were already their concern. He served in the *Una Sancta* section, and in another dealing with "The World of Nations." Inevitably, Temple was asked to draft the Oxford message on social questions and, at the end, he wrote for four and a half hours (until 1:15 a.m.) to produce it. Already he was the champion of unification, for the merging of Life and Work with Faith and Order, on the plea that Christian action must think through its theology, just as theology needs the dynamic of action. Always he proclaimed *unity rather than uniformity*, remembering Gore's advice. Yet he was resisted: the Bishop of Gloucester (A. C. Headlam), for example, accused him of "practically destroying" the Faith and Order Movement because he (Headlam) wanted it kept out of an ecumenical undertaking like a World Council.

Temple's view prevailed, and in 1938, at Utrecht, he became Chairman of a provisional committee of the World Council of Churches. Anglo-Catholic resistance continued with some strength, but he won the English Church's approval. In 1939, he wrote asking the Cardinal Secretary at the Vatican for exchange of information and unofficial consultation with Roman Catholic theologians, and the Vatican replied through the Apostolic Delegate in London that it "saw no obstacles in the way." In the other ecclesiastical direction, in 1943, he arranged for Garbett to visit the Moscow Patriarchate as a first step in reopening relations with the Church in the Soviet Union. [32]

The thorniest problem of Christian unity was within his own Church because the most actual and material attempt at it was the scheme for a Church of South India (soon to be an accomplished fact). This proposal was for the unification of four Anglican dioceses in South India with the Methodists, Presbyterians and Congregationalists in the area. Its basis was to be the four essentials of Catholic Christianity as set out by the Lambeth Conference ("Quadrilateral"): the Scriptures, the dominical sacraments of Baptism and Holy Communion, the ecumenical Creeds, and the historic Episcopate. The ministers, except for the first non-Anglicans while they lived, were to be ordained episcopally. Temple supported it, and favored a limited inter-communion for it with the Churches of the Anglican Communion. Seventeen years earlier, he had presented a report on it to the bishops of the Church. There was strong resistance by some Anglo-Catholic elements. There were even threats of schism, of "going over" to Rome, or of joining the Old Catholics. To one group of superiors in various religious orders, he replied that he would not meet with them until they withdrew such a threat. To all in the opposition, he observed that, while they were of the opinion that we cannot be in communion with any but those who can guarantee they hold "the full Christian faith," to him it was "axiomatic" that we should seek communion with all and sundry "unless we have ground for assurance that they do *not*" hold the "full faith."

One other wartime phase of his ecumenical leadership should be noted. This was the interdenominational "Religion and Life" movement. It was what Temple called "Social Evangelism" (*Social Witness and Evangelism*), started by the Anglican and Free Churches to witness to the relevance of Christian life and faith to the social issues trying men's minds and sapping their energies. This theological and social campaign was in the tradition of "COPEC," Life and Work, the Christian Social Council, and the British Council of Churches. It felt an added strength, faced as it was by a rapidly secularizing nation, when a Roman Catholic movement called "The Sword of the Spirit" joined them, making it an "interfaith" enterprise. To offer the Romans some common ground, Temple and others soon suggested a "Natural Law" approach to the moral theology of social problems of conscience. [33] This ended when the Romans, on second thought, withdrew from a dangerously contagious form of Christian fraternity!

Temple spoke to a great number of these meetings all over England, lecturing with startling, illuminating effect upon their whole agenda of concerns: the home, school, industry and business, the world of nations, and the world-wide Church. It was one of the major drains on his strength and life. In 1944, posthumously, a collection of eighteen of his major addresses, social and ecumenical, was published with the title, *The Church Looks Forward*.

Cut off from the Continental churches by the Second World War, Temple re-marshalled his forces and focused them at home

for the foundation of the British Council of Churches. In his
B.B.C. inaugural sermon in 1942, at a service in St. Paul's Cathedral, he insisted that "the primary need is for more clear and
united testimony to Christianity itself. The difference between
Catholic and Protestant is very small as compared to the difference between Christians and non-Christians." [34] He was at the
Amsterdam World Christian Youth Conference the sad summer
that ended in war, 1939. Said his successor, the Archbishop of
York, "Archbishop Temple probably did more than any one man
had ever previously done for Christian unity." [33]

◉ AMERICA   His brief visit to America in 1915, to give the
Paddock Lectures in New York, whetted his appetite for more.
On that occasion he had to sail the Atlantic through submarine-
infested waters. He happily accepted invitations to lecture at an
international Student Volunteer Movement meeting in Indianapolis in December, 1935, and to visit and lecture in several American universities. Mrs. Temple went with him. This time his
journey was safer than his visit. He had been warned that sentiment for and against Roosevelt's New Deal was running high and
that as a semi-official British dignitary he should walk and speak
softly. He spoke with meticulous although somewhat amused
care, sometimes openly amused. Privately, he expressed sorrow
over the New Deal's concessions to conservative economics; e.g.,
the "A. A. A." farm program which under a supply-and-demand
doctrine, had resulted in the destruction of real wealth (such as
pigs and cotton) for the sake of "free prices," as indeed, the artificial scarcity of the quota-and-subsidy price support programs have
continued to do. Publicly, he was circumspect. Nevertheless, the
more conservative wing of American newspapers, especially
Hearst's, peppered him with accusations of being "bungling and
mischievous," in a sort of Tommy-Go-Home campaign. The anti-
English lunacy of "Big Bill" Thompson, Mayor of Chicago, was
still getting a popular hearing among the Irish and some central-
southern European immigrant groups.

On his arrival he preached to four thousand at the Cathedral of
St. John the Divine in New York. At a Pilgrim dinner in his

honor he said of the Americans and the British, "We are made for friendship, both in the bewildering differences that so surprise us when we assume similarity, and the equally perplexing similarity which comes to contradict us if we assume that we are different."

The students at Indianapolis greeted his lectures (*Basic Convictions*) with nearly as much emotional excitement as they had given his friend Studdert-Kennedy ten years earlier, and with more intellectual response. Perhaps this was because both men followed the same "line": that salvation is social, and while we might be damned individually since isolation *is* damnation, we are saved as members one of another. At Harvard he gave the Belden Noble Lectures (*Christianity in Thought and Practice*). Princeton conferred an honorary degree of LL.D. (1936). [35] Between Chicago, their westernmost visit, and the East Coast, the Temples stopped off at various places. Having been importuned to attend an English Speaking Union dinner in Cincinnati ("no real address, just a friendly word"), he innocently annoyed a lot of people by rising to say, after a long introduction, that he was happy to be there, enjoyed the dinner, and was grateful especially because, in a strangely un-American way, they didn't expect him to make a speech. Then he sat down.

He later put first, in the order of his pleasures, a week he spent with about twenty of the clergy of the American Church at the College of Preachers at the National Cathedral in Washington, where he also preached. His lectures, *The Centrality of Christ*, were discussed vigorously, to his huge enjoyment; and the clergy there had a chance to see the fabled cleric giving off-the-cuff, accurate quotations from Aristotle in Greek, Augustine in Latin (his photographic memory "trick"), chuckling or laughing with high amusement, eating, walking, and listening. Except for his ecumenical trips to Switzerland and Utrecht, and one wartime venture still to be described, he made no other trips abroad beyond a journey with Mrs. Temple to Venice and Athens in 1938, *en route* to the consecration of a new cathedral in Cairo, and a short visit in Malta on the return journey. From the Amsterdam meeting in 1939 to his death in 1944, he never "officially" set foot off English soil again.

✿ MALVERN AND SOCIAL EVANGELISM   The Church Assembly made Temple chairman of its Commission on Evangelism,
and for him evangelism was something to be carried out by the
lay ministry as well as the clerical ministry. Therefore the laymen
were a special concern with him. Added to his eager drive for an
effective ministry of the laity on its own merits was his related
conviction that laymen are key figures today because modern
evangelism has to be social in its terms and methods, as well as
personal; and laymen, more than clergy, are the Christians who
are involved in, and operate, the social structures of the world,
economic and political.

When he thought of the laity he meant both men and women,
and he constantly struggled against the subordinate and falsely
humble place given to women in both Church and society. In
1918, he led the fight, a successful one, for the right of women
to sit in the Assembly. Seconded by Mrs. Temple's devoted service, he backed "women's work" in the Church as well as "men's
work," and strengthened the orders for deaconesses. He was convinced that deaconesses were ordained ministers. He never
changed his mind about either the principle itself or the strategy
of postponement, which he explained in a letter to a parson's
wife in 1916. "Personally I want (as at present advised) to see
women ordained to the priesthood. But still more do I want to
see both real advance towards the reunion of Christendom, and
the general emancipation of women. To win admission to the
priesthood now would put back the former and to most it would
put back the latter."

Apart from his role in the coal strike, probably the most dramatic episode in Temple's history was the Malvern Conference
of 1941. Four hundred people attended, including twenty-three
out of the ninety-eight bishops in the Church, fourteen deans,
twenty-one canons, fourteen archdeacons, ninety parish priests;
the rest were laity. It was first planned for London, but the blitz
was so fierce that the Government forbade it. Therefore they went
to the cold halls of Malvern College in the Midlands: hence the
name. It was early in the War, when England was enduring a

merciless bombing and the R.A.F. death rate was appalling. Talk of peace aims as well as war aims—the "purposive idealism of war"—went on in the papers, pulpits and forums. The key word of the day was "social reconstruction," and every promise was made that a true economic democracy would see to it that since a nation could feed and employ everybody in a war it would do it in peace. It was a daily tune. In this moral climate Prebendary Kirk of the Industrial Christian Fellowship got Temple's promise to gather and preside at a conference of churchmen on the "ordering of a new society." A German Nazi magazine ran a hideous caricature of him, showing him on the street with his gas mask, with the caption "England's Leading Christian On His Way To Tea With His Spiritual Brother, The Ambassador Of Bolshevismus."

W. G. Peck, one of the "Christendom group," who analyzed the problems of "Christian Sociology" in terms of a highly sacramental theology, was then giving full time to the I.C.F. He arranged to have papers read, mainly by spokesmen for his own "school," which was entirely satisfactory with Temple: Dorothy Sayers, Maurice Reckitt, T. S. Eliot, Middleton Murry, D. M. Mackinnon, H. A. Hodges, V. A. Demant. There were a couple by Sir Richard Acland and Kenneth Ingram. The two last named "stole the show." The more clearly reasoned, but also more academic, papers of the Christendom group (to whom Temple was actually closer because of their more explicit theological approach) were largely ignored. [36]

Acland's insistence that common ownership of the means of production is a fundamental Christian principle took the center of the stage. This, of course, was what made the newspaper headlines in England and America. Opposition to a position so baldly socialist was strong within the Conference, but after three days of debate, the Archbishop drafted an acceptable finding in which it was said that "the ultimate ownership of the principal resources of the community" in the hands of private owners "*may* be" a stumbling-block to a just society. The vote was "unanimous," however, only because it was *nemine contradicente*, for a large number present did not vote for or against. Important here, obviously, were the equivocating terms: "ultimate," "principal," and "may be." Temple's first draft said *"is"* rather than "may be" but the Conference majority voted to make the change.

In the United States the press naturally gave a prominent place to the Malvern news. The ecumenical journal *Christendom* devoted most of its 1941 summer number to the Malvern findings and a critical commentary upon them. Within a month's time after the Malvern meeting, a meeting to follow up its lead was called in New Haven, Connecticut, by the Church League for Industrial Democracy—the American opposite number to the Industrial Christian Fellowship. About three hundred and fifty came. It opened with a sermon in which Frederick C. Grant, the New Testament scholar, developed the theme that when speaking of the Kingdom of God "we are not talking about 'heaven' and neither was our Lord; He was talking, and we should talk, about the reign of God in the present world, here and now as well as hereafter." [34] The Acland amendment to the Malvern Declaration, proposing outright socialism, which had not been adopted at Malvern, was carried to adoption unanimously at New Haven. In his greetings to the American conference, Temple thought news coverage of Malvern might have startled those who were there; but, apart from the "journalistic fantasies," he was glad interest was created.

For Temple, who was in favor of a "mixed economy" with some private and some public enterprise (having given up the relatively more doctrinaire socialism of his pre-Manchester days), Malvern's cautious resolution was entirely satisfactory, even though it displeased the polar opposites of Right and Left. But, for all its care and balance, a compromise draft could not hold everybody who *in situ* voted for it. When the poet, Eliot, a quite conservative man, and Alec Vidler, editor of *Theology,* returned to London they reconsidered their votes and announced their *disapproval* of the resolution. The whole affair fixed widespread attention upon the Church and its wartime leadership, on the whole favorably. A year later, the Prime Minister who, such is England's genius, was a Conservative of conservatives, sent Temple's name to the King as Lang's successor in St. Augustine's

Chair. When George Bernard Shaw heard it, he said, "A realized impossibility."

Temple was a constant target for jokesters of the conservative or complacent sort. The Bishop of Gloucester, his antagonist in the ecumenical movement, took a slap at his idealism in 1943. "Your Grace, I find that in St. John the Divine's description of the New Jerusalem, there was no TEMPLE therein." [35] Temple probably roared with appreciative laughter. Henson said that he was "running gaily before the wind of Socialism," and later on he thought that Temple was lucky to die when he did, with the Socialist tide at flood, before it and his reputation had begun to ebb.[36]

Malvern had a strong follow-up, spear-headed by the I.C.F., although it was a bit tardy starting. Its real start may be laid in a crowded meeting in Albert Hall, London, in September of the next year. Temple spoke, and with him the Archbishop of York (Garbett); Sir Stafford Cripps, Lord Privy Seal; the Bishop of Bristol (C. S. Woodward); and others. Temple's address on Christian social concern was much along his usual lines. He never rode a hobby nor dealt with any one problem obsessively, as we may see, for example, in the serious support he gave a cause like the Howard League for Penal Reform. He did not merely oppose capital punishment (which he did in the National Council for Abolition of the Death Penalty), but he backed a wide range of constructive policies, as shown in his *Ethics of Penal Action* and the briefer *Ethics of Punishment*. So with other things besides the economic issues that concerned the I.C.F. As was said of Scott Holland, so it could almost be said of Temple, that he had "no message for tired souls."

At the Albert Hall meeting he made some brief yet unexpected remarks on the subject of credit reform. He suggested that credit has become as important to our economic life as currency, or more so, and that *neither* of them should be "minted" by such private sources as the un-nationalized banks. He proposed that all credit should be publicly issued and cancelled. This clearly resembled the "social credit" doctrines of Major Douglas which were espoused by the Christendom group, and a storm of denunci-

ation swirled up from business circles. (It shortly appeared that
Archbishop Garbett, who attended the meeting and sat with
Temple on the platform, was not so keen as Temple on the I.C.F.
program, and he definitely disliked his monetary views.)

Even the National Association of Manufacturers in the United
States set out to show that Temple was both ignorant and dangerous. The *Spectator* thought that the support outweighed the criticism, but there was most assuredly a lot of both. One important
result was the address he was invited to make, to elaborate his
views, to the Bank Officers' Guild the following February. The
I.C.F. "went to the country" with their issues. Temple, in the
midst of all his other duties as wartime Primate, spoke at his
health's cost to meetings in nearly all of the major cities of England and Scotland, a gruelling effort which certainly took a fatal
toll. Like President Roosevelt, he died in the penultimate year of
the War, 1944.

Undoubtedly Temple was driven by a powerful conscience and
loving concern; he would often say with much psychological wisdom, "What wears one out is not what one does but what one
doesn't do." Cosmo Lang is commonly said to have told Archbishop Garbett that he had resigned in order to make way for
Temple, but would never have done so if such an early death had
been foreseen. Conservative churchmen were grumbling for other
reasons. Dean Inge thought Temple a dangerous man, even
though Temple was godfather to Inge's son. He called Temple's
Thoughts in War-Time (1940) "a pitiful downfall of what was
once a fine and candid mind," and called his appointment to
Canterbury "a disastrous choice" for war-torn England.[37] [37]

Nevertheless, somehow within the merry-go-round of sermons,
travel, controversies, debates in the House of Lords, administration, and all the rest of it, his gift for conceptual thinking remained intact. It was demonstrated at a meeting of the Aquinas
Society in the Caxton Hall, London, in October, 1943. Victor
White, the Dominican, describes how Temple arrived late from
some public duty or other and delivered an amazingly perceptive
and shrewd lecture on Thomism and the half-dozen respects in
which, as he saw it, it does not measure up to modern needs. All
of this from a few notes scribbled on a slip of paper. (Five years

earlier, he had done the same thing at a meeting of the Thomas More Society of Roman Catholic lawyers, in a talk on medieval philosophy.) The critique of Thomism was taken down by short-hand notes, printed in *Blackfriars,* and then reprinted by the Society in pamphlet form, with a rejoinder by Father White. [38]

Once during the War he left England, a venture carried out without any fanfare. As Archbishop of York, he joined G. K. A. Bell (Bishop of Chichester, also a man of courage and social vision who, like Temple, preferred the barricades to the battle-ments), William Paton of the provisional World Council of Churches secretariat, and the Wesleyan leader, Henry Carter, in a trip to Holland in January, 1940, aimed at offering suggestions for a negotiation of peace. The prime mover was Bishop Berg-grav, the Lutheran Primate of Norway, and after they agreed on a memorandum, he took it on to Berlin. The Nazi authorities ignored it, and he returned to Oslo through England to become the Christian hero of the Norwegian resistance to Quisling-ism. Quick and thoughtless cries of "appeasement" by the belli-cose made all such explorations difficult: in another two years they were impossible, yet Temple never submitted to the "un-conditional surrender" doctrine, and Bishop Bell went on chal-lenging it to the very end. [39]

As a non-pacifist whose love-ethics were realistic enough to justify war under some circumstances (in, be it recognized, the era before nuclear weapons of mass extermination had reconsti-tuted the whole thorny problem), Temple kept his friendship with pacifists even at the height of jingo war sentiment. He often sat with the Cloister Group which met in the Lodge of Canon Charles Raven when he was Master of Christ's College, Cam-bridge. Speaking to the truth as he saw it, in love, he wrote a preface for a controversial wartime pamphlet, *Christ and Our Enemies,* by his longtime friend and Balliol classmate (jailed for war resistance in World War I), a Quaker-Anglican-Pacifist—Stephen Hobhouse. He defended the freedom and integrity of conscientious objectors, and in various ways debated the issues of pacifism in a consistently serious but respectful fashion. Shep-pard, in 1937, was so upset by Temple's criticism of the Peace Pledge that he put it to Dean Matthews whether he shouldn't leave the ministry, to which the reply was that they had not yet subscribed "to the dogma of the infallibility of the Archbishop of York!"

✿ AT THE END He had been enthroned at Canterbury in April on St. George's Day of 1942. [40] Just on the eve of his departing to America on a war comradeship errand, Lang pulled him back, disclosing his secret decision to resign. The War was at its height. The Battle of Britain had been turned in some degree by the Allies' strategic bombing; but just at that time, in Churchill's purple phrase, the war was truly a "mortal combat." As usual, he signalled his new role with a new book.

For the Penguin Press he readied his last book-length treatise, *Christianity and Social Order,* which promptly sold more than 100,000 copies. By 1958 more than 150,000 had been sold. Never had an Archbishop spoken so unmistakably for the conscience of Britain, or so fully and unsparingly. (Future historians will want to explore, through official papers if possible, what reasons there were for the almost "subliminal" association between the Primate and the Prime Minister. During the two and a half years of Temple's primacy there was only one contact recorded by Iremonger: Churchill's objection, personally, to Temple's appeal to the Government to reject any suggestion that Britain should shackle German prisoners of war merely in retaliation for the Nazi practice.) In the drama laden atmosphere of D-Day, June 6, 1944, he read his Ainslee Lecture in St. Martin-in-the-Fields undauntedly, *Christianity as an Interpretation of History.* In the House of Lords he championed the new Education Act of 1944 which brought in needed and wanted changes. Over the years (he sat in the House nineteen years), his coldness and skeptical attitude toward the Lords had modified, and so had their liking for him, if not their approval. The new Act rectified old injustices to Nonconformist schools, helped the Church's in a measure, and avoided a full-scale revolt of the Teachers' Union which disliked a provision in it for daily classroom prayers. [41]

Living was always a matter of "austerity" and often dangerous. He and Mrs. Temple were in the range of bombs more than once, especially the V-2's. Lambeth—once his boyhood home—had been badly hit; they had only a few rooms left for an "office and flat." Canterbury "got it bad" and the Temples won the inhabitants' love by "sticking," and helping in many ways. He pressed constantly for official and unofficial aid to the Jews victimized by Hitler's vicious policies. Through diplomatic and ecumenical Church channels he backed proposals for a negotiated peace, opposing the "unconditional surrender" policy. He visited the armed services, conducted prayer in industrial plants, corresponded with and for individual victims of grief or discrimination. He preached many Sundays in the churches of Croyden and East Kent where the bombing was bad. His broadcast sermons to troops in ships, in the African desert and Northern Italy brought such remarks as, "Now we understand for the first time what Christianity really is." A Labour Party leader said, in Canon Demant's hearing, that he envied the Church of England only one thing, its Primate whom he wanted as Prime Minister.[38]

Under all this pressure his gout was constantly acting up, and his suffering was great. All during the summer of '44, he suffered without let-up. His last public appearances were to attend a Retreat with his clergy on September 5, 1944, and then to deliver a Charge on evangelism to them at a Synod, September 18. He was brought there in an ambulance chair and instead of sitting, he stood on his one "good" leg as he spoke, and this worsened his condition. His last *pastoral* acts were on September 21-23, receiving each of his ordination candidates individually, as he lay in bed, and finally gathering them together around him for a final word. His death came in the morning of October 26, a few hours after the death of Princess Beatrice, last surviving child of Queen Victoria. He died without pain but unable to breathe. In a letter to friends, Mrs. Temple said, "I want to tell you that until half an hour before his death he was entirely happy and taking his usual interest in the affairs of the day, and we were hopeful that he was on the way to recovery from the infection that had so much lowered his strength and kept him in bed for some weeks." On his own 80th birthday, October 31, Cosmo Gordon Lang, his predecessor as Primate, officiated at the funeral in Canterbury. [42]

"Ministers of good things," said Richard Hooker, "are like torches, a light to others, waste and destruction to themselves." [39] Hensley Henson's description of him as "feminist, socialist and catholic" comes nowhere near the true man.[40] What he held before himself and tried to be is best summed up in a passage from his own Enthronement Sermon:

> "So let us set ourselves to gain a deepening loyalty to our Anglican tradition of Catholic order, Evangelical immediacy in our approach to God, and liberal acceptance of new truth made known to us: and let us at the same time join with all our fellow Christians who will join with us in bearing witness to the claim of Christ to rule in every department of life, and to the principles of His Kingdom."

That was William Temple: a man of (1) Catholic order, (2) Evangelical piety, (3) Liberal openness to new truth, (4) Ecumenical earnestness, (5) and Social concern in politics, economics, the arts, "every department of life." Dean Matthews doubted that "any other man has done as much to convince the general public that the Christian faith has a claim to be seriously considered by rational men, and that it has something important to say on the problems that confront contemporary society." [41] And *Punch* said, in the dark days of post-war doubts and premonitions (August 11, 1948): "If Christian sanity survives the modern world, none will deserve a greater share of the credit than William Temple." He was on any appreciative estimate one of the post-Reformation Anglican Communion's own "Four Great Doctors," with Richard Hooker, Joseph Butler, and F. D. Maurice.

Notes

1. Four primates had less than a year: Feologild (832), Aefsige and Beorthelm (959), and Thomas Bradwardine (1349); two for only a year or so: Robert of Jumièges (1051-52) and Matthew Hutton (1757-58); three for about as long as Temple: Simon Langham (1366-68), John Kemp (1452-54), Henry Dean (1501-03).

2. The only personally written and published essay of this kind by Temple himself is the introduction he wrote for E. G. Sandford's *Appreciation* of his father, Frederick Temple. It adds nothing to the meagre background data in the first volume of Snell's biography of Frederick. The brief ancestral sketch given here is based largely upon findings in E. G. Sandford, ed., *Frederick Temple: Archbishop of Canterbury* (2 vol.); the same author's *Frederick Temple: An Appreciation;* Bishop G. K. A. Bell's memoir in the Penguin edition of A. E. Baker's *William Temple and His Message;* F. J. Snell, *Early Associations of Archbishop [Frederick] Temple;* and *The Dictionary of National Biography.* It makes no use of and had no access to private family records. Dean Iremonger in his biography left such primary source material virtually untreated.

3. By straight count of the list in *Crockford's Clerical Directory 1959-60.* Enumerations vary slightly from writer to writer, although A. M. Ramsey's enthronement June 27, 1961 was announced as the 100th.

4. When J. M. Wilson, Canon of Worcester, wanted to see the records of the Sierra Leone affair he was refused permission by the authorities. There may be a bit of mystery in that suddenly ended, tragic story. (E. G. Sandford, *Frederick Temple,* Macmillan, N.Y., 1906, II.24 n.)

5. Curiously enough, the Dictionary of National Biography makes no reference to Sankey's short run as an assistant master at Colet Court.

6. His strongest musical negative in later years was, "I detest plainsong."

7. Many of those letters are preserved. Dean Iremonger found that the richest source of this kind, however, were his letters to his wife and to his brother Frederick. His brother was an engineer, specializing in sanitation and water works. He was once President of the Institute of

Sanitary Engineers. After a period in Birmingham he went out to India, where he married Frances Copleston, daughter of the Bishop of Calcutta. The Frederick Temples had five children of whom one was a son, Frederick Stephen, who followed the usual school path and University pattern, plus Trinity and Westcott House at Cambridge. Ordained, he first had a country ministry, then went to Hong Kong in 1953 as Dean of the Cathedral under Bishop Ronald Hall. In 1959 he returned to England as Chaplain to Archbishop Fisher.

8. These days were the last of his almost-Tory youth. He and his brother were delighted to be gentlemen-in-waiting for their father at the Coronation of Edward VII, and, indeed, William's radical social views were never at any time republican. It was only as an undergraduate that he acted as an all-out champion of the Establishment without reservations. Nonconformists were still "chapel folk" in his lexicon. Empire policy in general, the Boer War in particular, presented no problems of conscience . . . In short, he was intellectually curious but not yet quite critical.

9. On April 23, 1928, as a delegate in Jerusalem to the ecumenical missionary conference, he wrote to his wife: "I was drafting all morning, and seemed to be regarded as having done rather conspicuously my parlour trick of fitting everybody's pet point into a coherent document when they thought they were contradicting one another" (Iremonger, 396). He would draft a consensus, having listened carefully to the debate, and lay it before a conference with astonishing success. Sometimes, however, after a night's sleep, the participants were no longer quite so sure the "trick" worked well enough. This is what happened to T. S. Eliot and A. R. Vidler after they returned to London from the Malvern Conference. It must be acknowledged that he often moved too fast. At the C.O.P.E.C. meeting in Birmingham in 1924 he is said to have let a statement on capital punishment go out as a "considered decision" when it was not; and at Church meetings you could hear suspicious clerics "abundantly aware of the subtle brain behind that Pickwickian benignity of visage audibly wondering what 'Billy Temple is up to now'." (E. H. Jeffs, *Princes of the Modern Pulpit*, Abingdon, Nashville, 1931, 219). Dean Matthews of St. Paul's once said, "If William had presided over the Council of Nicea, Arius would not have left the Church." (C. H. E. Smyth, *Cyril Forster Garbett*, Hodder and Stoughton, London, 1959, 287).

10. It is often said, "Theological ideas are created on the Continent, corrected in England, and corrupted in America." The saying comes more often from Germans, or from Americans studying in Germany. If it has any basis in fact, Temple played no part in the theological process it describes. Like Maurice before him, he neither cited nor drew upon German theological sources—and only a few German philosophers. Almost alone among twentieth century, English-speaking theologians, he made virtually no use of such European "architects" of modern

Christianity as Schleiermacher, Kierkegaard, Ritschl, Troeltsch, Schweit-
zer, or of such later ones as Barth, Brunner, and Bultmann. Yet Temple
was not provincial nor a chauvinist. His lack of concern with theology
across the Channel appears to have been due to his Catholic and classical orientation. It should be noticed that his writings were, significantly,
just as bare of references to Roman Catholic and Orthodox as to Continental Protestants. He once told his wife that his highest wish was to
"master the great stream of classical theology," not the polemics of the
Reformers and the Counter-Reformers. The plain truth is that Temple
was every inch an Anglican, standing in between Romanism and Protestantism in the *via media* or bridge-church position, at what the French
scholar and Roman Catholic Father Tavard has called "the cross-roads"
(Georges Tavard, *Protestantism,* Hawthorn, N.Y., 1959, 91-106).

11. Two tangible monuments stand to his love of students. One is
William Temple House, Earl's Court, London: the only official Anglican
hostel for overseas students, which houses thirty to forty under auspices
of the Overseas Council of the Church Assembly. The other: William
Temple College, Rugby, for the study of theology and sociology and
social evangelism. It offers a two-year course and a one-year course, plus
week-end conferences, and corporate work with help in the devotional
life.

12. It was not mere personal favoritism. Bishop Gore in 1916 opposed Henson's nomination to Hereford because he thought him too
heterodox, but Davidson supported it and consecrated him.

13. During the discussion of Paget's refusal, Temple said he could
"assent" to the Virgin Birth honestly but it ought not to be in the
creed because it fastens attention on the wrong point. He still thought
so in *Foundations* in 1912. An interesting bit of "data" about religious
experience turned up in his report to friends later, when at St. James,
while attending a symphony in Queen's Hall he suddenly felt an absolute certainty about the Virgin Birth!

14. When Davidson died in 1930 Temple said, "Archbishop Davidson
was to me in a double sense my father's successor, for from the time
when he succeeded him in office he also became most truly a second
father to me" (RE, 108).

15. Temple's laugh was high and loud, hers quieter. Many of the
reminiscences about him center on his laughter. Sir Julian Huxley
recalls hearing his laugh before seeing him as he arrived late in a bomb
attack for a discussion of war aims, in London in 1941. On the other
hand, he could be stoic—as when he went ahead preaching the Three-
Hour Service on Good Friday, 1915, at St. James, when his mother had
just died. He did not let it be known because he didn't want the congregation feeling pity for *him* rather than Him.

16. One of the early ginger group was Maude Royden, who had
helped start *The Challenge.* She was, as her later years as a Nonconformist minister and preacher at the City Temple church showed, a

remarkable and stimulating person. She was on the Council of Life and Liberty, and in this affair Temple's record seems a little neglectful of principle for "unity's" sake. They were to meet at Cuddesdon, the theological college, but the Dean (let him remain nameless) refused to let her stay with them overnight—talk and board, but no bed—because the college's Anglo-Catholic clientele objected to women staying overnight under that roof. She resigned rather than be subject to such discrimination, and Temple, as Chairman, swallowed his convictions and let her return to London, alone.

17. In college he opposed disestablishment in an Oxford Union debate, Feb. 12, 1903, on Disestablishment and Disendowment. The *Isis* said he spoke with "characteristic intolerance," and *Oxford Magazine* thought he was "at his best" and "refreshing" because not pusillanimous! (C. H. E. Smyth, *Garbett,* 55)

18. Henson always disliked Temple, was plainly jealous. Promilitary, Erastian, Conservative, anti-Roman, anti-ecumenical, he was nearly Temple's opposite. As *he* thought, Temple regarded him as an "unteachable Conservative." He called Temple's role in Life and Liberty one of "casuistic facility and untiring eloquence" (*Retrospect of an Unimportant Life,* Oxford Univ. Press, London, I.206). Yet Temple's defenders would welcome Henson's diary entry Feb. 23, 1942, when Temple went to Canterbury: "His appeal is beyond all parallel manysided. The philosopher, the theologian, the social reformer, the party politician, the religious worker, the missionary, the advocate of reunion, the champion of oppressed minorities, the educationalist, the pacifist [sic]—all will feel that they have a title to look hopefully to the advent of a sympathizer in the Head of the Church of England." But he never could resist hitting at him: an interesting sample is his sneer at Temple's attempt to explain to common people the difference in Christian ethics between *agape* and *eros.* (E. F. Braley, *Letters of Herbert Hensley Henson,* S.P.C.K., London, 1950, 99)

19. His own preference in vestments was for the plainer ones, but as the years went by he gained—quite willingly—a facility for fitting in to many different and even elaborate practices. A single example could be the way he officiated at a Requiem in the monastery at Mirfield for Bishop Gore (whose cremation was a precedent for Temple's own choice in the matter). A faithful and invaluable aide was his domestic chaplain for twenty-one years, 1923-1944, Ian White-Thomson.

20. Humanly speaking, one can sympathize with Bishop Gore. After a meeting, at which Temple had kept his temper and Gore had lost his, as they walked down Victoria Street, Gore gloomy and ashamed, said, "It is a terrible thing to have a bad temper." Then he burst out at his friend's beaming smile: "But it's not so bad as having a good temper."

21. The Hearst Press in America said he ought to "be kept in confinement," but later, in the uproar over a speech of Temple's about financial reform, in the Second World War, a more than ordinarily

candid business man said, "After all, Throgmorton Street [like Wall Street] may be amused at the Archbishop's mistakes, but no honest churchman could ever be amused at the mistakes of Throgmorton Street." When Neville Chamberlain was Prime Minister, Temple, dealing with the unemployed in the North, said the nation should increase the "dole" (unemployment relief) rather than lower taxes. Chamberlain remarked, "I wish the Archbishop of York would mind his own business," to which Temple replied that saying what he did *was* his business!

22. Iremonger says (296), "The contrast between sacred and secular, which was one of the less profitable legacies of the Reformation, is now held to be false by all except a handful of Manichaeans." Unfortunately, there are more than "a handful" of such heretics still in and controlling the Church: the complaint that the Church should keep out of social issues is still commonly made, especially by conservatives whose social interests are often threatened by Christian social concern and witness.

23. Fairly consistently Temple defended the opinion that it is the Church's business to set forth principles, not to suggest or demand any particular operational application or program for the realization of the principles. He held to this in the face of frequent arguments that very often the real meaning of propositions of the "principle" or "middle axiom" kind cannot be made plain except by converting them into their operational terms. (It must be acknowledged that sometimes it is actually evasive and quite *un*principled to offer principles without programs. That Temple sensed this can be implied from an admission in *Church and Nation* (156), when discussing the prophet's task of witnessing to the ideal—with courage to take whatever may be the consequences in angry protest and reprisal. "It may require more courage than the office of king or statesman, and yet it is the easiest, because it is relatively simple.")

24. This is not a good word. In *The Church Assembly and the Church* (1930) Temple argued that it "is in no sense whatever the creation of Parliament." Although its powers were made legal by Parliament, the Assembly, he believed, "has no trace of Erastianism." It was a rather idealized image, which the facts have somewhat contradicted. He reminded critics that it was only ten years old.

25. Said Ernest H. Jeffs at that time, rather shrewdly from the Weslyan vantage point: "He might be described as a moderate Anglo-Catholic who claims the right to interpret the orthodox phrases in a Liberal sense, not excluding a decided Evangelical emphasis" (*Princes of the Modern Pulpit,* 225).

26. This English genius for toleration of difference and dissent is stridently proclaimed in theory in America but little respected in practice, as the McCarthyist spirit or the John Birch Society show. When Temple was enthroned, Hewlett Johnson ("the Red Dean") presided, and handed him his pastoral staff or shepherd's crook. He did so

again at the enthronement of Geoffrey Fisher in 1945, and (at the age of 87) once more at Archbishop Ramsey's enthronement in 1961. His security in Canterbury was, quite simply, due to the solemn oath required of the Archbishops to protect the Cathedral's rights and liberties. When Fisher visited the U.S. he was asked when he was going to "fire" Dean Johnson! At Ramsey's ascent to St. Augustine's chair there were delegates there from the Church in the Soviet Union. (In elevating anyone to bishoprics and deaneries the Prime Minister, on advice and after clearing with the nominee, sends his name to the Sovereign who tells the Cathedral chapter (Dean and Canons) who proceed to elect. If they don't (they nearly always do) they may lose their civil rights, lands, chattels, and go to prison!)

27. Even if what he said much of the time was not couched in the speech of the man in the street, its quality of prophetic relevance always made it seep down to all. The mass of the people knew he was their champion, saying important things, and they "understood" him. Said Reinhold Niebuhr, "The real fact is that Dr. Temple was able to relate 'religious insights and social order' more vitally and creatively than any other modern Christian leader." (*Nation,* Nov. 11, 1944, 159:585) But Temple claimed for his seventeenth century predecessor Laud that *he* was the people's Archbishop, too, even though he "stood for the older social ethics of a peasant civilization" (CSO, 44).

28. A partial explanation is that he left all of the treatment of Temple's philosophy to Dorothy Emmet, whereas she dealt only with the lectures themselves. In his article for the D.N.B. he repairs the omission, at least, by speaking of the astonishment generally felt at a busy Archbishop's feat of intellectual labor.

29. See J. M. Robertson, "Recent Research in the Fourth Gospel," *J. of Bib. Lit.,* 78 (1959) 242-52; T. W. Manson, in W. D. Davies and D. Daube, *The Background of the New Testament and Its Eschatology: Studies in Honour of C. H. Dodd,* Univ. Press, Cambridge, 1956, 219n 2. Temple always contended that it is "my conviction that the supposed contrast between the teaching of the Synoptists and St. John does not really exist" (RE, 74). In 1943 he said of the Fourth Gospel, "I personally believe [it] to be the surest historical guide of the four" (*Ibid.,* 225). His defense of its contents was as strong as of its historicity. He was consistently faith-minded or theological in his reading of the Bible, anticipating recent developments by leaving aside "the quest of the historical Jesus." In chapter eight of his *Readings in St. John's Gospel* he argued that its ill-will and invective against the Jews was something that tradition had hardened at a later stage and read back into St. John's account, after the conflicts of Jewish-Christians with orthodox Jews. But not many scholars would support his statement in 1922 at Manchester Cathedral that the St. John of the disciples was the author "and an eye witness of what he narrated."

30. This writer recalls, as a visitor in York in 1931, preaching in the Minster Square on a Saturday afternoon, from a weekly outdoor

pitch when it was the C. of E.'s turn. Whether through Temple's management or somebody else's, it came right after the half hour held by the "I.L.P." (Independent Labour Party), which meant that hordes lingered who would never have come to a Church pitch.

31. Some "ecumaniacs" felt that he seriously compromised his professions of desire for unity by declining to take part in common intercommunion eucharists. His belief was that intercommunion is the result of achieving real unity, not a means to it. But he was no stiff exclusionist. Canon Baker relates a case in which, in York, he asked Temple's permission to administer Holy Communion to a dying Methodist who had appealed through his Anglican wife. Said Temple, "I agree with you that the rubric at the end of the Confirmation service must be interpreted as applying [only] to members of the Church of England. And after all, one must be permitted to be a Christian sometimes" (*William Temple: An Estimate and Appreciation,* 108).

32. By 1961 Istanbul's ecumenical patriarch (Athenagoras, well known to American churchmen from his earlier years as a Greek archbishop in the U.S.) had invited observers from the World Council of Churches and the Roman Catholic Church to attend a Pan-Orthodox meeting to discuss, among other things, relations with non-Orthodox churches. And the Moscow patriarchate had decided to follow other Eastern bodies in applying to the World Council for membership.

33. This Natural Law inquiry was continued in some measure by a group including Anglicans such as Hodges and Hudson, Free Churchmen such as Alec Whitehouse and Nathaniel Micklem, the Roman Catholic theologian Victor White, O.P. They met for years at St. Deiniol's Library, Hawarden, in North Wales. This writer attended some sessions. The fruits of their effort to agree on a "rehabilitation" of the Natural Law concept were meagre: a pamphlet, *Natural Law: A Christian Reconsideration,* edited by Alexander Roper Vidler and W. A. Whitehouse, S.C.M., London, 1946, 45 pp.

34. Denominationalism and the sectarian and party spirit still sway small-gauge Christians—heedlessly acting as if the polemical problem of defending some version of the faith were still their leisurely, within-Christendom concern, when in fact we are in a post-Christian era when the real problem is apologetic—defending the faith itself. This is as much a need, Temple realized, within the "Christian" countries of the Atlantic world, as outside it. Indeed, the encounter with secular paganisms (e.g., Marxism or scientific humanism) is more serious than the encounter with religious paganisms (e.g., Buddhism or Islam). This fatal pettiness is seen in those "black" Protestants for whom "popery" is tantamount to demonism, and in the pseudo-Catholics of the Episcopal Churches who threaten to "swim the Tiber" if "the urge to merge" gets any stronger! By a kind of word-imperialism the inclusive title "Anglican" has taken on the factional meaning *Anglo-Catholic* in the American Church!

35. Iremonger (633) says he was given twelve honorary degrees by

eleven universities (two by Oxford). This writer has found ten of them: D.Litt., Oxford, 1918; D.D., Manchester, 1929; D.D., Durham, 1929; LL.D., Leeds, 1930; D.Litt., Sheffield, 1931; D.D., Cambridge, 1933 (the first ever conferred); D.C.L., Oxford, 1934; D.D., Dublin, 1934; LL.D., Princeton, 1936; S.T.D., Columbia, 1936.

36. It is striking that no mention is made of Temple in major theoretical works of the Christendom Group, such as V. A. Demant's *Religion and the Decline of Capitalism* (Faber and Faber, London, 1952), nor in memoirs such as M. B. Reckitt's *As It Happened* (Dent, London, 1941). Temple's satisfaction in the Christendom Group's careful theological approach did not extend to their general anti-socialist propaganda and proposals, which concentrated mainly on credit reforms. Iremonger remarks (433) that "he repeated his anxiety lest the Movement [begun at Malvern] should pass entirely into the hands of the Anglo-Catholics (at that time the most vigorous church group on behalf of social reform) or into the hands of the 'political left.' Many church leaders, he wrote, had more sympathy with the left than with the larger part of the right political wing, but 'we must be very careful that we do not give the impression that the Church is an agency for supporting left-wing politics, which are often based on presuppositions entirely un-Christian'." To Canon Tatlow he said, "there is a great deal of course in the Left wing movement which is no more Christian than that of the diehard Right." In the *Times* of Sept. 24, 1944, Temple complained of the way the press handled his addresses: "You very kindly included a rather full outline of those parts of my broadcast which might just as well have been uttered by a heathen, but you omitted the whole point of the sermon, which was that if these obligations are to be fulfilled or these hopes realized, we must win from God both the strength and the direction that we need."

37. As one who once held a curacy in the gift of the Dean and Chapter of St. Paul's, and therefore had to undergo Inge's deafness and sharp tongue at annual reporting interviews, the present writer finds the Dean's description of Temple exactly in character.

38. For reasons not known, to this writer at least, Temple gave up a plan he had formed in his later years personally to approach the Vatican with a proposal to bring Roman Catholic and Anglican scholars together to explore the possibilities of a common ground in the classical Natural Law concept, or a revision of it. Perhaps the failure of the Sword of the Spirit movement to continue cooperating with Religion and Life discouraged him. It should be noted that Temple himself usually spoke of "natural order" rather than Natural Law, and his address to the Aquinas Society suggests that he was at least not unaware of the difficulties experienced by the Hawarden study group.

39. One of the striking events of the War was a visit to Sweden by Bishop Bell in May, 1942, where he was called upon by two German pastors representing different elements. Hans Schönfeld, who had been

in the ecumenical secretariat, wanted for his group some assurance that if Hitler were overthrown, the Allies would deal with Germany for a peace settlement. The other pastor, Dietrich Bonhoeffer, confessed to Bell (with remarkable imprudence) that he was part of a plot to assassinate Hitler. Bell gave the information to the British ambassador in Stockholm and to Eden himself. Nothing was done in response. The assassination plot failed and Bonhoeffer, with his brother Klaus and a brother-in-law, were executed. (See G. K. A. Bell, "Background of the Hitler Plot," *Christendom,* Winter 1946, 9:65-72; also in *Contemporary Review,* Oct. 1945, 168:203-8; and *The Church and Humanity, 1939-1946,* Longmans Green, N.Y., 1946, 165-76.)

40. Not without some attempt to stave it off. Direct first-hand reports, naturally not documented, tell of Churchill's objection and of a deputation of eleven bishops to Downing Street to insist that Temple simply could *not* be translated from York, no matter how much Birdcage Walk and the City might want to disregard popular demand. It was a coalition government, and the Labour Party mobilized its mass support. Anthony Howard in the *New Statesman and Nation,* Oct. 5, 1957, said that Churchill revealed an antipathy for all of the clergy, but reluctantly acknowledged that Temple was "the half-crown article in a penny bazaar." The Bishop of London told Garbett at the time that he favored Temple for Canterbury but "William's prophetic gifts may be quenched if he has to speak for the whole Church" (Smyth, *Garbett,* 272). The fear, if such it was, proved groundless.

41. A real cause of tension between Temple and K. E. Kirk, the Bishop of Oxford, was Temple's (and Geoffrey Fisher's) concern for religion in the secular schools or council schools, as against Kirk's interest in building up *church* schools.

42. Humor, an unflagging trait all his life, has a somehow satisfying sign-off in this anecdote. As a believer in cremation for modern burials he left word to inter his body after burning. This was done quietly in the Cloister Garth (next to his father's grave) the morning after the great service, with no press or photographers present. After the clergy had gone, Mrs. Temple noticed that the urn was slightly askew in the grave and might topple when earth was thrown in. The undertaker went down to straighten it but couldn't quite scramble back out. Mrs. Temple and her secretary had to hold his hands and brace themselves to pull him up—a bizarre turn of events. She said later, "How amused William would have been" (Smyth, *Garbett,* 296). *Painted Windows* quotes him (189) as once saying that Dickens' *Pickwick Papers* could only be produced in a Christian country, that you could get satire in a pagan culture but "only in those countries where the morality of Christ has penetrated deeply do you get the spirit that loves the thing it laughs at."

43. There is a tendency, even in theological circles, to narrow and impoverish the term "theology" by restricting it to "systematics"—in

short, reducing its meaning to *doctrine*. But theology, or theologizing, does many jobs and its tasks have been more or less distinguished in the classical tradition of Christian learning under such heads as dogmatic, moral, ascetical, philosophical and pastoral. These are only convenient categories since obviously each branch, if it is mature and competent, operates with full reference to all of the others. And all of them presuppose biblical and historical foundations.

44. On one occasion Temple seems to have spoken of faith when he meant belief. Preaching to Repton schoolboys he told them, "Never forget that faith is an experiment; and if we want to be assured of the result we must first make the experiment" (SSTC, 127). Yet faith by his own showing is never a matter of qualified thought or merely tentative investigation.

45. Dorothy Emmet has said that Temple gave the impression of never being seriously puzzled. This is an overdrawn statement, for while he had his perplexities, like all of us, he gave an impression to some that he didn't, simply because his perplexities did not *shake* the faith-foundation from which he faced all questions. Such elemental and lifelong faith could cut a man off from the general run of poor mortals sometimes. The only time he failed in speaking to young people was at an S.C.M. conference, when he was Archbishop of York. On the subject "Why I Believe in God," he suddenly began to stumble and flounder for words, and the address was a flop. Later he confided to a friend: "You see, I have never known what it is to doubt the existence of God, and I felt I had no right to be speaking to that audience of young people." Nevertheless, it was *he*—the firm and utter believer—who was most listened to by a generation of young, skeptical, and questioning men and women. They heard the accents of a genuine faith. In William James' typology, Temple was definitely a once-born man, not twice-born; and, contrary to evangelical opinion, he was convinced that such Christians can reach depths of belief greater than the twice-born can.

46. The term "dialectical" is used by both idealists and materialists. It has to do with method. Temple explained it as "sometimes called critical and sometimes dialectical." As to its procedure: "Dialectic, in the end of the day, only means conversation or discussion. It is the attempt to reach truth by the putting of different points of view over against each other and trying to do justice to them all. It is the method which always refuses to dismiss any alleged fact or widely held belief on the ground that it will not harmonize with theories already adopted." He called it "a process of working round and round the available material until it is found gradually to fit into place and make a coherent scheme." And after all, "the real test is not usually to be found in the history of the discovery but in its subsequent vindication" (CTP, 20-3). In short, his concept of dialectic is nearer to Plato's than Lenin's or Hegel's; it is a *critical* method, comparing every idea to its contradiction in order to correct and strengthen it.

47. In a sermon "The Sin of Stupidity" he once said that "No nation has gone as far as England in its neglect and contempt for the intellect," and "the average Englishman has no interest whatsoever in Truth." (His text was I Cor. 14:20.) This sounds too hard and unfair; but he was speaking of coherent rather than analytical reason, which he called metaphysical, and in that sense was not far off the mark.

48. "Reason is not a term synonymous with Christianity. But Christianity by its own nature claims reason as its ally, its agent in the application of the principles of the Gospel to the affairs of life" (RE, 152).

49. Descartes' *cogito, ergo sum,* "I think, therefore I exist," was in effect *dubito, ergo sum,* "I doubt, therefore I exist." Temple's discussion shows no awareness of this but it is not weakened because of it. Temple's attack was on two scores: Descartes' method of universal doubt, which was so opposed to his own method of faith, and Descartes' solipsistic principle of thought's starting point. But Temple had no quarrel with doubt, as such. If it is honest, it is good. If it is jeering, it is bad. Doubt itself is neutral. What makes the difference is the moral variable. Jesus loved Thomas. "It is the doubting heart, not the doubting mind, that is sinful" (SSTC, 127).

50. This indicates the influence of Kant—of his method of logical discourse, although not of his theory of knowledge. Temple was extremely skeptical of the old pre-scientific logic, the formal and Aristotelian canons, such as the rule of the excluded middle. Indeed, he tended in practice to use what we might call an inclusive middle, holding that modern dynamics have shown that, far from its being true that A is never non-A, it is often the case that A is becoming non-A and vice-versa! This is a core insight of dialectical theory, of course. But, while skeptical of the ancient metaphysics and of easy rationalism, he did *not* mean that the real world itself is inchoate. In *Doctrine in the Church of England* (17) he said that "much in this world is irrational and strictly intelligible," but he meant only that human minds at this stage have to appreciate the flux of the universe (its indeterminacy) and how much they have yet to learn!

51. One or two writers have suggested that early in his life Temple confidently expected to draw such a blue-print, in spite of the pretension in such a venture, and in the end had to give it up. For example, the Roman Catholic writer W. D. Geoghegan, in a doctoral thesis, says that Temple's statement in *Theology* (39:233, 326-33) in 1939 that our unsettled times do not permit a "Christological" or "metaphysical" map of the universe shows that he had changed from looking at the Gospel as a "clue to a universal synthesis" to seeing it as a "source of world-transformation" (*Platonism in Recent Religious Thought,* Col. Univ. Press, N.Y., 1958). If he ever had any such hope, even in *Mens Creatrix,* he early saw its too ambitious nature. This kind of thing is usually said as part of the demonstrably mistaken argument that in the late Thirties Temple was a disillusioned Platonist! It is true that like

Plato he had a teleological worldview, and that like Plato he held to the kinship of mind and matter. Like Plato he gave the interaction of the individual and society a central place, but so did George Mead. Yet Plato also held Heraclitus' idea of flow and flux, as Marx did. But that doesn't make Marx an idealist! Long before the article in *Theology* he had completed two important shifts in his general method of thinking, already nascent in *Mens Creatrix*: from a near-Platonic idealism to (1) what he called dialectical realism, and (2) a process philosophy rather Whiteheadian, but no doubt more directly influenced by Samuel Alexander. He began as a liberal idealist much influenced by Edward Caird, and theologically liberal. He became a realist in philosophy, a "classical" Catholic in the ecumenical spirit, and a "centrist" in his theology. His *Nature, Man and God* has been described as a landmark in contemporary Christian thought (W. M. Horton, *Contemporary English Theology*, Harper, N.Y., 1936, 148-66.)

52. The delimited, unconstructive interests of radical empiricism and linguistic analysis, now regnant in British philosophy, were only getting a good start before he died, but they held no appeal for him. He learned to use speculative thought—"constructive" theology and philosophy aimed at relating the arts, religion, ethics and social questions. From this point of view his thinking had more in common with recent American and French philosophy than with British. (A bit of humor crops up in *Christianity in Thought and Practice* (26) when, rejecting the analytical G. E. Moore's idea that value can exist apart from its appreciation by persons, he uses a linguistic-sounding way of putting it: "The word 'good' as so used seems to me to be a noise and nothing else.") Temple's method of coherence or encirclement took shape as early as 1910 (FMT, 25 ff.). By coherence he meant (1) that the world of reality is objectively coherent—really hangs together, and (2) that the mind reaching out to know the coherent world can achieve coherent knowledge and understanding: indeed, he thought "truth" to be mind's discovery of itself—i.e., of coherence—in the objective world.

53. Modern theologians commonly acknowledge that to Temple goes the credit for shaping our view of the nature of revelation (e.g., see W. N. Pittenger, *The Word Incarnate*, 1959, p. 20). Temple combined the classical idea that God acts to communicate truths to men with the modern liberal idea that men by inner discernment, intuition or inspiration, find or "see" the truth. But Temple's strong conviction about the primacy of the divine initiative led him to set aside intuition and to favor inspiration—the "pneumatic" theory to account for the human response in the revelation-process. It was not a "special" inspiration in the sense of God's favoring some and cutting others out! (For an opposed view cf. A. Richardson, *Christian Apologetics*, 1947, pp. 145-7.) Perhaps the neatest statement of Temple's view is in *The Centrality of Christ* (33), where we find "that the area or *locus* of the revelation is at least usually an objective event, but that for the right

reading and interpretation of that event there is needed illumination of the Holy Spirit, so that actual and effective revelation takes place when there is a coincidence of the divinely guided event and the divinely illuminated mind, and for the fulness and effectiveness of revelation both factors are necessary." The factors in this definition are actually three: divine initiative, human response, and the Spirit's guidance and enabling—i.e., grace. He (Temple) attributed the germ of his treatment to Father H. H. Kelley, who said in his *The Church and Religious Unity* (1913), and *The Gospel of God* (1923), that *he* got it from W. Hermann's *Der Begriff den Offenbarung* (1887).

54. He called the attempt of philosophy to treat itself as something more than a method "the heresy of intellectualism," and held that the proper material for its operations is "human activities which are neither purely or not all intellectual." This is close to the recent English way of looking at philosophy as a method, and also close to "existentialism's" opinion that most of the problems of "formal philosophy" are abstract, devitiate and trivial compared to the great experiential themes of creative literature. On this view of philosophy, "It is clear at once that Ethics and Politics, and Aesthetics, will be exalted alongside Mathematics, as the typical activities of Mind, and that on the whole they may be more normative for Metaphysics. The Universe will be approached less as a problem (or theorem) in Geometry, more as a Drama or Symphony, and as a Society in process of formation" ("Symbolism as a Metaphysical Principle," *Mind,* 31:24). As to the "inductive" theory that we should proceed only from facts to theory, he insisted that facts lead to theories and theories are tested by other facts and theories. Thus the "induction vs. deduction" debate is merely precious because these exclusive methods "never represent the reality of living thought. All actual thinking proceeds in circles or pendulum-swings" (SSTC, 42).

55. He intended to apply this dynamic view of knowledge as a process to all knowing, not just to revelation. "No man ever yet knew the substance of any actual thing. What we know is never substance but activity" (RE, 69). He means that knowing is sense stimuli and responses, actions and reactions. Here is an "epistomological" reason for his preferring experiential to propositional theology—a preference which was completely dominant near the end, as we see in his *Theology* article for younger theologians, "Theology Today," in 1939.

56. Temple perceived the problem whether St. Paul was an incarnationist, even though he knew nothing of the reasons of textual critics for holding that the comma does not belong in the verse, or that another one should follow "God." In Chapter VII of *Christus Veritas* he argues that "on some occasions at least" Paul was an incarnationist and meant God when he called Jesus "Lord." While he allowed that we cannot say "beyond all doubt" that Paul was an incarnationist, he (Temple) was entirely convinced that Paul "fully believed in the Deity of the

Lord." He added that it is "impossible to doubt" that it was "the doctrine of the Johannine books" (which he loved so much). The comma problem never came to his attention. (Cf. F. C. Grant, *Ancient Judaism and the New Testament,* Macmillan, N.Y., 1949, 133-4.) The RSV now renders it rather weakly by omitting the comma, with a footnote offering the right reading: "In Christ God was reconciling the world to himself." But Temple was more alert than D. M. Baillie who, in *God Was in Christ* (1948), built a whole systematic theology on the wrong translation. Temple was very up-to-date in his devotion to the "theological Christ" rather than the "historic Jesus"—the faith about Jesus rather than the faith of Jesus—even if he could not agree that any biography of Jesus would be mainly a romantic fiction. However, in Temple's use of the New Testament there was never much critical sophistication, as based on a scientific textual apparatus. He used to speak quite blandly, for example, about our being so concerned with what John or Paul had to say that we were in danger of losing sight of the original historical teachings of Jesus Himself. Few scholars today would have that much confidence in our ability to arrive at His "original" teaching.

57. "I submit that the verdict of history is clear in condemnation of the traditional treatment of those who have been regarded as heretics or schismatics. No large alienated group, as far as I can recollect, has been won back by the method of anathema and excommunication" (PU, 3). In his preface to *Doctrine in the Church of England* he said, about Christian philosophy, "An official philosophy is a *monstrum horrendum.*"

58. Sometimes we read or hear characterizations of Temple which seem to put him in the camp of those who supposed that we could by reason make our way to faith; that the doctrines of the Christian creeds could be, as it were, the *conclusions* of logic based upon ordinary data, not needing the leap of faith at all. Thus described, Temple is often contrasted to Karl Barth. The following is worth quoting, to show that this representation is obviously mistaken: "The error of the Barthian school of theology—for that it contains error when judged by the canons of natural reason or Christian revelation I cannot doubt—is, like every other heresy, an exaggeration of truth. To deny the reality of moral progress, or that moral progress is an increasing conformity to the Divine, is wanton. To deny that revelation can, and in the long run must, on pain of becoming manifest as superstition, vindicate its claim by satisfying reason and conscience, is fanatical. But that revelation is altogether other than rational inference from previous experience is vitally important; that only by revelation and by surrender to its spiritual power can man be saved, is a profound and irrefragable truth. . ." (NMG, 396). Because of subsequent emphases in this volume, note several points of primary importance in Temple's outlook: (1) heterodoxy is not a moral fault, (2) there is moral progress, (3) it is

measurable by its approximation to the Divine Love, (4) revelation goes beyond but not against logic and morals, (5) it is faith's insights rather than reason's which can lift us above ourselves.

59. Iremonger (162) says that Thompson attacked Temple's *Repton School Sermons* for being apologetic and not critical enough. Perhaps Temple's marginal note had a bit of asperity in it!

60. Back in the eighth century St. Augustine started the use of a social analogy for the trinitarian doctrine of one God in three persons. He called the Godhead a divine *socius,* meaning a perfect society or community of persons, completely one in a life of interpersonal love and communion. Like many Englishmen (in modern times, e.g., Clement Webb and Leonard Hodgson) Temple leaned to this way of looking at God's being. The ancient doctrine of the Trinity in Christian faith goes beyond any idea of God as only a solitary, super-individual deity, all alone in his being because of his uniqueness. This three-in-one belief about God (Aristotle's "differentiated unity") is possibly the most distinctive faith-proposition in classical Christianity. Temple held that it carries a basically social "ontology" or view of primary being, the stuff ("ground or fountain") of things, because it asserts in effect that the source or ground of all existence, God Himself, ultimate Being Itself, is social and corporate, not private and individual. Reality is social. The antisocial falsifies reality, offends against "is-ness" as much as against "ought-ness." And furthermore, it follows that if and when human beings who are created in the Maker's image (*imago Dei*) act selfishly and individualistically, they deny not only God's but their own nature. For Temple, individualism is *unrealistic.* Says C. B. Moss, in *The Christian Faith* (1943, 50), "God is fundamentally a Society as well as a Being: the fact that man is a social animal is only a reflection of the divine being." While Temple was confident that the Trinity doctrine is more than "a piece of antiquated juggling"—a puzzle, yes, but not an idle one—he thought of it as "not primarily a solution of a problem but a summary of experience," the Church's experience which included (1) God as a Father of infinite majesty, (2) God staggering beneath a load too heavy for Him on the way from Jerusalem to Calvary, (3) God struggling and *pressing* against brute nature and the selfishness of men: i.e., Creator, Redeemer, Sanctifier. Temple confidently believed that God had not contrived mankind in order to *become* what He already was—a lover; rather he held, as a Trinitarian, that God possessed within His own Being the relations necessary for love. But being perfect Love, however self-sufficiently, the creation of man and his world were a necessary consequence of love's creativity.

61. For too many people the phrase, the "life" of Christ, refers to Jesus' biography. But for Temple (as for St. Paul in Romans 5:10) it meant God's saving power, His love.

62. Temple held that men cannot do evil for its own sake, that they always seek what is good even when it is only the "apparent good"

instead of the true good—which is, ultimately, what God's love calls for. Thus the man of malice, to take an extreme case, says in effect, "O evil, do thou be my good." This notion that men cannot sin perfectly, anymore than they can be perfectly virtuous, goes back to Boethius and earlier (NMG, 366).

63. In his Good Friday address, *Palm Sunday to Easter* (1942), he emphasized the shocking doctrine that God suffered for man, that "our sin costs God" and because He pays "the price of sin," He can freely forgive without lowering the moral standard. "If this side of the matter is not grasped, the Christian doctrine of free forgiveness is, as Hindus and Buddhists often say that it is, both immoral and demoralizing" (PSE, 6). Temple felt that this ethical shock was of greater religious importance than the *metaphysical* scandal in the paradoxical claim by faith that (to use current existential language) essence overcame existence by means of existence itself—i.e., as Tillich puts it, the infinite became finite to defeat the imperfection of the finite: God became man to overcome sin.

64. Just recently some theologians have tried to express this by calling Christ's nature "essential" manhood, prototypical, compared to the "existential" manhood of the rest of us: the perfectly human and the imperfectly human, the generically human and the particularly human. On the other side, Temple (UC, 85) pointed out, "If our Lord was truly Man, then He was also *a* man."

65. As he understood it, in the Church there was first the experience of Jesus Christ as God—then the doctrine. Temple found the first explicit deification of Jesus by St. Stephen, in his "Lord Jesus, receive my spirit" (Acts 7:59), not by St. Peter. And Stephen's death set off St. Paul's conversion (RE, 66).

66. Temple ignored the statement in the first of the Articles of Religion, that God "has no body, parts, *or passions*." The 39th Article never enslaved him. As we shall see, he also ignored the 38th's assertion that "the Goods and Riches of Christians are not common, as touching the right, title, and possession of the same." He was on this last matter nearer to the Anabaptists than to the merchant-Reformers!

67. Against any "vague theism," Temple stood squarely on biblical ground. He was not, for example, drawn by the metaphysical deity spoken of by philosophers like Spinoza, even though he acknowledged that Spinoza was indeed God-intoxicated. By Jewish-Christian standards Spinoza was an "atheist" because his deity was being rather than *a* Being, not a discrete Person. Tillich today draws the same comment that Spinoza invited.

68. Temple's patripassian theology had parallels in one way or another among other imaginative Christian thinkers in the nineteen twenties. For example, there was *The Hardest Part* by his friend Studdert-Kennedy, and *God and the Struggle for Existence* by Archbishop D'Arcy of Dublin. Archbishop Ramsey (*An Era of Anglican Theology,*

58) says that Temple pulled back a little from God's actually suffering, because he said the passivity view of God is *"almost* wholly false." But Temple always used qualifiers, even when he was quite convinced; it was a tactful and intellectually careful impulse—a sort of matter of polite utterance with him.

69. At various places throughout his writings Temple indicated his awareness of paradox in Christianity. In addition to a suffering deity and the power of sacrifice, he speaks often of victory by surrender, freedom through obedience, *Good* Friday, *felix culpa* (the happy sin that brings redemption), the "Fall" into spiritual stature, how law makes grace possible, how sin leads us to law, and so on.

70. Maurice had a much more Platonic or neo-Platonic explanation of how the Atonement was effected objectively. It was metaphysical and obviously similar to St. Paul's conception of mystical union with Christ, and of rising with Him into new life in the Resurrection. Sometimes Maurice spoke of our being in Christ by virtue of creation itself. At other times he made our membership in Christ a matter of redemption and restoration, in the manner of Irenaeus (*Against All Heresies,* 3), and the recapitulation theory of the Greek Fathers. In either case, he held that objectively and factually all men *are* a part of Christ. They are all already His own members when they come to Baptism. In spite of his alleged Platonism Temple made no use of this explanation of the objective side of the Atonement. Like Maurice he held to a metaphysical unity of men with God in Christ, but this unity was from creation and never broken. He thought of it as a Platonic "real universal." For him the salvation effected by the life and death of Christ was in the objective fact of the *revelation* of man's sonship to God, not in any new re-unification. For Temple men have never ceased to be children of God because of a "Fall"—whereas for Maurice they had had to be restored to that relationship by Christ's Incarnation. In Temple's theology the objective, new, and decisive fact effected by God for men was the revelation-by-demonstration of God's unchanging Love.

71. He saw it more as a stratagem of God, employed by Him in trying to end a lover's quarrel! Temple's summary of the history and basic issues of Atonement theory is almost without equal for lucidity and beauty, and extraordinarily helpful: in *The Faith and Modern Thought* (127-34).

72. Still another misunderstanding has grown up due to Temple's remarking, in a letter to Dorothy Emmet at the University of Manchester, that he had come to recognize the world as not rational but "strictly unintelligible" (Iremonger, 537-38). Standing by itself this would certainly be a reversal of all his thought! But what he actually said was that his thinking had been "driven" to a modification which was "not substantial" yet important. He felt that his process-and-value theology should be more dynamic than he had made it in the past, and that we should think of the world's unity by the analogy of a drama

rather than a picture. In a picture the parts are all present and the unity visible, but in a play the full meaning of even the first scene is not apparent until the final curtain: this he saw as a somewhat "greater emphasis on eschatology." Actually, the "play vs. picture" analogy was an old one with him; and from the start his work was filled with a sense of process. He was always saying we are as yet only in the middle of the play. And his remark about the world being "strictly unintelligible" meant *not entirely intelligible thus far*. It was not a declaration of despair and meaninglessness. In that same letter he also reasserted his lifelong conviction that men are "fellow-workers and agents" in the process of realizing value under the Logos or Creative Word.

73. For a while, around 1941, Temple was nearly discouraged about the "distance" between himself and the younger men in theology—a distance which seemed greater then than it would now. The world seemed hopelessly disordered and the "lust for dogma" was very strong, as a compensation. Iremonger records his saying, "I do not think I understand what some of our younger theologians are trying to get at, and I am quite certain that they do not understand me" (605). It was the young Anglo-Catholics, who fought him over his ecumenical theology, who most induced this feeling. But characteristically he began meeting and talking with them, and gained a closer understanding. E. K. Talbot wrote the Earl of Halifax that Temple was "the one bishop of the older generation to whom the younger theologians listen with respect and who carries authority with them" (Halifax, *Fulness of Days*, 168). He urged the young men in his article in *Theology* (1939) to tackle two tasks: (1) social theology for an era of social ethics and collective problems, and (2) conversion to the Christian faith and no mere reliance on general progress. He also highlighted two problems: (a) the relation of redemption to creation in theology—is there a Natural Order (Catholic view) or only a Natural Disorder (Protestant view); and (b) where is the decisive revelation coming, in revealed truths or revealing events—propositionally or experientially?

74. Alec Vidler (*Christian Belief*, 81) says that already before Baptism people "are children of God, Christ is their Head, they are heirs of eternal life," so that Baptism is what "brings them into the community where these hitherto hidden truths about all men are openly acknowledged and effectively realized." In his *Theology of F. D. Maurice* (100) he says, Baptism is the "enacted proclamation and assertion that what is true for mankind is true for this man and for that man." Maurice pointed out that the Tractarians spoke as if "those who were not baptized were not members of Christ" and as if human beings were "sons of God *only* because they were baptized men." Thus Eric Mascall (*Church Times*, May 6, 1949) said bluntly that "a baptismal rite which asserted or assumed that men are already children of God by their natural birth would stand condemned."

75. Temple explicitly rejected as unacceptable a solely subjective view

of the Incarnation-Atonement. He described such a view in the *Centrality of Christ* (35) as one which declares, "It is revelation, and revelation only. Nothing is done by it, but something eternal is disclosed."

76. Temple's Atonement was like Hastings Rashdall's in some ways (*Idea of Atonement in Christian Theology*, 1915). Canon Quick (*The Gospel of the New World*, 1944) came out to much the same view, but more elaborately. However, Rashdall's was a purely "exemplarist" formulation whereas Temple's was more inclusive and objective. As Temple looked at it, exemplarism can mean that Christ is an example of what can be, which he thought true, but also that Christ is an example or exemplification of what or who God *is*. He thought Rashdall's "a bad piece of theology" (Iremonger, 491).

77. Charles Gore, Temple's friend and mentor in many ways, had in his 1891 Bampton Lectures, *The Incarnation of the Son of God,* treated the Incarnation as the righting of a fallen world. It is amazing how often people who say readily enough, "Of *course* the Fall is a myth, not an historic event," nevertheless go right on thinking and speaking about human sin as something that *happened* rather than the natural, given self-centeredness that it is. Temple unmistakably opposed this antediluvian perspective. He saw in the "Fall" myth an ancient story about how mankind has developed upward morally (spiritually) from a subhuman, primitive, instinctual level of life to human rationality and morally responsible self-consciousness. In the Incarnation he saw that process lifted to a higher level of being.

78. The Jesuit paleontologist, Pierre Teilhard de Chardin, whose work has been published posthumously by an intellectuals' committee including Sir Julian Huxley and Arnold Toynbee, in spite of Vatican prohibitions (a "monitum") on the ground that Fr. Teilhard was close to heresy because he took evolution to be the key to history, is very close to Temple's process theology; of special importance are two volumes, *The Phenomenon of Man* (Macmillan, 1959) and *The Divine Milieu* (Macmillan, 1960). This priest-scientist was one of the discoverers of the "Peking Man" in the Gobi desert. He said: "I feel resolutely determined to devote myself by all possible means to the defense of the idea of the reality of a progress against every secular or religious pessimism."

79. In the Middle Ages no theological attention was paid to the Kingdom idea. This was a sad and evil world, only a testing way-station *en route* to "heaven." The concept was rediscovered and revitalized by nineteenth century theology. But in quite recent theology the old medieval indifference has gained a new foothold in Protestant as well as Catholic circles. It might be worthwhile to note here that in the biblical theology there are three distinguishable versions of Kingdom-faith or "eschatology"—i.e., beliefs about the end (*eschaton*) or last things toward which we should be reaching and are being drawn. In the order of their emergence in the biblical account they are (1) the

prophetic, (2) the apocalyptic, and (3) the gnostic. Each is worth a capsule characterization. The "prophetic" and history-embracing view of the future sees God's Kingdom as (a) a down-to-earth, sometimes gradually-growing reign, and (b) a viable order of the world's structures—not only of the hearts of men but of their day-to-day political and economic structures. The "apocalyptic" or irruptive view expects the kingdom to come into this world as an historical event, as the prophetic does, but its coming is thought to be *sudden,* in the twinkling of an eye, out of the blue. In some of its forms the apocalyptic or furturist hope included "gnashing of teeth" and great travail and destruction of life (see Mark 13), a catastrophic as well as sudden way of coming. The "gnostic" or esoteric view—the latest of the three to emerge—conceived of God's triumphal reign as consolidated only in the hearts of men, individually or privately, and subjectively; not at all a social-historical world order, but rather a matter of extricating souls *out* of history by a saving *knowledge,* often secret. All three kinds of eschatology—prophetic, apocalyptic, and gnostic—are to be found in some measure in the New Testament; the first two in the synoptic gospels (Mark, Matthew and Luke) and the third, in addition, in some parts of the Fourth Gospel and of the epistles. Temple's was positively the prophetic view, and he was certain that it was Jesus' view too. Temple gave it a modern sense of *development* not so plainly brought out in the prophets. But to the three descriptive-critical questions about the Kingdom—*what* is it like, *when* will it come, and *how*—his neo-prophetic answers were to the first "social," to the second "eventually," to the third "gradually."

80. He had no pre-scientific idea that the Kingdom is to be a millennium of social perfection. The Christian imperative is "to work for and prepare for the coming of the Kingdom on earth," but this cannot mean that we expect a certain social order to come and last for evermore, "till the earth gets cold and life impossible. We work for its *approximation* but the consummation is not and cannot be here" (CTT, 22).

81. Temple held that what was unique in Jesus' teaching about the Kingdom was His stubborn loyalty to the prophetic, this-worldly conception in the face of a popular, compensatory wish-fulfilling hope for a miraculous and quick triumph, and that the popular influence imposed itself on the gospel records. In like manner he held that in Jesus' view the Messianic role was one of vicarious and redemptive suffering; and in the Messiah (the Christ) the King and His Kingdom were already come, so that the "Second Coming" was, like apocalyptic, a popular overlay due to a clinging hope for a Victorious Conquerer—in a second appearance, since he clearly was not one in the first! While aware that many scholars find the origin of early Palestinian Christianity in the "seedplot" of apocalyptic, he was convinced that Jesus did not have that outlook.

82. He *thought* with and used the phrase of Georges Florovsky, "inaugurated eschatology," rather than C. H. Dodd's "realized eschatology" (e.g., CV, 148, 182; CFL, 24). The obvious fault in Dodd's phrase is its suggestion to the unwary or untutored that Jesus proclaimed a Kingdom already entirely here. Jesus' sayings about the Kingdom were not simple prolepsis, as many suppose; He did not speak of the Kingdom *as if* what was future were present—He said it was both, partially here already, fully yet to come.

83. Temple did not accept the interpretation in which Christ was to return in a "Second Coming" to "bring in" His Kingdom. As Temple understood the gospel accounts, Jesus was the inaugurator, not merely the herald, of the Kingdom: it was a present reality beginning with His incarnate presence in the world. He started this Kingdom with His sacrifice on the Cross, not with a second coming. Says Temple (KG, 36), "He is come. There is no different coming; He is come." And (38) thus his "answer to the apocalyptic critics of the day will be to say: Yes, surely Christ did expect His coming almost immediately; but it was not a *second* coming. There is nothing in His own language about a second coming. That all arises from the disciples' failure to rise to the full height of His teaching." By this he appears to have meant that having risen "on high" in the Ascension our Lord became present everywhere: that was the coming He foretold—His coming as Lord of all. It was not a second coming *locally* and *particularly*. J. A. T. Robinson supports this, in his *Jesus and His Coming* (SCM Press, London, 1957).

84. The process philosophy also has something in it akin to the medieval cosmological and teleological arguments for the existence of God, but Temple never put his eggs in that kind of metaphysical basket. He was much closer to the process-and-development principle in A. N. Whitehead's *Process and Reality* (Macmillan, 1930), Henri Bergson's *Creative Evolution* (Holt, 1911), Charles Hartshorne's *The Divine Reality* (Yale, 1948), and *Reality as a Social Process* (Free Press, 1953). But Temple would never be satisfied with Whitehead's treatment of the nature of ultimate reality, for example, for while *he* saw it explicitly as personal, Whitehead only added a hurried and unsupported addendum to that effect.

85. An example of stalemate theology would be much of what Reinhold Niebuhr has written. See his "Political Realism of Christian Orthodoxy," in *Reflections on the End of an Era* (Scribner, 1934).

86. Historically there were, according to Temple, four views of the Church and the Kingdom: (1) *Roman*—the Church *is* the Kingdom, and therefore merits absolute allegiance; (2) *Lutheran*—the Kingdom is invisible with an invisible Church membership, not to be visible until a "final consummation"; (3) *Calvinist*—the elect in the Church should be establishing the Kingdom in man's present social structures, in terms of obedience to the Divine Law; (4) *Orthodox* and *Anglican*—the Kingdom exists in the Church in the same way that the statue is in the

marble block, although hampered by the worldliness of the Church, working toward an apotheosis of the whole creation "that God may be all in all" (CaC, 55-6).

87. Speaking to the British Bible Society in 1943, he said he agreed with Goudge that there are two main doctrines of God and of the Church in the Bible. But, he said, "The essential instrument of God is the community of persons, and the Book is the instrument of the community." God first, then the Church, *then* the Bible. (RE, 225).

88. He knew it was a prolepsis on St. Paul's part: a prophetic vision of the future so intense and urgent that it foreshortens the time gap, causing him to speak of that which is to be as if it actually is now. So Jesus spoke of the "fulfilled Kingdom" in such passages as Luke 17:21.

89. William Temple never actually said "Baptism is ordination," but it is the logic of his views. He said, "Christ is the true Apostle; every Christian is by Baptism 'made a member of Christ,' a limb of His Body, so that his task is to fulfill some part of the purpose of Christ." He was quite clear that clerics and laics are *both* ministers; the former ordered specially to the Word and Sacraments, and the latter ordered mainly to the ministry of Work and Witness in the world.

90. In view of Temple's keen interest in philosophy, economics, and politics—indeed, most of the social sciences—it is an arresting fact that he did no reading in either anthropology or psychology. The former had not yet gained its present place in the intellectual world, but already in Temple's day psychology had become a common frame of reference. Freud, Adler, Jung, the behaviorists (e.g., Pavlov)—these and their works are practically unmentioned by him. He never "psychologized" people's thoughts and actions in terms of unconscious motivations, such as trying to discount conservatives as having "a need for authority," or, in the reverse direction, "explaining away" social radicals as unconsciously hating their fathers! This was partially due, no doubt, to a distaste for the presumption bound up in such judgments —but it still remains true that he was ignorant of the psychological disciplines themselves, both the "depth" schools and the empirical methods. However, it would be another matter altogether to say he was "naïve" about people because his discussions of man and personality were not psychologically sophisticated, unless it could be shown that his views were mistaken or distorted through his ignorance of the new disciplines. He seems to have been satisfied to recognize that psychology is a serious behavioral study, unable of itself either to provide or take away validation of theological and philosophical opinions (something which Freud ignored in his *Future of an Illusion*). Of psychology Temple said, equably, its "concern in relation to any belief is not to inquire whether belief is true, but to inquire what was the process of its formation" (TSPD, 20). To the claim, for example, that if prayer is auto-suggestion it is ineffective and bogus, he replied, *"non sequitur."*

91. A curious contradiction or lapse from this view of will may be

seen in *The Centrality of Christ* (72) where Temple, discussing sin as egocentricity, follows St. Augustine's notion that God's grace is needed to help a man *will to move his will!* His point was that a man cannot do it by any bootstrap power, cannot *will* to move his will, "because he doesn't want to." In short, his desires and his intelligence have not joined forces, he is unintegrated, not truly a person. Every act and element of sin reduces and impairs the person, the personality-level. But a certain lapse occurs here when Temple speaks of the will as "corrupted," because he has already shown that will is not an entity, and exists only as a function of unified mind and feeling. It is in these two latter phases that sin or self-centeredness works. His talk about "willing to will" is just as much a pointless tautology as asking whether "the power to choose has the power to choose," i.e., whether the will (which is freedom) is free! "Wanting" is what unharmonized desire does; willing is what desire and reason do together. Much confusion in theological discussion past and present has its source in St. Paul's sentence, Romans 7:19, a *locus classicus* for the analysis of sin. St. Paul was apparently saying that *will* was pitted against reason, that the "war" in his "members" was between his *will* and his mind. It would have been psychologically sounder, as Temple's theory of will indicates, to have written: "For I do not do the good I *wish* I wanted, but the evil I *wish* I did not want, but in fact *do* want, is what I do." In these modern times we realize that in an important sense people *always* do what they *want;* they always "practice what they believe in!" It may not be what they tell others they want, or even what they tell themselves they want—such is the human capacity for self-deception as well as for self-centeredness. But they do what they really want. Only when they want what their reason tells them they *ought* to want, will "will" be born; and will is *always* free because will *is* freedom!

92. Professor Bone continues this view: "A person is free and responsible to the extent that his character structure is integrated in terms of a personally developed hierarchy of essentially harmonious values. 'Values' is used as synonymous with life-purposes, aims, goals, motives, action-tendencies, etc. A person is *un-free* to the extent that his character is composed of structures which are in conflict with each other to express themselves, often in mutually contradictory values, as in character-neurosis" (H. Bone, "Notes on Integration, Freedom and Responsibility," *Review of Religion,* March, 1949, 13:259-63).

93. Temple was more "social" or solidaristic than Buber in his conception of the person. A careful scrutiny of Buber's writings shows a marked tendency to treat personal being as a *given* quality of the individual, even though only fulfilled or true to itself in relationship. But Temple held that it is a "social *product.*" "It is positively in the interaction of embryonic personalities with one another that the resultant personality is developed" (CTP, 68).

94. William Temple did not urge a return to the "organic" solidarism

of the medieval Catholic theologians. He had too much respect for democratic insights into the values of the individual, as perceived in post-medieval individualism. He regretted that in Christopher Dawson's uncritical loyalty to the Catholic tradition he could see "some of the most dangerous tendencies within Fascist thought" (CTP, 70). He preferred a more serious attempt to keep "freedom and fellowship side by side" in a dialectical analysis of the organic as a "thesis" and the individualistic as "antithesis"—and held to a "synthesis" of the two. The outlines of this synthesis, as we shall see, he thought he could already make out in a qualified socialism, and felt confident that history was working it out in fact (CTP, 43-4). He was close to the modern Anglican emphasis on personality, as seen in T. H. Green, Illingworth, Moberly, Richmond and Rashdall. In 1937 Ronald Smith's translation of Buber's *Ich und Du* appeared, on the *Zwischenmenschliche* relationship. Temple as a personalist was in complete agreement with Buber that both individualism and collectivism violate true community —collectivism because it "understands man only as a part," and individualism because it "understands only a part of man," for which cf. Will Herberg in his *Four Existentialist Theologians* (New York, 1958, 176-203). Tillich describes personal being dialectically as "individualization" and "participation," but the latter is less radical, more equivocal than Temple's, for Temple agreed with Maurice (*Lincoln's Inn Sermons*, 1891-2, II.51) that society is "essential" to humanity and the more individualistic people are the less human they are. At an earlier date (1924) Temple verged close to medieval, organic solidarism, for in *Christus Victor* (66) he said that the ego is "a focussing point in which nothing is focussed," and denied (71) that there is any "impenetrable core of self-hood" in a person. Maurice's *The Conscience* (1868) is an even earlier version of the "dialogic" doctrine of man!

95. "It is only, I think, in Russia, that this issue is at present being squarely faced . . . at least the Russians are perfectly aware that the primary problem concerns the nature of human personality" (CTP, 51-2).

96. This way of tying value to personality has been a part of both idealist *and* materialist thinking. Karl Marx and Nikolai Lenin repeated it constantly in their labor-theory of value, brought up to date by them from Catholic scholastic precedents. Thus in *Essays in Christian Politics*, defending a personal (labor) theory of economic value, he insisted that the real "enemy" is not materialism but a sub-personal doctrine of values. Emil Brunner puts it in colorful terms: all value apart from persons is a "phantasmagoria" (*The Divine Imperative*, 1936, 194-95). Edgar Brightman put it that "in personality is the only true intrinsic value we know or could conceive; all values are but forms of personal experience" (*Nature and Values*, 1945, 62). Temple discussed it frequently and consistently: his latest statement was, "Value, as it appears to me, consists in an interaction of mind and environment, but always

of such a kind that the mind is finding in the environment the objective occasion of its own satisfaction" (CTP, p. 26).

97. The philosophic reader can soon summarize Temple's answers as to the Whence, What and Where of value. As we have seen, value is *assigned* by persons. Value is for persons. However, in Temple's opinion this does not make value merely a function of a person's judgment. *Theologically* value is actual ultimately because of the divine will, and therefore value is primal. Things do not exist independently, with value as an attribute. Things exist as forms embodying the value or will or purpose of the Creator. As a voluntarist like Ockham, Temple reversed St. Thomas' view *(Summa Theologiae,* II-II, Q.5, A. 1 and 3). Aquinas thought a thing is good as far as it exists; Temple said it exists as far as it is good. This belief that only value has ultimate or "substantial" reality accounts for his virtualist doctrine of the Real Presence, as St. Thomas' transubstantiation resulted from putting "substance" before value. Temple thought that value is "actual" in the things valued; and "when I am hungry, what I want is the value as good of food; but this is not separable from the food." This is the essence of sacramentalism: the inter-reliance of the material and spiritual. God's creation is the actualization of Value or Will or Purpose. This is *the process of reality,* following a four-step route or "stages along Creation's way"—from matter to life to mind to spirit. "The universe is sacramental. Everything except the Creative Will exists to be the expression of that Will . . . The explanation of the Universe is to be found in the activity of a Creative Will." Temple concluded that there is only one self-explanatory principle, Purposive Will. That is theism. If it is untenable, the universe is inexplicable. "When in the causal regress we arrive at a will, the regress is at an end" ("Symbolism as a Metaphysical Principle," *Mind,* 30:124). At the finite and human levels of purpose, human persons are also involved in the process of creation, both as creatures and creators. At the human level, because of God's prior activity, values are "truly objective and discovered by the investigating mind—not created by it" (CTP, 29). And in the three categories of value—moral goodness (the *bonum*), truth (the *verum*), beauty (the *pulchrum*)—it is moral goodness which is supreme. Temple said that "Truth and Beauty are not, strictly speaking, absolute values . . . for there are circumstances in which it is better not to know the Truth, and there are instances of Beauty which in some circumstances had better not be apprehended. But Goodness is truly absolute; it could never be better that a man should be worse than he is" (NMG, xix). Value, he held, is ultimately ethical, not veridical or aesthetic.

98. Since Temple put goodness first and paramount in the three "eternal verities" of goodness, truth and beauty, it follows that truth is logically revealed through goodness; the reverse could not be so.

99. Temple here reflects his general evolutionary understanding of creation. He was much influenced by "epigenetic" or "emergent" views

of evolution, such as Samuel Alexander's (*Space, Time and Deity*, 1920) and C. Lloyd-Morgan's (*Life, Mind and Deity*, 1926)—the new "realists" who were dropping the idealist perspectives of Bradley and Green. This matured into the kind of process philosophy which Whitehead elaborated so effectively; it is seen in Jan Smut's "holism" (*Holism and Evolution*, 1926), the theology of Bethune-Baker (*The Way of Modernism*, 1927), and Lionel Thornton, an Anglo-Catholic (*The Incarnate Lord*, 1928). W. Norman Pittenger, the American theologian, is close to Temple and to these others named (*The Word Incarnate*, 1959, and *Theology and Reality*, 1955, esp. chs. 2 and 6). Theologically characterized, their view is "panentheistic"—i.e., they hold that everything exists *in* God (He is "the ground of being") but, as against pantheism, that God is more than and beyond the universe; God is "in but not of" His creation. Temple's process interpretations are set out at most length in *Mens Creatrix* (1917) and *Nature, Man and God* (1934). A quite recent religio-biological treatise is the one by Pierre Teilhard de Chardin, already mentioned (*The Phenomenon of Man*, 1959). The similarity of these various notions of "emergent" or "creative" evolution to the *Logos* doctrine of St. John, and the patristic idea of the work of the Eternal Son, will be obvious to students of historical theology.

100. Temple felt confident of his stand in this matter. "All the great theologians have always said that the love wherewith a man loves God or his neighbor is the Holy Ghost. It is not the *work* of the Holy Ghost only, it *is* the universal spirit at work in the hearts of His creatures" (CFL, 91). Mrs. Temple, after his death, said many times that he had hoped to live long enough to construct a coherent view of the Holy Spirit doctrine. If he had, it is a safe guess, it would have been along these lines—of moral and ascetical theology.

101. Temple liked to quote a parallel point made by his friend "Billy" Palmer, Bishop of Bombay, about the Ritschlian influence. It caused people, he remarked, to say "*I* believe in God" instead of "I believe in God" (SSTC, 29). He knew that love cannot be defined, only identified. Definition describes one thing in terms of another, or breaks it down descriptively. But love is a category, a primordial: like "blue" it can only be pointed to, or at, or named. It has to be experienced to be known. "Love cannot be defined; it can only be named; and its name is threefold—Father, Son, and Holy Ghost" (CV, 282).

102. Temple was, as we shall see, a "situationist" in his ethics, relative rather than absolutist: "Particular acts derive their value [righteousness] from their capacity to promote or to hinder the best relations between people, the relationship which must express their personality. All particular commands or prohibitions derive their value [righteousness] from their tendency to promote or to hinder the relationship of love on the widest possible scale" (CFL, 46).

103. He saw the good-with-the-bad, the ambivalence in the scientific temper. Its divorce of intellect and emotion results, as his will-theory

would suggest, in a weakening of values and purpose (judgment). It tries to be "neutral" or "dispassionate"—and this inculcates "a spectator attitude to life," to fit a purely descriptive discipline (RE, 213-14). Frustration is an ancient disease, but its modern form is due largely to "the absence of any sense of purpose in life" (*ibid.*, 215). He was much influenced by Josiah Royce's distinction between "the World of Observation" and "the World of Appreciation," which by more than fifty years anticipated C. P. Snow's *Two Cultures*! For this reason he emphasized the humanities in popular education. "The primary purpose of education is the formation of a purpose" (PSP, 10). By "purpose," as we have seen, he meant a redemptive or revolutionary goal of justice, not a hedonistic or prudential goal of *adjustment*. There are many things to which the Christian cannot make an adjustment! He believed that modern education is producing people who, while "taking high honors in their science examinations, are mentally puerile so soon as questions involving value—moral, social, aesthetic—are brought into discussion." (RE, 166).

104. "Reality seems to consist in a series of layers or strata, one above the other—not in space, of course, but logically—of such a kind that the lower is necessary to the existence of the higher, but only displays its full nature when the higher comes upon it and takes charge of it" (CTP, 54).

105. The notion of automatic progress, combined with a very thin gruel of theology almost like ethical culture, led many Liberal Protestants into a kind of disillusionment after the First World War, for which the "neo-orthodox" revival of Reformation doctrine was a chief corrective. Unfortunately, their recovery of classical Christianity has been something of a reaction socially. Reinhold Niebuhr has been a leader in this reaction. The semi-humanistic and Liberal Protestant version of the "social gospel" was, of course, never a part of the thinking of Roman Catholics or Anglicans, and *their* social-theological analysis has therefore sailed on a more even keel. The impression has grown up in America in the last quarter-century, cultivated by "neo-orthodox" conservatives, that the social-gospel forces were all naïve victims of this doctrine of automaticity. As a doctrine of progress it obviously did not do justice to the complexity and "unevenness" of human affairs. But so to characterize most Christian social thought is itself naïve and uninformed.

106. "Mainly our progress is extension of the Social Contract according to Hobbes and Glaucon, the agreement not to inflict or to suffer injuries; it is the substitution of enlightened selfishness for stupid selfishness. Of any emancipation from selfishness itself, or any attainment of perfect fellowship in self-surrender to the absolute good, our historic progress hitherto gives no promise whatsoever" (CV, 88). The social-contract references are to Thomas Hobbes' *Leviathan* and the Glaucon of Plato's *Republic*, Book II.

107. The quantitative change progressively from stupid to enlightened self-interest can be accounted for in terms of natural, human prudence; but the logic of all this is that in the "nodal" or "qualitative leap" from enlightened selfishness to disinterested love the power of grace is required.

108. It is difficult, especially outside professional theological circles, to establish the conceptual difference between "teleological" (end or goal theory) and "eschatological" (ultimate or last-things theory)—especially since the latter is a term nearly unheard of outside theology. Most thinkers use such terms as "theistic teleology." Among neophytes in theology, the term "eschatology" is used much too loosely and too much. It would clear the verbal decks if we could agree to let the philosophers' word for final cause or purpose stand for the last things of an historical kind, while the theologians' word would serve for the final or last things of God's purpose *beyond* history. The trouble with much that passes as Christian discussion nowadays is that the Kingdom of God is treated as if it were "eschatological" but not "teleological."

109. Temple's conception of "the Mind of the Maker" is far from deism's, in which God is supposed to have endowed His creation with certain built-in laws of development, then pulled the trigger to start the mechanism and let it go on its own. The analogy is more like the Bible's potter, shaping the material as well as providing it. He is an actor in His own drama, in two ways. First, He acts *indirectly* in history through the laws of the natural or created order, as in cause-and-effect and physical laws. Second, He acts *directly* in history—both specially as in the Incarnation, and continuously as in "the operations of grace" —i.e., the work of His immanent love, His Holy Spirit.

110. Whereas the Social Darwinists, such as William Graham Sumner and Herbert Spencer, were using the biological concept of "natural selection" and "the survival of the fittest" to rationalize and excuse individualism, competition, and a jungle ethic of each man for himself as the "natural" principle of life, Temple saw in their misuse of evolution a failure to understand the sociality of Darwin's thesis—that it is the fit *species* which survives, not individuals, and that the more individualistic the members of a species are the weaker the species. For this reason Temple embraced, within his providential theology, the theory of mutual aid which Prince Kropotkin had elaborated in his book with that title in 1920. However, Temple did not adopt the anarchist conclusions which Kropotkin drew from it.

111. Temple was clear in his own mind about this. "An individual is what it is in virtue of its relations; that is true; but we are not justified in concluding that apart from its relations it is nothing at all" (MC, 70). He argued that in a system ABC we have an interactive synthesis of alpha, beta, gamma. B and C *develop* alpha into A; A and C develop beta into B; A and B develop gamma into C. This is, of course, a characteristic bit of dialectic. "Every entity . . . contains something that

NOTES313

is unique, its own underived contribution to the sum of things whereby it becomes capable of action and reaction. This element of distinctiveness makes the core of every object. The failure of Determinism as an explanation of everything in general and of human conduct in particular involves, of course, the acceptance of real Indeterminism as part of our conception of Reality" (CV, 56; NP, 15). It is possible to hold that determinism, as he defined it, is really "mechanism," and that the Christian position is precisely determinist, as against the mechanistic extreme on the one hand and the libertarian extreme on the other. The "dialectical" view is that men are not completely determined (mechanism) nor completely undetermined (libertarianism), but are possessed of limited or conditional freedom (determinism—a cause-and-effect view). Either of the polar ideas is "an insult to personality" (NMG, 225), because they both make persons into "billiard balls," *things* subject only to external determination, since without both freedom and order people are helpless—in the one case as to choice of action, in the other as to any purpose or consequence.

112. This concept was more narrowly applied and perhaps more exactly applied by biologists than by Temple, whose thought on the subject came closer to William James'. James used the terms in this phrase for purposes of "philosophical anthropology," as Temple did.

113. None of this meant for Temple the necessary triumph of *uniformity* or the disappearance of pluralism in social life. Indeed, he was convinced that it was possible to preserve small and independent groups, but (dialectically) only if the bigger community took care to preserve and protect them—as it should. He was also aware that while unity is the secular trend, there are variations within it. Individuation out of primitive tribal solidarity has also been taking place.

114. Temple made use of Aristotle's ancient distinction between "efficient" and "final" causes. He thought that a lot of difficulty arises from the habit of thinking only of the *past* or "efficient" causation. Kant encouraged this habit in modern times. Limitation of the notion of "cause" to efficient causation is "a main source of the whole difficulty" (NMG, 226). Temple held that we should consider *final* causation too, pay serious attention to purpose or will rather than just the factors *already in the chain of cause and effect*. Every free act, once it is done, is itself an addition to the other factors of efficient causation, of course. But "final" cause (or *choice*) is a vital part of the total process.

115. He might have added that an earlier blow, after the Dutch one, had been struck by some English "Pilgrims" who fled to Holland and then, via England, to a New England in the American wilderness, rather than submit to the statutes of religious conformity!

116. A striking statement of this perspective in recent theology is G. D. Kaufman's in *The Context of Decision* (Abingdon, New York, 1961, 44): ". . . the most significant reality which we confront is not human sin but the God who acts to redeem us from that sin. Whereas

the analysis of man's sinfulness taken by itself might lead to despair of any possibility for real community among men, the revelation that God himself, creator of the heavens and the earth, is working in love to extricate man from his plight, restores hope for man and for human history. For 'if God be for us, who can be against us?' Doubtless sin and rebellion are still with us, but now we know that this empirical state of human existence is not the last word."

117. Temple, in speaking of this pseudo-objectivity of medieval rationalism, makes a very interesting historical judgment: "We cannot go behind the Reformation—that great *bouleversement* of human thinking, wherein it was for the first time fully recognized that each man is by nature the centre of his own universe, however true it be that his most urgent need is to discover that it does not revolve about him as its pivot" (NMG, 80).

118. It is evident that this point of view has little in common with the kind of "gospel evangelism" which concentrates on *getting* salvation. Neither is it in keeping with the advice of many moralists in the Christian tradition who have said that if there appears to be a conflict between your neighbor's welfare and protecting your soul's salvation, choose the latter and let love go! It is sufficiently exposed as an error by St. Paul's cry in Romans 9:13, "for the sake of my brethren I could wish that I myself were accursed and cut off from Christ."

119. Tritheism is *psychologically* inherent in the doctrine of the Trinity (not logically). It would be better to speak of "*God* the Father, *God* the Son, and *God* the Holy Spirit," than of *the* Father, *the* Son, and *the* Holy Spirit. We know God in His "roles" or different mighty acts: Creator, Redeemer, Sanctifier. "Father, Son, Holy Ghost—each name stands for the divine love in one of its necessary aspects" (CV, 275).

120. He called Pelagianism a form of "ethical atheism" (MC, 290), because it forgets or minimizes the fact that God's love is the only power that moves our wills, that "we love [only] because he first loved us." A bootstrap theory of ethical or moral power is a-theistic. His remark was made in his address to the Aquinas Society in 1944. Calling it *intrinsically* damnable is not quite consistent with his general view about the relativity of good and evil; evidently he used the word for emphasis.

121. This thesis of Temple's has inevitably caused some debate. As an explanation of how the at-one-ment is brought about by love's power without destroying freedom, it is convincing only to those who stand in some degree in the Christian tradition. It says that sinners (No-sayers) are so overwhelmed to find that God Himself has to suffer because of their selfishness that they give in. But this presupposes that they already believe that the Man on the Cross is God, in which case there is no need, *ex hypothesi,* to win them over! This, then, seems like a weakness in the theory—although no more perplexing than any other

way of accounting for Christian surrender, except possibly the super-natural-selection theory (God gives some the saving knowledge by direct illumination, withholds it from others—a gnostic idea), or the hysteria theory which accounts for sudden conversions in "gospel tents" under the pressure of shouted exhortations. It is to be noted that Temple is no sudden-conversionist himself, and he admits that knowledge of God's suffering will not "always and at once overcome selfishness," acting rather as a strong pull. But even so, as a theory of how *Christians* are more fully emptied of self, and more lovingly drawn into the fellowship of Christ, *it still presupposes faith as the door to conversion or life-change.* It is a problem with which he never grappled, probably because he simply assumed "Christendom" and at least a nominal belief in the divinity of Christ. A close look at his references to "conversion" will show that he always meant a fuller trust in God's love, not a new con-viction of God's existence or Christ's lordship! He himself never really had any doubts about the central Christian dogmas. His message was always directed to the deepening of men's faith rather than winning them to belief. And there is a considerable strain of opinion in his writings, implicitly, that "unbelievers" cannot be argued into believing anyway—that it is by the deep faith of present "believers" that others will be brought to the same mind. Who can say anymore? The leap of faith itself remains mysterious.

122. In a succinct summary of the soteriology in Ephesians, Temple spoke of how God made humans "with hearts and wills that cannot be coerced but can respond freely, in order that there might be a fellowship of love answering the love with which He made them." But then, he says, "they used their freedom for self-seeking." The past tense here (as an aorist) misrepresents the Ephesian writer's own thought; he should have said either "they *use* their freedom" or "they have used"—to avoid the suggestion that there was a time when they *started* to be selfish! People have always been self-centered; all animal creatures are, for with-out an ego-center they would be psychotic.

123. Says C. B. Moss: Original Sin "is not a good name, because, strictly speaking, original sin is not a sin at all, but a weakness leading to sin, just as a weak chest is not consumption, or weak eyes blindness" (*The Christian Faith,* S.P.C.K.-Morehouse Gorham, New York, 1943, 149). It is a pity that it hasn't been called Original Defect. In modern times there is a positive disadvantage to using a term which had its origin in illogic and pseudo-history. It may be that even "defect" is too unqualified, in view of the ego's ambivalent role—for it works as *creativity* as well as self-regard. The rabbinic *yetzer,* with its *tov* (good impulse) and *ha-ra* (evil impulse) was much better clinically. It is too bad that St. Paul put our discussion of sin off on the purely "odd" explanation in Genesis 3:1-7, nowhere else mentioned in the Bible. In this connection we might add that Temple would not accept the notion that finitude or creaturehood is the source of sin, or as Reinhold Nie-

buhr thought, a *combination* of finiteness and man's anxiety to transcend it (*Nature and Destiny of Man*, Scribner, New York, 1945, I. 251).
Temple held otherwise: "Inasmuch as finitude does not necessarily
involve self-centeredness, it cannot be said that the very principle of
the actual creation involved sin" (NMG, 501). He concluded that God's
creation allowed sin but did not "make" it, and that God also *uses* sin,
as and when it occurs, for creative ends.

124. Temple did not arbitrarily reject the religious use of myth. For
example, he held to the "Ascension" although we do not think our
Lord went *up* any more than we believe the earth is flat. He remembered that even the primitive Christians did not suppose God had a
left hand and a right hand (SSTC, 130-1). He thought, however, that
myths are archaic, and "no one ever did (or could) write a myth deliberately, because myth belongs to the stage when men had not learnt
to distinguish between historic and poetic truth" (letter to Bishop
Barnes, Iremonger, 491). He said, "the serious theologian never sets
anything aside without asking what (if anything) of spiritual value has
been faultily expressed here, and taking care to give it better expression." The Fall story is "a very good myth, curiously congruous with
evolution, because the Fall is (in the myth itself) a 'fall upwards,' seeing
that by it the knowledge of good and evil was obtained."

125. The medieval doctrine of the *donum superadditum* does this
more literally, possibly, than Reformation orthodoxy. But it is really a
case of six to one and a half-dozen to the other.

126. Temple's passionate concern with social justice and welfare, as
we shall see, was motivated by this insight into the "solidarity of sin."
He was eager for a good society as much for the sake of *persons* as for
society itself.

127. The gospels are concerned with sins, concrete and actual; St.
Paul focuses on sin, the generic and generalized, "original" form.
Unlike many theologians who talk only about sin-in-the-large, skirting
dangerous specifics, Temple tackled actual and particular sins, as well
as the broad theory-problem of sin *qua* sin. Nobody's toes get stepped
on when "sin" is denounced, as most prudent preachers soon discover.
It is the attack on "sins" that has always invited anger and the hazards
of prophetic witness.

128. Apropos is the limerick often cited in discussions of this ancient
theory as it appears in the modern form of Christian Science:

> There was a faith healer of Deal
> Who said, Although pain isn't real,
>   If I sit on a pin
>   And it punctures my skin,
> I dislike what I fancy I feel.

129. Josiah Royce, in his *Religious Aspect of Philosophy* (New York,
1887) took this line; so did Hastings Rashdall in his *Theory of Good*

and Evil (London, 1907). The first false answer, "maybe it is for the best, if we only knew," is commonly adopted with the bereaved. The second, that evil is self-existent, was tied by N. Berdyaev to his *ungrund* theory in *Freedom and the Spirit* (Scribner, 1935). Edgar Sheffield Brightman, at Boston University until his death a dozen or so years ago, was an eminent champion of the Finite God.

130. The suffering here is voluntary or *willing* suffering, of course. This is the suffering dramatized on the Cross. Temple saw no redemptive or ennobling consequences in compulsory, *un-*willing suffering. This is a point often overlooked by those who try to rest their protest against appeals to mercy (as, for example, in the euthanasia issue) on the "need of suffering."

131. Although willing to attribute the existence of cosmic evils directly to God's providence, Temple was strangely unwilling to carry his "good of evil" or tutelage doctrine far enough to account for moral evil (sin). This was, apparently, because he felt that any belief that sin is *inevitable* undercuts human freedom. He held that sin is not necessary, and therefore not God's doing; yet our weakness is part of God's arrangement, and it leads to sin. What God faced "was a probability so great as to be distinguishable only in thought from certainty," he declared, and in the next breath admitted that there is, as far as God's knowledge goes, no such thing as probability (NMG, 369). Many of us feel he squirmed unavailingly here, as other modern theologians have on the same point, trying to separate what is "necessary" from what is "inevitable."

132. It was roughly set out first in *The Faith and Modern Thought* (1910), and then in *Issues of Faith* (1917). In the Gifford Lectures (1934) he used much the same construction, even the same sentences and paragraphing, with little or no alteration or elaboration. Temple, had he lived to mid-century, would have opposed the "ontological theology" which de-personalizes God, and the growing indifference in theological circles to personal survival after death.

133. George Bernard Shaw said, "The practice of earth burial, with its cemeteries crowding the living out with the dead, its poisonous slow putrefactions, its risk of burial alive, and its cost, should be forbidden and replaced by cremation. It was discussed 80 years ago when I was a boy. Yet not even the cremation of an Archbishop (Temple: one of our best) has overcome our dread of doing anything that anyone else is not doing, nor the bigoted opposition of the Churches which preach the Resurrection of the Body without considering that a body can be resurrected from dust and ashes as feasibly as from a heap of maggots" (*Far-fetched Fables*, Dodd, Mead, New York, 1951).

134. This is an interesting objection since it so obviously suggests that it was subversive of morals, and a wiping out of "abiding consequences," *when God Himself* gave the world a "second chance" in the Incarnation, taking all of men's sins upon Himself and letting them

all off scot free by His undeserved mercy! Yet this charge, brought by some Buddhists and Hindus, he rejected—only to be troubled by it from a Christian source.

135. It is said that an Aberdeen graveyard has a headstone epitaph which illustrates:

> Here lie I, Martin Elginbrod;
> Have mercy on my soul, Lord God,
> As I would do were I Lord God,
> And you were Martin Elginbrod.

There are those who ask, "Why the Incarnation, if men are all saved whether or not they believe and behave?" What price Christ? The answer, certainly, is that God's saving action in Christ *revealed* the salvation of men, it is an accomplished fact, but it will not be realized in its fulness until they know it (hence the Church as mission) and respond. The Gospel is Good News, not a Good Deal. What depends upon our human response is not the fact of the new life in Christ but the "fulness thereof"—the joy and completion of conscious fellowship with God.

136. "As the flower turns to the sun, or the dog to his master, so the soul turns to God" (NMG, 487). Every motive and phase of worship "is gathered up in that emotion which most cleanses us from selfishness because it is the most selfless of all emotions—adoration" (HNW, 30). He even urged us to "Gaze, gaze upon God," with the suggestion that the purest prayer is wordless, the less "yakking" the better. And he especially distrusted *petitionary* prayer, asking God for things, because "if attention is diverted from God Himself to the self's satisfaction in being surrendered to Him, adoration is poisoned" (NMG, 390). By this standard—one commonly held in the great devotional tradition—most liturgical and non-liturgical worship falls to a fairly low level.

137. He more radically summed up his negations on the subject as: we do *not* pray to God (1) to correct His understanding, (2) to repair His memory, (3) to broaden His outlook, or (4) to implant new ideas (SSTC, 56).

138. After the New York State Supreme Court upheld the constitutionality of a prayer used to start the day in public schools, on the ground that it was non-creedal (pan-religious) and therefore does not violate separation of Church and State, the U.S. Supreme Court declared it illegal and unconstitutional, a violation of the First Amendment. Great issues in social philosophy may be raised by the Supreme Court's decision and the opinion upon which it was based, but the prayer itself was a frank petition of a selfish and tribal kind: for *me* first, then *my* school and teacher, then *our* country! Nothing about God's universal love and concern for all men, even our enemies!

139. "Many people are puzzled by the quite clear teaching of Christ that we should pray for our enemies. As far as I can judge . . . the whole difficulty arises from the supposition that if we pray for anyone

we must ask God to give him what he wishes to receive" (HNW, 34).

140. Temple once thought of calling his Gifford Lectures "A Study in Dialectical Realism," but he held off for fear it would suggest "an ambition to inaugurate a philosophical tradition." It has become one anyway! He was sure that only Christianity, in its sacramentalism, has a *theological* dialectic comprehensive enough to vie with Marxism for the minds of modern men. But since it is not altogether uncommon to hear people say that Temple was "tinged with Communism," it is important to emphasize that he repudiated it quite fundamentally because, as a naturalistic form of humanism, it *identifies* mind (or spirit) and matter, while Christian sacramentalism postulates only their unity. His other ground for rejecting the Marxian version of dialectical materialism was its limiting of mind to a mere function or reaction of matter, whereas Christianity would assign it a capacity for free and self-directing ideas (NMG, 488, 498). At the same time he knew what he was talking about and gave Marxism credit for "dialectical" and not gross or Scotch materialism—"the old-fashioned materialism, or what is called Mechanical Determinism" (CoC, 2). As long as Christianity remains idealistic and non-sacramental, it has little chance against Marxism in any scientific culture; this is a potential strength of Anglican and Roman Christianity. (There is a fine, succinct account of Temple's dialectical theory, but quite arbitrarily taken out of its sacramental context, in O. C. Thomas' *William Temple's Philosophy of Religion* [S.P.C.K. & Seabury, Greenwich, 1961, 33-9].) Philosophically, Temple was confident that Marxian materialism is bound "in the long run" to become some form of theism or pantheism. He claimed that "once the distinction between mind and matter is allowed, attention to the behaviour of mind is bound to bring men to an interpretation of experience in spiritual terms" (CoC, 6).

141. Through Anglican influence, chiefly Temple's, this concept has gained a wide currency. Thus D. M. Baillie says in his posthumous *Theology of the Sacraments* (Scribner, New York, 1957), using Temple's phrase "A Sacramental Universe," "This is a phrase that has been used a good deal in recent times, usually to indicate the idea that the sacraments in the specific sense are but concentrations of something very much more widespread, so that nothing could be in the special sense a sacrament unless everything were in a basic and general sense sacramental." And again, "Faith uses nature sacramentally" (42-6).

142. There are other passages in his works, parallel to this. See *Citizen and Churchman*, 101-2, and the passage in Gregory Dix's *The Shape of the Liturgy* (Dacre Press, London, 1945, 733): "The late Archbishop of Canterbury speaking on the Social Teachings of Christianity in the Albert Hall on September 26th, 1942, said . . . the offering of bread and wine—not wheat and grapes, as he emphasized—is the offering of human labour upon God's gifts." Dix added that this is perfectly true as eucharistic doctrine, but hard to read into the liturgy as it now

stands. Temple's point here was that the bread and wine we dare to lay on God's board is God's gift of wheat and grapes *mixed with human labor* into bread and wine. What are the conditions, uses, motives and goals of this human labor: are they appropriate to the action of eucharistic worship, are they worthy as offerings? This view of the oblation is a parallel to the idea of "congealed labor" being "in" commodities, in the medieval scholastic and modern Marxian versions of the labor theory of value.

143. His irenic temper and historical perspective may be seen in his comment that transubstantiation was, to start with, a genuine effort to "spiritualize" the gross "Dark Ages" idea of the Real Presence. While it is "quite impossible to hold, because the terms in which it was formulated no longer represent the way in which any human being thinks," such Aristotelian terms were the best available in the medieval conceptual armory.

144. "To express my own thought accurately I must say, not that the Bread and Wine symbolize, or are symbols of, the Body and Blood of Christ, but that sacramentally (i.e., symbolically and instrumentally) they *are* his Body and Blood; that is to say, within the sacramental action that is their value and therefore their reality" (TSPD, 159). In logical keeping with his non-substantial view of the Presence he opposed "fasting communions," favored encouraging frequent non-fasting reception instead, and said he had been told by Archbishop Davidson that "Mr. Keble all his days paid no observance to any such rule" (*ibid.*, 163).

145. He was always loyal to the Anglican self-image but knew that it has its psychological hazards. He saw to it that they were recognized in the *Report on the Unity of the Church* of the 1930 Lambeth Conference (114): "This very combination . . . sometimes creates an impression of vagueness and indecisiveness which others are able to avoid. Yet we believe that such difficulties are incidental to that mode of corporate life which, as we are persuaded, exhibits the divine operations of the one Spirit."

146. Along with freedom to dissent theologically (or politically) he was open to *assent* of either kind, if sincerely experimental. If a man accepts some Church teachings without personal perceptions of them, solely on the ground that the Church is likely to be right, it is "a free exercise of judgment concerning the good" and so far spiritually valid (NMG, 348).

147. He once wrote to Bishop Barnes of Birmingham, a militant Modernist, that, as with Liberalism, "I regret the existence of a special organization of Modernists . . . [for] to separate out the people specially concerned with it weakens their leavening capacity, and stiffens others in resistance" (Iremonger, 492).

148. At one point, in 1928, he grew rhapsodic about the English Church in particular, perhaps revealingly since it was not his usual

manner. He said, "The Church of England, like other Churches, has often failed to be completely Christian . . . but it has never failed to be utterly, completely, provokingly, adorably English" (GCE, 6).

149. Temple regarded national churches as an historical and epochal feature, the other two as more permanent and characteristic. The principle of the supremacy of Scripture seemed to him to have been subordinated by the Protestants to the *duty* (not primarily the "right") of private judgment about the truths of the Bible as well as the merits of Church teaching (ECP, 199). It is this "critical" norm which accounts for the greater development of radical biblical scholarship among Protestants than Catholics. Temple wanted private judgment exercised humbly in the fellowship of the Church—a very Anglican, non-sectarian view!

150. For non-episcopalians a great deal hangs, of course, on the soundness of the opinion that bishops are the heirs and successors of the Apostles. Temple never indicated any interest in, or engaged in debate upon, the issue often raised about whether the *administrative* authority of bishops, as distinguished from presbyters, is primitive and "Scriptural" or, indeed, if they *were* distinguished in the primitive Church. We have seen how his method was to assign authority to the living Church rather than—in case of conflict or doubt—to the accounts in the Bible. His view of the solution of the issue was a more pragmatic one: "The Christian Society, it is universally agreed, had adopted the Episcopate as its sole channel of ministerial Order as early as A.D. 200. Some hold that this had always been its principle, some that in the early days the episcopal, presbyterian and congregationalist principles were followed side by side. Between these two I do not seek to judge . . . By one means or by many the Church sought to remain in full continuity with its life in those early days; and after a few generations . . . is found agreeing in using the Episcopate in its continuity of succession and consecration, as its central principle of Order. The Anglican Communion still uses the Historic Episcopate in that way" (TSPD, 103-5).

151. It seems clear that in Temple's opinion a commissioned ministry, receiving its power from Christ and its authority from the Church, is of the *esse*—but not so for the Episcopacy.

152. His case for calling them "ordained" was that deaconesses are, like the clergy, "set apart in perpetuity and endowed with answering grace by the laying on of hands and prayer in ordination." At the same time he denied that this is creating a fourth order of the historic three-fold ministry of bishops, priests, and deacons. There is no inconsistency, as Dean Iremonger's account might suggest. A deaconess' vows, even if lifelong and under manual blessing, are no more an additional order of the ministry than a nun's or brother's in a religious order. An overseas bishop at the end of World War Two actually ordained a deaconess first to deacon's orders, then to priest's. Temple died too soon to discuss the merits of that case, but it is a safe guess that for the reason given

above he would have supported the decision of the Lambeth Conference to persuade the good bishop to cease and desist.

153. Philip Napier Waggett, S.S.J.E. (d. 1939), a Cowley monk who ministered to the poor of London and Capetown, became a distinguished war chaplain, wrote extensively on religion and science, and eucharistic theology. (Archbishop Fisher referred in his Cambridge Sermon on intercommunion to Temple's phrase but erroneously gave a "Fr. Kelly" as its source, instead of Waggett. Presumably Fisher meant H. M. Kelly, S.S.M., of Kelham. Cf. *A Step Forward in Church Relations,* Church Assembly, London, 1946, 11.)

154. He offered a little comfort in the thought that, sinful as schism is, it is often a state *within* the Church, and for this reason not as bad as apostasy and infidelity which are actual separations from the Body. And on this score, he thought, there is "no guilt of schism in those who are loyal to the teaching which they have received," and certainly none in those converted from heathenism by denominational missionaries (CLF, 13). Temple, with his greater horror of schism than of heresy or heterodoxy, is closer here to the Eastern than to the Western outlook.

155. The same problem arises in America where the National Council of Churches is under constant fire from reactionary agitators of the "lunatic right" for its "red pronouncements" on various social concerns affecting the people of the churches.

156. He repeated this view more than a decade later (1933): "Some day, no doubt, in a very remote future, the question of union with Rome will become practical. At present I regard it as almost infinitely remote . . ." (Iremonger, 419). There are signs in the early Sixties that his use of "almost infinitely remote" may have been unduly pessimistic. At least the readiness of Roman Catholic theologians to discuss ecumenical questions has been much more in evidence than in Temple's day, especially since the first session (1962) of the Second Vatican Council.

157. Usage has freighted a term like "super-state" with totalitarian and imperialist connotations which were the farthest thing from his mind when he said this. The later emergence of Hitlerism introduced new "resonances" into the forum of debate about social policy. What he meant is here described in some detail in Chapter Twelve. During the Second World War he wrote to an army chaplain that while the Pope had no sympathy for Fascism, "an authoritarian organization of religion is always bound to find itself lined up on the whole with authoritarian politics, and while the Roman Church will always support democratic formalism and the power of the majority, it will have little concern for the moral rights of minorities"—i.e., theirs is an unwholesome kind of democracy. Furthermore, he said, "The Roman Catholics treat grown-up people permanently as children and that is a frame of mind which inevitably overflows into politics" (Iremonger, 419-20).

158. This was part of a sermon at Repton School, in 1913, on "The Sin of Stupidity." The next year in a Repton sermon on "The Economy

of History" he said that "the Papacy in its great days was the noblest effort that mankind has yet made; nothing to equal it in loftiness of aspiration or thoroughness of scientific reasoning can elsewhere be found among the political achievements of men; but it had not in it all that was to mark the Kingdom of God, and it received not the promise" (SSTC, 217).

159. He did not foresee the radical post-war polarization of the power conflict, communism vs. capitalism. At least, if he did, he nowhere made his foresight explicit.

160. Kenneth Latourette says that the three Gospel-less lands, claiming political independence, are Afghanistan, Nepal and Outer Mongolia. But Bhutan has never had a Christian mission, while Nepal does —in Katmandu. (Cf. K. S. Latourette, *The Christian World Mission in Our Day*, Harper, New York, 1954, 7.)

161. Here Temple's cast of mind was more Catholic than Protestant —as an heir of that Spanish theologian Victoria of the Sixteenth Century who first argued that heathens who *reject* the faith are not therefore condemned. (All along it had been agreed that those who never hear it are slated for Limbo.) Victoria succeeded in pleading that culture-tied blindness is a sort of "invincible ignorance"—so that a confirmed pagan is excused! But it was not until the encyclical *Quanto Conficiamur* of Pius IX in 1863 that there was an official acknowledgement that those who are non-believers in "good faith" are blameless. Most Protestant missionaries by 1863 may have thought that way too, but they did not talk or act that way!

162. Toward the end, after two world wars, and the appearance of fascism and communism, he had a keener appreciation of the non-theological factors than he had shortly after the 1910 revolution against the monarchy in China, under Dr. Sun Yat Sen. He believed that massacres were avoided in that revolution because most of the leaders were educated in Christian mission schools, and hoped for more and more Christian influence there (SSTC, 134-5).

163. Professor Tawney shortly afterwards left for several months in China, to study the agrarian economy under the pressures of political and ideological change. His report, filled with shrewd prophetic warnings, was being written as this writer joined him in London, as his student. That report is *Land and Labour in China* (Harcourt, New York, 1932). A. J. Toynbee has at various times and places aroused resistance, especially in Israel and among Zionists, by asserting that there is a fatal contradiction in all Semitic religions in the worship of a God who is both loving and jealous. He has held that the notion of God's jealousy leads to a monopolistic view of salvation and to a tribalistic, in-group spirit which finds expression in such social evils as nationalism. The Christian faith, a Semitic offshoot or "heresy," has not always freed itself from either spiritual or social claims to be a *chosen people*: "particularism" in both salvation-doctrine (e.g., "Heaven

or Hell") and social philosophy (e.g., "Herrenvolk" or "Americanism") was certainly no part of Temple's theology.

164. This last point about teen-agers was made by Temple in connection with his efforts for the new Education Act of 1944, and has a somewhat limited meaning for Christians today. (Not that every teacher and pastor could not echo it for reasons of his own!)

165. This may be a counsel of despair, of course, *if* Christian witness has to be made through *fellowship* and *sharing,* and *if* the laity are not "weanable" from individualism to more social and corporate attitudes. It poses one of the centrally important questions in all strategic considerations of evangelism.

166. Temple nowhere discussed the classical issue in moral theology and Christian ethics— Is a thing right and good because God wills it, or does He will it because it is right and good? To this writer there is no sign of a case for either view made in Temple's published work. However, in view of his chosen and deliberate realism epistomologically, which he held along with an ultimately idealistic metaphysics, it seems a reasonable conclusion that he would have favored the first or voluntaristic view, as Ockham did, that God's will decides the objective value of things. Against this interpretation of his position, however, stands an unelaborated statement, in the midst of another topic, to the other effect: "A thing is not right because God commands it; God commands it because it is right" (UC, 94).

167. Many ethical analysts have tried to hold that the two are not coterminous—that a "deontological" or duty ethic (such as Kant's formalism) which asks what is right as the determinative question, is different from a "teleological" or goal ethic (such as Aristotle's Good Man) which asks what is good or what is nearest to the ideal. The ultimate identity of the two may be seen quickly enough when we ask ourselves which standard Christian ethics tests decisions by: right or good? Clearly Christian duty is to obey the law of love, and clearly the goal or highest good of the Christian ethic is to obey the law of love. The distinction between a Beatific Vision ethic like Bonaventure's, which is supposed to be teleological, and a loving-obedience ethic like Luther's, which is supposed to be deontological, obviously has to do with two different psychological orientations, not with ethical decisions about conduct. Nor is one any more controlled by sanctions and "long run" considerations than the other. Temple's position was stated in *Nature, Man and God* (408-9).

168. St. Paul could summarize the Summary of the Law in neighbor-love rather than God-love because God is the constant, always-there Neighbor. The usual remark that the "second half" of the Summary follows from the first is not as penetrating as the view that the first included the second.

169. This could not be taken to mean that the Atheistic Debauchee is doing no wrong if he *feels* none. That is pure subjectivism. Temple rejected purely "emotive" theories of ethics: "Moral judgment is not

concerned with feelings of the critic, but with the quality of the act or the agent" (ECP, 122). Even a desert island is part of "the quad" God oversees. The drunken atheist is *not* alone, theologically regarded, as Temple usually insisted; therefore he is always a member of society—at least, he is always *in relationship* objectively with the divine Person, even when not with any human person. But at the level of human consciousness, where the moral sense emerges creatively, the isolated man *might* not "feel" any sense of wrongdoing. *Mens Creatrix* is the most disjointed and poorly constructed of Temple's work, and Dorothy Emmet senses an inconsistency here in his island example (in Iremonger, 536). It overstated and under-refined his thought. (However, her suggestion that there may be "intrinsic goods" apart from "personal relationships" simply misses Temple's *theological* point that nothing exists outside God's purpose and evaluation. Temple never said that values are *interpersonal*—only that they are values in relation *to* persons. And it was the moral sense, not right and wrong, which he said is produced in human society.)

170. A closer examination of Temple's use of "love" shows why he comes very close sometimes to speaking as if love and justice are different principles. In discussing moral goodness in a fairly careful way he said, of the commandment to love our neighbors, that "love is not at our command" and "if there is no love the will cannot force us" to fulfill the commandment (NMG, 195-6). It seems pretty clear that he conceived of love—Christian love, or *agape*—as an emotional, not a volitional leaning towards others. Most scholars take love in the New Testament to be the reverse of Temple's view, so that a Christian fulfills the law of love to the neighbor even if he does not *like* him. Says C. E. B. Cranfield, New Testament love refers to "the will rather than to emotion" (in A. Richardson, ed., *Theological Word Book of the Bible*, Macmillan, New York, 1951, 121-36).

171. In the same way he was influenced by Plato to think of ethics as the morality of *private* relationships, and politics as the morality of *social* relationships, but actually he knew that they are one and the same—value considerations.

172. He agreed with Kant that "you can because you should"—that "ought" entails or presupposes "can." Some Christian moralists (e.g., Reinhold Niebuhr) have appeared, in effect, to deny men any moral ability because of their opposition to bootstrap humanism and their over-corrective emphasis on man's incapacity. Many Calvinists and Lutherans have portrayed Augustine's view of man's moral capacity as "total depravity, total inability." Most of this is obvious exaggeration. Temple held two things about man's moral powers: (1) man has (acquires) a given or natural ability to choose the good and act upon it; (2) his moral powers as to both conscience and commitment are weak and in need of grace, not only to get him off his self-center (original sin) but also to strengthen him against sin.

173. All serious Christian scholars are aware that there is a bit of

complexity in the so-called "second half of the Summary of the Law" (Luke 10:27b), the command to love the neighbor as the self. Are we to love him as *much* as we love ourselves? Or equally and along with ourselves? Or in the same *way* as ourselves? Or as much as and in the same way, but *instead* of ourselves? It has been discussed often in the classical tradition. Temple seems to have contradicted himself on this question, or at least to have lost consistency. In a 1912 discussion he said that we are to seek each our own interest only when and because it would advance the welfare of our neighbor and society, thus basically subordinating the self to fellowship. He went on to say, "So far as I can see there can be no obligation to self"—which at first seems nihilistic in the fashion of oriental *nirvana,* and unChristian (KG, 48). But a prior point he had made saved him from that error—that the self *alone* has no claims, which implies that the self *in relationship* does have claims. Later, in Chicago in 1936, he approached the issue by reminding us that no one can love the neighbor as oneself without divine grace, and then said flatly: "But in no case is the agent called upon to prefer the interest of his neighbor to his own; he is required to put them on the same level, and this will include the assertion of his own interest . . ." (CTP, 103). Needless to say, to this writer the second (Chicago) statement seems a serious lapse from agapeic ethics if it is taken to mean, as it could be, that the self's interests are not to be set aside for the neighbor's sake.

174. One should be alert to the dangers in his apparent view that common sense and conscience are always dependable. He had stated it earlier in *Mens Creatrix* (201). There he accepts too easily the claim that "the medicinal lie" of nurses and doctors to dying patients is a right action. But in any case he is on good ground in denying that *any* lie is wrong regardless of circumstances—"medicinal lies" can often be the most loving thing and therefore the right thing.

175. Surely here in this context Temple by his own logic should have enclosed the word "steal" in quotation marks, to keep his meaning constant.

176. Again, by his logic, Temple should not have used "nearly" or "perhaps" here. The clear meaning of what he said about the relativity of ethical decisions is that only love is *always* right and good, only malice is *always* wrong and evil.

177. Temple, following Sir David Ross' distinction in *The Right and the Good* (1930) between moral right and moral good, attributed rightness to "acts" and goodness to "actions." The distinction is not merely a play on words, but it has little significance in this treatment of his ethical thought. He never spoke of good or bad "things" and right or wrong "actions," because no *thing* could be evil, as such, anyway. He held that "it is not permissible for any Christian to say that anything [e.g., sex] that God has made is inherently evil" (CFL, 43). Thus it is theologically impossible to regard any material or physical thing as

always evil. This leaves only the question whether any act or action is inherently evil. To this Temple replied, in effect, "No, nothing except malice—ill will or unlovingness."

178. The influence of the Cambridge analyst, G. E. Moore, led Temple to adopt what he (rather inaccurately) called the "common sense" doctrine that "right" means "productive of the best possible consequences." This is Moore's "optimific" theory of right. Temple thought he found it in substance in Plato's *Republic* (457 B), but put himself on shaky ground in saying so. Neither Temple nor Moore, in this writer's view, paid enough respect to the cautionary statement of the optimific principle—right is that which appears most productive of good in the *foreseeable* consequences. Unlike Moore, Temple for theological reasons asserted positively that "the law of love" is the measure of the "best possible" of consequences.

179. As a very young man Temple took a stern and absolutist line, very Kantian. He became more relativistic as to conduct as he grew older. But even as a schoolboy he had the heart of it. He wrote to his father, "If a man really believes in God, he cannot do wrong" (Iremonger, 20). Such a man can make mistakes but to the extent that he loves God he will not *do* wrong, deliberately do *wrong*.

180. He was not over-simple about it. He recognized that the regularities of nature are related to moral action—that "we can make no plans and form no purposes unless we count upon the regularity of natural process" (BC, 12). Indeed, this is why there is no *moral* difficulty in facing the calamities that come upon men through natural orderliness.

181. This first key, universality, would be a contradiction of Temple's relativism except that he was prepared only to find *principles* given, not rules or applications. Cultural anthropology, however, would give neither Temple nor the Natural Law theologians any support for their hope of finding any universals at the level of principle, except for "do the good, avoid the evil" (which is logically inherent in the ethical quest), and prohibitions of things like murder and perjury (which are actions in a particular form that a particular culture has proscribed: e.g., "murder" is not defined the same way universally, perjury is not, and so on).

182. As the title of his sixth chapter in *Christianity and Social Order* he used "Natural *Order*," not "law." Perhaps the most striking observation is that both the term and the concept of Natural Law are not even mentioned in his Gifford Lectures.

183. This writer can only say that Temple here is like most Christian moralists, sadly unaware of the depth and extent of human variety and cultural relativity, and to speak of "automatic" insight, *even in the hypothetical absence of sin,* fails to do justice to what social scientists have learned about "the sociology of knowledge."

184. Here he was consciously approving the thesis of Jacques Mari-

tain in *Scholasticism and Politics* (Macmillan, New York, 1940). Maritain's was a more abstract version of the personalism represented by the French writer and social radical Emmanuel Mounier in *The Personalist Manifesto* (Longmans, Green, New York, 1938). See also Temple's opinion of Maritain's personalism as having a better flavour than St. Thomas' version, in *Malvern 1941* (14), and his estimate of Maritain in *What Christians Stand For in the Secular World.*

185. In all three lands the State was a one-party monolith which had dispensed with parliamentary direction. Great importance attaches, of course, to their differences: Germany's was a race-party, Russia's a class-party, Italy's a frankly statist-party. But all were alike in dictatorship, in rejecting political democracy.

186. As a concomitant, he always held that personality, too, is a Christian product. The Greeks and Latins had no conception of personality in our modern sense, and hence so much profitless confusion in efforts to "explain" the three-persons Greek metaphysic of the Trinity. A *persona,* as in a dramatic action or play, was "a part played by a person, rather than a person who played the part" (CiC, 79).

187. They hardly call for treatment here, but we might note two other features of Temple's democratic standard: (1) the voice of the people is *not* the voice of God—it is almost certain to be wrong in some measure, but its errors are less dangerous than those of any minority; and (2) democracy is a set of dynamic principles, not any particular political system—whether a limited monarchy or a republic or a socialist soviet. He recognized, incidentally, that there are peoples in the world not yet ready for democracy or even asking for it (RE, 144).

188. He wrote this in the autumn of 1926 after his encounter with the Prime Minister's anger at Temple's part in the Coal Strike. Clearly his use of "inconceivable" is intended to apply to England's democracy: he was aware even that early of the totalitarian trends on the Continent.

189. It is interesting to observe that he paid considerable attention to the contractual theory of the State's origin, implicit in all anarcho-syndicalist doctrines which aim at dispensing with the State, but he never seemed to catch on to the essentially "contractual" theory of the pre-political community itself. The contractual theory of the State in Hobbes and Rousseau is often applied, at least by inference, to human association as such, as in all radical individualism which treats the individual as the primary reality and society as something merely derivative. In one place Temple mentions this pre-political contractualism, but little more (CS, 43-5). He remarks, quite correctly, that the social contract theory deals with the origin "sometimes of Society, sometimes of Government. And the fact that this distinction has not always been observed arises from the fact that many thinkers have identified Society with the State." His illustration of the contractual origin of society itself is that of Glaucon in the second book of Plato's *Republic.*

190. The contract theory is mythological, like the Fall in Genesis. There was no one point in time when a contract was made, just as there was no point when "mankind" made a decision to disobey God. And just as Temple raised questions as to the adequacy of the Fall myth, so he questioned the contract myth. "The Contract theory is not even good myth" (CS, 88; CaC, 24). He preferred to base his theory of the State, as of Society, on a positive theology of creation.

191. He would have welcomed the racial integration laws in America, for example, on the ground that they both checked the evils of segregation *and* tended to convert the will of the people toward non-discrimination. It is certainly often the case that as people are brought by law to cease and desist from certain unsocial practices, they begin to lose their taste for them. Political or social freedom, like everything else, is a relative good—not good universally or unconditionally.

192. Speaking of social policy, Temple said: "I see quite well how Love may be the motive prompting creation; but I do not see how Love, as Love and nothing else, is to be creative. Love needs Power if it is to create or accomplish anything. And the difference between Love and Power is proved in our experience by the fact that the two do not vary together. If a man is drowning and two men try to save him, one may love him more, but if he is muscularly weak he will help him less than the other who is stronger, though his love is not so great" (CS, 32-3).

193. This was written before the sharp development of a new nationalism in Soviet Russia and the communist countries elsewhere, including China. It was also before the communist parties began allying themselves with nationalist movements against colonial powers. Many Marxist critics condemn the communists for their "reversion to nationalism," but this particular point would not have been pressed by Temple. His distrust of "cosmopolitanism" as a remedy for nationalism and national egoism anticipated even the term, or name, with which the Russian Communist Party denounced the same error under Stalin, after the Second World War—in the Soviets' renewal of a place for national sentiment in their scheme of things (CTP, 98).

194. He always regretted the Lutheran influence in the English Reformation's Church-State arrangement. While he did not think Luther intended it, he nevertheless brought about a subjection of the Church to the German civil powers (CiC, 67). Near the end of his ministry, in the second great war with Germany, he even thought that the Lutheran rejection of all "natural theology" led to a separation of Christian criticism from civil policy. "It is easy to see how Luther prepared the way for Hitler" (*Malvern 1941*, 13).

195. His idea here was that people should first be married by a justice of the peace or other civil officer, the clergy ceasing to do "the State's business" (TSPD, 48). In *The Centrality of Christ* (93) he held that the Church should keep to its ideal, never granting holy matri-

mony to any person who has a partner to a former marriage still living, whether the "innocent" party or not. At the same time he was positive that our Lord never intended "to legislate for His Church in this matter of marriage" (STPD, 45). To many readers Temple never succeeded in making a very impressive case for this unusual departure from his principles of love, relativism, and the *gradual* realization of the ideal in the actual. Earlier, in 1912, he had argued that the Church should maintain a higher standard of marriage than the State, which rightly cuts its cloth according to what is *generally* possible now—whereas the Church can sustain a level possible to Christians under grace, preserving the ideal for all, the future-possible (KG, 88).

196. He confessed that it is "the claim to possess a Revelation at once unique, final and universal, which makes the Church a perennial source of difficulty to any State which does not avowedly accept that Revelation as the guide of its actions. At one time the State in England made such an avowal" (CaC, 5). Luther, of course, had tried to make the Prince *summus episcopus* on the assumption that he would always be a Christian—and so it was in England's Reformation. And is no more, in either land.

197. His last remarks on the subject came as a result of a challenge by the then Lord Privy Seal at a meeting in Albert Hall in 1942, when Temple was on the platform with him. Cripps asked, "Are you ready for Disestablishment and Disendowment?" But Temple was never convinced that the greatest good would come from disestablishment. A renewed call from "disestablishmentarians" in December of 1955 brought the Roman Catholic *Herald* to say: "The tradition of establishment has proved to be a powerful spiritual and moral factor in the country . . . Bound up with the Christian throne, the Church of England has . . . been a growing rather than a declining Christian influence . . . We find it hard to see how God's truth will be better served by a disestablishment which would make our society formally secularist" (*Time,* Dec. 12, 1955, 66:88-9).

198. He seems to have evolved his *schema* without any sociological sophistication, simply by logic and observation, combined with theological reference. For example, in his use of "community" he does not distinguish it from "society" as Frederick Toennies distinguished *gemeinschaft,* or primary cultural unity, from *gesellschaft,* or secondary structural unity. But the basic common sense of such concepts in sociology is evident in the fact that Temple *thought* them without using them consciously or formally, by putting his "communities" into a total scheme also including associations and fellowships.

199. Students of New Testament theology and ethics will recognize at once that the typology here corresponds closely to the technical distinctions which have developed between *eros,* or emotional, satisfaction-seeking love; *philia* or selective, discriminating friendship-love; and *agape* or attitudinal, disinterested love. Families and nation-states are

highly emotional forms of group-egoism—sometimes apparently almost irrational and sacrosanct. Associations, in which something of self-interest is being sought even though it entails giving something, too, are like *philia:* there is reciprocity and mutual interest, but the membership lasts only as long as the need is met. *Fellowships* are so disinterested and self-denying that they are easily regarded as fanatical by those who are not "called" to be members. Temple drew no such parallel with the forms of love, but it is there just the same. Indeed, he claimed that "an association is not of its essence self-regarding," but he is not very convincing about it. He admits that they are "neither intensely egoistic nor capable of great generosity" (CTP, 95-6). In any case, Temple does not make the unrealistic attempt to call upon Christians to live only by the third principle of membership, i.e., to live only at the level of grace; he realized that, at the level of nature and history, God's creative process works through all three kinds of love and relationships.

200. Even in his ecumenical writings he never seemed quite to come to grips with the question whether the Church as a fellowship takes precedence over the nation. It does, by his logic. For practical purposes he always held that Christians are not disloyal to the wider Christian fellowship when they go to war for their countries, if they are sincerely convinced of the rightness of their cause and do not deny that their enemies are their Christian brothers. Apparently his main reason for putting the nation highest among historical loyalties was a feeling that anything wider was unrealistic. "There is, as a rule, no practical means of serving the human race except by serving some section of it" (CiC, 102). But his own vision of increasing world unity seems to have allowed that the "rule" would operate less and less in the future. Granted that "mankind" is a non-empirical construct, and granted the need of a *theological* foundation for limiting the State's authority and rights, could there not—in all fairness to non-theological thinkers—be a humanistic as well as theistic construct of this kind?

201. Nowhere, apparently, does he deal with or try to answer the socialist claim that the higher standard of living in capitalist society, compared to feudalism's, is due to technology and not to the system.

202. There is no record of his having read G. V. Plekhanov's *Role of the Individual in History,* or such non-communist analyses as Venable's *Human Nature: The Marxian View* (Knopf, New York, 1945).

203. Temple's point here is validated only by his *theological* presuppositions, by his faith-propositions about history as God's creative process and man as a spiritual being. He was not unaware that Marxists would answer his question by "explaining" Jesus and the early Christians in terms of socio-economic conditioning. E.g., see Karl Kautsky's *Origins of Christianity* (1908), and Ludwig Feuerbach's *Essence of Christianity* (1841). The subjectivity of the latter was especially alien to Temple's method.

204. This Christian, biblical-Johannine materialism or sacramentalism

was a constant theme throughout his life. It is first recorded in the Cambridge Lenten lectures in 1912 (KG, 120), but it shows up in one context or another repeatedly. Cf., as instances, *Personal Religion and the Life of Fellowship* (1926, 17), *Nature, Man and God* (1932, 478), *Readings in St. John's Gospel* (1939, I.xx), *Centrality of Christ* (1935, 57), *What Christians Stand For in the Secular World* (1944, sec. 3).

205. The "detachment" idea is based on vss. 24, 31 and 35, all interspersed remarks in a discussion of sex, marriage and divorce. They are based on his early expectation of an immediate *parousia*, which he later dropped. Christian asceticism, after a short period of eremitic practice, became social in the monasteries, forswearing private property—but not corporate wealth. The Gospel, as in the Beatitudes, speaks of poverty but not of *destitution* as good; modest possessions—neither penury nor the wealth of those in kings' houses. The have-nots are not favored over the haves—only the have-enoughs over the have-too-muches! Lady Poverty for the Franciscans was really Dame Destitution, but Jesus was of the poor rather than of the beggars. Personal voluntary poverty may be *safer* for some people, spiritually, but it is not the way of ethical responsibility in the wider fellowship of society.

206. "The Bolshevik effort to unite men internationally on the basis of economic interests against other groups similarly based is definitely retrograde, because the unity of a nation is richer in content than the unity of an economic class, and its fellowship is proportionately more valuable. The values won in the nationalist phase of history must not be lost as we consciously and definitely enter on the international" (CS, 158). On his Australian tour in 1910, however, he was still of the opinion that class-loyalty need not involve "class-selfishness" (PSR, 58). Later he was willing to allow that particular persons might manage to have the first and avoid the latter, but that as a general thing they couldn't.

207. In conversation with this writer, in York, Temple once said about the Thirty-eighth Article ("the Riches and Goods of Christians are not common, as touching the right, title and possession of the same; as certain Anabaptists do falsely boast") that it made him a "heretic" because he believed our wealth is by right and ultimate title common, only *temporarily* assigned to private persons as a concession to sin's working.

208. The development he refers to is the increasing proletarianization of the "petty bourgeoisie" and the pauperization of the workers. The exact opposite has taken place, of course.

209. Temple had true sympathy for this rather pragmatic epistemology, which has developed out of scientific experience; Percy Bridgmann's *Logic of Modern Physics* (Macmillan, New York, 1927) is an early classic in the development of the "operational" theory of knowledge.

210. The phrase, middle axioms, was possibly an unfortunate one, since by definition an "axiom" is a self-validating, non-derivative

proposition, and cannot stand in the "middle" between something logically prior to it and a subsequent derivative. But it expressed his meaning. Its use has been encouraged in America, especially by John Bennett. J. H. Oldham appears to have been the first to use it. (*The Church and It's Function in Society*, Willett, Clark, Chicago, 1937, 193-94, 222.)

211. Temple here anticipated recent shifts in economic analysis from profit-maximizing to other theories of business behavior based on principles such as viability and balanced aspirations, which include moral and spiritual values. Cf. Kenneth Boulding, *A Reconstruction of Economics* (Wiley, New York, 1950), and N. W. Chamberlain, *A General Theory of Economic Process* (Harper, New York, 1955).

212. The document *What Christians Stand For in the Secular World* ought not, perhaps, to be in his bibliography, but it is included here because it is commonly listed as Temple's, and he *did* write it. Actually, like so many other things, he wrote it as a summary of the findings of a group called the Christian Frontier, of which he and the lay theologian Joseph Oldham were the leaders. This same ecumenical group published the *Christian News-Letter*, in which the document made its first appearance.

213. He was thinking of what we might call the problem of the Six Ms in our highly interdependent economy. A wage-raise in steel increases prices in everything; a strike of truck drivers can lose millions in nationwide commerce; bankers can paralyze business by cutting off credit. The economy is an integrated mechanism. We have the Men—the labor needed, in overabundance as automation proceeds; we have Materials—the natural resources to process and manufacture into consumer goods; we have Machines—the modern, fabulously efficient means of production, steadily enhancing the productivity of labor; we have Management—the enterprise and brains and know-how to carry on the process (owners nowadays hire their brains as they their brawn); we have the Markets—the need or consumer demand. However, to make demand effective there must be Money—purchasing power distributed in sufficient volume through wages, salaries and dividends. Money is the life-blood of the corporate economy. The total balance of this intricate economic mechanism, and its smooth functioning, cannot be entrusted blindly to faith in some "automatic harmony" or "natural" laws such as govern sun-spots and tidal waves. It has to be rational in its totality as well as in its separate sectors, and rationally coordinated.

214. In many places for many years Temple said there are *four* such fundamental principles, but for some reason not explained he omitted the fourth one in the plan of *Christianity and Social Order*. The fourth one was always "the power of sacrifice." (PRLF, 65-8.)

215. The chief sources for Temple's program are: *Christianity and Social Order*, 101-22; *The Hope of a New World*, esp. 46-63; "The Archbishop's Resolution" (*Malvern Conference Findings*); "What Must

Christians Do Now?" *Christian Century,* Oct. 9, 1940 (English title, "Begin Now"); *The Church Looks Forward,* esp. 110-69; *The Church and the Social Order* (I.C.F. pamphlet of an address in Glasgow, September, 1941).

216. A somewhat "dated" point of which Temple made a lot was his insistence that profit-seeking business precipitates war by its competition for markets and its pressure on governments to gain control. Thus "the predominance of the profit motive is itself a cause of war" (HNW, 17). He and his contemporaries were constantly faced with the grim realities of colonialism and economic tensions in the world between the big capitalist powers. Temple took seriously the warnings in saturation theories like J. A. Hobson's *(Imperialism,* 1908; *Work and Wealth,* 1914; *Rationalization and Unemployment,* 1930), that domestic markets are limited by the amount of wages (purchasing power) available, and that dynamic business has to go abroad (a) to sell or trade profitably, and (b) to reinvest profitably. The Pilgrim Trust study of the "hard core" of unemployment, which Temple chaired, brought this out forcibly. Less than twenty years after his death, the dominant form of conflict and tension has become primarily a power and ideological rivalry, although it is not without its economic interests. It is still true, of course, that the development of raw-materials countries into manufacturing countries is contracting the commodity market for the big Western powers in their thrusts abroad—an ominous fact that now is hidden by their cold-war expenditures, which provide jobs for the garrison economy that would not otherwise be available. But if "peace should break out" and these economies were then forced to distribute enough purchasing power to consume at home *all* of the goods produced by their industries, the "saturation" problem would confront them again as it did in the pre-war Thirties. The population explosion also helps them to ease the tension between the present system's capacity to produce and its capacity to consume. But as time goes on this "solution" will be seen to be a disaster. And the "backward" or underdeveloped nations will give less and less welcome to foreign capital and goods. All of these things, combining with the astronomical increase of productive capacity which nuclear power will bring, will force the issue into the open: Shall production be limited to consumer capacity, or consumption be expanded to producer capacity? The first of these policies, the present one, Temple argued, is a reversal of the "natural" order. To him the wage-system, or "labor market" theory of wage payments, seemed outmoded and dangerous. And he realized that in a socialist society there is no threat of over-production, i.e., of producing more goods than its people can consume according to the rules of the economic game.

217. Temple, true to his sense of the development of collectivism, saw little future for small-scale business in merchandising or manufacturing. He wanted a place always left for private enterprise and initiative and

for the free play of choice and interest they facilitate; but he was aware that something like "three fourths of the businesses which are started go into liquidation within three years." (The name "profit system" does not fit a large proportion of private enterprises, as most people might be surprised to learn.) Temple regarded most little firms as sentimental hindrances to "progress and science in the art of management" and a cause for much unemployment due to their failure. He was frankly in the Big Business camp. And over and beyond his social realism he had the classical Christian feeling that one's right to enjoy the profits of an enterprise was established by the "partnership" born of assuming the risks and liabilities entailed: limited liability investment was to Temple a heads-I-win, tails-you-lose morality in which the investor stands to gain if it succeeds, but only loses what he paid in if it fails, with no responsibility to anybody else.

218. Late medieval Schoolmen allowed a continuing interest on loans to profit-making ventures, if they were profitable, on the ground that the lender was a partner. They were loans for *commoditum*, not *usum*. Temple's originality here is in putting a limit on the profit to be given to this particular kind of partner—the investor—by applying the Just Price to money. And he was essentially consistent enough to apply it to land too, by cutting out private landlordism in all except agricultural and ex-urban residential sites.

219. Laski's view appears sporadically throughout his works. Many Labour Party people favored it. Benevenisti's is treated in his *Iniquitous Contract* (London, 1937). Josiah Stamp speaks of it in his *Christianity and Economics*. E. Rignano's is in the translation of his book by W. J. Shutz, *The Social Significance of the Inheritance Tax* (New York, 1924).

220. A "debenture" is the English term for a bond with a fixed rate of interest and a fixed date of maturity, for expiration and repayment. The British government in the early Forties had responded to the protests of farmers by a Tithe Act under which (to Temple's satisfaction) the tithes immemorially distrained upon farmers by some rectory churches were converted into lump sums and paid off for good and all by the State. The farmers were then required to repay the government in installments until they were debt-free. The old Church tithes were like most investments in respect, at least, of their being an endless levy.

221. Temple never got around to working out the further details. We may imagine that he would have had to see that some kind of investment-partnership should be granted to the governmental social-security and cooperative group-insurance institutions, whereby saving for rainy days and retirement could earn income at a rate at least comparable to the profits being paid out in wages and salaries during active employment.

222. The present writer happened to be lunching with Mrs. Temple in 1946 in London on the day following a visit to Downing Street of English churchmen of the major communions, led by Archbishop Fisher.

They complained about the losses their churches were suffering. Mrs. Temple said, "William will be turning over in his grave. Poor William, poor Church." Even the *Times* was acid, saying that the Church was frightened because while it knew it was only losing about a shilling *per capita* of its claimed members, it also knew it couldn't get a penny from most of them in voluntary support.

223. He insisted on labor's right to strike as long as it was on the outside of the company, looking in. At the same time he was so keen on justice to all that he doubted the right of labor to engage in sympathetic strikes *outside* the industry. Innocent third parties must be protected. And in any case "all strikes are symptomatic of our civilization." As a socialist he opposed the trade-union, class-conflict outlook, wanted to wipe out economic classes instead of perpetuating a bargaining structure. However, Temple had some doubts about labor's readiness to take a full part. "Labour has historically been very reluctant to accept a share in the control of industry or the direction of its policy. It is doubtful whether Labour at present would generally accept its proportion of places on the Boards of Directors or make a very good use of those places if it did" (HNW, 54). He explained that unions are a nineteenth-century phenomenon based on a class-ordered society, "structurally and psychologically ill-adapted for the chief opportunities of today." And, he added, "it is as difficult to overcome the vested interests of Labour organizations, and those who gain a living by working in them, as it is to overcome the capitalist vested interests which Labour rightly denounces. The source of the trouble is not wealth; it is sin— which is the perquisite of no class . . ." (HNW, 60-1).

224. Temple spoke frequently and sharply on the commodity theory of labor. To the extent that any system rests on it, he said, it "is an immoral and vicious economic system" (CTP, 66-7). He argued that if we want to hire a man's labor we have to hire *him.* "Our industrial system today does not rest on the commodity view of labour: a multitude of factors have come in to modify it. But *we have not yet explicitly repudiated it or adopted another principle in its place"* (CV, 204).

225. In the famous encyclical of Leo XIII on social justice, *Rerum Novarum* (1891), it was said, "Each requires the other; capital cannot get along without labor, nor labor without capital." As a matter of fact, this is correct. But in its context it was a claim that *laborers* cannot get along without *capitalists,* a system of class collaboration, which (as the socialist economies show) is untrue. That logical slip-over, a semantic confusion, sometimes knowingly employed, was what Temple was protesting. On one occasion, however, in an address in Washington, he forgot himself and said of capital, management and labor—all three, "if one of them withdraws its cooperation the process stops" (CoC, 112). Here he was guilty of Ruskin's "pathetic fallacy" of attributing personal quality to material things, a fallacy he always abhorred. (Cf. Peter Drucker, *Landmarks of Tomorrow,* New York, 1958, 98 ff., for a management consultant's forecast of "a society without either capitalist

or proletarian," only the middle class of employed professionals.) Temple quite logically rejected the argument that private property is necessary to personality *if the property is capital.* He could follow Aristotle and Aquinas that personal things should be privately possessed, and he was even prepared to allow that the kind of capital (tools) the ancients used was of a size and kind that made it personal. But modern, mass-production machinery has to be corporately used, is not by nature private, and therefore Temple proposed to make its ownership consistent with its nature and use. (Socialism is not brought about by socialists, although they add a certain amount of ideological pressure based on objective changes already occurring. It is science and technology that do it, with their built-in interdependence.)

226. All sorts of economic research and problem-solving were coming up against monetary and fiscal "sleeper" questions. For example, the International Labor Conference of the I. L. O. in Geneva in 1937 had concluded: "Economic prosperity and social security depend more on monetary policy than on any other single factor" (*Malvern Torch,* I.C.F., London, March, 1943).

227. In the furor that arose after Temple's proposals were made public, one banking expert wrote him: "The joke about financial questions, generally speaking, is that nobody knows the technical answers to them. If somebody will start giving the moral answers, we may get somewhere" (Iremonger, 579). That is what Temple was doing.

228. Ralph M. Hawtrey, once secretary of the British Treasury, said that banks "lend by creating credit. They create the means of payment out of nothing" (*Encyc. Brit.,* 14th ed., 15:698). When Marriner Eccles headed the Federal Reserve System in the U.S., he was asked before the House Banking and Currency Committee (Sept. 30, 1941), "Mr. Eccles, how did you get the money to buy those $2,000,000,000 of government securities?" He replied, "We created it, out of the right to issue credit money." Eccles explained: "The banks can create and destroy money. Bank credit is money. It is the money we do most of our business with, not with that currency which we usually think of as money." Says the article on banking in the *Encyclopedia Britannica,* "Banks create credit. It is a mistake to suppose that bank credit is created to any important extent by the payment of money into the banks. A loan made by a bank is a clear addition to the amount of money in the community." For further light on Temple's proposal, consider these quotations from *The American Individual Enterprise System* (McGraw-Hill, New York, 1946), published for the National Association of Manufacturers (399 ff.): (1) "Money is to the economic system what blood is to the human body." (2) "The process by which a bank creates a bank deposit is quite simple . . . When [it] is entered in the deposit account, new money has been created . . . The new deposit is new money." (3) "How far banks should be permitted to go in this creation of money has long been a matter of public concern." (In the U.S. the Federal Reserve's credit ratio is binding on member banks by law, and it

varies with business expectations. Small depositors, $10,000 and under, are now protected by federal insurance from bank collapse through over-extension. In the socialist economies money is issued according to the volume of wealth produced, and used on a sort of postage stamp principle to move goods to the consumer and then cancelled. Monetary inflation or deflation is deliberate, in a managed economy.)

229. Hartley Withers (*Archiepiscopal Economics*, Individualist Book-shop, London, 1942, Post-War Questions No. 18) also appealed to the Parable of the Talents in Matthew 25 as "divine approval of profit earning," to discredit Temple's proposal to eliminate bank profits from credit creation, as well as to "wither" investors' profits from the production of actual goods and services.

230. Rumor has it that his expert advice on the costs of bank-loan service came from Sir John Maynard Keynes, his friend, who was the most distinguished economist of that era, a Cambridge academician as well as a Director of the Bank of England. As all students know, Keynes' influence on fiscal policy has radically altered the pattern of economic legislation in Britain and America.

231. Says John Gunther in *Inside Europe Today* (Harper, New York, 1961): "Western Europe has probably moved closer toward economic unity in the last twenty-five years than in the previous five hundred, and the beginnings of integration on the political level are almost sure to follow. It is a striking fact that the frontiers of the Common Market are almost precisely those of the empire of Charlemagne, except for the boot of Italy."

232. See E. F. Hecksher ("Protection," *Encyc. of Social Sciences*): "Indeed, as long as trade meant the giving away of commodities in exchange for those received, it was scarcely conceivable that it would be considered advantageous to acquire as few commodities as possible in exchange for those given away. But when people began to think in terms of money exchange, they came to look upon money as the aim and end of trade; imports then became dangerous as depleting the community of 'treasure,' while exports were invaluable as increasing the stock of money."

233. At Oxford he had been a Protectionist, but not for the sake of higher profits. He even joined the Tariff Reform League in order to push the goal of tariff protection, as a wall behind which to safely finance social welfare without danger of being undercut by cut-throat competition from low-standard colonial producers (often backed by British capitalists!). He was unpopular because of this, even though he admitted protection would make England poorer, not richer, because of his insistence that it was worth it. Yet he always repudiated the mercantilist doctrine, and applauded at least the chief aim of the Free Trade of Cobden and Bright—which was real wealth, not money.

234. Strong as his conviction was about world federalism, he had equally strong convictions about credit creation. Therefore he was in favor of a Bank for International Settlements, but opposed a World

Bank ("an enormous instance of irresponsible power") as long as banks create credit and control it.

235. His views on riparian rights, if he ever developed any, were not published.

236. At Coronation Eucharists the King or Queen personally places the oblation on the altar, the symbolism being that the whole people's wealth is given back to Him from Whom it has been received and Whose it is. It is the ritual acknowledgement that (a) the Crown has the stewardship, as representing the people, and (b) the whole common wealth is God's.

237. Temple understood that the popular modern *re*-conception of "stewardship" is a sub-Christian version. It vests God's grant of possession (not ownership) in the hands of private individuals, instead of in the community or people. The patristic writers were more biblical; they treated the whole social order as having the stewardship, with individuals or families being sub-tenants of parts of it, according as the rulers ("patriarchs") divided it. But with the rise of feudalism the Aristotelian principle of private ownership and public benefit (chivalry and *noblesse oblige*) reversed the biblical conception. Properly understood, individual possessers ("owners") are not stewards on behalf of their neighbors; they are only stewards for God, *via* the community's wisdom and sufferance. God does not give His wealth to some *rather than to others,* expecting the rich to be "generous" to His other children!

238. Like Winston Churchill who was a Single Taxer, Temple knew of Henry George's critique and took it to heart.

239. He wanted tradition safeguarded by exempting agricultural estates from death duties, and abolition of urban ground-landlords by drastic duties. "I should forbid the sale of urban land except to the public authority" (HNW, 59).

240. The only directly challengeable element of data in Temple's case for a conditional (relative) justification of war is this statement: "Our Lord recognizes the right of kingdoms of this world to fight" (RE, 176). It is not necessary to his argument and is obviously a moot and interpretive statement.

241. This writer should state his own decision so that if it biases his account of this phase of Temple's thought, it may be corrected for. His is a non-pacifist, anti-war position based on a pragmatic and relativist assessment of the evils of nuclear war *versus* any gains that might be at stake in a given conflict. His position, like Temple's, is on the side of the classical Just War doctrine and against the pacifist doctrine, but in applying the Just War's precondition of "proportionate good" he finds that war today uses, or could too easily slip into using, nihilistic means which subvert any good end in view.

242. Temple always challenged the view that the Sermon on the Mount taught non-resistance (rather than non-violent resistance). He held that it *implied* the use of non-violent resistance, rather than an active resistance. But in any case, he held that the Sermon and the

gospels did *not* teach non-resistance to evil. Compare the non-resistance interpretation in Reinhold Niebuhr's *Interpretation of Christian Ethics* (Harper, New York, 1935, 158 ff.) to Martin Luther King's view (like Temple's) in the sixth chapter of *Stride Toward Freedom* (Harper, New York, 1958).

243. Temple thought it a pity that in English we have to translate both *zoe* and *psyche* by the same word. The *psyche* or "breath of life" can sometimes be given up for the *zoe* which bears our eternal life.

244. He obviously doubted that any *group*, whether a whole nation or some smaller sector of it, would ever in fact be altruistic, sacrificing its own good for another's, even though he allowed for it logically. But his principle of creative process and his "optimistic hypothesis" provided more, surely, than a logical basis for the possibility. If individuals can grow in fellowship through enlightened self-interest, so can communities and associations.

245. Temple always assumes that the war in question is defensive and non-vindictive; that Christian ethics can never justify wars of aggression, only justify the "innocent party" in war (and, as we have seen, he was quite clear that nobody's hands are quite clean, even at best). He knew but rejected the pacifist opinion that since there is no simple war of defense, without some guilt on both sides, there can be no just war. He maintained that even if a nation has been guilty of sins of omission or commission, it cannot add to its past faults by becoming guilty of the new fault of inaction in the face of aggression (TWT, 9).

246. This is obviously dated, alike in its language and its substance. Nowhere in anything he wrote is there any sign that he foresaw nuclear or thermonuclear weapons. Temple would have been most likely to agree that when "guns" ceased to be the comparison, and nuclear weapons succeeded molecular, a nodal or dialectical point or *leap* was reached, making a qualitative difference, so that the debate is no longer over a merely *quantitative* difference in war's destructiveness. In short, mass-extermination weapons are not merely bigger guns, and to think they are reveals a lack of value-perception. He foresaw, of course, that society was bound to eliminate the "merchants of death" who not only privately manufactured for profit but *traded* in arms in the interbellum period. All that has been brought to an end by international agreements and national controls.

247. This was the same poem in which the better known line ran, "In the Spring a young man's fancy lightly turns to thoughts of love." The couplet ran:

> Till the war drums throbbed no longer,
> and the battle flags were furl'd
> In the Parliament of Man,
> the Federation of the world.

References

(Full data on Temple's works will be found in the Bibliography. Here only the assigned code initials are used. Other books are given by abbreviation after their first mention.)

INTRODUCTION

1. *Malvern 1941*, 224.
2. C. Smyth, *Cyril Forster Garbett*, Hodder & Stoughton, London (1959), 275.
3. David Walker, in *Church Quarterly Review*, 161 (Oct.-Dec. 1960), 479-99.

CHAPTER I
Theology as a Method

1. CTP, 38.
2. Iremonger, p. 18.
3. SSTC, 47.
4. CTP, 37.
5. SSTC, 43.
6. Iremonger, 605.
7. *An Era, etc.*, 146-47.
8. CRG, 10. Cf. Anselm's *Proslogium*, ch. 1.
9. TSPD, 6-7.
10. St. Matthew 7:11.
11. NMG, 441.
12. RE, 231.
13. *The Knowledge of God and the Service of God*, Scribner, New York (1939), 38.
14. RE, 245.
15. MC, 86.
16. SSTC, 43.
17. CLF, 21.
18. RE, 93.
19. Iremonger, 40.
20. W. R. Matthews, in Baker's *W.T.*:

An Estimate, etc., James Clarke and Co., Ltd., London, 22.
21. O. C. Quick, *The Gospel of the Modern World*, James Nisbet & Co. Ltd., London (1944), xii.
22. CTP, 11-12.
23. As in the liturgical "Last Gospel," St. John 1:14.
24. BC, 23.
25. Canon Baker, in RE, 4.
26. J. Baillie and H. Martin, *Revelation*, Faber & Faber, London (1937), 107.
27. FMT, 28.
28. NMG, 44.
29. CN, 123.
30. ECP, 21.
31. CTP, 34.
32. CV, 175.
33. St. John 14:9.
34. Iremonger, 155.
35. His Beckly Lecture, in RE, 216.
36. TSPD, 14.
37. NMG, 35.
38. SSTC, 54.

CHAPTER II
God's Search for Man

1. St. Mark 8:27.
2. MC, 317.
3. RSJ2, 231.
4. MC, 341.
5. NMG, 399.

6. RE, 98.
7. CV, 153.
8. NMG, 290 ff.
9. CV, 221.
10. *Ibid.*, 153.
11. RSJ2, xxxi.
12. CV, 134.
13. NMG, 478; also RSJ2, xx; MA, 17; PRLF, 17.
14. NMG, 478.
15. CV, 275.
16. NMG, 435.
17. CV, 275.
18. RE, 91.
19. CV, 116.
20. RSJ2, 385.
21. RSJ1, 18.
22. *Ibid.*, 231.
23. TSPD, 29.
24. RSJ2, 359.
25. *Theology*, 39 (Nov. 1939), 233, 326-33.
26. RSJ2, viii.
27. DCE, 16-7.
28. CoC, 59.
29. NMG, 481.
30. FMT, 143.
31. IF, 54.
32. FMT, 133.
33. *Ibid.*, 136-7.
34. *Ibid.*, 137-42.
35. NMG, 469.
36. *Ibid.*, 403.
37. RE, 121.
38. CRG, 42.
39. NMG, 469.
40. RSS, 21.
41. MC, 337.
42. CV, 262.
43. *The Word Incarnate*, Harper, New York (1959), 4.
44. *Ibid.*, 243.
45. St. John 5:17.

CHAPTER III
Kingdom and Church

1. CWP, 30.
2. NMG, 512.
3. MC, 343.
4. RSJ2, xxxi.
5. RE, 265.
6. Iremonger, 164.
7. RE, 227.
8. CWP, 30-1.
9. ECP, 24.
10. MC, 337.
11. CFL, 128.
12. Iremonger, 420.
13. *Ibid.*, 605.
14. *Relations Between the Younger and the Older Churches*, International Missionary Council, New York (1928), 148.
15. MC, 334.
16. CV, 200.
17. Iremonger, 387.
18. MC, 345.
19. CaC, 57.
20. Iremonger, 487.
21. KG, 4.
22. *Oxford War-Time Papers*, No. 9, Humphrey Milford, London (1914), 7.
23. CV, 169.
24. *Ibid.*, 157.
25. Acts 2:44-45, and 4:34-37.
26. PRLF, 20-1.

CHAPTER IV
Personality in Fellowship

1. CFL, 11.
2. NMG, 234.
3. RSJ2, 238.
4. MC, 167.
5. CV, 38.
6. NMG, 238.
7. *Ibid.*, 244.
8. *Theology*, 32 (Jan. 1936) 187, 10.
9. CTP, 50.
10. NMG, 211.
11. CoC, 111.
12. CTP, 68.
13. CFL, 117.
14. NP, 5.
15. CV, 199.
16. *Report on the Jerusalem Conference*, International Missionary Council, New York (1928), I. 379.
17. TSPD, 202.
18. RE, 60.

19. NMG, 416.
20. *Ibid.*, 165.
21. St. Matthew 5:46.
22. RSJ2, 231.
23. NMG, 405.
24. CFL, 104.
25. *Ibid.*, 103.
26. NP, 91.
27. HNW, 123.
28. MC, 285.

CHAPTER V

History, Freedom, and Necessity

1. CV, 93.
2. J. A. T. Robinson, "The Christian Hope," in D. M. Mackinnon, *Christian Faith and Communist Faith*, Macmillan, New York (1953), 217.
3. CV, 6.
4. John Baillie, *The Idea of Progress*, Oxford University Press, London (1950), 95.
5. PRLF, 15.
6. *Theology*, 37 (Jan. 1936) 8-17, 187.
7. NMG, 278.
8. *Ibid.*, 396.
9. CLF, 165.
10. RE, 260.
11. CLF, 40.
12. CFL, 87.
13. *Ibid.*, 91.
14. A. J. Toynbee, *Study of History*, Oxford University Press, London (1935-54), IV. *passim*.
15. NMG, 501.
16. *Ibid.*, 265-7, 294-95; CiC, 22; MA, 9.
17. NMG, 227.
18. MC, 69-70.
19. "Anti-Duhring," *Handbook of Marxism*, ed. Emile Burns, International Publishers, New York (1935), 255.
20. NMG, 403.
21. CoC, 73; NMG, 469.
22. CFL, 100.
23. NMG, 242.
24. *Ibid.*, 239.
25. MC, 170.

26. CSO, 59.
27. "The Idea of God," *Spectator*, April 4, 1931, 146:538.
28. "Thomism and Modern Needs," *Blackfriars*, March, 1944, 25:89.

CHAPTER VI

Grace and Sin

1. NMG, 485.
2. FMT, 7.
3. CSO, 50.
4. CTT, 23.
5. NMG, 397, 400.
6. *Ibid.*, 390.
7. CoC, 73.
8. *Ibid.*, 73-4.
9. CV, 26.
10. *Ibid.*, 214.
11. CoC, 19.
12. CV, 74.
13. NP, 38.
14. CoC, 64.
15. NMG, 362.
16. KG, 65.
17. NMG, 509.
18. FMT, 118.
19. NMG, 509-10.
20. IRRE, 22-3.
21. *Ibid.*, 6.
22. *Ibid.*, 3.
23. CFL, 81; NMG, 469.
24. FMT, 167.
25. CFL, 82.
26. RSJ2, 310.
27. NMG, 469.

CHAPTER VII

Worship and Sacraments

1. BC, 23.
2. CaC, 101.
3. CoC, 80.
4. CFL, 19.
5. *Christian News-Letter*, Feb. 1944.
6. HNW, 27.
7. *Ibid.*, 32.
8. ECP, 212.
9. CFL, 110.
10. RSJ1, 91.

11. *Clue to Christian Education,* Scribner, New York (1950), 122.
12. TSPD, 23.
13. NMG, 36.
14. HNW, 69.
15. NMG, 477.
16. *Ibid.,* 478.
17. *Ibid.,* 498.
18. HNW, 70-1; CaC, 101-02.
19. *Summa Theologiae,* III, Q.76, A.5.
20. TSPD, 159.
21. RSJ1, 81.
22. DCE, 171.
23. RSJ1, 98.
24. TSPD, 146.
25. *W.T.: An Estimate etc.,* 108. (Reference 20, Chap. I.)

CHAPTER VIII
Anglicanism and Orders

1. CiC, 40.
2. *Ibid.,* 42.
3. *Idem.*
4. GCE, 2.
5. *Ibid.,* 3.
6. TSPD, 74.
7. *Ibid.,* 79.
8. GCE, 7.
9. CHC, 48-9.
10. CLF, 4.
11. GCE, 10.
12. TSPD, 118.
13. CLF, 25.
14. TSPD, 110.
15. *York Diocesan Leaflet,* July, 1931.
16. TSPD, 110.
17. *Ibid.,* 112.
18. *Ibid.,* 80.
19. Iremonger, 452.
20. GHC, 51.
21. Kenneth Ingram, ed., *Youth Looks at Religion,* Philip Allan, London (1932), 165.

CHAPTER IX
Reunion and Rome

1. Iremonger, 406.
2. ECP, 202-03.

3. PU, 3.
4. CU, 10-11.
5. TSPD, 91.
6. *Ibid.,* 134.
7. TR, 10.
8. TSPD, 129.
9. RSJ2, 327.
10. TSPD, 126.
11. *Resolution,* Convocation of Canterbury, Jan. 22, 1932.
12. *Priesthood and South India,* Council for the Defense of Church Principles, London (n.d.), 11.
13. CLF, 20.
14. Iremonger, 592.
15. HNW, 111.
16. PRLF, 33.
17. CW, 5.
18. RE, 156.
19. Begbie, *Painted Windows,* Mills and Boone, New York (1922), 187.
20. *Ibid.,* 186.
21. *Ibid.,* 186-87.
22. CLF, 32.
23. SSTC, 154.
24. CLF, 31.

CHAPTER X
The Church Is Mission

1. BC, 79.
2. *Ibid.,* 78-9.
3. CFL, 124.
4. CTT, 3.
5. HNW, 105.
6. CLF, 85.
7. *Ibid.,* 87-8.
8. PRLF, 81.
9. BC, 77.
10. *Ibid.,* 74.
11. *Ibid.,* 71.
12. Toynbee, *op. cit.,* VII.428.
13. *The World Quest,* Church Assembly, S.P.G., London (1936), 107.
14. *Christian Message in a Non-Christian World,* Harper, New York (1938), ix.
15. *Ibid.,* 287.
16. BC, 80.

17. KG, 100.
18. Iremonger, 396.
19. PRLF, 83.
20. CaC, 57.
21. RE, 205.
22. *Ibid.*, 203.
23. HNW, 105-06.
24. CaC, 61.
25. *Ibid.*, 101.
26. HNW, 107.
27. *Ibid.*, 70.

CHAPTER XI

Morals and Natural Order

1. Lectures 7, 8, 9, and 16.
2. CTP, 26.
3. KG, 42.
4. *Ibid.*, 67.
5. *Ibid.*, 59.
6. NP, 57.
7. "The Philosopher," in Iremonger, 535.
8. NMG, 211.
9. CTP, 51.
10. MC, 182.
11. *Ibid.*, 181.
12. KG, 48.
13. CFL, 82.
14. CSO, 75.
15. *Idem.*
16. NMG, 405.
17. *Ibid.*, 169.
18. CFL, 92.
19. CN, 134.
20. *Ibid.*, 135.
21. NMG, 173.
22. *Ibid.*, 250.
23. RE, 173-74.
24. MC, 132.
25. Cf. CFL; CW.
26. ECP, 123.
27. CFL, 46.
28. PRLF, 61.
29. CSO, 79.
30. HNW, 66-7.
31. CSO, 82.
32. *Existentialism and Humanism*, tr. Philip Mairet, Methuen, London (1948), 26, 89.

CHAPTER XII

Society and Church

1. PC, 65.
2. CSO, 62.
3. CHC, 55.
4. CSO, 65.
5. CIH, 12.
6. TWT, 23.
7. *Malvern 1941*, 12.
8. CS, 45.
9. CaC, 28.
10. CHC, 76-7.
11. ECP, 49.
12. CSO, 66.
13. *Ibid.*, 64; CHC, 80 ff.
14. ECP, 12-18.
15. CS, 43-90.
16. *Ibid.*, 90.
17. ECP, 32-41.
18. *Ibid.*, 39.
19. *Idem.*
20. CN, 64-8.
21. CWP, 26-7.
22. KG, 33.
23. CS, 139.
24. HNW, 68.
25. *Idem.*
26. CLF, 174.
27. HNW, 23.
28. CaC, 29.
29. *Summa Theologiae*, II.2, Q.42, A.2.
30. CS, 153.
31. *Ibid.*, 157.
32. *Ibid.*, 158.
33. *Idem.*
34. CHC, 72.
35. CaC, 69.
36. CS, 196-97.
37. *Ibid.*, 195.
38. CLF, 130.
39. CaC, 67.
40. CTP, 81-112.
41. TWT, 25.
42. CTP, 97.

CHAPTER XIII

Socialism and Ideology

1. CSO, 19.
2. ECP, 54.

3. CS, 83.
4. *Ibid.*, 78.
5. PRLF, 61.
6. CSO, 101.
7. ECP, 44.
8. *York Quarterly*, Jan., 1939.
9. *General Report*, S.P.C.K., London (1908), II.100-01.
10. M. B. Reckitt, *Maurice to Temple*, Faber & Faber, London (1947), 151; W. G. Peck, in *W.T.: An Estimate etc.*, 64; C. E. Hudson and M. B. Reckitt, *The Church and the World*, George Allen & Unwin, London (1938), III.162.
11. PSP, 12.
12. KG, 79.
13. ECP, 44.
14. CSO, 102.
15. *The World Quest*, 103.
16. CCom, 12.
17. *The World Quest*, 102.
18. KG, 119.
19. CSO, 18.
20. HNW, 49.
21. KG, 119-20.
22. *Idem.*
23. IF, 66.
24. CoC, 104.
25. ECP, 46.
26. CoC, 106; CSO, 18.
27. HNW, 61.
28. NMG, 513.
29. CSO, 32.
30. ECP, 29; CSO, 96.
31. CSO, 36.
32. NMG, ix, 487-88.
33. CS, 82-3; NMG, 59.
34. WCSF, sec. 4.
35. MC, 66-7.
36. HNW, 52.
37. CSO, 101-02.
38. W. G. Peck, *Christendom: A Journal of Christian Sociology*, 13:56, 234.
39. CSO, 87.
40. *Malvern 1941*, 220.
41. *Ibid.*, 222.
42. CSO, 101-02.
43. ECP, 43.
44. CaC, 30.
45. ECP, 65.
46. CaC, 8.
47. RSS, 58-60.

CHAPTER XIV

Economic Reconstruction (1)

1. CLF, 116.
2. CoC, 101.
3. CSO, 18.
4. CN, 36.
5. *Malvern 1941*, 218; RE, 203.
6. CLF, 110.
7. CaC, 77.
8. CSO, 21.
9. *Ibid.*, 19.
10. *Malvern 1941*, 216-18.
11. *Ibid.*, 10.
12. *Ibid.*, vii.
13. Joseph Fletcher, *Christianity and Property*, Westminster, Philadelphia (1947), 203.
14. *The Challenge*, Anglican Fellowship for Social Action, Montreal, Nov., 1944.
15. CLF, 123.
16. WCSF, sec. 3.
17. PRLF, 61.
18. *Idem.*
19. HNW, 17, 103.
20. TWT, 114.
21. New York, 1941.
22. CSO, 100.
23. *Ibid.*, 108-21.
24. CLF, 122.
25. CaC, 84.

CHAPTER XV

Economic Reconstruction (2)

1. CLF, 114.
2. HNW, 62.
3. *Ibid.*, 51.
4. CSO, 111.
5. HNW, 54.
6. *Idem.*
7. CSO, 111.
8. "London Financial Press Attacks Primate's Stand," *Montreal Star*, Oct. 3, 1942.

9. HNW, 62.
10. *Idem.*
11. CSO, 106.
12. "Begin Now," par. 3.
13. *Malvern 1941*, 219.
14. CFL, 47.
15. CFL, 126.
16. HNW, 56.
17. *Idem.*
18. *The Challenge, ut supra.*
19. CSO, 116.
20. *Idem.*
21. *Idem.*
22. HNW, 56.
23. CLF, 128.
24. HNW, 57.
25. CSO, 114.
26. HNW, 43.
27. CSO, 115.
28. *Ibid.*, 114-15; HNW, 42-4.
29. CLF, 116.
30. *Idem.*
31. HNW, 53.
32. CSO, 13.
33. *Ibid.*, 118.
34. *Ibid.*, 119.
35. *Ibid.*, 120.
36. *Idem.*
37. Quoted by Sidney Dark, *Malvern Torch*, March, 1943.

CHAPTER XVI

War and the Sanctity of Life

1. CWP, 18.
2. Iremonger, 543.
3. TWT, 6.
4. *Ibid.*, 9.
5. CTP, 110.
6. CJW, 22.
7. *Ibid.*, 26-7.
8. CTP, 83.
9. TWT, 32.
10. CTP, 110.
11. *Ibid.*, 91.
12. *Idem.*
13. *Ibid.*, 91-2; ECP, 18.
14. CWP, 20-1.
15. *Ibid.*, 14.
16. Jeremiah, 6:14.
17. CW, 16; CLF, 40.

18. TWT, 11-14.
19. ECP, 18.
20. *Is Christ Divided?*, 10.
21. TWT, 43.
22. *Idem.*
23. HNW, 81.
24. CaC, 13-19.
25. ECP, 38.
26. CHC, 87 ff.
27. RE, 130-33.
28. HNW, 96.
29. RE, 126.

CHAPTER XVII

Postscript

1. *D.N.B. 1941-50*, Oxford University Press, London (1959), vii.
2. D. R. Sharpe, *Walter Rauschenbusch*, Macmillan, New York (1942), 203.
3. DCE, 1.
4. Iremonger, 503.
5. NMG, ix.
6. Iremonger, 65, 619.
7. *Contemporary English Theology*, Harper, New York (1941), 148 ff.
8. NMG, xxvii.
9. *Systematic Theology*, University of Chicago Press (1951), II.31.
10. K. E. Kirk, in *Church Quarterly Review*, CXX (July 1935), 301.
11. J. C. Bennett, in *Anglican Theological Review*, XXV (July 1943), 263.
12. William Nicholls, SCM Press, London (1958), 25.
13. "Theology Today," *Theology*, XXXIX (Nov. 1939), 327-28.
14. FMT, 152-54.

APPENDIX: BIOGRAPHICAL SKETCH

1. Robert Sherwood, *Roosevelt and Hopkins*, Harper, New York (1948), 10.
2. Nov. 13, 1944, IV:19, 1.
3. E. H. Jeffs, *Princes of the Modern Pulpit*, Abingdon, Nashville (1931), 214.
4. Iremonger, 499.

5. *Fellow-Men: A Gallery of England, 1876-1946*, Dent, London (1948), 49.
6. E. G. Sandford, ed., *Frederick Temple*, Macmillan, New York (1906), I.13.
7. F. J. Snell, *Early Associations of Archbishop Temple*, Thomas Whittaker, New York (n.d.), 76.
8. *Idem.*
9. *Idem.*
10. A. C. Benson, *Life of Edward White Benson*, Macmillan, New York (1899), II.394.
11. Iremonger, 18.
12. CLF, 119.
13. Iremonger, 35.
14. *Frederick Denison Maurice*, by his son Frederick, Scribner, New York (1884), II.35.
15. *General Report*, of the Congress, SPCK, London (1908), II.100-01.
16. PSP, 24.
17. In Stephen Paget and J. M. C. Crum, *Francis Paget*, Macmillan, London (1913), 108-22. No mention is made of the Temple ordination affair.
18. *Painted Windows*, Putnam, New York (1922), 187.
19. A. M. Ramsey, *An Era in Anglican Theology: From Gore to Temple*, Scribner, New York (1960), 160.
20. Adam Fox, *Dean Inge*, J. Murray, London (1950), 157.
21. E. F. Braley, *Letters of Herbert Hensley Henson*, SPCK, London (1950), 136.

22. *Ibid.*, 160.
23. NMG, 170.
24. Iremonger, 205.
25. See Iremonger, 222-50, and Temple in *Church and Nation* (1915) and *Citizen and Churchman* (1941).
26. A. E. Baker, ed., *William Temple: An Estimate and Appreciation*, J. Clarke, London (1946), 103.
27. *Op. cit.*, 173, 189.
28. Iremonger, 399.
29. G. K. A. Bell, *Randall Davidson*, Oxford University Press, London (1935), II.1209.
30. Page 53.
31. *Anglican Theological Review*, 25 (July 1943) 3.
32. Iremonger, 399.
33. C. F. Garbett, *In An Age of Revolution*, Hodder & Stoughton, London (1952), 267.
34. *The Witness*, 24 (March 16, 1941) 32, 8-9.
35. Braley, *op. cit.*, 239.
36. H. H. Henson, *Retrospect of an Unimportant Life*, Oxford University Press, New York (1950), III.276.
37. Fox, *op. cit.*, 127, 250.
38. *New English Weekly*, Nov. 2, 1944, 20-1.
39. Quoted by Bishop Bell, in Baker's *William Temple and His Message*, 47.
40. Henson, *op. cit.*, II.293.
41. Baker's *W.T.: An Estimate etc.*, 7.

Bibliography

In the first edition of his *William Temple's Teaching* (Penguin, 1946) Canon Baker said that there were "more than seventy" items under Temple's name in the British Museum Catalogue. Actually, there were ninety-two separate and different items, exclusive of re-editions. A glance at the list given here shows that both Baker and the B. M. fall far short of an adequate survey of extant Temple materials. In his biography Dean Iremonger lists only the major books.

The list which follows, more nearly complete than any published to date, includes 317 items, 221 from Temple's own pen and 96 from others. This comes nowhere near the fullest requirements of technical bibliography. Only the books are annotated. It is to be hoped that a research student will soon make a study of Temple's contributions to the weekly *Challenge,* of which he was editor and a contributor from 1914 to 1918. None of his writing there is included in this bibliography. (Files for general research purposes are available in the B. M. and in the Bodleian at Oxford.) His editorial essays in *The Pilgrim,* 1920 through 1927, published quarterly by Longmans, Green of London, are all given because they are less occasional in character. A surprisingly large number of master's and doctor's theses about Temple are available in American theological school libraries.

None of the myriad reviews of Temple's books, which appeared in magazines and journals, has been included. (There is a good list of reviews for three of his major works in Owen Thomas' book, included in this bibliography.) The reviews were not invariably laudatory. Only a representative selection of news stories has been included, from metropolitan weeklies but not from dailies. Left out are all the pieces, hundreds of them, which appeared in parish and diocesan papers, in Convocation and Assembly proceedings (e.g., synod addresses), and in archdiocesan gazettes and provincial quarterlies. In the thirties William Temple received much newspaper attention, although—of course—nothing like as much as went to a little Hollywood child actress, Shirley Temple.

The present bibliography, if it were exhaustive according to the author's knowledge, would include over 500 items. Someday somebody will compile a complete listing. In the course of such an apparently dull and unrewarding enterprise some interesting things could be unearthed. For example, in the January, 1925 issue of *The Pilgrim* (5:178-94), immediately preceding one of Temple's editorials, was an essay by Canon Baker entitled "Nature, Man and God," with some of the same ideas and structure found developed later in Temple's Gifford Lectures of that same title.

Where dual appearances allow, American rather than English titles and editions are given preference, if they came out at the same time; but always the earlier one is chosen. Titles which have appeared more than once, without any change in the material, are listed only once. Temple often used fairly generous sections of his material two, three, and even four times. Ordinarily articles are omitted if they appeared later as part of a book. A few privately printed things have been cited by Baker and Iremonger, such as "Abstract Speculation," read at the Oxford Jowett Society in 1901; "Robert Browning," printed in 1904; "The Province of Science," 1904. None of these is listed since they are not available in the usual library stocks.

J. F.

BOOKS*

BC *Basic Convictions*. Harper, New York, 1936. 81 pp.
Addresses at the twelfth quadrennial convention of the Student Volunteer Movement, Indianapolis, 1935. Reality of God, obligation of worship, the Cross and the world's need, the "divine constraint" of missions. Evangelical emphasis.

CoC *Centrality of Christ*. Morehouse-Gorham, New York, 1936. 115 pp.
Four lectures at the College of Preachers, Washington, D.C. Revelation, sin and atonement, the Incarnation, Christianity related to ethics and politics. (English edition, *The Preacher's Theme Today*.)

CtC *Challenge to the Church*. S.P.C.K., London, 1917. 83 pp.
An account of the National Mission of Repentance and Hope, in 1916; meaning of repentance, Christian hope, the Gospel in the world.

CiC *Christ in His Church*. Macmillan, London, 1925. 156 pp.
Charge at a primary visitation, Diocese of Manchester, 1924. The Church as the Body of Christ, the Incarnation, sacraments, miracles, vocations, Catholic and Evangelical life, relations to the State, democracy and world politics, the devotional life.

CV *Christ the Truth*. Macmillan, New York, 1924. 341 pp.
English edition entitled *Christus Veritas*. Sequel to *Mens Creatrix*. Theological rather than philosophical in method, a contribution to a "Christo-centric metaphysic." Nature of God and of man, the Godhead of Jesus, His Person, the Spirit and the Church, eternity and history, worship and sacraments, the Atonement, love and the Trinity.

* See separate listings for pamphlets, symposia, etc.

CFL *Christian Faith and Life.* Macmillan, New York, 1936. 139 pp.
His famous Oxford Mission addresses, 1931. What we mean by God, Christ in history, moral standard, sin and repentance, the Crucifixion, the Holy Spirit, prayer and the sacraments, Christian society. By 1944 it had had eleven printings.

CSO *Christianity and Social Order.* Penguin Books, New York, 1942. 94 pp.
The Church's right and duty to "interfere" in social questions, how it should do so, its past social role, primary and derivative Christian social principles, the "Natural Order" and a priority of values. An appendix deals with a specific program of social reconstruction in capital ownership, industrial democracy, investment, credit, land, and international trade. Now available in SCM edition, London, 1950, 126 pp.

CS *Christianity and the State.* Macmillan, London, 1928. 198 pp.
Henry Scott Holland Memorial lectures. The principles involved, historical and past theories, internal and external relations of the State. Appendices on Canon Raven's *Creator Spirit,* and Church-State relations.

CTP *Christianity in Thought and Practice.* Morehouse-Gorham, New York, 1936. 112 pp.
The Moody Lectures at the University of Chicago. Philosophy and religion, personality in theology and ethics, ethics for individuals and groups.

CRG *Christ's Revelation of God.* SCM, London, 1925. 63 pp.
What our Lord presupposed, what He taught by speech and by action. Shows Temple's use of the Bible, his exegetical temper and methods. Three lectures to a student conference.

CV *Christus Veritas.* Macmillan, London, 1924. 285 pp.
See *Christ the Truth.*

CTT *Church and Its Teaching Today.* Macmillan, New York, 1936. 49 pp.
The William Belden Noble lectures at Harvard, on the nature and task of the Church, theology, and modern thought.

CN *Church and Nation.* Macmillan, London, 1915. 204 pp.
The Paddock lectures at the General Theological Seminary in New York, May, 1915. Freedom, Church and State, justice and liberty, holiness and catholicity, the citizenship of heaven, God in history. Appendices on the apocalyptic consciousness, moral and spiritual authority, education and justice, orders and catholicity, Providence.

CLF *Church Looks Forward.* Macmillan, New York, 1944. 193 pp.
Posthumous collection of his latest addresses, twenty-five in all. Many subjects: reunion, education, war and Christian fellowship, crisis in the West, sex and venereal disease, individualism, property, economic order, capitalist finance, industrial management. Chapter 21 on economics is of high importance.

CaC *Citizen and Churchman.* Eyre & Spottiswoode, London, 1941. 111 pp.
> On Church-State relations, the churchman's role as a citizen; an appendix on questions for group study.

ECP *Essays in Christian Politics and Kindred Subjects.* Longmans, Green, London, 1927. 228 pp.
> Essays mostly from editorials in *The Pilgrim*: politics, truth and tradition, faith and authority, marriage, gambling, Coué, Shakespeare, Shaw, modernism, ministry of healing, the Church of England, worship.

FMT *Faith and Modern Thought.* Macmillan, London, 1910. 172 pp.
> His first book. Intercollegiate Union lectures, London, on grounds of belief in God, revelation and faith, historic bases of Christianity, the Person of Christ, the Atonement, the problem of evil, the Spirit and the Church, eternal life.

FG *Fellowship with God.* Macmillan, London, 1920. 243 pp.
> Sermons in Westminster Abbey, Eton, Rugby, Repton, Cambridge. Peace, idolatry, the Holy Spirit, the sacraments, priesthood, sacrifice, the Incarnation. They show Temple's preaching skill on a non-academic level.

HNW *Hope of a New World.* Macmillan, New York, 1941. 125 pp.
> B.B.C. talks and other addresses. The old world passing, God and freedom, prayer and its answer, social justice, a Christian civilization, hope for the future, principles of reconstruction, evangelism, God's sovereignty.

IF *Issues of Faith.* Macmillan, London, 1917. 69 pp.
> An exposition of the third paragraph of the Apostles' Creed: the Holy Ghost, the Church, the communion of saints, forgiveness of sins, the Resurrection.

KG *Kingdom of God.* Macmillan, London, 1912. 143 pp.
> The founding of the Kingdom, religion and ethics, the Kingdom and the world, other world views, the divine judgment. Lectures for the Christian Evidence Society, Cambridge.

LBP *Life of Bishop Percival.* Macmillan, London, 1921. 389 pp.
> A labor of love for the Bishop of Hereford's memory. Percival was Temple's Godfather, one time headmaster of Rugby, a radical in politics, defender of the writers of *Foundations*.

MC *Mens Creatrix: An Essay.* Macmillan, London, 1917. 367 pp.
> Planned and partially written while Temple was a don at Queen's College, Oxford. A philosophical or "natural theology" approach to the Christian faith, to be studied with *Christus Veritas,* and compared to *Nature, Man and God,* written fifteen years later.

NMG *Nature, Man and God.* Macmillan, London, 1934. 530 pp.
> The Gifford Lectures at Glasgow, 1932-33 and 1933-34. Calling his position "dialectical realism," he works out his philosophy of religion

thoroughly on knowledge, history, truth and beauty, ethics, process and value, freedom and determinism, revelation, finitude and evil, grace and freedom, eternal life and the sacramental view of the world.

NP *Nature of Personality.* Macmillan, London, 1911. 120 pp.

Six lectures in Oxford: materialism and agnosticism, personal being, rights and duties, the will and its freedom, original sin and moral duty, the social process, personality in the universe, the triune personality in the Godhead.

PRLF *Personal Religion and the Life of Fellowship.* Longmans, Green, London, 1926. 87 pp.

The doctrines of God and history, the place of the Church in the creed, worship and fellowship, discipleship and politics and economics, the Church and the Kingdom, the primary need of conversion.

PC *Plato and Christianity.* Macmillan, London, 1916. 102 pp.

Plato's general philosophy, his ethics and politics, and their relation to Christianity. Oxford University Extension lectures in Christ Church, August, 1915.

PTT *Preacher's Theme Today.* S.P.C.K., London, 1936. 87 pp.

See *The Centrality of Christ.*

PSP *Principles of Social Progress.* Australian Student Christian Union, Melbourne, 1910. 68 pp.

The general principles of Christian social concern, education, democracy, and Christianity at work through social process.

RSJ1 *Readings in St. John's Gospel: First Series, Chapter I-XII.* Macmillan, London, 1939. 1-204 pp.

"With St. John I am at home." Not a systematic commentary or exegesis; intended for devotional meditations. The Fourth Gospel as "the profoundest of all writings."

RSJ2 *Readings in St. John's Gospel: Second Series, Chapters XIII-XXI.* Macmillan, London, 1940. 207-412 pp.

This and the first volume were translated into Chinese by W. B. Djang, for overseas Chinese. Hong Kong, 1952.

RE *Religious Experience, and Other Essays and Addresses.* J. Clarke, London, 1958. 265 pp.

Collected by his friend and editor, Canon A. E. Baker, with an excellent critical and biographical introduction.

RSS *Repton School Sermons: Studies in the Religion of the Incarnation.* Macmillan, London, 1913. 334 pp.

Chapel talks for schoolboys, but readable for all. The preface about youth is of interest, as well as the expository sermons themselves.

SSTC *Studies in the Spirit and Truth of Christianity.* Macmillan, London, 1914. 234 pp.

Religious experience, the power of tradition, doubt, energy, the sin of stupidity, the economy of history. University and school sermons.

TWT *Thoughts in War-Time.* London, Macmillan, 1940. 149 pp.

War and pacifism, the supposed sanctity of life, a just war, peace aims and war aims, theology today, faith and freedom. An appendix by Canon B. H. Streeter.

TSPD *Thoughts on Some Problems of the Day.* Macmillan, London, 1931. 206 pp.

The charge at Temple's primary visitation, York. Faith in God, the Church's witness, the Anglican heritage, reunion and the validity of orders, eucharistic doctrine.

UC *Universality of Christ.* SCM, London, 1921. 105 pp.

Lectures at an S.C.M. conference: Christology, comparative method, possibilities of a universal religion, Christ as the completed revelation, and Christianity pragmatically regarded.

PAMPHLETS

CK *Call of the Kingdom.* National Mission of Repentence and Hope, S.P.C.K., London, 1916. 32 pp.

CWP *Christ and the Way to Peace.* SCM, London, 1935. 31 p.

CWS *Christian and the World Situation.* New Commonwealth, London, 1935. 20 pp.

CD *Christian Democracy.* SCM, London, 1937. 46 pp.

CH *Christian Hope of Eternal Life.* S.P.C.K., London, 1941. 7 pp.

CM *Christian Marriage: To Those Who Desire Marriage in the Church.* Church Literature Association, London, 1943. 8 pp.

CR *Christian Responsibility and Social Problems.* Industrial Christian Fellowship, London, 1935. 8 pp.

CSS *Christian Social Service* (the Beckly Lecture). Epworth Press, London, 1929. 16 pp.

CU *Christian Unity and Church Reunion.* S.P.C.K., London, 1943. 19 pp.

CCom *Christianity and Communism.* S.P.C.K., London, 1938. 16 pp.

CW *Christianity and War.* No. 1 in "Papers for War-Time." Oxford University Press, London, 1914. 12 pp.

CWT *Christianity and War*: A Word for Teachers. S.P.C.K., London, 1915. 15 pp.

CIH *Christianity as an Interpretation of History* (William Ainslee Memorial Lecture). Lyman and Company, London, 1944. 22 pp.

CEB *Church and the Education Bill.* B. H. Blackwell, Oxford, 1906. 12 pp.

CSoc *Church and the Social Order.* Industrial Christian Fellowship, London, 1941. 32 pp.

ComK *Coming of the Kingdom.* Liverpool Diocesan Board of Divinity, Liverpool, 1917. 24 pp.

CJW *Conditional Justification of War.* Hazell, Watson & Viney, Ltd., London, 1940. 32 pp.

DCP *Democracy: Its Claims and Perils.* P. S. King, London, 1926. 16 pp.

DEGL *Distinctive Excellences of Greek and Latin.* John Murray, London, 1930. 20 pp.

EFP *Education for Peace.* Birbeck College, London, 1941. 14 pp.

EC *Education of Citizens.* Parents' National Educational Union, London, 1905. 12 pp.

EPA *Ethics of Penal Action.* National Association of Probation Officers, London, 1934. 40 pp.

EP *Ethics of Punishment* (John Howard Anniversary Sermon). Howard League for Penal Reform, London, 1945. 16 pp.

FHS *Fellowship of the Holy Spirit.* S.P.C.K., London, 1917. 12 pp.

FS *Fellowship of Service.* S.P.C.K., London, 1936. 12 pp.

FMN *Freedom of Men and Nations.* Macmillan, London, 1924. 16 pp.

FTP *Freedom, Truth and Peace.* Oxford University Press, London, 1942. 10 pp.

GCE. *Genius of the Church of England.* Church Publications Board, London, 1928. 15 pp.

GEP *Genius of English Poetry.* Oxford University Press, London, 1939. 15 pp.

GF *Go Forward*: Thoughts on the National Crisis. S.P.C.K., London, 1915. 15 pp.

HW *Holy War.* S.P.C.K., London, 1916. 15 pp.

IRRE *Idea of Immortality in Relation to Religion and Ethics.* Independent Press, London, 1932. 23 pp.

IMRP *In Memoriam: Ronald Poulton.* Macmillan, London, 1915. 24 pp.

LM *Layman Has a Ministry.* National Council of the Episcopal Church, New York, n.d. 12 pp.

LL *Life and Liberty*: A Call to Prayer. Macmillan, London, 1917. 19 pp.

LC *Living Church.* No. 2 Life and Liberty Paper. S.P.C.K., London, 1918. 12 pp.

MG *Majesty of God.* S.P.C.K., London, 1930. 14 pp.

MM *Malvern Manifesto* (the "Archbishop's Resolution"). Church League for Industrial Democracy, New York, 1942. 8 pp.

MP *Manual of Prayers for War-Time.* A. R. Mowbray, London, 1939. 35 pp.

MA *Materialism and Agnosticism.* SCM, Melbourne, 1910. 19 pp.

MCSH *Message of Comfort, Sympathy and Hope.* Church Assembly, London, 1942. 4 pp.

NMJ *Nazi Massacres of the Jews and Others.* Gollancz, London, 1943. 9 pp.

NCC *Needs and Claims of the Church of Christ.* S.P.C.K., London, 1917. 16 pp.

NN *Number 9, Oxford Papers for War-Time.* Humphrey Milford, London, 1915. 8 pp.

OLP *One Lord, One People.* Lutterworth Press, London, 1941. 23 pp.

ONC *Our Need of a Catholic Church.* S.P.C.K., London, 1915. 12 pp.

PSE *Palm Sunday to Easter.* Morehouse-Gorham, New York, 1942. 45 pp.

PNPB *Plea for the New Prayer Book.* S.P.C.K., London, 1927. 29 pp.

PBC *Prayer Book Crisis.* S.P.C.K., London, 1928. 31 pp.

PV *Prayer for Victory:* What It Means. Church Literature Association, London, 1940. 8 pp.

PP *Problem of Power.* Industrial Christian Fellowship, London, 1944. 8 pp.

PU *Problems of Unity.* S.P.C.K., London, 1940. 8 pp.

RCS *Relation of Church and State.* S.P.C.K., London, 1930. 24 pp.

RIEL *Resources and Influence of English Literature.* National Book Council, London, 1942. 24 pp.

SWE *Social Witness and Evangelism* (the Beckly Lecture). Epworth Press, London, 1947. 32 pp.

SAB *Spirit and Aims of Britain in War.* S.P.C.K., London, 1940. 8 pp.

SER *State in Its External Relations.* Macmillan, London, 1932. 46 pp.

SVD *Spiritual Value of Democracy.* Macmillan, London, 1932. 46 pp.

SCB *Statement of Christian Belief.* S.P.C.K., London, 1943. 8 pp.

STSPD *Syllabus of Thoughts on Some Problems of the Day.* Macmillan, London, 1931. 15 pp.

TS *Thanksgiving Service in Westminster Abbey.* Church Literature Association, London, 1927. 25 pp.

TSR *Theology, the Science of Religion.* Blackwell, Oxford, 1914. 16 pp.

TMN *Thomism and Modern Needs.* Aquinas Society of London, Blackfriars, London, 1944. 14 pp.

TR *Thoughts on Reunion.* Church of Ireland Printing Company, Dublin, 1935. 22 pp.

WCSF *What Christians Stand for in the Secular World.* SCM, London, 1944, 16 pp.

WMCDN *What Must Christians Do Now?* Christian Century, Chicago, 1940. 7 pp.

WDG *Why Does God Allow War?* S.P.C.K., London, 1941. 7 pp.

WC *World Call.* Missionary Council Bulletin III B, Church Assembly, London, n.d. 8 pp.

Symposia

"Biographical Introduction" (57 pp.), in E. G. Sandford, Ed., *Frederick Temple*: An Appreciation. Macmillan, New York, 1907.

Chairman's Introduction, in *Doctrine in the Church of England*: Report of the Commission Appointed by the Archbishops in 1922. Macmillan, New York, 1938.

"Christian Cooperation for Justice and Peace," in *A Christian Basis for the Post-War World*, ed. H. Williams. Morehouse-Gorham, New York, 1942.

"Christian Faith and the Common Life," in *Christian Faith and the Common Life*. Oxford Conference Book, Willett, Clark, Chicago, 1938.

"Christian Hope of Eternal Life," in *The Christian Hope of Eternal Life*. S.P.C.K., London, 1936.

"Christian Way Out," in *The Christian Way Out*. Witness Publishing Company, Chicago, 1932.

"Christianity Today: Social and Christian Ethics" (16 pp.), in *The History of Christianity in the Light of Modern Knowledge*. Harcourt, Brace, New York, 1929.

"The Church," in *Foundations*: A Statement of Christian Belief in Terms of Modern Thought, by Seven Oxford Men. Macmillan, New York, 1912.

"Comment," in *Religion in Life*. R. S. King, London, 1944.

"Competition: A Study in Human Motive," in *Competition*. Macmillan, London, 1917.

"Declaration of Nationalization," in *General Report* (Pan-Anglican Conference, London, 1908) Vol. II. S.P.C.K., London, 1909.

"Divinity of Christ," in *Foundations, ut supra*.

"Epilogue," *ibid.*

"Godhead of Jesus," in *Fundamentals of the Faith*, Temple, Storr, Bernard and Mozley. Palmer & Sons, London, 1922.

"Historical Christian Fellowship," in *The Relation Between the Younger and the Older Churches*. International Missionary Council, New York, 1928.

"In Time of War," with C. E. Raven, in *Is Christ Divided?* Penguin, New York, 1943.

"Introduction" (23 pp.), in *Christ and Our Enemies*, Stephen Hobhouse. S.P.C.K., London, 1944.

"Introduction," in *Men Without Work*. Pilgrim Trust, London, 1938.

"Introduction," in *The Recall to Religion*, S. C. Carpenter, V. A. Demant, A. E. Taylor, and others. Eyre & Spottiswoode, London, 1937.

"Introduction," in *The Teaching Church*. S.P.C.K., London, 1928.

"Introduction," in *Towards a Christian Order*. Eyre & Spottiswoode, London, 1942.

"Life and World as a Single Whole," in *More Points of View*: A Second Series of Broadcast Addresses. Allen & Unwin, London, 1930.

"Memoir," in *The Gospel of the New World*, O. C. Quick. Nisbet, London, 1944.

"Missions and Politics: Their Mutual Relevance," *The World Quest*. Church Assembly, S.P.G., London, 1936.

"Nature of Government," in *Some Aspects of the Women's Movement,* ed., Zoë Fairfield. SCM, London, 1915.

"Pacifists and Non-Pacifists," in *Is Christ Divided? ut supra.*

"Place of the Assembly in the Church's Life," in *The Church Assembly and the Church.* Foreword by Cosmo Gordon Lang. Church House, London, 1930.

"Poetry and Science," in *Essays and Studies by Members of the English Association.* Second Series, Vol. 17, Oxford University Press, London, 1932.

"Primary Need, Conversion," in *Religion and Life,* ed., W. Paton. King and Staples, London, 1945.

"Problems of Society," in *Christ and Human Need.* SCM, London, 1912.

"Reply," in *Youth Looks at Religion,* ed., Kenneth Ingram. P. Allan, London, 1933.

"Revelation" in *Revelation,* ed., John Baillie & Hugh Martin. Faber & Faber, London, 1937.

"Review of the Conference" in *Malvern 1941: The Life of the Church and the Order of Society.* Longmans Green, London, 1941.

"Some Implications of Theism" in *Contemporary British Philosophy,* ed., J. M. Muirhead. Macmillan, New York, 1924.

"Special Task of the Church" in *The Church Looks Forward.* Morehouse-Gorham, New York, 1942.

"Statement of the Case for Evangelism" in *The Christian Life and Message to Non-Christian Systems of Thought and Life.* International Missionary Council, New York, 1928.

"Studdert-Kennedy: The Man and His Message" (32 pp.) in *G. A. Studdert-Kennedy,* by His Friends, ed., J. K. Mozley. R. R. Smith, New York, 1929.

"Survey of the Problem" in *The Recall to Religion, ut supra.*

"Three Features" and other addresses, in *The Proceedings of C.O.P.E.C.* (Conference on Politics, Economics and Citizenship). Longmans Green, London, 1924, 12 vols.

"Universal Church" in *Religion in Life, ut supra.*

"What Does Man Know of God?" in *God and the World Through Christian Eyes,* ed., L. Hodgson. SCM, London, 1933, 2 vols.

"Worship and Life" in *How Christians Worship,* ed., J. Eric Fenn. SCM, London, 1942.

ARTICLES, ADDRESSES, SERMONS

"Aid to Goebbels," *Christian Century,* LIX (November 11, 1942), 1381-82.

"Archbishop Lord Davidson," Eulogy Sermon, Bishopthorpe Parish Church, Sunday after Ascension, 1930.

"Back to Unity," *University of Toronto Quarterly,* (October, 1934), 15-21.

"Begin Now" (see *What Must Christians Do Now?*).

"Case for the Church Enabling Act," *Spectator*, CXXII (May 31, 1919), 692-93.

"Christian Conception of History," *Pilgrim*, VI (October, 1925), 87-100.

"Christian Education in Elementary School," *Economic Review*, XVII (January, 1907), 1-12.

"Christian Social Doctrine," *Spectator*, CLXVI (January 24, 1941), 83.

"Christian Social Principles," *Pilgrim*, III (April, 1923), 337-46.

"Christian Unity," *Second World Conference on Faith and Order*, Edinburgh, August 3, 1937.

"Christian Unity: The Theological Background," *Pilgrim*, I (October, 1920), 106-16.

"Christianity and the Empire," *Pilgrim*, VI (July, 1926), 447-57.

"Christianity and Marriage," *Pilgrim*, III (July, 1923), 459-74.

"Christianity and Politics," *Pilgrim*, IV (April, 1924), 329-41.

"Christianity as a Historical Religion," *Theology*, XXXII (January, 1936), 8-17.

"Christians in the Secular World," *Christian Century*, LXI (March 1, 1944), 269-71.

"Christmas Broadcast," incl. in Baker's *Religious Experience, ut supra*.

"Church and Education," *Pilgrim*, V (April, 1925), 330-40.

"Church and the Labour Party," *Economic Review*, XVIII (April, 1908), 190-202.

"Church and the Social Crisis," *Christian Century*, LIX (October 7, 1942), 1209-11; also, *Vital Speeches*, IX (October 15, 1942), 23-5.

"Church in the Bible," *Bible House*, London (October 8, 1943).

"C.O.P.E.C.," *Pilgrim*, IV (July, 1924), 454-67.

"Coué and St. Paul," *Pilgrim*, III (October, 1922), 96-110.

"Creation and Redemption," *Cambridge Review* (June, 1925).

"Death Penalty," *Spectator*, CLIV (January 25, 1935), 112-21; reprinted, *Spectator*, CXCVI (June 29, 1956), 880.

"Dick Sheppard," *Spectator*, CLIX (November 5, 1937), 792.

"Divine Constraint of Christian Missions," *Missionary Review of the World*, LIX (March, 1936), 119-21.

"Divine Source of Liberty," *Hibbert Journal*, XXXVI (October, 1937), 1-13.

"Education and Religion Among Working-men," *Constructive Quarterly*, II (March, 1914), 188-96.

"Educational Science," *Nature*, XCVIII (November 23, 1916), 238-40.

"Faith and Authority," *Pilgrim*, II (January, 1922), 212-22.

"Faith and Freedom," *Vital Speeches*, I (July 1, 1925), 644-48.

"Fellowship," *Pilgrim*, I (July, 1921), 462-68.

"Future of Germany," *Fortnightly Review*, CLVI (November, 1941), 405-13.

"Gambling and Ethics," *Pilgrim*, IV (January, 1924), 219-28.

"God and the State," *Pilgrim*, V (October, 1924), 86-95.

"Has Europe a Future?," *Pilgrim*, II (July, 1922), 456-66.
"How Can We Find God?," *Christian Century*, XLVI (February 28, 1929), 291-92.
"Idea of God," *Spectator*, CXLVI (April 4, 1931), 537-38.
"Industry and the Community," *Pilgrim*, VII (October, 1926), 331-39.
"In the Beginning God," World Conference of Christian Youth, Amsterdam, July 24, 1939.
"Kingdom and the King," *Pilgrim*, IV (October, 1923), 103-05.
"Life and Liberty Movement," *Contemporary Review*, CXIII (February, 1918), 161-68.
"Love of God Our Hope of Immortality," *Hibbert Journal*, XIV (April, 1916), 539-50.
"Loyalty," *Pilgrim*, VII (January, 1927), 212-20.
"Moral Foundations of Peace," *Contemporary Review*, CXVIII (July, 1920), 65-70.
"My Point of View," B.B.C. Broadcast, February 10, 1930.
"National Education," *Pilgrim*, II (April, 1922), 334-43.
"New Problems in Economics," *Contemporary Review*, CXLI (April, 1932), 409-14.
"Objects and Methods of Education," *School and Society*, IV (October 14, 1916), 571-85.
"Perils of a Purely Scientific Education," *York Quarterly* (Summer, 1932).
"Philosophy of the Incarnation," sermon, University of Cambridge, 1918.
"Plato's Vision of the Ideas," *Mind*, XVII (October, 1908), 502-17.
"Prayer and Conduct," *Pilgrim*, I (April, 1921), 337-43.
"Presidential Address," *Library Association Record*, XXXIX (June, 1937), 287-90.
"Principles of Reconstruction," *Fortnightly Review*, CLIII (May, 1940), 456-61.
"Principles or Ideals," *Pilgrim*, III (January, 1923), 218-25.
"Problem of the Press," *Pilgrim*, V (July, 1925), 446-54.
"Problem of the Schools," *Pilgrim*, VI (January, 1926), 210-20.
"Relations Between Church and State," *Contemporary Review*, CXXXIV (August, 1928), 154-60.
"Religious Experience," *Guardian* (July 9, 1914).
"Resources of Literature," *Pilgrim*, VI (April, 1926), 331-39.
"Sacramental Principle," *Pilgrim*, I (January, 1921), 218-27.
"Sealed Book," lecture, Blackpool, August, 1923.
"Social Justice," *Vital Speeches*, VII (December 1, 1940), 114-17.
"St. Joan, Shakespeare and Shaw," *Pilgrim*, V (January, 1925), 208-17.
"Symbolism as a Metaphysical Principle," *Mind*, XXI (October, 1922), 467-77.
"Thanksgiving Service Address: In Memory of William Paton," *International Review of Missions*, XXXIII (January, 1944), 10-12.

"Theological Background for Christian Unity," *Pilgrim,* I (October, 1920), 106-16.

"Thomism and Modern Needs," *Blackfriars,* XXV (March, 1944), 81-2; 86-93.

"Truth and Tradition," *Pilgrim,* II (October, 1921), 96-107.

"Unitarianism and the Gospel," *Moslem World,* XXV (December, 1935), 1-3.

"Value of Philosophy to Religion," *Journal of Philosophical Studies,* III (July, 1928), 345-48.

"What Christians Stand for in the Secular World," *Christian News-Letter* (December 28, 1943).

"What Must Christians Do Now?" *Christian Century,* LVII (October 9, 1940), 1242-44.

"World's Need of the Church," *Constructive Quarterly,* VII (March, 1919), 1-10.

BIOGRAPHICAL WORKS

Baker, A. E., Introduction, *Religious Experience.* London: James Clarke and Co., 1958.

Begbie, E. H., "Gentleman with a Duster," *Painted Windows.* New York: Mills and Boon, 1922.

Bell, G. K. A., "William Temple: Memoir," in A. E. Baker's *William Temple and His Message.* New York: Penguin Books, 1946 (not in revised edition of *William Temple's Teaching,* London: J. Clarke, 1949 and Philadelphia: Westminster, 1951).

Dark, Sidney, *The People's Archbishop.* London: J. Clarke, 1942.

Green, V. H. H., *From St. Augustine to William Temple:* Eight Studies in Christian Leadership. London: Latimer House, 1948.

Iremonger, F. A., *William Temple, Archbishop of Canterbury:* His Life and Letters. London: Oxford University Press, 1948.

Iremonger, F. A., "William Temple (1881-1944)," *Dictionary of National Biography 1941-1950.* London: Oxford University Press (1959), 869-873.

Jeffs, E. H., *Princes of the Modern Pulpit in England.* Nashville: Cokesbury, 1931.

Otter, Anthony, *William Temple and the Universal Church.* London: SCM, 1949.

CRITICAL TREATMENTS

Anonymous, *Some Economic Thinking about Malvern* (mimeograph). Compiled from expressions received by the National Association of Manufacturers, New York, 1941.

Bennett, J. C., "William Temple," *Anglican Theological Review,* XXV (July, 1943), 257-71.

Bodgener, J. H., "Archbishop's Tract for the Times," *London Quarterly Review,* CLXIX (April, 1944), 134-38.

Craig, Robert, "William Temple and the Prospects of a Reasonable Christology," *Anglican Theological Review,* XLI (January, 1959), 52-62.

Emmet, Dorothy, "The Philosopher," in F. A. Iremonger's *William Temple, ut supra,* 521-39.

Fletcher, Joseph, "Drama of the Dogma," *Witness,* XXVIII (February 1, 1945), 24: 6-8.

Fletcher, Joseph, "Meaning of the Malvern Declaration," *Christendom* (US), VI (Summer, 1941), 339-51.

Fletcher, Joseph, "William Temple," *Handbook of Christian Theologians.* New York: Meridian Books, 1963.

Geoghegan, W. D., *Platonism in Recent Religious Thought.* New York: Columbia University Press, 1958.

Gesell, John, "Beyond 'Nature, Man and God'," *Anglican Theological Review,* XLII (July, 1960), 234-46.

Goudge, H. L., "Some Modern Teaching on Freedom," *Church Quarterly Review,* CXXII (April, 1936), 1-18.

Horton, W. M., *Contemporary English Theology.* New York: Harper & Bros., 1936.

Matthews, W. R., ed., *William Temple:* An Estimate and Appreciation. London: J. Clarke, 1946.

Miller, R. C., "Is Temple a Realist?," *Journal of Religion,* XIX (January, 1939), 44-54.

Mozley, J. K., *Some Tendencies in British Theology.* London: S.P.C.K., 1951.

Pittenger, W. N., *The Word Incarnate.* New York: Harper & Bros., 1959.

Ramsey, A. M., *An Era in Anglican Theology:* From Gore to Temple. New York: Charles Scribner's Sons, 1960.

Reckitt, M. B., *Maurice to Temple.* London: Faber & Faber, 1947.

Roberts, David, "Temple the Scholar," *The Witness,* XXVIII (February 1, 1945), 24: 11-13.

Shepherd, M. H., "Temple on the Eucharist," *The Witness,* XXVIII (February 1, 1945), 24: 13.

Thomas, O. C., *William Temple's Philosophy of Religion.* London-Greenwich: S.P.C.K.-Seabury, 1961.

Walker, David, "William Temple, Archbishop of Canterbury," *Church Quarterly Review,* CLXI (October-December, 1960), 479-99.

Webb, C. C. J., *A Century of Anglican Theology.* Oxford: Blackwell, 1923.

Widgery, A. G., *Contemporary Thought in Great Britain.* London: Williams and Norgate, 1927.

Portraits in Words and Pictures

Barry, F. R., "New Primate," *Spectator*, CLXVIII (February 27, 1942), 199.

Christendom (US), X. Portrait (Winter, 1945), xvi.

Current Biography (an annual), "William Temple." 1942.

Davies, D. R., "Recollection," *London Quarterly Review*, CLXXIII (October, 1948), 307-11.

Discovery, XIII. Portrait (September, 1932), 273.

Hunter, L. S., "In Memory," *Spectator*, CLXXIX (November 7, 1947), 587.

Illustrated London News, "Dr. Temple, New Primate." (March 7, 1942. The best, liveliest photos of Temple, especially cover picture.)

Jennings, R., "William Temple at School," *Nineteenth Century*, CXXXVI (December, 1944), 261.

Leiper, H. S., "William Temple, Man and Friend," *Christendom* (US), X (Winter, 1945), 9-13.

Life, XII. Portrait (April 20, 1942), 41.

Lloyd, Roger, "William Temple's Legacy," *Churchman*, CXL (January 1, 1946), 1, 14.

Lowry, C. W., "Temple as a Friend," *The Witness*, XXVIII (February 1, 1945), 24: 10-11.

Lowry, C. W., "William Temple," *Christendom*, VII (Winter, 1943), 26-41.

Lowry, C. W., "William Temple, Thinker and Theologian," *Christendom* (US), X (Winter, 1945), 5-8.

Missionary Review, LIX. Portrait (February, 1936), 66.

Moberly, Walter, "Memorial: William Temple," *Oxford*, I (Winter, 1945), 55-59.

Mott, J. R., "William Temple, Ecumenical Leader," *Christendom* (US), X (Winter, 1945), 1-4.

Nature, CXLIX. "Archbishop of Canterbury." (February 28, 1942), 241.

Newsweek, VI. Portrait (December 14, 1935), 20.

Newsweek, XIX. Portrait (June 8, 1942), 66.

Niebuhr, Reinhold, "Dr. William Temple and His Britain," *Nation*, CLIX (November 11, 1944), 584-86.

Niebuhr, Ursula, "Memories of William Temple," *The Witness*, XXVIII (February 1, 1945), 24: 8-10.

Oldham, G. A., "A Tribute," (sermon) *Living Church*, CX (January 14, 1945), 2: 10-11.

Peck, W. G., "The Social Witness of William Temple," *Christendom: A Journal of Christian Sociology*, XIII (December, 1944), 56: 234-36.

Publishers' Weekly, CXLVI. Obituary (November 4, 1944), 1848.

Review of Reviews, LXXXVI. Portrait (September, 1925), 12.

Saturday Review, CL. Caricature (October 11, 1930), 447.

Smith, W. L., "William Temple," *Canadian Forum*, XXII (May, 1942), 41-43.

Survey Graphic, XXXI. Portrait (January, 1942), 16.

NEWS ACCOUNTS AND EDITORIALS

"Airways Advertising on Temple's Creed," *Christian Century*, LIX (November 11, 1942), 1381-82.

"Archbishop and Article 231," *New Statesman and Nation*, III (March 12, 1932), 326.

"Archbishop of Canterbury Dies," *Living Church*, CXIX (November 5, 1944), 19: 9-15.

"Archbishop of York," *Newsweek*, XI (May 23, 1938), 24.

"Archbishop Sees Light," *Saturday Review*, CLX (October 5, 1935), 269.

"Archbishop's Diatribes," *Saturday Review*, CLX (December 21, 1935), 619.

"Britain Loses Great Liberal Leader," *Newsweek*, XXIV (November 6, 1944), 76.

"Canterbury Controversy," *Newsweek*, XXXII (July 26, 1948), 70.

"Canterbury Pilgrim," *Time*, XXXIX (May 4, 1942), 64.

"Canterbury Tale," *Newsweek*, XIX (May 4, 1942), 67.

"Canterbury Outdoes Beveridge for Little Man," *Newsweek*, XXI (February 22, 1943), 66.

"Church of England Gets a New Leader," *Senior Scholastic*, XL (March 9, 1942), 5.

Dark, Sidney, "Crisis in the Church," *New Statesman and Nation*, XXIII (January 31, 1942), 73.

Dark, Sidney, "What Can He Do?" *New Statesman and Nation*, XXIII (February 28, 1942), 136-71.

"Death of Canterbury," *Time*, XLIV (November 6, 1944), 60.

"Election of the Primate of All England," *John Rylands Library Bulletin*, XXVI (May, 1942), 233-36.

"English Archbishops Urge Social Cures," *Literary Digest*, CXVIII (July 14, 1934), 10.

"From York to the U.S.," *Time*, XXVI (December 16, 1935), 37.

"Funeral of Dr. Temple," *Illustrated London News*, CCV (November 11, 1944), 551.

"Known for Speaking Mind," *Newsweek*, XIX (March 2, 1942), 54-55.

"Letter to the Pope," *Time*, LII (July 26, 1948), 40.

"New Primate and New Portents," *Christian Science Monitor* (April 18, 1942), 7.

"New Primate Enthroned with Pomp," *Life*, XII (June 1, 1942), 34-5 (a similar "spread" in *Illustrated London News*, CC (May 2, 1942), 509).

"Prelate and Prophet," *Time*, LII (October 18, 1948), 75.

"Prime Minister and the Archbishop," *New Statesman and Nation*, VII (January 27, 1934), 108.

"Reformist in Canterbury," *Newsweek*, XX (October 5, 1942), 46-47.

"Religious Leaders Stress Loss," *Christian Century*, LXI (November 15, 1944), 1332.

"Visit from York," and Portrait, *Newsweek*, VI (December 14, 1935), 20.

"Visiting Prelate Social Crusader," *Literary Digest*, CXX (December 7, 1935), 18.

"What Can He Do?" in *New Statesman and Nation*, XXIII (February 28, 1942), 136-37.

"What Can Archbishop Temple Do?" *Christian Century*, LIX (April 8, 1942), 451.

"William Ebor Becomes William Cantuar," *Christian Century*, LIX (March 4, 1942), 267.

"William Temple," *Missionary Review of the World*, LIX (February, 1936), 66.

"William Temple," *Newsweek*, IX (January 2, 1937), 11.

"William Temple," *Christian Century*, LXI (November 8, 1944), 1280-81.

"William Temple, Militant Christian," *Christian Science Monitor* (August 29, 1942), 7.

"York to the U.S.," *Time*, XXVI (December 16, 1935), 37.

"York to Canterbury," *Time*, XXXIX (March 2, 1942), 43-44.

Selected Readings

Baker, A. E., *William Temple's Teaching*. Philadelphia: Westminster Press, 1951; and London: J. Clarke, 1949; but see also *William Temple and His Message*, London and New York: Penguin Books, 1946, same author.

Tatham, F. H. C., *The Wisdom of William Temple*, decorations by Sylvia Green. London: A. R. Mowbray, 1949.

Warner, H. C., *Daily Readings from William Temple*. London: Hodder & Stoughton, 1948.

Index

366

19860